ST. IRENAEUS OF LYONS
AGAINST THE HERESIES

Ancient Christian Writers

THE WORKS OF THE FATHERS IN TRANSLATION

EDITED BY

WALTER J. BURGHARDT

THOMAS COMERFORD LAWLER

JOHN J. DILLON

No. 55

ST. IRENAEUS OF LYONS AGAINST THE HERESIES

TRANSLATED AND ANNOTATED

BY

DOMINIC J. UNGER, O.F.M. CAP.

Late of St. Patrick Friary
Saint Louis, Missouri

WITH FURTHER REVISIONS

BY

JOHN J. DILLON

VOLUME I
Book I

PAULIST PRESS
New York, N.Y./Mahwah, N.J.

COPYRIGHT © 1992
BY
CAPUCHIN PROVINCE OF MID-AMERICA

Library of Congress Cataloging-in-Publication Data

Irenaeus, Saint, Bishop of Lyons.
    [Adversus haereses. English]
    Against the heresies/St. Irenaeus of Lyons; translated and annotated by
Dominic J. Unger with further revisions by John J. Dillon.
        p.   cm.—(Ancient Christian writers; no. 55–)
    Translation of: Adversus haereses.
    Includes bibliographical references and index.
    ISBN 0-8091-0454-7 (v. 1)
        1. Gnosticism—Controversial literature—Early works to 1800.   2. The-
ology, Doctrinal—Early works to 1800.   I. Unger, Dominic J.   II. Dillon, John J.   III. Title.   IV. Series: Ancient Christian writers; no. 55,
etc.
BR60.A35   no.55, etc.
[BR65.I63]
270 s—dc20
[239'.3]   91-40838
                                                                                        CIP

Published by Paulist Press
997 Macarthur Boulevard
Mahwah, New Jersey 07430

PRINTED AND BOUND IN THE UNITED STATES OF AMERICA

CONTENTS

NOTES

INDEXES

ST. IRENAEUS OF LYONS
AGAINST THE HERESIES

BOOK I

INTRODUCTION

1. An earlier volume in this series presented a translation of the *Proof of the Apostolic Preaching*,[1] one of the two works of Irenaeus which have survived in their entirety. With this volume the series begins publication of Irenaeus's principal work, his *Exposé and Overthrow of What Is Falsely Called Knowledge*. It is this work, commonly called *Adversus haereses*, or, *Against the Heresies*, which establishes Irenaeus as the most important of the theologians of the second century and merits for him the title of founder of Christian theology.[2]

2. The *Adversus haereses* is a detailed and effective refutation of Gnosticism, and it is a major source of information on the various Gnostic sects and doctrines.[3] In recent years this aspect of Irenaeus's writings has received increased attention, stimulated in part by the discovery in 1946 near Nag Hammadi in Upper Egypt of a large collection of ancient Gnostic texts in Coptic.[4] Included in this find were some previously lost works which Irenaeus and others used in their polemical anti-Gnostic writings, as well as some works not hitherto known even by title or description. The richness of this find has not yet been fully explored. Studies thus far, however, substantiate the centuries-old belief in the reliability of Irenaeus as a source.

3. The importance of Irenaeus as a writer of the early patristic era lies, of course, not so much in what he tells us of the Gnostics as in his clear and convincing descriptions of the doctrines of the Church, and in the fact that he is the first Christian writer to give a relatively complete and systematic treatise on theology.[5] Certainly, he does not have the systematic development of doctrines found in the scholastic or modern theologians; but in view of the early times in which he lived, he treats systematically what today we call the treatises on the One and Triune God, on Creation, on Christ the Savior, on the Church, on Salvation, and on the Resurrection. In many cases he has a rather coherent and unified treatment of individual doctrines; e.g., his

treatise on the Church and on tradition in Book 3. Particularly noteworthy is that Irenaeus had a pivotal topic which unified all his other
teachings—Jesus Christ as universal Recapitulator. He really placed
Christ as the cornerstone of his theological edifice. This put a marvel-
ous unity into all his theological thought.[6] Another source of unity is
his constantly recurring theme of the salvation of men and women,
which is a continuous and gradual process until it reaches the magnifi-
cent glory of the body. Of course, the truly basic and ruling idea
levelled against the Gnostics in the total work of Irenaeus is the existence of only one, true, and all-perfect God. The *Adversus haereses*,
composed in five books over a number of years, was written to show
the errors of the Gnostics. At the same time, however, Irenaeus, who
was a firm believer in the teaching authority of the Church, in the
importance of apostolic succession, and in a primacy of Rome, followed the principle that a clear presentation of the truth is itself a
forceful refutation of error. The fact that Irenaeus was a loyal follower of tradition did not make him stagnant; no, his was a creative
genius. Some scholars write as if there were no development possible
in theology according to Irenaeus.[7] But development is certainly possible and, actually, Irenaeus made great strides over his predecessors;
for instance, in and because of his doctrine about recapitulation of all
things in Christ. His is not merely a restatement pure and simple of
Scripture and tradition. While he is not generally known as a great
stylist, he accomplished his purpose remarkably well.

TITLE AND AUTHENTICITY

4. The short title for Irenaeus's main work, *Adversus haereses*, was
known in Greek to Eusebius, Basil, Maximus, and Photius.[8] That
short form, however, was not the original title, which Eusebius gives
as *Elegkhos kai anatrope tes pseudonumou gnoseos*.[9] Irenaeus himself
says in the prefaces to Books 2, 4, and 5 that this longer form is the
title, and there are allusions to the longer form in his Books 1 and 2.[10]
The *anatrope* in the title obviously refers to "overthrow" or "refutation" of the heresies by the use of arguments based on reason, Scrip-

ture, and tradition."[11] From Irenaeus's purpose and procedure in Book 1, it is equally clear that *elegkhos*, which can be translated either "exposé" or "refutation," here means a refutation by exposure of the errors. The final phrase of the title, *tēs pseudōnumou gnōseōs*, "of the falsely called knowledge," or, "of what is falsely called knowledge," is found in 1 Timothy 6.20.

5. Irenaean authorship of the *Adversus haereses* is firmly established and universally accepted.[12] There are many citations of, and quotations from, the work in the writings of others, from Hippolytus and Tertullian, contemporaries of Irenaeus, to St. John of Damascus. The original Greek text has long been lost, but the work, as we have it, preserved in an early and quite literal Latin translation, is the complete work, and all parts of it are genuine.[13]

TIME OF COMPOSITION

6. The years in which Irenaeus wrote the *Adversus haereses* cannot be determined precisely, and at most some general indications may be noted of the periods in which at least some parts of the work were composed.

7. It is clear that Irenaeus did not write the work all at one time, and that the period of composition extended over a number of years. The reading of the heretical books which Irenaeus consulted entailed much labor. Each book of the *Adversus haereses* supposes a slow process of elaboration of many elements.[14] There are in the work some signs of interruption. Irenaeus sent the books singly to a friend of his as each was finished. From the preface to Book 3 it is certain that he had already sent Books 1 and 2 to his friend. Similarly, the preface to Book 4 indicates that Book 3 had already been sent, and the preface to Book 5 indicates that Book 4 had been forwarded. And since Irenaeus at the end of his Book 1 promises another book, it is probable that he dispatched Book 1 before doing Book 2.

8. Some parts of the work give the impression of having been written during a period when the Church was spared from external persecution. There seems to be an indication in 4.30.1 that Christians were

at the Emperor's court; and in 4.30.3 the Christians were enjoying a peace that seems to be credited to the Romans. In fact, the composition of a work of such proportions would almost seem to require a period of cessation from political persecutions. There was such a period during the reign of Emperor Commodus (180–92), that is, in the latter half of Pope Eleutherius's pontificate and the first part of Pope Victor's. In the famous catalogue of the Roman bishops given by Irenaeus in 3.3.3, Eleutherius is the last one mentioned. It is a safe assumption that Eleutherius was still reigning and that Book 3 was finished before the completion of Eleutherius's pontificate in 188 or 189.

9. Some historians believe that Book 2 was written during a persecution, that is, under Marcus Aurelius (161–80), because in 2.22.2 Irenaeus writes of persecutions of the just as if they are then going on. Books 1 and 2, then, may have been written before 180. The fact that in 3.21.1 Irenaeus speaks of the Greek version of the Old Testament done by Theodotion would not upset such a dating. Though authors have usually held that Theodotion's version appeared around 180,[15] modern scholars are sure that what goes by the name of Theodotion's version is not all from him at that late date. The revision of the Septuagint (hereinafter LXX) began already in the first century,[16] and so Irenaeus could have used Theodotion's version prior to 180.

Irenaeus's Readers

10. The friend to whom Irenaeus sent the books of *Adversus haereses* had asked him to write this work because he had for a long time desired to study Valentinianism.[17] This friend was most likely a bishop. Irenaeus admits that his friend is in many ways more competent than he, and he speaks of him as having the obligation of stemming the tide of error.[18] Irenaeus promised this work as a help to safeguard those who are with his friend, to whom his friend can explain the matters in more detail.[19] This supposes someone with a flock to care for. In the preface to his Book 5, Irenaeus writes of obeying the precept of his friend. This would seem to indicate that his

friend was at least of equal rank. But it is clear that this friend was not the only one Irenaeus hoped would read his work. Near the end of Book 1 he writes: "You, too, and all those who are with you are now in a position to examine what has been said and to overthrow their wicked and unfounded doctrines. . . ."[20] In the preface to Book 5 he speaks of his friend and "all who will read" the book.

11. Neither the name nor the region of the friend addressed by Irenaeus is known. The friend obviously knew Greek, for the *Adversus haereses* was written in Greek. Seemingly, he was also in a place where Greek was used generally, and where the Ptolemaean and Marcosian versions of Gnosticism were raging. Since Irenaeus wrote in Greek, some have suggested that his addressee was not in Gaul or in Rome, but somewhere in the East, perhaps in Alexandria or in Asia Minor. But if Irenaeus had been writing to someone in the East, he would scarcely have spent so much time on Western Gnosticism. Moreover, he often refers to the traditions of the presbyters of Asia Minor in language suggesting that these were not known to readers. In 1.13.5 he narrates an incident about "a certain deacon from among our people in Asia," by which he seems certainly to imply that his readers are not in Asia. In 1.26.1 he reports that Cerinthus taught in Asia; again, the implication is that his readers are not in Asia. For a similar reason, the references to Antioch and Alexandria in 1.24.1 would seem to exclude those places.

12. Gaul as well would hardly seem to be the locale of the readers— not because Irenaeus wrote in Greek, but because he probably would not have spoken of the people of Lyons as barbarians[21] if he had been writing to someone near there. He wrote at great length about the Marcosian heresy because it had become quite rampant in the Rhone valley, and he was able to study it in detail. But he seems to have written for people in some other area where that heresy had infiltrated.

13. That other area may well have been Italy, perhaps even Rome itself. Rome cannot be excluded because of the Greek language. Hippolytus wrote in Greek at Rome for the Romans. The fact that Hippolytus not very many years after the composition of the *Adversus haereses* used that work as a main source and quoted from it at length, could be an indication that Irenaeus sent his work to Rome or somewhere near there. It is a fact that Irenaeus wrote several letters to

Rome. Also, his manner of referring in 1.25.6 to the heretic Marcellina and her influence in Rome may be another indication that Irenaeus's readers were there.

PURPOSE AND PLAN OF *ADVERSUS HAERESES*

14. Irenaeus intended to offer his friend means for refuting the Gnostics. Since he believed that a clear exposition of error is in itself a refutation of that error,[22] he devoted Book 1 of the *Adversus haereses* entirely to exposing the heresies. In the other four books of his work, he advanced positive arguments against the heresies. Though the whole work is essentially a refutation of heresy, it contains much positive theology about divine revelation.

15. Some scholars seem to hold that Irenaeus initially had in mind only a short work, and that he changed his plans as he proceeded.[23] Irenaeus observes in 1.31.4 that his exposé of the heresies has been long, and he promises a "subsequent book." But there is no sign there of change in plans. He had intended from the start to give an exposé of the heresies and then to refute them positively. At the end of Book 2, he speaks of several other books that will follow.[24]

16. The basic plan of the *Adversus haereses* has already been noted. An exposé of the heresies is given in Book 1. In Book 2 there is a refutation of the heresies, chiefly the fundamental tenets of the Gnostics about two gods, by arguments drawn from reason. The next two books continue the refutation, Book 3 with arguments drawn mainly from the words of the apostles, Book 4 with arguments based mainly on the Lord's words. In Book 5 Irenaeus deals mostly with the salvation of the body, a doctrine which the Gnostics sharply denied.

17. This present volume contains only Book 1. The first eight chapters of the book give an account of Valentinianism as taught by Ptolemaeus. Chapter 9 is a short refutation of that heresy, and Chapter 10 presents a summary of the Catholic Rule of the Truth. Chapter 11 is an exposé of the errors of Valentinus and his disciples. Chapters 12–22 contain a long treatment of Marcosianism. Then, beginning with Simon Magus, the arch-heretic, there is a description of the heresiarchs

of various branches of Gnosticism and their disciples in Chapters 23–27. Finally, Chapters 28–31 describe the errors of sects that do not seem to have had definite heresiarchs.[25]

STYLE

18. In the preface to Book 1, Irenaeus apologizes for his style: "From us who live among the Celts and are accustomed to transacting practically everything in a barbarous tongue, you cannot expect rhetorical art, which we have never learned, or the craft of writing, in which we have not had practice, or elegant style and persuasiveness, with which we are not familiar."

19. He underrates his abilities. It is true that his writing is frequently marred by prolixity, repetition, and involved constructions. Even so, his prose has a number of excellent qualities. In general his style is simple and forceful. He is precise in the choice of words, as can be seen, for example, in this series of clauses in 2.30.9: ". . . whom the Law announces, whom the prophets herald, whom Christ reveals, whom the apostles hand down, in whom the Church believes." He is noted also for his variety. He uses four different words to express the idea of preaching, and at least eight different verbs, with various shades of meaning, to express the fact that one thing is a copy of another. In Book 1, to make sure that the reader is aware that he is describing erroneous doctrines and not his own view, he uses phrases such as "they say" very often, but he employs at least fifteen different verbs for this. He is a master of figurative language and concrete illustrations, which are always apt and concise. Book 2 in particular abounds with examples. At times he rises to heights of genuine eloquence.[26] Scattered throughout the five books one finds many concise statements that have become classic, many of them jewels. Here are some examples: "He might indeed have been invisible to them because of His eminence, but He could by no means have been unknown to them because of His providence" (2.6.1); "God's friendship bestows imperishability on those who strive for it" (4.13.4); ". . . so that He might become the Son of man, in order that man in turn might become

a son of God" (3.10.2); "Where the Church is, there is God's Spirit; and where God's Spirit is, there is the Church" (3.24.1). There are all shades of irony in Irenaeus, from light pleasantry to caustic thrusts,[27] as well as some very severe condemnations of heretics. Nevertheless, his general tone is one of calmness and modesty. As has already been indicated, the general plan of the work as a whole is clear and methodical. The same can be said of the plan of each book, despite the author's frequent digressions.

20. What Irenaeus lacks as a stylist, he makes up for in thought. He displays a broad knowledge of Catholic doctrine and a clear and sure grasp of it. Though he gives us a disclaimer about writing ability, his work in fact merits the praise that St. Jerome gave when he referred to the *Adversus haereses* as a work of "most learned and eloquent style."[28]

SCRIPTURE AND TRADITION

21. For Irenaeus, the main witnesses to the Truth are Scripture and tradition.

22. The divine inspiration of the Scriptures is stressed time and again.[29] "The Scriptures are perfect, inasmuch as they were spoken by God's Word and Spirit" (2.28.2); "one and the same Spirit who heralded through the prophets . . . He Himself announced through the apostles" (3.21.4); "the Word . . . gave us the fourfold Gospel" (3.11.8); "the Scriptures are divine."[30] Not only the prophets, but the entire Old Testament is prophetic,[31] because the Holy Spirit spoke through all the writers just as He did through the prophets; the writers were His instruments. Moreover, the New Testament is as inspired and divine as the Old Testament, being equally the word of the Spirit.[32] The Scriptures are without error, "perfect," and "the mainstay and pillar of our faith."[33]

23. Though Irenaeus does not mention a list or canon of the books of the Bible, one can make a fairly complete list from his citations.[34] He cites all the Old Testament books except Judith, Esther, 1 and 2 Chronicles, Ecclesiastes, Canticle of Canticles, Job, Tobit, Obadiah, Nahum, Zephaniah, Haggai, and 1 and 2 Maccabees. But from a pas-

sage in Book 1 it is clear that he knew of Tobit, Nahum, and Haggai.[35] He also knew of the twelve minor prophets as a unit.[36] Of the New Testament, Irenaeus quotes or uses every book except Philemon and 3 John. Although some scholars have questioned whether he used James, Jude, and 2 Peter, in notes to the pertinent passages, I shall show that it is more than probable that he did.[37]

24. In Book 4, Irenaeus cites a sentence from Hermas (*Mandatum* 1), introducing it with the formula "the writing (*graphē*) says."[38] Because of the *graphē*, a word frequently used for Scripture, some scholars have concluded that Irenaeus considered the work of Hermas to be part of the Bible. The conclusion is not warranted. Irenaeus uses *graphē* also with reference to the letter of Pope Clement.[39]

25. Except perhaps for the use of Henoch in 4.16.2, Irenaeus did not use apocryphal books. But he actually quotes an apocryphal text on Christ's descent into "hell" six times, variously ascribing it to Jeremiah, to Isaiah, and to "the prophets."[40] He also quotes two sayings attributed to Jesus which are not in the canonical books.[41]

26. For Old Testament passages, Irenaeus generally used the Septuagint, though at times his text approximates the Hebrew more closely. For the New Testament, the Greek of the excerpts and the Latin version of Irenaeus have a Scripture text different from that of modern critical editions. Irenaeus's Bible text seems to have been substantially that of the Western family. Still, it is difficult here to be certain of readings. In Book 1, in which we have long passages in Greek, when Irenaeus quotes Scripture he often is quoting the heretics, and hence these passages are not sure guides for the text of Irenaeus's Bible. Moreover, the Greek text is from excerpts of Irenaeus in the works of other authors, who may have adjusted the scriptural quotations to their scriptural texts. For Books 2 and 3 we have for the most part only the Latin version. The Latin translator, as Dom Chapman has proved, made his own translation from the Greek of Irenaeus, following the Greek slavishly even in word order.[42] Similarly, the Armenian translator of Books 4 and 5 translated the Greek of Irenaeus, though at times later scribes made some adjustments in the scriptural passages.[43]

27. Harvey strongly defended the theory that Irenaeus was acquainted with the Scriptures in the Syriac version and translated from that into Greek. There would seem to be no solid reason for

that. The Western readings in the Old Syriac came by way of Tatian's *Diatessaron*. But Irenaeus appears to have used the Western text which was current in the West and which came to be used everywhere in the second and third centuries.[44] The difference in readings can at times be explained by the use of a harmonized version of the Gospels. Irenaeus probably made use of some kind of harmony in the Gospels, but whether he used Tatian's is disputed.

28. Irenaeus at times quotes the same scriptural passage in different ways; for instance, he cites Matt. 11.27 three different ways in Book 4.[45] Such variation could have been due to citation from memory; or it is possible he used various manuscripts of the Bible. He may also have had a kind of hexapla, as the Hebrew transcriptions of Gen. 1.1 in *Proof* 43 might indicate.[46] For the Messianic texts of the Old Testament, he need not have quoted the Bible directly, for there were collections of such texts for use by Christian writers.[47] Possibly Irenaeus took these texts from Justin's *Syntagma*, a work now lost. The use of *Testimonia* collections might account for false attributions by Irenaeus such as that of Numbers 24.17 to Isaiah in A.H. 3.9.2 and that of the *Magnificat* to Elizabeth in 4.7.1.[48]

29. Usually Irenaeus insists on the literal sense of Scripture. He holds that it is wrong to twist texts from their natural meaning by combining them with other texts that do not fit.[49] Truth itself must be the ultimate rule of interpretation.[50] One must have regard for the style of the Scriptures. Even the punctuation must be correct.[51] Obscure passages of the parables must not be interpreted by other obscure passages, but by such as are clear and certain.[52] The Gnostics indulged in exaggerated allegorical interpretations, and Irenaeus at times uses their weapon against them. But with him the allegorical interpretations are just ornaments added to the solid literal witnesses. The Scriptures are so vast in meaning that one should not be perturbed if he or she does not understand them all.[53]

30. Scripture, then, is an excellent source for the Rule of Faith. It is divine and must be believed. But the Scriptures are not always clear, nor did all of Scripture exist from the beginning. Hence it is not an absolute Rule of Faith.[54] Scripture is ultimately subject to the criterion of tradition, of the doctrine of the Church, of the Rule of Truth itself.

31. Irenaeus uses a variety of names to designate tradition, a variety based on the various aspects of the same reality: tradition, tradition of

the apostles, tradition which derives from the apostles, tradition of the Truth, the preaching, the preaching of the Truth, the body of the Truth, the Rule of the Truth, or of the Faith, the doctrine, the doctrinal system.

32. Tradition must be derived from the apostles.[55] Any tradition outside this apostolic tradition must be resolutely rejected.[56] The condition and warranty for this is uninterrupted succession of bishops throughout the Church from the apostles and their disciples[57] so that every church throughout the world teaches one and the same unchangeable doctrine—tradition must really be catholic.[58] Moreover, the apostolic tradition must be verified in particular in the church at Rome, because that church has a preeminence over the others, and for that reason all the other churches, if truly apostolic, must agree with the Roman.[59]

33. Since tradition existed before the writings of the New Testament[60] it is an absolute source of revelation. It is the teaching of the living Church, which would have existed even if nothing had been committed to writing.[61]

Manuscript History

34. It is to be regretted that we do not have the original Greek for this important work. What of the original Greek we have today has been saved in the works of other writers who copied long passages from Irenaeus.[62] Much of Book 1 has been preserved by Epiphanius, who tells us that he copied verbatim and notes the fact when he merely condenses. Hippolytus used Irenaeus extensively and made sizable extracts from him. Eusebius has preserved some precious snatches, as has also Theodoret of Cyrus, who used Irenaeus copiously for his treatise on heresies. Some passages are extant in St. John of Damascus's *Sacra parallela*, and a few in the Catenae. There are several fragments in the Oxyrhynchus papyrus 405 and some longer but corrupted sections in the Jena papyrus. References to these various sources and to other minor sources are provided in the notes on the passages in question.

35. The loss of the complete text of Irenaeus's Greek is a mystery to scholars. The Greek text was available to the translators of the Armenian version in the sixth century, and in the eighth century when it was excerpted for the *Sacra parallela*. In the ninth century Photius read a copy at Baghdad; this copy could have disappeared in the sacking of Baghdad in 1258.[63]

36. For the *Adversus haereses*, then, we are for the most part dependent on the ancient Latin version, which provides for us the entire text. There are nine manuscripts, though not all are complete.[64] The manuscripts can be grouped into two distinct families. The oldest family is represented by the Clermont, Voss, and Stockholm manuscripts. The second family is represented by the Arundel and other manuscripts.

37. The Clermont manuscript (C), which was found in the Jesuit college of Clermont, is now in the Preussische Staatsbibliothek in Berlin. It originated in the ninth century in the monastery of Corbie. Its Irish script is accounted for by the fact that St. Columbanus founded the monastery at Luxeuil around the year 590, and the monks of that monastery established the monastery of Corbie around the year 660. This monastery has all five books of the *Adversus haereses*, but ends at chapter 26 of Book 5. Thus it lacks the final ten chapters of the work. There is also a rather long lacuna from chapter 13.4 to chapter 14.1 in Book 5.

38. The Voss manuscript (V) is in the library of the University of Leiden. It was at one time owned by Sir Thomas Voss, an English humanist. Written in 1494 in England, it has the last ten chapters of Book 5, but it has the same lacuna as the Clermont manuscript in chapter 13 of Book 5.

39. The manuscript (H [Holmiensis A 140]) kept in Stockholm was bought by Queen Christina of Sweden in 1650. Written at the end of the fifteenth century, it is judged to be a copy of the Voss manuscript.

40. The Arundel manuscript (A) is in the British Museum. It was written in 1166 from a model in La Grande Chartreuse and for which a Florus of Lyons (d. 859/860) wrote a prologue, which is extant in this Arundel copy. The manuscript is incomplete, ending with chapter 31 of Book 5.

41. The Vatican Library has four manuscripts with the Latin version of the *Adversus haereses*. Vatican manuscript Latin 187 (Q) was

written in 1429 or shortly before; it belongs to the second family of manuscripts. Vatican manuscript Latin 188 (R) depends on Latin 187 and was written during the pontificate of Nicholas V (1447–55). Another manuscript, Ottobonensis (Latin 752), normally designated O, which also depends on Latin 187, was copied between 1429 and 1440. The fourth manuscript at the Vatican, Ottobonensis (Latin 1154), normally designated P, was written around 1530.

42. The manuscript of Salamanca (Latin 202), normally designated S, was written before 1457, when John of Segovia gave it to the University of Salamanca.

43. The three manuscripts that Erasmus used are lost; they certainly belonged to the second family.[65] The humanist Passerat, who edited Book 1 and the beginning of Book 2 of the *Adversus haereses,* is said to have used a "very ancient manuscript." Loofs thought that this was simply the Voss manuscript, and that Passerat had not read it directly but through Feuardent, who, Loofs thought, had also used the Voss manuscript. M. L. Guillaumin has written that this is by no means certain. Rather, it seems to her that both Feuardent's vetus codex and Passerat's codex antiquissimus differed from each other and from the Voss manuscript. More recently L. Doutreleau has argued that Loofs's views should be upheld in this matter and that the codex Passeratii is nothing more than an illusion of the past.[66]

44. The relative value of these families and their manuscripts is somewhat in doubt today. The editors of Books 4 and 5 of the *Adversus haereses* in the *Sources chrétiennes* series made a careful study of the Armenian translation and compared it with the Latin manuscripts. They found that the Arundel manuscript is much more often in agreement with the Armenian version than are other Latin manuscripts. Since they thought the Armenian version was very faithful to the original, they preferred also the Arundel manuscript.[67] Prior to this, scholars quite generally, including F. Sagnard, who originally had edited Irenaeus's Book 3 for *Sources chrétiennes* in 1952, gave preference to the Clermont manuscript. And I am not so sure that this view should be altogether disregarded. I agree with B. Botte, who submits that the Clermont manuscript merits first place and can prevail even against both the Voss and Arundel manuscripts, but needs to be controlled in every case by, and at times corrected in favor of, the Armenian version and the Arundel manuscript.[68]

45. All in all the Latin text of the *Adversus haereses* is preserved as well as virtually any ancient document. There was no second Latin version, though some were misled on this point by a citation in Agobard's *De iudaicis superstitionibus*,[69] which differs from the normal translation. The quotation in Agobard is in fact a fragment that Rufinus had translated from the Greek of Eusebius.

46. The old Latin version of Irenaeus is noted for its slavish literalness. For this reason, though it is not without translator's errors and copyists' mistakes in the manuscripts, it is valuable for establishing the original text of Irenaeus. In many cases one can grasp the real sense of the Latin only by first translating it back into Greek.[70] The Latinity is of a corrupt kind, abounding in barbarisms and solecisms. It is clear that at times the translator did not understand the meaning of the Greek. Though scholars are not agreed on how well the translator knew Greek or Latin, it would seem on balance that he knew Greek but did not know Latin very well. The Latin text frequently retains the syntactical construction of the Greek, even to the point of attempting the Greek definite article with a demonstrative or relative pronoun construction. Had the translator known Latin well, he would scarcely have done that unless he was intent on preserving for posterity the language structure as well as the thought of Irenaeus. This does not seem likely.

47. Some scholars have suggested that Irenaeus himself made the Latin translation.[71] Irenaeus, however, would hardly have missed his own meaning, as the translator did in fact do at times. Some have also suggested that Tertullian made the translation. The language of the Latin version, however, is simply not that of Tertullian, but rather of a barbaric type, Celtic in origin.[72] Tertullian seems to have used the translation, for there are passages from it, some of them verbatim, in his *Adversus Valentinianos*. When the ancient version has a faulty rendition, so does Tertullian, even in minute peculiarities, so that the agreement cannot be explained by mere accident.[73] The instances in which Tertullian agrees with the Greek against the Latin do not militate against this remark; rather, these instances would seem to indicate that Tertullian at times saw the errors in the Latin and corrected them, apparently with the aid of a Greek copy.

48. The Latin version seems to have been made not long after Irenaeus's time, that is, in the earlier decades of the third century,

when Gnosticism was still a force to be reckoned with, since there would appear to have been little reason for making such a translation except as a weapon against Gnosticism. The majority of scholars have held to this early dating.[74] In more recent years it has been suggested that the translation was made in the latter half of the fourth century, probably in North Africa. The argument here is that Augustine quotes from the translation and is the first to do so.[75] Obviously, this involves contradiction of the evidence noted above regarding Tertullian's use of the translation. In any case, the translation could have existed, and have been used for some time, without having been quoted verbatim. Moreover, it seems almost incredible that a translator of the fourth century would have used so many archaic expressions, with which the Latin version abounds, and slavishly retained so many Greek constructions.

49. *Armenian version*. In the sixth century the entire *Adversus haereses* was translated, from the Greek, into Armenian. Only Books 4 and 5 of the work are extant.[76] We will discuss this version more at length in the Introduction to Book 4. There are also some important independent fragments in Armenian for other parts of the work. For a discussion of the Armenian fragments of Book 1 see SC 263.101–7.[77]

50. *Syriac version*. Some parts of the *Adversus haereses*, but not the entire work, were translated into Syriac.[78] Some fragments of this version are extant; in general the help they provide in establishing the text of Irenaeus is minimal. For a somewhat different evaluation of the Syriac fragments, at least for Book 1, see Doutreleau's remarks in SC 263.109–11.

Printed Editions

51. Erasmus was the first to put out a printed edition of the *Adversus haereses*, in 1526 at Basel. It is the *Editio princeps*, but it has only the Latin text, without any Greek fragments. In addition, it lacks the last five chapters of the work. A number of reprints were made of this edition during the next half century, till 1571. Nicolas Desgallards (Gallasius) published an edition in 1570 at Geneva in which he in-

cluded the Greek excerpts found in Epiphanius. At Paris in 1575, F. Feuardent published a new edition; he used only the Latin but added the last five chapters from the Voss manuscript and supplied the text for a number of the lacunae in Erasmus's edition. For a later edition, in 1596 at Cologne, Feuardent added over forty Greek fragments found in various Greek writers. Meanwhile in 1575, J. de Billy (Billius) made a new translation of the first eighteen chapters of Book 1 as preserved by Epiphanius. His translation is printed in the seventh volume of Migne's *Patrologia graeca* below the older Latin version.

52. More than a century later, in 1702, J. E. Grabe, a learned Prussian who had settled in England and changed from Lutheranism to Anglicanism, put out an edition at Oxford, adding many Greek fragments. He introduced the use of the Arundel manuscript in printed editions.[79] A few years later, in 1710, the Benedictine R. Massuet put out an edition at Paris. He used the Clermont manuscript and preferred its readings. N. Le Nourry had already noted the existence of the Clermont manuscript in 1697.[80] Massuet used all the Greek fragments available and added a scholarly introduction. The Massuet edition became the popular edition, especially through its inclusion in Migne's *Patrologia graeca* 7.

53. Efforts were subsequently made to issue a more critical edition. First A. Stieren put out a two-volume edition between 1848 and 1853 at Leipzig. Then in 1857 W. W. Harvey put out one in Cambridge. Harvey had the advantage of the newly discovered Greek text of Hippolytus's *Refutation of All Heresies,* and a good number of Syriac fragments as well as a few Armenian fragments. He collated the three main manuscripts (Clermont, Voss, Arundel) of the Latin version. Though the Harvey edition has a number of defects, it was used quite generally by scholars.[81] In 1907 U. Mannucci began a still more critical edition at Rome, but only the first two books ever appeared. Another edition of the first book appeared when J. S. A. Cunningham submitted a doctoral dissertation in May 1967 at Princeton University entitled, *Irenaeus: Adversus haereses I: A New Edition of the Latin Text.* The excellent French series of patristic writings, Sources chrétiennes (hereinafter SC), has published a critical edition of the Latin text, together with all the excerpts and fragments extant, and with a French translation and ample scholarly notes. The series began with Book 3 which was published in 1952 by the Dominican F. Sagnard (SC 34).

When Sagnard died, the work was taken over by a team of several scholars. Here is the publishing history of this acclaimed text and French translation:[82]

SC 100 *Irénée de Lyon: Contre les hérésies*. Book 4, edited and translated by A. Rousseau, B. Hemmerdinger, C. Mercier, and L. Doutreleau, 2 vols., 1965.

SC 151 *Irénée de Lyon: Contre les hérésies*. Book 5, edited and translated by A. Rousseau, L. Doutreleau, and C. Mercier, vol. 1: Introduction etc., 1969.

SC 152 *Irénée de Lyon: Contre les hérésies*. Book 5, edited and translated by A. Rousseau, L. Doutreleau, and C. Mercier, vol. 2: Text and translation, 1969.

SC 210 *Irénée de Lyon: Contre les hérésies*. Book 3, edited and translated by A. Rousseau and L. Doutreleau, vol. 1: Introduction etc., 1974.

SC 211 *Irénée de Lyon: Contre les hérésies*. Book 3, edited and translated by A. Rousseau and L. Doutreleau, vol. 2: Text and translation, 1974.

SC 263 *Irénée de Lyon: Contre les hérésies*. Book 1, edited and translated by A. Rousseau and L. Doutreleau, vol. 1: Introduction etc., 1979.

SC 264 *Irénée de Lyon: Contre les hérésies*. Book 1, edited and translated by A. Rousseau and L. Doutreleau, vol. 2: Text and translation, 1979.

SC 293 *Irénée de Lyon: Contre les hérésies*. Book 2, edited and translated by A. Rousseau and L. Doutreleau, vol. 1: Introduction etc., 1982.

SC 294 *Irénée de Lyon: Contre les hérésies*. Book 2, edited and translated by A. Rousseau and L. Doutreleau, vol. 2: Text and translation, 1982.

54. In preparing the present translation of Book 1, I have used the edition of Harvey, always comparing it where pertinent, however, with Holl's critical edition of Epiphanius.[83] In the notes to the text I have added the references to the various works in which the excerpts and fragments of the Greek can be found.

55. The divisions of chapters and paragraphs in this translation are

based on those in the editions published by Massuet, Stieren, and Rousseau and Doutreleau. Although the chapter headings are for the most part my own, I have tried to fit the wording of the chapter headings to the contents of the chapter as far as possible. Past editors of the Latin text have kept the tables of contents and the chapter headings as found in the manuscripts for their historic value, even though they have little value for understanding Irenaeus. They do not come from Irenaeus himself. The tables of contents for the first four books were, however, already in the Greek manuscripts before the Latin and Armenian translations. The chapter headings were added later, possibly in the fifth or sixth century, and then not always correctly or exactly. The manuscripts for Book 5 do not have a table of contents or chapter headings. These were introduced for Book 5 in the edition of Desgallards in 1570, but later editors made various changes.[84]

56. Of the modern translations, the following were consulted: 1) the German by E. Klebba in *Bibliothek der Kirchenväter*[2] 3–4 (Munich 1912); 2) the following English translations: first, by A. Roberts and J. W. H. Rambaut, as revised and annotated by A. Cleveland Coxe, in *Ante-Nicene Fathers* 1 (Buffalo 1886)—this translation is quite faulty in places; and second, the translation of principal passages, with notes and arguments, published by F. R. Montgomery Hitchcock, *The Treatise of Irenaeus of Lugdunum against the Heresies* (2 vols., London 1916); 3) the Italian by Vittorino Dellagiacoma in *S. Ireneo di Lione. Contre Le Eresie* (I Classici Cristiani, 2 vols., Siena 1968[2]).[85]

AGAINST THE HERESIES

PREFACE

Certain people[1] are discarding[2] the Truth and introducing deceitful *myths and endless genealogies,* which, as the Apostle says, *promote speculations rather than the divine training that is in faith.*[3] By specious argumentation, craftily patched together,[4] they mislead the minds of the more ignorant and ensnare them by falsifying the Lord's words.[5] Thus they become wicked interpreters of genuine words. They bring many to ruin by leading them, under the pretense of knowledge,[6] away from Him who established and adorned this universe, as if they had something more sublime and excellent to manifest than the God *who made heaven and . . . all things in them.*[7] By cleverness with words they persuasively allure the simple folk to this style of searching, but then, absurdly,[8] bring them to perdition by trumping up their blasphemous and impious opinion against the Creator.[9] In this matter[10] they just cannot distinguish what is false from what is true.

2. Error, in fact, does not show its true self, lest on being stripped naked it should be detected. Instead, it craftily decks itself out in an attractive dress, and thus, by an outward false appearance, presents itself to the more ignorant, truer than Truth itself, ridiculous as it is even to say this.[11] With regard to such people, one[12] greater than we has said: "An artful imitation in glass is a mockery to a precious stone, though it is an emerald and highly prized by some people, so long as no one is at hand to evaluate it and skillfully expose the crafty counterfeit. And when copper is alloyed to silver, what man, if he is unskilled,[13] will readily be able to evaluate it." Therefore, we will see to it that it will not be our fault if some are snatched away, like sheep by wolves, whom they would fail to recognize because of the treachery of the sheepskin,[14] since they speak the same language we do, but intend different meanings. Of such the Lord admonished us to beware.[15] And so, after chancing upon the commentaries of the disciples of Valentinus—as they style themselves—and after conversing with some of

them and becoming acquainted with their doctrine, we thought it necessary to inform you, our dear friend, about these portentous and profound "mysteries" which not all grasp,[16] because not all have purged their brains.[17] Thus, having learned of these mysteries yourself, you can make them clear to all your people and warn them to be on guard against this profundity of nonsense and of blasphemy against God.[18] To the best of our ability we will give you a concise and clear report on the doctrine of these people who are at present spreading false teaching. We are speaking of the disciples of Ptolemaeus, an offshoot of the Valentinian school.[19] We will also offer suggestions, to the best of our limited capacity, for refuting this doctrine, by showing how utterly absurd, inconsistent, and incongruous with the Truth their statements are. Not that we are accustomed to writing books, or practiced in the art of rhetoric; but it is love that prompts us to acquaint you and all your people with the teachings which up till now have been kept secret,[20] which, however, by the grace of God have at last come to light. *For nothing is covered that will not be revealed, and nothing hidden that will not be known.*[21]

3. From us who live among the Celts[22] and are accustomed to transact practically everything in a barbarous tongue, you cannot expect rhetorical art, which we have never learned, or the craft of writing, in which we have not had practice, or elegant style and persuasiveness, with which we are not familiar. Rather, you must welcome in charity what in charity we write to you—simply and truthfully and unaffectedly. You yourself, as one more competent than we, will develop these points, receiving from us, as it were, only the seeds and beginnings. In the broad range of your mind you will reap abundant fruit[23] from our brief statements, and will forcefully present to your people what we have reported but feebly. Finally, we have made every effort not only to make clear to you their doctrines—which you have long sought to learn—but also to supply you with aids for proving it false. You, in like manner, will generously serve the rest, in keeping with the grace given you by the Lord, so that men and women no longer may be led astray by the specious argumentation of those people, which is as follows.

CHAPTER 1
THE VALENTINIANS' ABSURD EXPLANATION
OF THE ORIGIN OF THE AEONS.

1. They[1] claim that in the invisible and unnameable heights there is a certain perfect Aeon[2] that was before all, the First-Being, whom they also call First-Beginning, First-Father, and Profundity.[3] He is invisible and incomprehensible.[4] And, since he is incomprehensible and invisible, eternal and ingenerate, he existed in deep quiet and stillness through countless ages.[5] Along with him there existed Thought, whom they also name Grace and Silence. At one time this Profundity decided to emit from himself the Beginning of all things. This emission would be as a "seed" which he decided to emit and deposit as it were in the womb of Silence,[6] who coexisted with him. After she had received this "seed" and had become pregnant, she gave birth to Mind, who was both similar and equal to his Father who emitted him; and he alone comprehended his (Father's) greatness. This Mind they also call Only-begotten, Father and Beginning of all things.[7] Truth was emitted at the same time he [Mind] was. Thus these four constitute the first and principal Pythagorean Tetrad,[8] for there are Profundity and Silence, then Mind and Truth. This [Tetrad] they also style the root of all things. But when this Only-begotten perceived for what things he was emitted, he in turn emitted Word and Life, since he was Father of all who were to come after him and the beginning and formation of the entire Fullness. Thereupon by the conjugal union of Word and Life, Man and Church[9] were emitted. That is the principal Ogdoad, the root and the substance of all things, known among them by four names, Profundity, Mind, Word, and Man, because each of these is male and female; thus, in the first case, First-Father was united in marriage to Thought whom they call Grace and Silence;[10] then Only-begotten, that is, Mind, to Truth; next Word, to Life; finally Man, to Church.

2. Since these Aeons themselves were emitted for their Father's

glory,[11] they in turn wished to glorify the Father by something of their own. So they sent forth emissions through conjugal unions. After Man and Church had been emitted, Word and Life emitted ten other Aeons, whose names are these: Profound and Mingling, Ageless and Union, Self-producing and Pleasure, Immobile and Blending, Only-begotten and Happiness. These are the ten Aeons which they assert were emitted by Word and Life. Moreover, Man himself, together with Church, emitted twelve Aeons, to whom they give these names: Advocate and Faith, Paternal and Hope, Maternal and Love, Praise and Understanding, Ecclesiastic and Blessedness, Desired and Wisdom.[12]

3. Such are the thirty Aeons of their erroneous system. They are enveloped in silence and are known to no one.[13] This indivisible and spiritual Fullness of theirs is tripartite, being divided into an Ogdoad, a Decad, and a Dodecad.[14] And for this reason Savior—for they do not wish to call him Lord—did no work in public for thirty years,[15] thus manifesting the mystery of these Aeons. They also assert that these thirty Aeons are most plainly indicated in the parable of the laborers sent into the vineyard;[16] for some are sent about the first hour, others about the third hour, others about the sixth hour, others about the ninth hour, others about the eleventh hour. Now if the hours mentioned are added up, the sum total will be thirty; for one, three, six, nine, and eleven make thirty. Thus they hold that the Aeons have been indicated by these hours. Besides, they claim that these are great and wonderful and unutterable mysteries, which they themselves bear as fruit. And if anywhere anything of the many[17] things mentioned in the Scriptures can [be drawn to these things, they wish to] accommodate and adapt them to their fabrication.[18]

CHAPTER 2
THE DEFECTION OF WISDOM OUTSIDE THE FULLNESS AND HER RESTORATION BY LIMIT. THE EMISSION OF CHRIST AND THE FORMATION OF JESUS.

1. So they tell us that First-Father of theirs is known only to Only-begotten, that is, to Mind, who was born of him.[1] To all the rest he is

invisible and incomprehensible. According to them, Mind alone enjoyed himself in contemplating Father and exulted in considering his immeasurable greatness. He was thinking of communicating Father's greatness also to the rest of the Aeons, how vast and great he is, and that he is without beginning, immeasurable and incapable of being seen. But at the will of Father, Silence restrained him, because she wished to get them all to have the mind and the desire to seek after their First-Father mentioned above. The rest of the Aeons, too, were in some manner quietly desiring to see the one who emitted their "Seed" and to be informed about their Root who was without beginning.

2. But the last and youngest Aeon of the Dodecad emitted by Man and Church, namely, Wisdom, advanced far ahead of all of them and suffered passion, though without the embrace of Desired, her consort. The passion began in Mind and Truth[2] but spread as by infection to this estranged Aeon [Wisdom] under the pretense of love,[3] but in reality out of temerity,[4] because he had no fellowship[5] with perfect Father, as even Mind did. The passion consisted in seeking after Father; for he wished, so they say, to comprehend his greatness. But then he was not able, inasmuch as he undertook an impossible affair, and he fell into extreme agony because of the immense height[6] and unsearchable nature of Father and because of the affection for him. Since he was ever stretching forward to what was ahead,[7] he would at last have been swallowed up by his charm and resolved into the entire substance[8] unless he had met the power that strengthens all things[9] and safeguards them outside the unspeakable greatness. This power they also call Limit. By it they say he was restrained[10] and strengthened, and when with difficulty he had been brought to his senses and was convinced that Father is unfathomable, he laid aside the first Intention[11] together with the subsequent passion which had arisen from that amazing admiration [for Father].

3. Some of them,[12] however, describe the passion and return of Wisdom in this[13] mystical fashion. After she had undertaken the impossible and unattainable affair, she brought forth a formless substance, namely, such a nature as a woman could bring forth.[14] When she looked at it, she was filled first with grief on account of the unfinished nature of her offspring, then with fear lest her very existence should come to an end.[15] After that she was beside herself and

perplexed as she sought the cause [of her offspring] and how she might conceal her.[16] While involved in these passions, she changed her mind and tried to return to Father. When she had made the bold attempt for some time and her strength failed, she entreated Father. The other Aeons, too, especially Mind, made supplication together with her.[17] Hence, they claim, material substance took its beginning from ignorance and grief, fear and bewilderment.[18]

4. Afterwards Father, by means of Only-begotten, emitted the above-mentioned Limit as part of no conjugal couple, [but] bisexual.[19] For they hold that sometimes Father emits with Silence as consort,[20] then again he is above both male and female.[21] This Limit they call Stake, Redeemer, Reaper, Limiter, and Restorer.[22] They claim that Wisdom was purified by this Limit and strengthened and restored to her own consort [Desired].[23] For, after Intention, together with her subsequent passion, had been separated from her, she herself remained[24] within the Fullness, but her Intention with her passion was separated by Limit and fenced out[25] and kept outside of it. Intention is a spiritual substance, possessing some of the natural tendency of an Aeon, but she is formless and shapeless, because she had received nothing.[26] For this reason they say she is a weak and feminine fruit.[27]

5. After[28] Intention had been separated outside the Fullness of the Aeons, and its Mother had been restored to her own conjugal partner, Only-begotten in accord with Father's forethought again emitted another conjugal couple, namely, Christ and Holy Spirit, for the stabilization and support of the Fullness, lest any of the Aeons have a similar misfortune [as Wisdom].[29] Through them they say the Aeons were perfected. For, they claim, Christ taught them the nature of their conjugal union, that they would be able to know the comprehension of Ingenerate.[30] He also announced among them the knowledge of Father [Profundity], namely, that he is immeasurable and incomprehensible, and that he can be neither seen nor heard. He is known only by Only-begotten.[31] Father's incomprehensible[32] nature is primarily the cause for the permanent existence of the rest of the Aeons; but what can be comprehended of him, namely, his Son,[33] is the cause of their origin and formation. These things, then, Christ performed among them as soon as he had been emitted.

6. The [one] Holy Spirit taught them to give thanks that they had all been made equal, and he introduced [them to] the true rest.[34] They say that in this manner the Aeons were made equal in form and mind, since all became Minds and all Words and all Men and all Christs. In like manner, the female Aeons all became Truths and Lives and Spirits and Churches. Thereupon,[35] they tell us, when all the Aeons had been strengthened and brought to perfect rest, they sang hymns amid much rejoicing to First-Father, who himself took part in the great exultation.[36] Then, in gratitude for this benefit, the entire Fullness of the Aeons, with one will and mind, and with the consent of Christ and Spirit and the approval of their Father,[37] collected and combined whatever most beautiful and brilliant each one had in himself. These things they fittingly blended together and carefully united into one. To the honor and glory of Profundity[38] they made this emission the most perfect beauty and constellation of the Fullness, the most perfect fruit, Jesus. They also gave him the name Savior and Christ, and patronymically, Word, and All, because he is emitted from all. And as an honor to themselves, they emitted together with him Angels of the same nature[39] to be his bodyguard.

CHAPTER 3
THE VALENTINIANS MISUSE THE SCRIPTURES IN SUPPORT OF THEIR ERRORS.

1. Such, then, are the dealings in the inner circle of the Fullness, as they tell them.[1] Such, too, was the misfortune of the Aeon who suffered passion and nearly perished when, because of her search after Father, she was involved in much material substance.[2] Such was the stabilization, after her agony,[3] by Limit, Stake, Redeemer, Reaper, Limiter, and Restorer. Such was likewise the later origin of the Aeons, namely, of the first Christ and Holy Spirit, both of whom were emitted by Father after the repentance of Wisdom. Such was the formation of the second Christ—whom they also style Savior—a creation

out of the combined contributions [of the Aeons]. These things, however, were not declared openly, because not all are capable of grasping
this knowledge.[4] They were pointed out mystically by Savior through
parables to those who were able to understand them. Thus, the thirty
Aeons are pointed out, as we said above,[5] by the thirty years during
which they say Savior did not work in public[6] and by the parable of the
workers in the vineyard.[7] Paul, on his part, very clearly and frequently
names these Aeons, and even preserves their rank, when he speaks
thus: *To all generations of the age* [aeon] *of ages* [aeons].[8] Even we
ourselves at the giving of thanks,[9] when we say: "To the ages [aeons]
of the ages" [aeons],[10] are said to point out those Aeons. Finally,
whenever the word Aeon or Aeons occurs [in Scripture], they maintain there is reference to their Aeons.

2. The emission of the Dodecad of the Aeons is indicated [they
claim] by the fact that the Lord was twelve years old when he disputed
with the teachers of the Law;[11] likewise, by the choice of the apostles.[12]
Besides, the other eighteen Aeons were revealed by the fact that after
his resurrection from the dead, he is said to have spent eighteen
months with his disciples.[13] Likewise, the ten Aeons are pointed out by
iota, the first letter of his name. For this reason Savior said: *Not one
iota or one tittle shall be lost . . . till all is accomplished.*[14]

3. Now the passion experienced by the twelfth Aeon is pointed out,
they say, by the apostasy of Judas, the twelfth of the apostles, when the
betrayal took place.[15] Also by the fact that [Jesus] suffered in the
twelfth month;[16] for they profess that he preached one year after his
baptism.[17] Furthermore, this is most clearly manifested by the case of
the woman with the hemorrhage, since, after she had suffered for
twelve years, she was healed by Savior's coming, when she touched
the hem of his cloak. And because of that, Savior said: *Who touched
me?*[18] By this he taught the disciples the mystery that had taken place
among the Aeons and the healing of the Aeon that had suffered passion. For that power was pointed out through her who had suffered
for twelve years, inasmuch as she was straining forward and her material substance was flowing out into immensity, as they say. And unless
she had touched that Son's cloak, that is, the Truth of the First Tetrad,
which is indicated by the hem, she would have been resolved into the
universal substance.[19] But she stopped and rested from her passion;

for, when the power of the Son went out—this they hold is the power of Limit—he healed her and removed the passion from her.

4. Moreover, they assert that Savior, who was made from all things, is the All. This is proved by the following passage: *Every male who opens the womb;*[20] for he, being the All, opened the womb of Intention of the Aeon who suffered passion when she was cast out of the Fullness.[21] He also calls this second Ogdoad, of which we shall speak a little later. They say that for this reason Paul said explicitly: *But he is all;*[22] and again: *To him and from him are all things;*[23] and further: *In him the whole fullness of deity dwells;*[24] and: *All things are recapitulated in Christ* through God.[25] Thus they interpret these and similar passages.

5. Likewise[26] they show that their Limit, to whom of course they give various names, possesses two activities: that of supporting and that of separating. Inasmuch as he supports and strengthens he is Stake; inasmuch as he separates and divides he is Limit. They say Savior indicated his activity as follows. First, that of supporting when he said: *Whoever does not bear his own cross [stauros] and come after me, cannot be my disciple;*[27] and: *having taken up the cross, follow me.*[28] Next, that of dividing when he said: *I have not come to bring peace, but a sword.*[29] They say that also John [the Baptist] pointed out the same when he said: *His winnowing fork is in his hand, to clear the threshing floor, and he will gather the wheat into his granary but the chaff he will burn with unquenchable fire.*[30] By this he pointed out the activity of Limit; for the winnowing fork, they explain, is Stake who surely consumes all material things as fire consumes chaff, but purges those who are saved, as the winnowing fork does the wheat. Also the apostle Paul, they say, makes mention of this Stake in the following: *For the word of the cross [stauros] is folly to those who are perishing, but to those who are saved, it is the power of God;*[31] and again: *But far be it from me to glory except in the cross [stauros] of . . . Christ, by whom the world has been crucified to me, and I to the world.*[32]

6. Such things, therefore, they assert about their Fullness and the formation of the universe.[33] They do violence to the good words [of Scripture] in adapting them to their wicked fabrications. Not only from the words of the evangelists and apostles do they try to make proofs by perverting the interpretations and by falsifying the explanations, but also from the law and the prophets.[34] Since many parables

and allegories have been spoken and can be made to mean many things, what is ambiguous they cleverly and deceitfully adapt to their fabrication by an unusual explanation.[35] Thus they lead away from the Truth into captivity those who do not guard a firm faith in the one Father Almighty and in one Jesus Christ,[36] the Son of God.[37]

CHAPTER 4
THE FORMATION OF ACHAMOTH AND OF THE MATERIAL WORLD FROM HER PASSION.

1. The things that they said are outside the Fullness are as follows:[1] Intention of the Wisdom that dwells above, whom they call Achamoth,[2] and who together with her passion was separated from the Fullness,[3] was of necessity boiling over in places of shadow and emptiness;[4] for she was excluded from the light and the Fullness, being formless and shapeless, as if abortive, because she did not receive anything [from a male parent].[5] Moreover, Christ on high had pity on her and, having stretched himself beyond Stake,[6] by his own power formed only the formation which is according to substance, but not that which is according to knowledge.[7] When he had accomplished this, having withdrawn his power, he returned and so forsook her, in order that she, aware of her passion which had been caused by her separating from the Fullness, might desire the better things, since she retained some fragrance of immortality[8] which had been left her by Christ and Holy Spirit. Therefore, she too is given two names: Wisdom patronomically, for her parent is called Wisdom; and Holy Spirit, after the Spirit of Christ. But when she had obtained a form and had become intelligent, she was immediately deprived of the Word, that is, Christ, who invisibly attended her. So she set out in search of the Light that had forsaken her, but she was not able to apprehend it, because she was restrained by Limit. And while Limit was thus[9] restraining her from the impulse of going farther, he shouted out "Jao." From this, they say, came the name Jao.[10] When she was not able to go beyond Limit, because she was completely involved in passion and had been left outside alone, she fell into every kind of varied and different

passions that exist. She suffered grief, on the one hand, because she could not apprehend [the Light]; on the other hand, fear, lest she should lose life also just as she had lost the light; finally, perplexity. But all of these were enveloped in ignorance.[11] In these passions, however, she did not suffer a change as her mother, the first Wisdom and Aeon; no, her nature was opposed to knowledge.[12] At the same time another emotion came upon her, namely, of returning to him who gave her life.

2. This [emotion], they say, became the origin and substance of matter from which this world was constituted.[13] By way of illustration, from her amendment every soul of the world and of Demiurge took its origin; but from her fear and grief, all other things had their beginning. From her tears came every moist substance; from laughter, luminous substance; from grief and consternation, the corporeal elements of the world. For at all times she would weep and grieve, they tell us, because she had been left alone in the darkness and emptiness; at other times, when she thought about the light that had left her, she would relax and laugh; at still other times she would fear or be perplexed and bewildered.

3. What is all this? We have here, then, a great tragedy and a phantasy, as each one of them pompously explains[14]—one this way, another that way—from what kind of passion and from what element, material substance took its origin. Rightly, it seems to me, are they unwilling to teach these things to all in public but only to those who are able to pay a large sum for such mysteries! For no longer are these things similar to those about which Our Lord said: *You received without paying, give without pay.*[15] No, they are abstruse and portentous and profound mysteries, acquired with much toil by lovers of falsehood. Really, who would spend all his wealth in order to learn that the seas and the springs and the rivers and all liquid substance took their origin from the tears of Intention, the Aeon who suffered passion; and light, from her laughter; and the corporeal elements of this world, from her consternation and distress?

4. I myself wish to contribute something to their prolific retinue. When I see that there are fresh waters, such as springs, rivers, rains, and the like, but that the waters of the seas are salty, I think that not all the waters were emitted from her tears, because a tear has only a salty quality. Therefore, it is clear that salty waters are the ones that were

emitted from her tears. In all probability, however, in her great agony and distress she also perspired. Now, because of this, according to their hypothesis, one must assume that springs and rivers, and any other sweet waters, took their origin from her perspiration.[16] It is, namely, unbelievable that both salty and sweet waters came from her tears which have only one quality. It is more credible that some are from her tears, the others from her perspiration. Furthermore, since some waters in this world are hot and pungent, you ought to know what Intention did and from what member these were emitted! Indeed, such products fit in well with their hypothesis.

5. When,[17] therefore, their Mother had endured every passion and had with difficulty raised herself up, she turned to supplicate the Light, that is, Christ, who had left her, so they say. He, since he had returned to the Fullness, was probably unwilling to descend a second time. So he sent Advocate to her, that is, Savior, to whom Father had given all his power, and into whose power he had given over all things.[18] The Aeons followed his example, so that by him might be created all things, visible and invisible, Thrones, Divinities, and Dominions.[19] He was sent to her together with his coeval Angels.[20] They relate that Wisdom when she met him, first covered herself with a veil out of reverence,[21] but, having gazed upon his entire prolific retinue,[22] she took courage from his appearance and ran towards him. He then formed for her the formation that is according to knowledge[23] and healed her passions by removing them from her and not neglecting them;[24] for it was not possible to annihilate them, as those of the first Wisdom, because they were already possessed of aptitude and power.[25] But having separated them, he mingled and consolidated them, and changed them from an incorporeal passion into incorporeal substance.[26] Then he so fitted them with such adaptability and such a nature that they might enter composite beings and bodies, and so there would be two substances,[27] the one, coming from the passions, evil; the other, coming from the amendment, liable to suffering. Because of that they speak of Savior's having created by his own power.[28] They teach, too, that when Achamoth had been freed from passion and had with joy received the contemplation of the lights which were with him, that is, of the Angels that were with him, and had yearned after

them,[29] she brought forth fruits after their image,[30] a spiritual offspring, born after the likeness of Savior's bodyguard.

CHAPTER 5
THE FORMATION OF DEMIURGE AND OF MAN.

1. According to them,[1] therefore, there existed these three substances: The one out of passion, the material substance; the other out
of the amendment, the ensouled substance; the third, which she herself conceived, the spiritual substance.[2] In that manner she was engaged in their formation. She could, however, not give form to the
spiritual substance, because it was of the same substance as she. She
was, however, engaged in giving form to the ensouled substance
which was made out of her amendment, that is to say the physical
substance, and she produced on the outside the teachings received
from Savior.[3] First, they say, she gave form out of her ensouled substance to the God, Father and King[4] of all things, also of those who are
of the same nature as he, that is, of the ensouled substances—which
they also call the right-handed—and of the substances [that came] out
of passion and matter—which they also call left-handed.[5] For, they
assert, he gave form to all things that exist after him,[6] to which he was
secretly urged by his Mother. Hence they also call him Mother-
Parent, Fatherless,[7] Demiurge and Father. They call him Father of the
right-handed, that is, of the ensouled substances; but Demiurge of the
left-handed, that is, material substances; and King of the universe. For
when Intention wished to make all things to the honor of the Aeons,
she, or rather, Savior through her, made images of them [the Aeons];[8]
and she preserved the image of the invisible Father from the fact that
she was not known to Demiurge; but he [Demiurge] preserved the
image of the Only-begotten Son,[9] and the Archangels and Angels
who were made subject to him preserved the image of the rest of
the Aeons.

2. Accordingly,[10] they assert that he became Father and God of all

things outside the Fullness, inasmuch as he is the Maker of all the ensouled and material beings. For it was he who distinguished the two substances that were confused and made corporeal out of incorporeal things. He made the heavenly and earthly things, and became the Maker of the material and ensouled beings, of the right-handed and the left-handed, of the light and the heavy, of those that tend upwards and of those that tend downwards. He made also seven heavens,[11] above which he himself exists. On this account they style him the Hebdomad, but his Mother Achamoth is the Ogdoad, since she preserves the number of the original and primary Ogdoad of the Fullness. They affirm that the seven heavens are intelligent,[12] and they opine that they are Angels, and even Demiurge himself they opine is an Angel like God. Likewise, paradise is above the third heaven, and is a fourth Archangel with power. From him Adam received something while he dwelt in it.[13]

3. Demiurge imagines,[14] they assert, that he made the totality of these things by himself, whereas he made them inasmuch as Achamoth[15] [his Mother] emitted them. He made the heavens without knowing the heavens; he fashioned man without knowing Man; he brought the earth to light without understanding the Earth. In like manner, they assert, he was ignorant of the images of the things he made, even of his Mother herself. He imagined that he himself was all things. His Mother, they say, was the cause of that false notion of his,[16] because she wished thus to promote him as the head and beginning of her own substance and Lord over all affairs. This Mother they also call Ogdoad, Wisdom, Earth, Jerusalem, Holy Spirit, and Lord, in the masculine gender.[17] Her dwelling is the intermediate region. She is indeed above Demiurge, but below or outside the Fullness until the consummation.[18]

4. So,[19] they say that the material substance consists of three passions: fear, grief, and perplexity.[20] The ensouled substances received their constitution out of fear and amendment.[21] On the one hand they want the Demiurge to have his origin from amendment, but every other ensouled substance, such [as the souls] of irrational animals, of wild beasts, and of men [came] from fear. On this account Demiurge, too weak[22] to recognize any spiritual substance, thought that he alone was God, and declared through the prophets: *I am God . . . and besides me there is no one.*[23] Further, they teach that the wicked spiritual sub-

stances[24] came from grief. Hence, the devil whom they also call World-Ruler,[25] demons,[26] and every wicked spiritual substance, originated from grief.[27] But Demiurge, they say, is the son of their Mother [Achamoth], whereas World-Ruler is a creature of Demiurge. World-Ruler has knowledge of what is above himself, because he is the spirit of wickedness, but Demiurge is ignorant of them, inasmuch as he is ensouled. Their Mother dwells in the regions above the heavens,[28] that is, in the intermediate state, Demiurge dwells in the heavenly place, that is, in the Hebdomad;[29] but World-Ruler, in our world. The corporeal elements of the world, as we already remarked, came from consternation and distress, as from a more ignoble source.[30] Thus they teach, the earth came into being according to the condition of perplexity; the water came into being according to the movement of fear;[31] air, according to the consolidation of her grief;[32] while fire, which causes death and corruption, was inherent in all these elements, according to their teaching, just as ignorance lay hidden in these three passions.

5. After the world had been created,[33] Demiurge in turn made the earthly[34] element of man. He did not make him from this dry earth, but from the invisible substance, from the fusible and fluid matter; then, they decree, into this part he breathed[35] the ensouled element. This is he who was made *after the image and likeness.*[36] The material element is *after the image,* by which it comes near to God,[37] though it is not of the same substance as he; the ensouled element is *after the likeness.* Hence his substance was also called the Spirit of life,[38] since it came from a spiritual emission. Finally, he was clothed in a skin-like garment;[39] and this, they say, is the fleshy element that can be perceived by the senses.

6. Furthermore,[40] they declare that Demiurge himself was ignorant of the offspring of Achamoth, their Mother, which was conceived by virtue of her contemplation of the Angels who surround Savior, and which was spiritual like the Mother. Secretly, without his knowledge, she deposited this [offspring] in him that through him it might be planted as a "seed" in the soul which came from him, and thence in this material body;[41] and, having been borne in them as in a womb and grown, it might become fit for the reception of perfect knowledge.[42] So Demiurge, as they assert, was ignorant of the fact that the spiritual man, together with his breath of life,[43] was planted in him by Achamoth by means of an unutterable power and forethought. For just as

he was ignorant of his Mother, so also of her offspring. This same offspring is, according to them, Church, the antitype of Church on high. Such, then, according to their idea, is man: his soul is from Demiurge, his body is from the earth, his fleshy element is from matter, and his spiritual element is from his Mother Achamoth.

CHAPTER 6
THE THREEFOLD ELEMENT IN PERSONS. THE FORMATION OF SAVIOR. SALVATION IS THROUGH KNOWLEDGE, HENCE GOOD WORKS ARE USELESS.

1. There are, therefore, three elements. First the material, which they also call the left-handed, and which they say must necessarily perish, inasmuch as it is altogether incapable of receiving a breath of incorruptibility.[1] Second, there is the ensouled element, to which they also give the name right-handed. Inasmuch as it is between the spiritual and the material, it will go over to that element to which it has an inclination. Third, the spiritual, which has been sent forth that here below it might take on form, having the ensouled element as a consort and having been disciplined together with it in conduct. And this spiritual element, they say, is *the salt . . . and the light of the world.*[2] For even the ensouled element[3] needed sentient things as means of discipline. For this reason, they say, the world too was created and Savior came to this ensouled element that he might save it, since it had self-determining power.[4] For, they assert that he took the firstfruits from those whom he was going to save: from Achamoth, the spiritual; from Demiurge he put on the ensouled Christ; from the Economy[5] he clothed himself with a body of the ensouled substance, which was prepared with ineffable skill, so that it might be visible and tangible and passible.[6] But he did not take on any material element,[7] since material substance is incapable of receiving salvation. The consummation will take place when every spiritual element has been formed and perfected by knowledge.[8] The spiritual element is the spiritual persons who possess the perfect knowledge about God, and have been initiated into the mysteries of Achamoth; and they assume that they themselves are these.[9]

2. Really, the ensouled persons are disciplined by ensouled measures; they are the ones who are made steadfast by works and bare faith, and so do not have perfect knowledge. They claim that we of the Church[10] are these persons. So they declare that good conduct is necessary also for us; otherwise it is impossible to be saved. They themselves, however, so they dogmatize, are spiritual, not by conduct, but by nature, and so will be saved entirely and in every case. For just as the earthly element cannot partake of salvation—for they say it is incapable of receiving salvation—so, on the other hand, the spiritual, which they maintain they constitute, cannot take on corruption, regardless of what practices they may have engaged in. By way of illustration, gold when deposited in mud does not lose its beauty, but preserves its own nature, since mud can in no way injure gold. In the same way they themselves, so they indeed claim, neither suffer harm nor lose their spiritual substance regardless of what material practices they may be engaged in.[11]

3. Because of this doctrine,[12] the most perfect among them shamelessly do all the forbidden things, about which the Scriptures give guarantee *that those who do such things shall not inherit the kingdom of God.*[13] Food sacrificed to idols they eat without scruple,[14] thinking they in no way defile themselves by it. And they are the first to assemble at every heathen festival held in honor of the idols for the sake of pleasure,[15] with the result that some do not abstain even from the spectacle loathsome to God and men where men fight wild beasts and each other[16] in homicidal fashion. Others give themselves up to carnal pleasures immoderately. Carnal things, they say, must be given to the carnal, and spiritual to the spiritual.[17] Some secretly defile those women who are being taught this doctrine by them. The women who had often been seduced by some of them, but were afterwards converted to the Church of God, confessed that too,[18] along with the rest of their errors. Some, even publicly and without any shame, took away from their husbands whatever women they loved passionately and took them as their own wives. Others, finally, who in the beginning feigned to dwell chastely with them as with sisters, were exposed as time went on when the "sister" became pregnant by the "brother."

4. Moreover, they indulge in other foul and godless practices, against which we guard ourselves because of the fear of God and do not sin even in thought or word. For this they run us down as uncul-

tured and ignoramuses. Themselves, however, they extol by calling[19] themselves perfect and the children of election. Indeed, they say that we receive grace for use only, and so it will be taken away again; they, however, have grace as a proper possession, which came down from above, from the unspeakable and unnameable conjugal couple, and so it will be increased for them.[20] For this reason, they say, they must always and in every way put into practice[21] the mystery of the conjugal union. Of this they persuade unthinking people by quoting verbatim as follows: "Whoever is in the world[22] and does not love some woman to the extent of being married to her, is not of the truth[23] and will not attain to the truth. On the other hand, whoever is of the world[24] and is married to a woman will not attain the truth since he is married to the woman out of concupiscence."[25] And for this reason, for us whom they call ensouled persons[26] and claim are of the world, continence and good conduct are necessary, in order that through these we might come to the intermediate region. For themselves, however, who are called spiritual and perfect, this is by no means necessary; for it is not good conduct that leads one into the Fullness; no, it is the "seed" which is sent forth from there immature, but is perfected here below.

CHAPTER 7
THE THREE CLASSES OF PERSONS
AND THEIR ETERNAL LOT.

1. When,[1] however, all the offspring have attained perfection, they say that Achamoth, their Mother, will withdraw from the intermediate region and will enter the Fullness and receive Savior as her spouse, who was made out of all [the Aeons], that the conjugal union between Savior and Wisdom, that is, Achamoth, may take place. These are the bridegroom and the bride,[2] but the bridal chamber[3] is the entire Fullness.[4] The spiritual persons, moreover, having put off their souls and having become intellectual spirits, will enter the Fullness without being apprehended or seen, and will be given as brides to the angels who surround Savior. Even Demiurge himself will go into the region of his Mother, Wisdom, that is, into the intermediate region.

The souls of the righteous will likewise rest in this intermediate region. For nothing of an ensouled nature enters Fullness.[5] When these
things have taken place in that manner, they teach that the fire which
lies lurking in the world will blaze forth and be aflame, and having
destroyed all matter will itself all be consumed along with matter, and
pass into nothingness.[6] They declare that Demiurge was ignorant of
all these things before the coming of Savior.

2. There are those who say that Demiurge produced even Christ as
his own son but also of an ensouled nature,[7] and that he spoke of him
[Christ] through the prophets. Moreover, this is he who passed
through Mary just as water passes through a tube.[8] It was on him that
Savior, who belonged to the Fullness and was made from all the
Aeons, descended in the shape of a dove[9] at his baptism. In him, too,
was the spiritual "seed" of Achamoth itself. Our Lord, then, as they
assert, was composed of these four elements—having preserved, however, the type of the original and primary Tetrad:[10] first, of the spiritual element, which was from Achamoth; second, of the ensouled
element, which was from Demiurge; third, of Economy, who was
prepared with ineffable art; and fourth, of Savior, who was the dove
that descended on him [Jesus]. He remained impassible—inasmuch as
he is inapprehensible and invisible it would be impossible for him to
suffer—consequently, when he was led to Pilate, Christ's Spirit, who
had been deposited in him, was taken away.[11] But neither did the
"seed" that he received from his Mother suffer, for it too was impassible, being spiritual and invisible even to Demiurge. For the rest,
according to them, the ensouled element in Christ suffered, as also he
[Jesus] who was prepared by way of mystery[12] because of the Economy, in order that through him the Mother might display the type of
the Christ on high, of him, namely, who extended himself beyond
Stake and made Achamoth's formation according to substance.[13] All
these things they say are types of the things above.

3. They assert, furthermore, that the souls which possess the
"seed" of Achamoth are superior to the rest. For this reason they are
also loved more than the others by Demiurge, who, being ignorant of
the real reason, thinks they are such because of himself. Consequently, he also classified souls as prophets, priests, and kings. They
explain, too, that this offspring spoke many things through the prophets,[14] inasmuch as it was of a more exalted nature. The Mother, too—

rather she through Demiurge and through the souls made by him—
spoke[15] many things about the Aeons on high. Moreover, they divide
the prophecies into various classes: one portion they hold was spoken
by the Mother, another by the offspring, and still another by Demiurge. In the same manner, Jesus had his prophecies partly from Savior,
partly from his Mother, partly from Demiurge, as we shall show as our
work proceeds.

4. Furthermore, Demiurge, inasmuch as he was ignorant of the
things that were above him, was moved in regard to the things that
were spoken, but treated them with contempt, thinking that various
things were the causes: either the prophetic spirit—which possessed a
certain motion all its own—or mere man, or the admixture of the
baser materials.[16] Thus he remained ignorant of those things until
Savior's coming.[17] But when Savior came, Demiurge learned from him
all the things, and with all his strength gladly drew near to him. He is
the centurion of the Gospel who said to Savior: *For I too have soldiers
and slaves under my authority, and whatever I command, they do.*[18] He
will carry out the Economy[19] relative to this world until the time
appointed, mostly because of his concern for Church, but also because
he is aware of the prize in store for him, namely, that he will advance
to his Mother's region.

5. They suppose that there are three classes of people[20]—the spiritual, the ensouled, and the earthly[21]—as Cain, Abel, and Seth were; and
from these [one arrives at] the three natures by considering them no
longer as individuals but as a class.[22] The earthly indeed goes into
corruption; but the ensouled, if it chooses the better things, will rest in
the intermediate region; if, however, it chooses the worse things, it
too will go to regions similar [to the worse things]. Moreover, they
dogmatize that the spiritual people whom Achamoth has planted as
"seeds" from then until now in just souls, and which have been disciplined and nourished here below—because they were sent forth immature—and have finally become worthy of perfection, will be given
brides to the Angels of Savior, while their souls will of necessity rest
forever in the intermediate region together with Demiurge. Again,
subdividing the souls, they say that some are good by nature and some
evil by nature. The good are those that are capable of receiving the
"seed," whereas those evil by nature are never capable of receiving
that "seed."[23]

CHAPTER 8
THE VALENTINIANS PERVERT THE SCRIPTURES IN ORDER TO PROVE THEIR FABRICATIONS OUTSIDE THE FULLNESS.

1. Such is their system which neither the prophets preached, nor the Lord taught, nor the apostles handed down. They boast rather loudly[1] of knowing more about it than others do, citing it from non-scriptural works;[2] and, as people would say, they attempt to braid ropes of sand. They try to adapt to their own sayings in a manner worthy of credence,[3] either the Lord's parables, or the prophets' sayings, or the apostles' words, so that their fabrication might not appear to be without witness. They disregard the order and the connection of the Scriptures and, as much as in them lies, they disjoint the members of the Truth. They transfer passages and rearrange them; and, making one thing out of another, they deceive many by the badly composed phantasy of the Lord's words that they adapt.[4] By way of illustration,[5] suppose someone would take the beautiful image of a king, carefully made out of precious stones by a skillful artist, and would destroy the features of the man on it and change around and rearrange the jewels, and make the form of a dog, or of a fox, out of them, and that a rather bad piece of work. Suppose he would then say with determination that this is the beautiful image of the king that the skillful artist had made, at the same time pointing to the jewels which had been beautifully fitted together by the first artist into the image of the king, but which had been badly changed by the second into the form of a dog. And suppose he would through this fanciful arrangement of the jewels deceive the inexperienced who had no idea of what the king's picture looked like, and would persuade them that this base picture of a fox is that beautiful image of the king. In the same way these people patch together old women's fables,[6] and then pluck words and sayings and parables from here and there and wish to adapt these words of God to their fables.[7] We have already said how much of these words they adapt to the things within the Fullness.

2. How much, likewise, they attempt to appropriate[8] from the Scriptures to the things outside of their Fullness is [clear from] the following. The Lord, they say, in the last times of the world[9] came to

suffer for this reason, that he might manifest the suffering that came
upon the last of the Aeons and, by this end, make visible the purpose of
the dealings[10] concerning the Aeons. They tell us that the twelve-year-
old virgin, the daughter of the ruler of the temple, whom the Lord
visited and raised from the dead,[11] is a type of Achamoth, to whom
their Christ stretched himself forward and gave her form, and led her
to the perception of the light which had forsaken her. The Savior
appeared to her when she was outside the Fullness, as by the fate of an
abortion. Paul is said to have asserted this in his First Letter to the
Corinthians: *Last of all, as to one untimely born, he appeared also to me.*[12]
Likewise, in the same letter he pointed out the coming of Savior with
his coeval angels to Achamoth: *The woman ought to have a veil over her
head, because of the Angels.*[13] And, that Achamoth put a veil over her face
because of reverence when Savior came to her, Moses clearly manifested by putting a veil over his face.[14] Also the sufferings which she
endured, they assert, the Lord pointed out on the cross. In this way,
when he exclaimed: *My God, my God, why have you forsaken me?,*[15] he
recalled that Wisdom was deserted by the light and was hindered by
Limit from advancing any farther. Her grief he manifested when he
said: *My heart is very sorrowful,*[16] even to death;[17] her fear when he said:
My Father, if it is possible, let this cup pass from me;[18] and her perplexity
when he said: *And what shall I say,*[19] I do not know.

3. They teach that he pointed out the three classes of people as
follows: First the material class when to him who said: *I shall follow
you,*[20] he replied: *The Son of Man has nowhere to lay his head.* Second the
ensouled class when to him who exclaimed: *I will follow you, but let me
first go and say farewell to those at my house,*[21] he said: *No one who puts
his hand to the plow and looks back is fit for the kingdom of heaven.* This
one was the middle class, as also he who though he confessed having
kept most of the laws of holiness, did not wish to follow but was
overpowered by riches to such an extent as never to attain perfection.[22] This one they hold was in the class of the ensouled people. The
spiritual class [he pointed out] when he said: *Leave the dead to bury
their own dead; but as for you, go and proclaim the kingdom of God;*[23] and
when he said to Zacchaeus the tax collector: *Make haste and come
down; for I must stay at your house today.*[24] These, they declare, belong
to the spiritual class. The parable of the leaven,[25] too, which the
woman is said to have hidden in three measures of meal, they say,

manifests the three classes. According to their teaching, the woman is Wisdom; the three measures of meal, the three classes of people, the spiritual, the ensouled, and the earthy. The leaven is Savior himself. Paul, too, very clearly spoke of the earthly, the ensouled, and the spiritual when he said in one place: *As was the earthly, such also are the earthly;*[26] and in another place: *But the ensouled man does not receive the things of the Spirit;*[27] and in still another place: *But the spiritual man judges all things.*[28] That the ensouled man does not receive the things of the Spirit they assert he said of Demiurge who, since he was ensouled, knew neither his Mother, who was spiritual, nor her offspring, nor the Aeons in the Fullness. Paul showed, furthermore, that Savior received the firstfruits of those whom he was to save, when he said: *And if the firstfruits are holy, so is the whole lump.*[29] Now they teach that the firstfruits are the spiritual class whereas the lump is we, that is, the ensouled church, which lump he assumed and raised up[30] with himself since he was the leaven.

4. Likewise, that Achamoth strayed outside the Fullness, was given a form by Christ, and was sought by Savior, he indicated, they claim, when he said that he came to the sheep that had gone astray.[31] For the sheep that had gone astray, they explain, is said to be their Mother. From her "seed," they hold, the Church here below was planted. The straying is her stay outside the Fullness amid all sorts of passions, from which they hold matter was made. The woman who sweeps the house and finds the drachma,[32] they explain as referring to Wisdom on high, who had lost her Intention but later found it when all things had been purified by Savior's coming. For this reason according to them she is reinstated in the Fullness. Simeon, they say, who took Christ in his arms and gave thanks to him and exclaimed: *Lord, now you may let your servant depart in peace, according to your word,*[33] was a type of Demiurge who, when Savior had come, learned of his change [of region] and gave thanks to Profundity. The statement about Anna the prophetess who was announced in the Gospel, and who, after living seven years with her husband, spent the rest of her life as a widow until she saw Savior and recognized him and spoke of him to all,[34] most plainly points out Achamoth, who after looking on Savior for a little while, with his coeval angels,[35] spent all the rest of the time in the intermediate region, waiting for him, until he would come and reinstate her to her own conjugal union: *Yet Wisdom is justified by her children;*[36] and

by Paul as follows: *Yet among the mature we speak wisdom.*[37] They assert, too, that Paul spoke of the conjugal unions within the Fullness. He manifested them by the one passage where, when writing of the conjugal union in this life,[38] he said: *This mystery is a profound one. I am saying it refers to Christ and the Church.*[39]

5. Further, they teach that John, the disciple of the Lord, indicated in so many words the first Ogdoad. This is what they say. John, the disciple of the Lord, wishing to narrate the origin of all things,[40] according to which Father emitted all things, proposes a kind of beginning, the first thing begotten by Father, whom[41] he called Son[42] and Only-begotten God,[43] by whom Father emitted all things as through a "seed." They say that Word was emitted by this Only-begotten and in him was emitted the whole substance of the Aeons, whom Word himself formed later. Since, then, he speaks of the first origin [of things], he does well to start his doctrine with the Beginning, that is with the Son and the Word. He writes as follows: *In the beginning was the Word, and the Word was with God, and the Word was God. He was in the beginning with God.*[44] First, he distinguishes these three: God, Beginning, and Word. Then he unites them in order to show the emission of each one singly, namely of Son and of Word, and the union of Son to Word, and of both to Father. For the Beginning is in Father and from Father; but Word is in Beginning and from Beginning. Therefore, he said well: *In the beginning was the Word,* for he was in Son. *And the Word was with God,* for he was also Beginning. And consequently: *The Word was God,* for whatever is born of God, is God. *He was in the beginning with God,* shows the order of the emission. *All things were made through him, and without him was made not a thing,*[45] for the Word was made the cause of the form[46] and origin of all the Aeons that came after him. *But what was made in him was life.*[47] Here he indicated also the conjugal couple.[48] *For all things,* he said, *were made through him,* but the Life, in him. She [Life], then, who was made in him is more closely related to him than the things that were made through him; for she is associated with him, and through him bears fruit. For when he continues: *And the Life was the Light of Men,*[49] though he now speaks of Men,[50] he indicated also Church by the like name, so that by the one name he might manifest the union of the conjugal couple. For Man and Church spring from Word and Life. Besides, he called Life the Light of Men, because they were enlight-

ened by her. Paul says the same thing: *For anything that becomes visible is light.*[51] Since, therefore, Life is manifested and gave birth to Man and Church, she is called their Light. By these words, then, John clearly manifested among other things the second Tetrad, Word and Life, Man and Church. But he also indicated the first Tetrad; for, when he told about Savior and asserted that all things outside the Fullness were made by him, he said that he [Savior] is the fruit of the entire Fullness.[52] For John said that he [Savior] is the Light which shone in the darkness and was not comprehended by it, since in forming out of passion all the things that were made, he remained ignorant of them.[53] John also called him Son and Truth and Life, and Word-become-flesh. He asserted: *We have beheld his glory, glory as of the Only-begotten, full of grace and truth,*[54] which was given to him by Father. John, however, put it thus: *And the Word became flesh and dwelt among us, and we beheld his glory, the glory of the Only-begotten of the Father, full of grace and truth.*[55] So he carefully points out also the first Tetrad when he speaks of Father and Grace, Only-begotten and Truth. Thus John speaks of the first Ogdoad, which is the Mother of all the Aeons; he speaks namely of Father and Grace,[56] of Only-begotten and Truth, of Word and Life, of Man and Church. Thus Ptolemaeus puts it.[57]

CHAPTER 9
REFUTATION OF THE GNOSTIC USE
OF THE SCRIPTURES.

1. You see, then, my friend, the method they use. By it they deceive themselves, because they try to set up[1] their fabrication by misusing the Scriptures. On this account, I have presented their very statements,[2] that in them you might recognize the craftiness of their method and the wickedness of their error.[3] In the first place, if John had intended to point out the Ogdoad on high, he would have preserved the order of the emission and would have set down the first Tetrad among the first names, since, according to them, it is most venerable, and he would have joined the second Tetrad in the same way, that by the order of the names the order of the Ogdoad would

have been manifested, and not after so long an interval as if he had forgotten about the first Tetrad and then, when he remembered it, placed it last. Secondly, if he had wanted to point out the conjugal couples, he would not have passed by the name of Church. Or else, in regard to the rest of the conjugal couples he would have been satisfied to mention the males, since the females could be implied, so that he might have observed uniformity among all of them. Or, if he had enumerated the companions of the other Aeons, he would have indicated the consort also of Man, and would not have left it up to us to divine her name.

2. Manifest, then, is the false fabrication of their exegesis. To be sure, John preached one God Almighty, and one Only-begotten Christ Jesus, through whom he says *all things were made*.[4] This is the Word of God,[5] this is the Only-begotten,[6] this the Maker of all things, this *true Light who enlightens every man*,[7] this the Maker of the world,[8] this the one who *came into his own*,[9] this the one who *became flesh and dwelt among us*.[10] But these men speciously distort the exegesis, and they hold there is an Only-begotten by virtue of an emission, whom they call Beginning; but they hold that another became the Savior; and still another became Word of the Only-begotten Son; and another became Christ who was emitted for setting the Fullness right. They wrest each of the sayings from the Truth. They misuse the names and transfer them to their own system, so that, according to them, John does not mention the Lord Jesus Christ in these passages. For if he did speak of Father, Grace, Only-begotten, Truth, Word, Life, Man, and Church, according to their system, he spoke of the first Ogdoad, in which there was yet no Jesus or Christ, John's teacher. But the Apostle himself made it clear that he did not speak of their conjugal couples, but of Our Lord Jesus Christ, whom he knew to be the Word of God. For, by way of resuming what he said in the beginning about the Word,[11] he adds: *And the Word became flesh and dwelt among us*.[12] Now, according to their system, the Word did not become flesh, since he never even went out of the Fullness; but Savior did [become flesh], the one who was made out of all [the Aeons], who was generated later than the Word.[13]

3. Learn,[14] then, foolish people, that Jesus who suffered for us, who dwelt among us, this very same one is the Word of God. Certainly, if any other of the Aeons had become flesh for our salvation, in all

probability the Apostle would have spoken of that other Aeon. But if the Word of the Father, who descended, is the one who also ascended, namely the Only-begotten Son of the one God,[15] who according to the Father's good pleasure became flesh for the sake of men, then John is not speaking of anyone else, nor of the Ogdoad, but of the Lord Jesus Christ. For, according to them, Word did not directly become flesh; but Savior put on an ensouled body,[16] they say, which was fashioned out of the Economy by an unutterable forethought, so that he might become visible and tangible. Flesh,[17] however, is the ancient handiwork made by God out of the earth as in Adam. But it is this which John points out that the Word of God truly became. So he broke up their first and principal Ogdoad. For, since the Word and Only-begotten and Life and Light and Savior and Christ and Son of God, and this same one become incarnate for us, have been shown to be one and the same, the fabrication of their Ogdoad has been broken up. And with this broken up, their entire system falls through—this empty allusion for the defense of which they mistreat the Scripture.[18]

4. After having entirely fabricated their own system, they gather together sayings and names from scattered places and transfer them, as we have already said, from their natural meaning to an unnatural one.[19] They act like those who would propose themes which they chance upon and then try to put them to verse[20] from Homeric poems, so that the inexperienced think that Homer composed the poems with that theme, which in reality are of recent composition. Actually many are so misled by the contrived sequence of the verses that they question whether Homer may not have composed them thus; for example, if one would write as follows the Homeric lines about Hercules who was sent by Eurystheus to the dog in Hades. For the sake of illustration it is not forbidden to cite these verses, since in both cases the attempt is similar, even identical:

When thus it had been spoken, there was sent from his house
   deeply groaning
Hercules powerful hero, with brilliant deeds acquainted,
By Eurystheus, the son of Sthenelus, Perseus's offspring,
That from Erebus he might fetch the dog of dark Hades.
So, like a mountain: bred lion he went, confident of his prowess,
Rapidly through the city while all his friends followed after,

Unmarried maidens and youths, also much experienced old men,
Bitterly weeping for him as one going forward to death.
Therefore Hermes together with blue-eyed Athena did send him;
For she knew how the heart of her brother was suffering with
    grief.[21]

What simple-minded person would not be misled by these verses
and believe that Homer composed them in that manner for that very
theme? One who is well-versed in Homeric themes will recognize the
verses, but he will not recognize the theme, since he knows that some
of them were spoken of Ulysses, others of Hercules himself, others of
Priam, others of Menelaus and Agamemnon. However, if he takes
them and puts each one back into its own [theme],[22] he will make their
fabricated theme disappear. In the same way, anyone who keeps unchangeable in himself the Rule of the Truth[23] received through baptism will recognize the names and sayings and parables from the
Scriptures, but this blasphemous theme of theirs he will not recognize.
For even if he recognizes the jewels, he will not accept the fox for the
image of the king. He will restore each one of the passages to its
proper order and, having fit it into the body of the Truth,[24] he will lay
bare their fabrication and show that it is without support.

5. Since the ending[25] is wanting to this drama, in order that one who
completes their farce may add a devastating argument, we have
thought it well to show, in the first place, in what respects the fathers
of this myth themselves differ from each other, coming as they do
from different spirits of error. And indeed, from this fact one can very
accurately recognize—even before giving a demonstration[26] [of their
error]—the firm Truth preached by the Church[27] and the falsehood
fabricated by those people.

CHAPTER 10
THE RULE OF THE TRUTH IS ONE IN THE CHURCH
THROUGHOUT THE WORLD.

1. The Church,[1] indeed, though disseminated throughout the
world,[2] even to the ends of the earth, received from the apostles and

their disciples the faith in one God the Father Almighty, the Creator of heaven and earth and the seas and all things that are in them;[3] and in the one Jesus Christ, the Son of God, who was enfleshed for our salvation;[4] and in the Holy Spirit,[5] who through the prophets preached the Economies, the coming,[6] the birth from a Virgin, the passion, the resurrection from the dead, and the bodily ascension[7] into heaven of the beloved Son,[8] Christ Jesus our Lord,[9] and His coming from heaven in the glory of the Father[10] to recapitulate all things,[11] and to raise up all flesh of the whole human race,[12] in order that to Christ Jesus, our Lord and God, Savior and King, according to the invisible[13] Father's good pleasure,[14] *Every knee should bow [of those] in heaven and on earth and under the earth, and every tongue confess* Him,[15] and that He would exercise just judgment[16] toward all; and that, on the other hand, He would send into eternal fire[17] the spiritual forces of wickedness,[18] and the angels who transgressed and became rebels, and the godless, wicked, lawless, and blasphemous people; but, on the other hand, by bestowing life on the righteous and holy[19] and those who kept His commandments[20] and who have persevered in His love[21]—both those who did so from the beginning[22] and those who did so after repentance—He would bestow on them as a grace the gift of incorruption and clothe them with everlasting glory.[23] 2. The Church, as we have said before, though disseminated throughout the whole world, carefully guards this preaching and this faith which she has received, as if she dwelt in one house. She likewise believes these things as if she had but one soul and one and the same heart;[24] she preaches, teaches, and hands them down harmoniously, as if she possessed but one mouth.[25]

For, though the languages throughout the world are dissimilar, nevertheless the meaning of the tradition is one and the same.[26] To explain, the churches which have been founded in Germany do not believe or hand down anything else; neither do those founded in Spain or Gaul or Libya or in the central regions of the world.[27] But just as the sun, God's creation, is one and the same throughout the world, so too the light, the preaching of the Truth, shines everywhere and enlightens all men who wish to come to the knowledge of the Truth.[28] Neither will any of those who preside in the churches, though exceedingly eloquent, say anything else (*for no one is above the Master*[29]); nor will a poor speaker subtract from the tradition. For, since the faith is one and the same, neither he who can discourse at length about it adds to it, nor he who can say only a little subtracts from it.[30]

3. The fact that some know more by virtue of their intelligence,[31] and some less, does not come about by their changing the doctrine itself; for example, by thinking up another God besides the Creator, Maker, and Nourisher of this universe, as if He were not sufficient for us; or another Christ, or another Only-begotten. It does come about, however, by bringing out more fully the meaning of whatever was said in parables and adapting it exactly to the doctrine of the Truth;[32] and by explaining God's dealings and Economy,[33] which He made for the sake of the human race; by making clear that God was long-suffering in regard to the angels who transgressed by rebellion,[34] and in regard to the disobedience of men; by announcing why one and the same God made some things temporal, others eternal, and some heavenly, others earthly; by understanding why God, who is invisible, appeared to the prophets, not under one form, but differently to different prophets; and by indicating why several covenants were made with the human race; by[35] teaching what the real nature of each of the covenants was; and by searching out why God *consigned all things to disobedience that He may have mercy on all;*[36] by acknowledging gratefully[37] why the Word of God became flesh[38] and suffered; by announcing why the coming of the Son of God was in the last times, that is, why the Beginning appeared at the end;[39] by unfolding as much as is contained in the Scriptures about the end and the things that are to come; by not passing over in silence why God made the Gentiles, who were despaired of,[40] joint heirs and fellow members and joint partakers with the saints;[41] by proclaiming how this mortal body will put on immortality, and this corruptible body, incorruption;[42] and by preaching in what sense God says: *Those who were not a people are "my people"; and she who was not beloved is "my beloved";*[43] and in what sense He says: *For the desolate has more children than she who has a husband.*[44] Surely, in regard to these points, and others similar to them, the Apostle exclaims: *Oh the depth of [the] riches and [the] wisdom and [the] knowledge of God! How unsearchable are His judgments and how inscrutable His ways!*[45] No; [the difference] does not come about by thinking up, over and above the Creator and Maker, a Mother of theirs and His, the Intention of the Aeon who went astray, and thus to arrive at so great a blasphemy. Nor [does it come about] by feigning the Fullness which is

above even this Mother, which at one time counted only thirty, but now an innumerable tribe of Aeons, as these teachers, truly devoid of divine knowledge,[46] assert. The reason is that, as was said previously, the entire Church has one and the same faith throughout the whole world.

CHAPTER II
THE SYSTEM OF VALENTINUS AND HIS FOLLOWERS.

1. Now let us look at the unstable doctrine of these men and how, since there are two of them,[1] they do not say the same things about the same subject, but contradict themselves in regard to things and names. For example, Valentinus, the foremost, having adapted the principles from the so-called Gnostic heresy to his peculiar system of doctrine, defined it[2] as follows.[3] There is an unnameable Duality, whose one part is called Unutterable, and the other Silence. Next, out of this Duality a second Duality was emitted whose one part he named Father [Mind] and the other Truth.[4] Now from this Tetrad were produced Word and Life, Man and Church. So there existed the first Ogdoad. He says that from Word and Life ten powers were emitted, as we have said before; but from Man and Church, twelve. One of these, having gone astray and become degenerate,[5] was the cause of the rest of the affairs.[6] He explained that there were two Limits, the one between Profundity and the rest of the Fullness, separating the Aeons who were generated from Father who was ingenerate; the other separating their Mother [Wisdom] from the Fullness. But Christ was not emitted by the Aeons within the Fullness; he was brought forth by the Mother, after she had gone out of the Fullness, with some shadow, because of her memory of better things.[7] He, being masculine, severed the shadow from himself and entered the Fullness; but his Mother, though she was left with shadow and was devoid of the spiritual substance, brought forth another son. This is Demiurge, whom he also calls the all-powerful of all things under him. Together with him, he dogmatized, was emitted also a left-handed ruler. In this he agrees with those falsely called Gnostics,[8] of whom we shall speak later. As for Jesus, at

times he says that he was emitted by him who was separated from their Mother and united with all the rest, that is, by Desired; at times, by him who reentered the Fullness, that is, by Christ; at times, by Man and Church. Holy Spirit, he claims, was emitted by Truth for the purpose of testing the Aeons and making them productive, and for this he enters them in an invisible manner. So through him the Aeons produce the plants of truth.[9] Those are the things that he said.

2. Secundus[10] teaches that the first Ogdoad is a right-handed Tetrad and a left-handed Tetrad. He also teaches that one is called Light, the other Darkness, and that the rebel and degenerate power is not from the thirty Aeons, but from the fruits of these.

3. Another renowned teacher of theirs,[11] who was extending himself toward a greater height and a more profound knowledge, explained the first Tetrad as follows: "There is before all things a certain First-Beginning, a First-unthinkable,[12] who is both unutterable and unnameable. I call him Oneness. With this Oneness there coexists a power to which I give the name Unity. This Unity and Oneness, being one, without bringing forth [outside themselves] brought forth Beginning of all things, intelligible, ingenerate too, and invisible.[13] This Beginning our language styles Monad. With this Monad there coexisted a power consubstantial with it, which I call Unit. These Powers—Oneness, Unity, Monad, Unit—brought forth the rest of the emissions of the Aeons."

4. Woe, woe! Alas, alas! Indeed such a tragic exclamation of names is truly in place, relative to such a concoction of names,[14] and such boldness as his to add the names to his falsehood without blushing. For when he says: "Before all things there existed a certain First-Beginning, a First-unthinkable, whom I call Oneness," and again: "With this Oneness there coexists a Power, which I name Unity," he most clearly confesses that what he said is a fabrication and that he himself added to the fabrication the names that heretofore were not attached by anyone else. And unless he had had the boldness to do this, according to him, truth would today not have a name. Nothing,[15] therefore, prohibits anyone else from proposing names for the same system[16] as follows: There is a certain royal First-Beginning, First-unthinkable, First-non-substantial Power, First-ever-forward-rolling.[17] However, with this one there coexists a Power, which I call a Gourd; with this Gourd there coexists a Power, to which I give the name Utter-

Emptiness. Now this Gourd and Utter-Emptiness, since they are one, brought forth a fruit, without bringing it forth—a fruit everywhere visible, edible, and delicious, which in our language we call a Cucumber. With this Cucumber there coexists a consubstantial Power,[18] to which I give the name Pumpkin.[19] These Powers—Gourd, Utter-Emptiness, Cucumber, and Pumpkin—begot the rest of the multitude of delirious Pumpkins of Valentinus. For if one must accommodate to the first Tetrad this terminology, which is applied to things in general, and if one must give names according to one's pleasure, who forbids the use of these names,[20] since they are much more credible and in vogue and known by all?

5. Others, however, called their primary and original Ogdoad by the following names.[21] First, First-Beginning; second, Unthinkable; third, Unutterable; and fourth, Invisible. And from First-Beginning, Beginning was emitted in the first and fifth place; from Unthinkable, Incomprehensible was emitted in the second and sixth place; from Unutterable, Unnameable was emitted in the third and seventh place; from Invisible, Ingenerate was emitted in fourth and eighth place. This is the Fullness of the first Ogdoad. That they might appear more perfect than the perfect and be more knowledgeable of the truth than the Gnostics,[22] they hold that these Powers existed before Profundity and Silence. Against them one might justly exclaim: "Oh you nonsense-blabbering pumpkins! You blameworthy and untrue sophists!" Even in regard to Profundity there are many and different opinions among them. Some say that he is without conjugal consort, being neither male nor female,[23] nor anything at all.[24] Others claim that he is both masculine and feminine, and ascribe to him the nature of a hermaphrodite. Still others assign to him Silence as consort that there might be a first conjugal couple.

CHAPTER 12
TENETS OF THE FOLLOWERS OF PTOLEMAEUS AND COLORBASUS.

1. Now, the more knowledgeable followers of Ptolemaeus[1] claim that Profundity has two consorts, which they also call dispositions,[2]

Thought and Volition, because first he thought of what he would emit, as they say, then he willed it. Hence from these two dispositions and powers, Thought and Volition, which had formed a kind of union, there came forth as from a conjugal union the emission of Only-begotten and Truth. These two proceeded as types and images of Father's two dispositions, the visible of the invisible, Mind of Volition, and Truth of Thought. So the image of supervenient Volition was masculine, but the image of ingenerate Thought was feminine, since Volition became a kind of power of Thought. For Thought was always thinking of the emission but was not able by herself to bring forth what she thought of. When, however, the power of Volition supervened, then she emitted what she was thinking of.

2. Do not these men seem to you, my dear friend, to have had in mind the Homeric Zeus more than the Sovereign of the Universe. Zeus was not able to sleep on account of his anxiety while he was planning how he might honor Achilles and destroy the Greeks.[3] He [the Sovereign], however, has accomplished whatever He willed at the same time that He thought of it; and He thinks of whatever He wills at the same time that He wills it. Whatever He wills He thinks of, and whatever He thinks of He wills, since He is all thought, all will, all mind,[4] all eyes, all ears, the whole fountain of all good things.

3. Those,[5] however, who are considered the more intelligent among them say that the first Ogdoad was not emitted by steps, one Aeon by another; but, they assure us, the emission of the six Aeons was all together and at one time by the First-Father and his Thought, as if they themselves had acted as midwives when these were being generated.[6] No longer do they say that Man and Church were generated by Word and Life; but Word and Life, by Man and Church. They express it in the following manner. When First-Father thought of emitting something, this something was called Father; since however what he emitted was true, it was given the name Truth; but when he wished to manifest himself, it was called Man. Those whom he first thought of emitting were given the name Church. Man spoke the Word; this is the first-born Son. But Life followed upon Word. And so the first Ogdoad was completed.

4. They quarrel much among themselves about Savior, too.[7] Some claim that he was generated from all the Aeons, for which reason he is

also called the Well-pleasing, because the entire Fullness was pleased to glorify Father through him.[8] Others claim that he was emitted only by the ten Aeons who came from Word and Life, that on account of this he was called Word and Life, and that he kept the name of his parents. Still others claim that he was made from the twelve Aeons who sprang from Man and Church; and hence he professes himself to be the Son of Man, as if he were a descendant of Man. Still others claim he was made by Christ and Holy Spirit, who were emitted for the support of the Fullness;[9] hence he is called Christ, keeping the name of the Father by whom he was emitted. Others, finally, claim that Man is called the First-Father of all [the Aeons] and First-Beginning and First-unthinkable. And this is the great and hidden mystery[10] that the Power which is above all others and contains all others is called Man. And for this reason Savior called himself the Son of Man.

CHAPTER 13
THE DECEITFUL ARTS AND WICKED PRACTICES OF MARCUS.

1. A certain member of their company, Marcus by name,[1] who boasts of correcting his teacher,[2] is also very skilled in magical imposture. By this means he deceived many men and not a few women, and converted them to himself as to one most learned and most perfect,[3] possessed of the greatest power from invisible and unnameable regions. In truth, he was the forerunner of the Antichrist. For example, he combines the buffooneries of Anaxilaus[4] with the craftiness of so-called magicians. As a result those who have no sense and have lost their mind think he is working wonders.

2. As he feigns to give thanks over the cup mixed with wine,[5] and draws out at great length the prayer of invocation,[6] he makes the cup appear to be purple or red so that it seems that Grace, who is from the regions which are above all things, dropped her own blood into that cup because of his invocation, and that those who are present greatly

desire to taste of that drink, so that Grace, who was invoked by this magician, might rain upon them too. Moreover, having handed mixed cups to the women, he commands them to give thanks over them in his presence. And when this has been done, he himself brings forward another cup much larger than that over which the duped woman gave thanks, and pours from the smaller cup, over which thanks had been given by the woman, into the one which he himself brought forward. At the same time he says over it these words: "May Grace who is before all things, unthinkable and unspeakable, fill your inner self[7] and increase in you her own knowledge, by planting the mustard seed in good ground."[8] By saying some such words and driving the wretched woman to madness, he appears to have worked wonders, namely, that the large cup was filled from the small one, even to overflowing. Still other acts similar to these he performed and deceived many and drew them after himself.

3. It is probable that he possesses even some demon as a familiar, through whom he himself seems to prophesy,[9] and through whom whatever woman he considers worthy to partake of his Grace he makes prophesy. Especially about women he is concerned, and that, about those who are well-dressed and clothed in purple and who are very rich, whom he often attempts to seduce. Flatteringly he says to them: "I want you to partake of my Grace, because the Father of all always sees your Angel in his presence.[10] But the dwelling place of your Greatness [angel][11] is within us. It behooves us to be united. First receive Grace from me and through me. Adorn yourself as a bride awaiting her bridegroom that you may be what I am, and I may be what you are. Put the 'seed' of light in your bridal chamber. Take from me the bridegroom. Receive him [in yourself] and be received in him.[12] Look, Grace is descending upon you. Open your mouth and prophesy."[13] Now, if the woman should answer: "I have never prophesied and do not know how to prophesy," he will again utter some invocations to the amazement of the duped woman. He says to her: "Open your mouth and say anything whatsoever and prophesy." Thereupon she becomes puffed up and elated by those words, her soul becomes aroused at the prospect of prophesying, her heart beats faster than usual. She dares idly and boldly to say nonsensical things and whatever

happens to come to mind, since she has been heated by an empty wind. (This is what one superior to us said about such people,[14] "A soul that is heated by empty air is bold and impudent.") From now on she considers herself a prophetess and thanks Marcus for having given her of his Grace. She tries to reward him not only by the gift of her possessions—in that manner he has amassed a fortune—but by sharing her body, desiring to unite herself with him in every way so that she may become one with him.

4. But some of the most faithful women, who have the fear of God and could not be deceived—whom he tried to beguile like the rest by commanding them to prophesy—rejected and condemned him, and withdrew from such company.[15] They knew very well that the gift of prophecy does not enter man through Marcus, the magician. On the contrary, upon whomever God sends his grace from above, they are the ones who possess the God-given prophetic power and then speak where and when God wills, but not when Marcus commands. For whoever commands is greater and of higher authority than the one who is commanded, since the one rules, but the other has been made subject. If, then, Marcus commands, or someone else—since they all have the custom of drawing lots at the banquets[16] and of commanding one another to prophesy, and, in keeping with their own desires, of prophesying for their own benefit—the one who commands, though he is a man, will be greater and of higher authority than the prophetic spirit. This, of course, is impossible. On the contrary, such spirits that are commanded by these men and speak whatever the men wish are perishable and weak, bold and impudent, sent by Satan to deceive and destroy those who have not kept that vigorous faith, which they had received through the Church in the beginning.

5. Furthermore,[17] often these women returned to the Church of God and confessed that this Marcus concocts love potions and charms[18] for some of them, though not for all, in order to insult even their bodies; and that they were violated in body by him, and on their part loved him very erotically. So it happened that a certain deacon from among our own people in Asia,[19] who while giving Marcus hospitality in his own house fell victim to such a misfortune. His wife, who was very beautiful, was defiled in mind and body by this magician. For

a long time she traveled about with him. When, however, with much effort the brothers converted her, she spent the whole time doing penance[20] amid weeping and lamentation over the defilement she had suffered through this magician.

6. Some of his disciples, too, who wandered about among them, deceived many silly women and defiled them.[21] They boasted of being so perfect that no one was able to come up to the greatness of their knowledge, not even were one to mention Peter or Paul, or any other of the apostles, and that they knew more than all others and alone imbibed the greatness of the knowledge and the unspeakable Power; they themselves are on a height above all Power, and so they are free to do all things without fear of anyone in regard to anything. For, because of the redemption,[22] they cannot be apprehended by, and are invisible to, the Judge. But even if he should apprehend them, standing in his presence they would say these words together with the redemption: "O Coadjutor of God and of the mystic Silence who is before all the Aeons, through whom[23] the Greatnesses always behold the Father's face,[24] using you as their guide and usher, they [Greatnesses] draw their forms up above."[25] (These forms she [Achamoth] in her great daring had fancied, and on account of First-Father's goodness produced us as their images while contemplating the things on high as in a dream.) "See, the Judge is at hand and the herald orders me to defend myself. You, however, acquainted as you are with the affairs of both, present to the Judge the case of both of us as if it were one cause." Now as soon as the Mother heard these pleas, she put on them the Homeric helmet of Hades so they could escape from the Judge without being seen.[26] And suddenly she draws them up and introduces them into the bridal chamber and restores them to their own consorts.[27]

7. Such things as these they prattled and practiced also in our own regions around the Rhone[28] and deceived many women. Some of these women who had had their consciences seared[29] made a confession;[30] some are even ashamed openly to do this; and others gradually withdrew themselves in silence and despaired of the life of God;[31] some of them apostasized completely; others waver between both courses and experience what the proverb says: "They are neither outside nor in-

side." Such is the profit they have from the "seed" of the children of "knowledge."

CHAPTER 14
THE MARCOSIAN SYSTEM IN NUMBERS AND LETTERS.

1. This Marcus,[1] therefore, claimed that he alone is the matrix and receptacle of Silence of Colorbasus,[2] inasuch as he is Only-begotten. The seed[3] that was deposited in him he brought forth in the following manner. The most exalted Tetrad came down to him from the invisible and unnameable regions in the shape of a woman, since, as he says, the world could not have endured her masculine nature. She revealed who she was and also the origin of all things. This she had never before revealed to anyone whether of the gods or of men. To Marcus alone she explained it as follows. When Father, who is without a father,[4] unthinkable and immaterial in substance, who is neither male nor female, first wished that the unspeakable be spoken and the invisible be given form, he opened his mouth and brought forth Word similar to himself. Word stood beside him and manifested to him who he was, since he had appeared as the form of the invisible.[5] The enunciation of the name developed in the following manner. He [the Father] pronounced the first word of his name, which is Beginning [*Arkhē*]; it was a combination[6] of four characters. He joined a second to it which was also a combination of four letters. Next he pronounced the third; this consisted of ten characters. And the combination that he pronounced after these had twelve characters.[7] So the pronunciation of the whole name consisted of thirty letters, but four combinations. Each of the characters had its own letters, its own impressions, its own pronunciation, shape, and images; and not one of them [characters] perceives the form of that [combination] of which itself is a character.[8] Moreover, none knows its own [combination], nor does it know[9] the pronunciation even of its neighbor's name. On the contrary, what it pronounces, it does so as if it were pronouncing

the whole; it believes that it names the whole. For each of them, since it is a member of the whole, names its own sound as if it were the whole; and they do not cease sounding until they come to the last letter of the last character that pronounces itself alone.[10] The restoration[11] of all things will take place, he said, whenever all have descended upon the one letter, and sound one and the same pronunciation. He supposes the Amen, which we pray in unison, to be the image of this pronunciation. But the sounds, he claims, are those which formed the Aeon that is immaterial and ingenerate. They are likewise the forms which see the face of Father unceasingly, which the Lord calls Angels.[12]

2. Those names of the characters which are common and can be told he named Aeons, Words, Roots, Seeds, Fullnesses, and Fruits.[13] He said we must believe that each one of them, and whatever is peculiar to each one, is contained in the name Church. Now of these characters the last letter of the last character voiced itself, and its sound,[14] going forth according to the image of the characters, begot its own characters.[15] From these he says all the things that are here below were prepared, and the things that were before these[16] were begotten. Indeed, on the one hand, the letter itself, whose sound followed the sound here below, he asserts, was again taken up by its own combination in order to complete the whole; but the sound remained here below as if cast out. On the other hand, the character itself,[17] from which the letter together with its pronunciation came down, the Tetrad says, is made up of thirty letters, and each of the thirty letters has in itself other letters, from which the name of the letters [to which they belong] is coined. And again, these other letters are named by still others, and these by others, so that the multitude of letters runs into infinitude. By the following you may understand more clearly what I have said.[18] The character delta contains in itself five letters, that is, delta itself, epsilon, lambda, tau, and alpha. Now these letters are again written by other letters,[19] and these others by still others. If, then, the entire substance of delta runs into infinitude, letters continually begetting other letters, and following each other, how much greater than that character is this sea of letters? And if the one letter is so infinite, think of the profundity of the letters which make up the entire name of First-Father [Profundity] according to the teaching of Marcus's Silence. Hence Father, knowing his incomprehensible nature, gave to

each one of the characters, which he also called Aeons, the power to utter its own pronunciation, because the single Aeon was not capable of uttering the whole.

3. Further,[20] the Tetrad explained these things to him as it said: "I also wish to show you Truth itself. I have brought her down from the dwellings on high that you might look on her unveiled and learn of her beauty and also hear her speak and admire her wisdom. See, then, alpha and omega are her head on high; beta and psi are her neck; gamma and chi are her shoulders with hands; her breast is delta and phi; epsilon and upsilon are her diaphragm; zeta and tau are her stomach; eta and sigma are her private parts; theta and rho are her thighs; iota and pi are her knees; kappa and omicron are her legs; lambda and xi are her ankles; mu and nu are her feet." (This, according to the magician, is the body of Truth; this is the shape of her character; this the impression of her letter. And he calls this character Man. He claims that it is the source of every word, the beginning of every sound, the expression of all that is unspeakable, and the mouth of taciturn Silence. This indeed is her body.) "You, however, lift the thought of your mind higher and from the Mouth of Truth hear the self-begetting Word who dispenses Father's gift."

4. When that Tetrad had spoken these things, Truth looking at Man and opening her mouth uttered a word.[21] The word became a name, and the name was the one that we know and speak, Christ Jesus. As soon as she had spoken it, she was silent. When Marcus, however, waited for her to say more, the Tetrad appeared and said: Have you considered as contemptible the word from the mouth of Truth? This word which you know and seem to possess is not a name of old, for you merely possess its sound; you are ignorant of its power. For Jesus indeed is a symbolical name,[22] having six letters and being known by all who belong to those who are called.[23] The name, however, which is among the Aeons of the Fullness has many parts, being of another form and of another type; it is known by those companions [of Savior], whose Greatnesses [angels] are always with him.

5. Know,[24] then, that these your twenty-four letters are symbolical emissions of the three powers[25] which embrace the entire number of characters on high. You are to consider the nine mute letters[26] as belonging to Father and Truth, because these are mute, that is, they are unspeakable and unutterable. The eight semivowels,[27] as belonging

to Word and Life, because they are, as it were, intermediate between the mutes and the vowels, they receive the emission from the Aeons above; but an ascent from those below.[28] The vowels too are seven. They belong to Man and Church, because the voice that came forth through Man formed all things; for the sound of the voice clothed them with form. So Word and Life possess eight [of the letters]; Man and Church, seven; Father and Truth, nine. Since, however, the reckoning was deficient, he who was superfluous in Father descended, having been sent forth to the one from whom he had been separated, to set right the deeds, in order that the unity of the Fullness, since it was endowed with equality, might produce in all of them one Power which was from all.[29] And thus he who had the seven letters received the power of him who had the eight; and all three regions were made alike in respect to number, being Ogdoads. When these came together three times, they manifested the number twenty-four. The three characters,[30] too, which he asserts[31] belong to the three Powers in conjugal pairs, become six. From these flow the twenty-four characters, having been quadrupled by the number of the unspeakable Tetrad. This, then, adds up to the same number as is said to belong to the Unnameable. These, however, are borne by the three Powers according to the likeness of the Invisible. The characters which we call double letters[32] are images of the characters of these [three Powers]. When these double letters are added to the twenty-four characters by virtue of analogy [to those on high], they make the number thirty.[33]

6. The fruit of this count and arrangement,[34] he asserts, is the one that appeared in the likeness of an image.[35] He who after six days ascended the mountain as the fourth one[36] became the sixth one,[37] that is, the one who descended upon and was contained in the Hebdomad,[38] since he was the symbolical Ogdoad and had in himself the entire number of the characters. This number, the descent of the dove, which is the alpha and the omega, manifested when he came to his baptism; for the number of the dove is eight hundred and one.[39] For this reason, too, Moses said that man was made on the sixth day.[40] Likewise, the Economy [Jesus] was made on the sixth day, the day of Preparation,[41] on which[42] the last man appeared to regenerate the first man. Of this Economy the sixth hour was the beginning and the end,

since on this hour he was affixed to the cross. For perfect Mind understood the number six, since he had the power of creating and regenerating, and he manifested to the children of light[43] the regeneration which was achieved by means of that symbolical number which appeared in him [the last man].[44] Hence he asserts that the double letters also contain the symbolical number.[45] In fact, the symbolical number when added to the twenty-four characters completes the thirty-letter name.

7. As Marcus's Silence said, he [the symbolical number] used as a minister the Greatness of the seven numbers, that the fruit of the self-devised plan might be made manifest.[46] "Indeed for the present," she said, "consider the symbolical number [Jesus], he who was formed by the symbolical number, and who was, as it were, divided or cut in two and remained outside. He, by his own power and intelligence, through his own production, and in imitation of the Hebdomad's power breathed life into this world of seven powers and made it the soul of the visible universe. Therefore, he too used this work as if it had been made by him of his own free will. But the other [works], inasmuch as they are imitations of the inimitable things, minister to the Mother's Intention.[47] And so the first Heaven pronounces the alpha; the second, the epsilon; the third, the eta; the fourth, which is the middle number of seven, pronounces the value of iota; the fifth, the omicron; the sixth, the upsilon; the seventh, which is also the fourth from the middle, cries out the character omega." The Silence of Marcus assures us of this, talking nonsense but saying nothing true. "All these powers," she adds, "embracing each other, together voice and glorify him by whom they were emitted. And the glory of the sound is wafted upwards to First-Father." Indeed, she asserted that the sound of this glorification, when borne to earth, becomes the Maker and Parent of the things upon the earth.[48]

8. He takes his proof for this from newborn infants, whose soul, as soon as they come forth from the womb, cries out the sound of each of the characters. Therefore, just as the seven Powers glorify Word, he says, so the soul of these infants, weeping and mourning over Marcus, glorify him. On this account David also said: *By the mouth of infants and sucklings you have perfected praise;*[49] and again: *The heavens are*

telling the glory of God.[50] For this reason, too, when the soul is in suffering and distress for its own purgation,[51] it cries out omega as a sign of praise, in order that, when the soul on high recognizes its kin,[52] it might send help to it.

9. Such is the nonsense he has spoken about Name which is all, which is composed of thirty letters; about Profundity, who received an increase from the letters of this name; about Truth's body with its twelve members, each of which consists of two letters; about the voice of her who spoke without speaking; about the interpretation of the Name that has not been spoken; and about the soul of the world and of man, insofar as they possess the Economy who is according to the image. Next we shall tell you how the Tetrad showed Marcus an equal-numbered power from among the names, so that none of their words,[53] my friend, that have come to our knowledge may be hidden from you. This is in accord with your repeated request.

CHAPTER 15
THE ACCOUNT OF SILENCE TO MARCUS ABOUT THE GENERATION OF THE TWENTY-FOUR CHARACTERS AND OF JESUS.

1. To continue,[1] their all-wise Silence announced the origin of the twenty-four characters as follows. Unity exists together with Oneness. From these, according to what we said above, there are two emissions, Monad and One. When these were added to the two, there were four, since two times two are four. Again, when two and four were added, they disclosed the number six. Moreover, when these six were multiplied by four, they brought forth the twenty-four forms. These names in the first Tetrad are considered the holiest and could not be spoken; they are known only by the Son, though Father also knows what they are. The other names, however, which are pronounced with solemnity and faith are these: Unutterable (*Arrētos*) and Silence (*Sigē*), Father (*Patēr*) and Truth (*Alētheia*). The sum total of this Tetrad is twenty-four characters. For the name Unutterable (*Arrētos*) has seven letter; Silence (*Seigē*), five; Father (*Patēr*), five; and Truth (*Alētheia*), seven. Now when these are added together,

namely, twice five and twice seven, they fill out the number twenty-four. In like manner, the second Tetrad, Word (*Logos*) and Life (*Zōē*), Man (*Anthrōpos*) and Church (*Ekklēsia*), manifest the same number of characters. Likewise the name of Savior, which can be uttered, that is, Jesus (*Iēsous*), has six letters, but his name which cannot be uttered has twenty-four letters.[2] The name "Christ the Son" (*Huios Khreistos*) has twelve letters; but the name of Christ that is unutterable has thirty letters.[3] And for this reason he asserts that he is alpha and omega in order to indicate the dove,[4] since this bird had that number.[5]

2. Jesus,[6] he asserts, has the following ineffable origin. The second Tetrad came forth as a daughter from the Mother of all things, that is, from the first Tetrad,[7] thus the first Ogdoad resulted. From this proceeded the Decad. In this way a Decad and an Ogdoad were made. The Decad, then, having been added to the Ogdoad and multiplied by ten produced the number eighty. The number eighty, in turn, multiplied by ten begot the number eight hundred. As a result, the entire number of the letters, having proceeded from the Ogdoad to the Decad, is eight plus eighty plus eight hundred. For the name of Jesus, according to the number to which the letters correspond, is eight hundred and eighty-eight. And so you have clearly [stated] also the supercelestial origin of Jesus.[8] For this reason the Greek alphabet has eight units, eight decades, and eight hundreds. Thus it reveals the number eight hundred eighty-eight, that is Jesus, who was composed of all the numbers.[9] For this reason, too, he is called alpha and omega, thus indicating his origin from all. They have this explanation too. When the various units of the first Tetrad were added together according to the progression of numbers, the number ten appeared; for one, two, three, and four, when added up, make ten. This is written I, and this they hold is Jesus. Moreover, Christ [*Khreistos*], he said, consisting of eight letters, points out the first Ogdoad, which when multiplied by ten, and that result again by ten, and all added together, begot Jesus. Besides, he asserts that Christ the Son, that is the Dodecad, is spoken of. For Son is a name of four letters [*Huios*] and Christ [*Khreistos*] of eight, which when added together manifest the greatness of the Dodecad. In addition, he asserts before the symbol of this name, that is, Jesus, appeared to his sons,[10] men were steeped in great ignorance and error. But when the six-letter Name appeared—who clothed himself in flesh, in order to be apprehensible by man's

senses, and who possessed in himself these six and twenty-four letters[11]—their ignorance was dispelled when they knew him, and they
ascended from death to life. Thus for them the Name was born as a
way to the Father of Truth.[12] For, as he claims, the Father of all things
resolved to dispel the ignorance and to destroy death. Now the knowledge [received] from him was the dispelling of the ignorance. For that
purpose the man was chosen,[13] who was made according to his will and
according to the image of the Power on high.[14]

3. The Aeons proceeded from a Tetrad.[15] In the Tetrad there were
Man and Church, Word and Life. When, therefore, powers had
emanated from these Aeons, as he asserts, they begot the Jesus who
appeared on earth. The Angel Gabriel took the place of Word; Holy
Spirit, of Life; the power of the Most High, of Man;[16] but the Virgin
indicates the Church. And so in his [Marcus's] judgment, the man
according to the Economy was engendered through Mary. The Father
of all things chose[17] this man through Word, as he passed through her
womb, in order to make himself known. When he came to the water
for baptism, there descended on him as a dove[18] the one who had
ascended on high and who filled up the number twelve. In him existed
the "seed" of those who were planted together with him,[19] and who
descended and ascended together with him. Moreover, he asserts, this
power which descended is Father's "seed,"[20] which has in itself both
Father and Son, and the unnameable power of Silence which is known
through them, and all the Aeons. And this is Spirit who spoke by the
mouth of Jesus, confessed himself to be Son, manifested Father, and
when he descended upon Jesus, was made one with him. He asserts
that Savior, who was made because of the Economy, destroyed death,
but made known his Father, the Christ.[21] He says, therefore, that Jesus
is the name of Man who was made because of the Economy; and it was
given after the likeness and form of Man who was about to descend
upon him. So when he [Jesus] apprehended him [Man from on high],
he was in possession of Man and Word and Father, and of the Unutterable One, and of Silence and Truth and Church and Life.

4. Such things really are too much for even a "Woe" and "Alas"
and every exclamation of sadness and grief. For who would not hate
the deplorable[22] contriver of such falsehoods, when he sees the Truth
made into an idol by Marcus and branded with the letters of the

alphabet? The Greeks confess that it is only recently—relative to what was from the beginning, which is expressed by "Yesterday and the day before yesterday"[23]—that first they received sixteen letters through Cadmus. Then, as time went on, they themselves invented others; at one time the aspirate, at another the double letters; last of all, Palamedes added the long letters to the rest.[24] By inference, before these letters were made by the Greeks, Truth did not exist! For the body of Truth, according to you, Marcus, was begotten later than Cadmus, and so later than those who existed before him. It is also begotten later than those who added the rest of the characters; later than yourself, because you alone reduced to an idol her whom you call Truth.[25]

5. Furthermore, who will put up with your Silence who garrulously utters such things, who gives a name to the Unnameable, who explains the Unspeakable, who searches out the Unsearchable; and who asserts that he who you claim is incorporeal and invisible opened his mouth and sent forth Word as one of the composite animals; and who asserts that Word, though he is like him who emitted him and became the image of the Invisible, consists nevertheless of thirty characters and four combinations [of letters]? Then Father of all things will consist in accordance with his resemblance to the Word, as you say, of thirty characters and four combinations. Or who will put up with you who confine the Creator of all things, the Framer and Maker, the Word of God, to figures and numbers—now thirty, now twenty-four, now only six—and then divide Him into four combinations and thirty characters? With you, who reduce to the number eight hundred and eighty-eight the Lord of all things who established the heavens,[26] as if He had become like the alphabet? With you who subdivide into a Tetrad, Ogdoad, Decad, and Dodecad the Father, who comprehends all things, but is Himself incomprehensible.[27] With you, finally, who by the multiplications of these numbers explain the Father's nature, which, as you say, is unutterable and unthinkable? You yourself become a false Daedalus[28] and the wicked architect of the Power that is supreme over all things, by giving a name to him who is incorporeal and immaterial, and by building his essence and substance out of many letters, the ones begetting the others. And the power, which you assert is indivisible, you divide into consonants and vowels and semi-vowels.

You falsely ascribe the unutterable element [of these letters] to Father of all things and to his Thought, and so you thrust into the worst blasphemy and greatest impiety all those who put their trust in you.

6. Both rightly and fittingly, therefore, in view of your boldness, has the divinely inspired elder and preacher of the Truth burst forth against you in the following poetic lines:[29]

> Marcus, maker of idols, observer of portents,
> Skilled in astrology and in all arts of magic,
> Whereby you confirm your erroneous doctrines.
> Showing wonders to whomever you lead into error,
> Showing the works of the apostate Power,
> Marvels which Satan, your father, teaches you always
> To perform through the power angelic of Azazel,[30]
> Using you as the precursor of godless Evil.

Such are the words of the God-loving elder. We, however, shall attempt briefly to run through the rest of their mystical teachings, though they are long; and things that have long remained hidden, we shall bring into the open. In this way we hope they can easily be refuted by all.[31]

CHAPTER 16
THE ABSURD INTERPRETATIONS OF THE MARCOSIANS.

1. These men associate the origin of their Aeons with the straying and finding of the sheep,[1] as they make it into one thing and endeavor to explain it in a more mystic manner by reducing all things to numbers. They assert that all things consist of monads and dyads. They add up the numbers from one to four and thus beget the Decad. In fact, one, two, three, and four added up bring forth the number ten of the Aeons.[2] Again, when the Dyad proceeded [by twos] from itself up to Symbol [Six], that is two plus four plus six, it manifested the Dodecad. Further, if in the same way we add up the numbers [by twos] from two until ten, the number thirty is manifested,[3] in which are contained the

Ogdoad, Decad, and Dodecad. But the Dodecad they call passion
because it contains the symbolical number [six] which accompanies it
[the Dodecad].[4] For that reason a defection occurred in regard to the
number twelve. The sheep skipped away and went astray.[5] Then, they
assert, the apostasy from the Dodecad took place. In the same way,
they divine one Power perished when it defected from the Dodecad.
This is the woman who lost her coin and, having lighted a candle,
found it again.[6] Accordingly, when the numbers that are left over—
namely, nine in reference to the coins and eleven[7] in reference to the
sheep—are multiplied by each other, the number ninety-nine is the
result, because nine multiplied by eleven makes ninety-nine. And for
this reason, they say "Amen" contains this same number.[8]

2. I shall not shrink from declaring to you their other interpretations in order that you may recognize their fruit everywhere. They
hold that the character eta together with the symbolical number constitutes an Ogdoad, inasmuch as it is the eighth in line from the first
letter. Then again, when one counts up the number of their characters
till eta, without the symbolical number, they manifest the Triacontad.
For if one begins with alpha and finishes the count of the characters
with eta, omitting the symbolical number and adding together the sum
of the letters, he will find the number of the Triacontad. To illustrate,
up to epsilon the total is fifteen; then by adding the number seven to
that, the number twenty-two is obtained; then by adding to these eta,
that is eight, the most wonderful Triacontad is completed. And because of this they declare that the Ogdoad is the Mother of the thirty
Aeons. Since, therefore, the number thirty is combined from the three
powers [Ogdoad, Decad, and Dodecad], when it is multiplied by
three, it makes ninety; for three by thirty is ninety. Again, this same
triad when squared makes nine. Thus the Ogdoad begets the number
ninety-nine. And since the twelfth Aeon, when it defected, left the
eleven above, they say appropriately that the form of the letters has
been so prepared that they are a symbol of the Logos.[9] For the lambda
is the eleventh of the letters, but that is the number of the Triacontad.
And it corresponds to the image of the Economy on high, since from
alpha, omitting the symbolical number, until lambda, the sum of the
letters in immediate succession, adding also the lambda, is ninety-
nine. It is quite clear from the very shape of the character of the
lambda, which in point of order is in the eleventh place, that it de-

scended to search for one like itself in order to complete the number twelve; and having found it, it was completed. For the lambda, as it were, having gone in search of the character like itself, and having found it and snatched it to itself, filled up the place of the number twelve, since the mu is composed of two lambdas. By means of their knowledge, then, they too flee from the place of the ninety-nine, that is, Degeneracy, which is the type of the left hand; however, they strive after the one, who, when added to the ninety-nine, transfers them to the right hand.[10]

3. Well do I know, my friend, that as you run through these things, you will have a good laugh on such would-be-wise foolishness of theirs. They really deserve our pity, these men who by means of the alphabet and numbers so coldly and violently tear to pieces so great a religion, the greatness of the truly unexpressable Power, and the so great Economies of God. These men have apostatized from the Church; they believe such old women's tales;[11] they are truly self-condemned.[12] Paul commands us to avoid such after the first and second admonition.[13] And John, the Lord's disciple, made their condemnation stronger by wishing that we do not even give them a welcome. *For he who greets them,* John asserts, *shares in their wicked works;*[14] and rightly: *For there is no welcome,* says the Lord, *for the wicked.*[15] Really, more impious than every impiety are these people who claim that the Maker of heaven and earth, who alone is the all-powerful God, above whom there is no other God, was emitted from degeneracy, which in turn was emitted from another degeneracy, so that according to them he is the emission of a third degeneracy.[16] Such a doctrine we must really exhale from ourselves and execrate.[17] We must, moreover, flee far from such people. And the more they boldly affirm and rejoice in their fictions, so much the more should we realize that they are under the influence of the Ogdoad of wicked spirits.[18] By way of illustration, people who fall into a fit of frenzy, the more they laugh and think themselves well and do all things as people who are in good health, and some things even better than people who are in good health, so much the sicker are they. In the same way these men, the more they think themselves to be superwise and exhaust themselves, as do those who overstretch the bow, so much less wisdom do they have. For when the unclean spirit of foolishness had gone out of these people and when later he found them occupied, not with God, but with worldly ques-

tions, he took with himself seven other spirits more wicked than himself;[19] and he infatuated the minds of these people so much that they thought they were capable of thinking of being above God; and he fittingly prepared them for complete derangement.[20] Then he put in them the wicked spirits' Ogdoad of foolishness.

CHAPTER 17
THE MARCOSIAN THEORY THAT CREATED THINGS WERE MADE AFTER THE PATTERN OF THE INVISIBLE BEINGS.

1. I wish[1] to explain to you how they claim that this creation was made after the pattern of the invisible beings by Demiurge's Mother, who used him as an instrument, though he was ignorant of this. They assert, first, that the four elements, fire, water, earth, and air, were emitted as images of the Tetrad on high.[2] Now if the energies of these four elements—namely, heat and cold, dryness and humidity—are added together, they image the Ogdoad exactly. Out of this [Ogdoad][3] they enumerate ten powers as follows: seven spherical bodies, which they also call the heavens; then the sphere that encircles these, which they name the eighth heaven; after these, the sun and moon. Since these amount to ten, they claim that they are the copies of the invisible Decad, which proceeded from Word and Life. The Dodecad is indicated by the so-called zodiacal circle; for according to them, the twelve zodiacal signs most clearly foreshadow the Dodecad, the daughter of Man and Church. And since the highest heaven was linked to the movement of the whole group [of heavens] and bore down on their sphere, and by its gravity acted as a counterbalance to their speed, the result was that it made the cycle from one sign to another in thirty years.[4] So they claim it is a copy of Limit who encircles their Mother, whose name is Thirty. The moon, in turn, since it encircles its own heaven in thirty days, images the thirty Aeons by the number of days. The sun, too, since it runs through its orbit in twelve months and, returning to its starting point, completes the circle, manifests the Dodecad by its twelve months. And even the days, since they are

measured by twelve hours,[5] are a type of the Dodecad. But even the hour, the twelfth part of a day, they assert, is arranged in thirty parts as an image of the Triacontad. Also the circumference of the zodiacal circle itself consists of three hundred and sixty degrees, because each of the zodiacal signs has thirty degrees. And thus, they say, by means of this circle, the image is preserved of the relation between the twelve and the thirty.[6] Furthermore, they assert that the earth is divided into twelve zones, and in each zone it receives perpendicularly a special power from the heavens.[7] It also begets offspring that are similar to the power that sends down the influence.[8] They assure us that this is a most evident type of the Dodecad and its offspring.

2. In addition to this, they hold that[9] Demiurge wanted to imitate the infinite, eternal, immeasurable, and timeless nature of the Ogdoad on high. When, however, he was not able to make a copy of the Ogdoad's permanent and perpetual nature, since he himself was a fruit of Degeneracy, he broke down the Ogdoad's eternal nature into times, seasons, and numbers of many years, since he thought he was imitating the Ogdoad's infinite nature by a multitude of times.[10] At this point, when Truth escaped his reach, they say that he became a follower of falsehood.[11] And so when the times have run their course, his work will come to ruin.

Chapter 18

The Marcosians Distort Passages of the Pentateuch to Support Their Fabrications about Creation.

1. In saying[1] such things about the creation each one of them, as far as he is able, thinks up every day something more novel.[2] None of them is perfect if he does not produce among them the greatest lies. So it is necessary that we point out and refute whatever passages of the prophets they transpose and adapt. Moses, they assert, when he began the account of creation, pointed out the Mother of all things in the very beginning when he said: *In the beginning God created the heavens and the earth.*[3] Therefore, as they say, by naming these four—

God and beginning, the heavens and the earth—he expressed the types of their Tetrad.[4] He also indicated its invisible nature when he said: *Now the earth was invisible and unformed.*[5] They hold that the second Tetrad, the offspring of the first Tetrad, he announces, by naming the deep and the darkness, in which there were both water and the spirit that hovered over the water.[6] Then he proceeded to mention the Decad: the light, the day, the night, the firmament, the evening, the morning, the dry land, the sea, the plants, and in tenth place the trees.[7] In that way, by the ten names, he indicated the ten Aeons. The power of the Dodecad was typified thus: by naming the sun, the moon, the stars, the seasons, the years, the sea monsters, the fishes, the reptiles, the fowl, the quadrupeds, the beasts, and after all these, man as the twelfth.[8] Thus they teach that the Triacontad was spoken of by the Spirit through Moses. Moreover, man too, who was formed according to the image[9] of the Power on high, possesses in himself a power that comes from one fountain. This fountain is situated in the region of the brain, from which flow four powers according to the image of the Tetrad on high, and which are called first, sight; second, hearing; third, smell; fourth, taste.[10] Moreover, the Ogdoad, they assert, is indicated by means of man thus: He has two ears and two eyes, two nostrils and a double taste—bitter and sweet. Besides, the entire man, they teach, possesses the entire image of the Triacontad in this way: He bears the Decad in the fingers of his hands; he bears the Dodecad in his entire body, which is divided into twelve members. But they divide the body [of man] just as they divide the body of Truth, about which we have spoken already.[11] Now the Ogdoad, since it is unspeakable and indivisible, is thought to be hidden in the bowels!

2. Again, they assert that the sun, the great luminary, was made on the fourth day[12] because of the number of the Tetrad. Likewise, the curtains[13] of the tabernacle that Moses made, which were made of linen—blue, purple, and scarlet[14]—manifested the same image [of the Tetrad]. They maintain, too, that the long priestly robe, which was adorned with four rows of precious stones,[15] symbolizes the Tetrad. And, plainly, if there are any other such things in the Scriptures that can designate the number four, these, they assert, were made because of the Tetrad. The Ogdoad, in turn, is manifested as follows: They say that man was formed on the eighth day[16]—sometimes they hold that he was made on the sixth day, sometimes on the eighth day, unless they

mean that his earthly part was formed on the sixth day, but his fleshly part on the eighth day; as a matter of fact, they distinguish those two things. Some also hold that one man was made bisexual *after the image and likeness of God*,[17] and he is the spiritual man; the other one was formed from the earth.[18]

3. Likewise, the disposition in regard to the ark for the deluge, in which eight persons were saved, most clearly points out, they assert, the Ogdoad which brings salvation.[19] This same Ogdoad is symbolized by David inasmuch as he was the eighth by birth among his brothers.[20] Furthermore, the circumcision which took place on the eighth day[21] manifests the circumcision of the Ogdoad on high. In short, they say that whatever is found in the Scriptures that can be drawn to the number eight fulfills the mystery of the Ogdoad. They assert, moreover, that the Decad is symbolized by the ten nations, which God promised to give to Abraham as a possession.[22] It is manifested, too, by the disposition concerning Sarah, when after ten years she gave her handmaid Hagar to Abraham, that from her she might bear a son;[23] likewise, the servant of Abraham who was sent to Rebecca and gave her ten bracelets of gold at the well[24] and her brothers who detained her for ten days;[25] furthermore, Jeroboam who received ten scepters;[26] the ten curtains of the tabernacle;[27] the columns that were ten cubits high;[28] the ten sons of Jacob who were sent into Egypt the first time to buy grain;[29] the ten apostles to whom the Lord appeared after his resurrection when Thomas was not present[30]—all these, according to them, typify the invisible Decad.

4. The Dodecad, concerning which also the mystery of the passion of Degeneracy took place, from which passion they hold all things visible were made—this Dodecad is strikingly and manifestly found everywhere [in the Scriptures]. For instance, the twelve sons of Jacob,[31] from whom came the twelve tribes;[32] the embroidered oracular breastplate with the twelve stones and the twelve bells;[33] the twelve stones which were placed by Moses at the foot of the mountain;[34] the twelve stones placed by Joshua in the river[35] and another set of twelve stones on the other side of the river;[36] the twelve bearers of the ark of the covenant;[37] the twelve stones which Elijah used to make the altar of holocaust for the heifer;[38] and the number twelve of the apostles. In short, whatever has the number twelve they say designates their Dodecad. Finally, the union of all these, which is called Triacontad, they

attempt to demonstrate by the ark of Noah which was thirty cubits high;[39] by the thirty guests among whom the first place was assigned to Saul by Samuel;[40] by the thirty days during which David concealed himself in the field, and by the [thirty] men who entered the cave with him;[41] by the length of the holy tabernacle, which was thirty cubits.[42] And if they find any other numbers like these, they earnestly strive to demonstrate their Triacontad by them.[43]

CHAPTER 19
THE MARCOSIANS ALLEGE THE SCRIPTURES PROVE THAT FIRST-FATHER WAS UNKNOWN BEFORE CHRIST'S COMING.

1. I considered it necessary[1] to add to these things also whatever they attempt to persuade us of concerning their First-Father, who was unknown to all before Christ's coming. They select passages from the Scriptures in order to prove that Our Lord announced another Father beside the Creator of the universe, who, as we have already mentioned, they impiously say was the product of Degeneracy. For instance, the words of the prophet Isaiah: *But Israel does not know me, and the people do not understand me,*[2] they adapt to refer to the ignorance about the invisible Profundity. Also the passage of Hosea: *There is no truth in them and there is no knowledge of God,*[3] they violently stretch to mean the same thing. And this: *No one understands, no one seeks for God. All have turned aside, together they have gone wrong,*[4] they refer to the ignorance about Profundity. And this passage of Moses: *No one shall see God and live,*[5] they would make believe refers to that Profundity. 2. Really, they lie when they say that the Creator was seen by the prophets yet hold that this passage: *No one shall see God and live,*[6] was said of the Greatness that is invisible to all and unknowable. That this passage: *No one shall see God and live,* was said of the invisible Father and Creator of the universe, is evident to us all. That it was by no means said of their falsely excogitated Profundity, but of the Creator who is also the invisible God, will be shown in the course of our treatise. Likewise, Daniel signified this same thing when, as one

who did not know, he asked the angel for an explanation of the parables. Moreover, the angel, hiding from him the great mystery of Profundity, said to him: *Go, Daniel, for the words are sealed up until those who are intelligent understand, and those who are white are made white.*[7] And they boast that they themselves are the ones who are white and quite intelligent.

CHAPTER 20
THE MARCOSIANS USE APOCRYPHAL AND SPURIOUS WRITINGS, AND THEY PERVERT THE GOSPELS.

1. Besides those passages,[1] they adduce an untold multitude of apocryphal and spurious writings, which they have composed to bewilder foolish men and such as do not understand the letters of the Truth. For this purpose they adduce this falsification: When the Lord was a child and was learning the alphabet, his teacher said to him—as is customary—"Pronounce alpha." He answered: "Alpha." Again the teacher ordered him to pronounce "Beta." Then the Lord answered: "You tell me first what alpha is, and then I shall tell you what beta is."[2] This they explain in the sense that he alone understood the Unknowable, whom he revealed in alpha as in a type.

2. Further, they falsely fit to that standard some of the things put in the Gospel; for example, the answer he [the Lord] gave to his Mother when he was twelve years old: *Did you not know that I must be about my Father's business?*[3] They assert that he announced to them, Father, of whom they were ignorant. For this reason, too, he sent forth his disciples to the twelve tribes to preach the God who was unknown to them.[4] Likewise, to the person who addressed him as "good Master,"[5] he confessed the truly good God by saying: *Why do you call me good? One is good, the Father in the heavens.*[6] By the heavens, they say, he meant the Aeons. Again, when he was asked: *By what power do you do this?*[7] he did not answer but confounded them by putting a question to them instead.[8] By not answering them, they declare, he manifested Father's unspeakable nature.[9] Moreover, when he said: "They have often desired to hear one of these discourses, but they had no one who

would speak to me,"[10] they speak of one who manifested by the word *one* the truly one God, whom they had not known. Furthermore, when he drew near to Jerusalem and wept over it, he said: *Would that even today you knew the things that make for peace! But now they are hidden from you.*[11] By the word *hidden* he manifested the hidden nature of Profundity. And again when he said: *Come to me, all who labor and are heavy-laden, and learn of me,*[12] he announced the Father of Truth [Profundity]. These men say that he promised to teach them what they did not know.

3. Finally, as the highest proof[13] and, as it were, crown of their system, they adduce this text:[14] *I praise you, Father, Lord of heaven and earth,*[15] *that you have hidden these things from the wise and understanding, and revealed them to babes; yea, Father, for such was your gracious will. All things have been delivered to me by my Father; and no one knew the Father except the Son, neither [did anyone know] the Son except the Father, and anyone to whom the Son might reveal him.*[16] By these words, they assert, he clearly showed how before the Son's coming no one knew the Father of Truth, whom they have falsely invented.[17] They wish to construe this so that the Maker and Creator was always known by everyone, but that the Lord said these things about Father who is unknown to all. Still they announce him!

CHAPTER 21

THE HERETICAL NOTIONS ABOUT REDEMPTION.

1. The tradition about their redemption turns out to be invisible and incomprehensible, inasmuch as this is the mother of the incomprehensible and invisible beings.[1] And so it is unstable and cannot be told simply or in one word, because each one of them hands it down just as he wishes. For there are as many redemptions as there are mystery-teachers of this doctrine. When in the proper place we shall expose them, we shall tell how this false picture was injected by Satan in order to deny the baptism of rebirth unto God, and to destroy the entire faith.[2]

2. Redemption, they say, is necessary for those who have received perfect knowledge that they may be reborn into the power that is

above all things. For otherwise it is impossible to enter within the Fullness, since it is this [redemption] which leads them into the depth of Profundity.[3] For they maintain that the baptism of the visible Jesus was unto remission of sins; but the redemption of Christ who descended upon Jesus was unto perfection, since they suppose that the former was ensouled but the latter spiritual. And the baptism of John was preached for repentance, but the redemption of Christ [who descended on him] was given for perfection. And of this he said: *I have another baptism to be baptized with; and I hasten vigorously to it.*[4] Moreover, they say that the Lord presented this redemption to the sons of Zebedee when their mother asked that one might sit on his right and the other on his left in his kingdom, and he answered: *Are you able . . . to be baptized with the baptism with which I must be baptized?*[5] Paul, too, they assert, has often indicated in express terms the redemption which is in Christ Jesus.[6] That is the redemption which they hand down in such a varied and discordant manner.

3. Some of them prepare a bridal chamber and complete the mystic teaching with invocations on those who are being initiated.[7] What was performed by them, they assert, is a spiritual marriage, after the likeness of the conjugal unions on high. But others lead them to water and while baptizing them pronounce these words over them: "[I baptize you] into the name of the unknown Father of the universe, into Truth, the Mother of all, into him who descended upon Jesus, into the union and redemption and participation of the powers."[8] Still others pronounce some Hebrew names over those who are being initiated in order to bewilder them still more. These are: Basyma cacabasa eanaa irraumista diarbada caëota bafabor camelanthi."[9] The interpretation of these words is this: "That which is above the Father's every power, which is called Light and good Spirit and Life, I invoke because you reigned in the body." Others, again, invoke the redemption upon them thus: "The name which has been hidden from every Deity, Dominion, and Truth, with which Jesus the Nazarene clothed himself within the regions of the light of Christ—of Christ who lives by the Holy Spirit for the angelic redemption." The name of the restoration is this: "Messia ufar magno in seenchaldia mosomeda eaacha faronepseha Iesu Nazarene." The interpretation of these words is this: "I do not divide the spirit, the heart, and the supercelestial, merciful power. May I enjoy your name, O Savior of Truth." Such are the formulae

spoken by those who do the initiating. But he who has been initiated replies: "I have been confirmed, I have been redeemed; and I redeem my soul from this world and from all things derived from it in the name of Jao, who redeemed his own soul unto a redemption in the living Christ." Then the bystanders pronounce these words over them: "Peace be to all upon whom this name rests." After this they anoint with balsam[10] the one who has been initiated, because they say that this ointment is a type of fragrance which is widespread on the Aeons.[11]

4. There are those who say that it is useless to lead the people to the water. So they mix oil and water together. This they put on the heads of the ones to be initiated, pronouncing at the same time some invocations similar to those we have mentioned. This, they hold, is the redemption. They, too, anoint with balsam. Others, however, reject all these things. They assert that the mystery of the unspeakable and invisible Power ought not to be consecrated by visible and corruptible creatures; nor the mystery of the unthinkable and incorporeal, by the sentient and corporeal. [They maintain] that the very knowledge of the unspeakable Greatness is perfect redemption; for, since both degeneracy and passion came from ignorance,[12] the entire substance which came from ignorance is destroyed by knowledge; and so knowledge is the redemption of the inner man. And this redemption is not corporeal, since the body is corruptible; nor is it ensouled, since the soul also is from Degeneracy and is, as it were, the dwelling of the spirit. Therefore, the redemption too must be spiritual; for the inner, spiritual man is redeemed by knowledge. And this deeper knowledge of all things is sufficient for them. And that is the true redemption.[13]

5. There are others who redeem the dying[14] at the very moment of their departure by putting oil and water, that is, the above-mentioned ointment with water, on their heads, while pronouncing the above invocations. The purpose of this is that these [dying] might become incomprehensible and invisible to the Principalities and the Powers, and that their inner man might ascend above the invisible things; and though their body is left in the created world, the soul is sent forward to Demiurge. They instruct them that, after they have died, when they come to the Powers, they are to speak as follows: "I am a son of Father, of Father who is preexisting. I am a son in the Preexisting one.[15] I have come to see all things that belong to me and to others

(which, however, do not belong to others entirely, but to Achamoth, who is a female)." She made these things for herself. So they got their origin from the Preexisting one, and I am returning to my own, whence I came.[16] By means of such words they say that he will escape from the Powers. Then he comes to the attendants of Demiurge and says to them: "I am a precious vase,[17] more precious than the female who made you. Though your Mother is ignorant of her root, I know myself, and I know whence I am, and I call upon incorruptible Wisdom who is in Father and who is the Mother of your Mother who had no Father nor a male consort.[18] A Female [Achamoth] who herself came from a Female [Wisdom] made you without knowing her own Mother, but thought that she was all alone. I, however, call upon her Mother."[19] When the attendants of Demiurge hear these things, they are very much upset and condemn their root and the origin of their Mother. They [the dead], however, break their bonds, that is, the soul,[20] and go into their own possessions. These, then, are the things that have reached us concerning the "redemption." But since these men differ among themselves both in doctrine and in tradition, and since those of them who are acknowledged as the more modern endeavor to excogitate something new every day and to produce something that no one has ever thought of, it is difficult to describe all of their opinions.

CHAPTER 22

DEVIATIONS OF THE HERETICS
FROM THE ANCIENT FAITH.

1. The Rule of the Truth that we hold is this:[1] There is one God Almighty, who created all things through His Word; He both prepared and made all things out of nothing,[2] just as Scripture says: *For by the word of the Lord the heavens were made, and all their host by the breath of His mouth.*[3] And again: *All things were made through Him and without Him was made not a thing.*[4] From this *all* nothing is exempt. Now, it is the Father who made all things through Him, whether visible or invisible,[5] whether sensible or intelligible, whether temporal

for the sake of some dispensation or eternal.[6] These[7] He did not make through Angels or some Powers that were separated from His thought.[8] For the God of all things needs nothing.[9] No, He made all things by His Word and Spirit, disposing and governing them and giving all of them existence. This is the one who made the world, which indeed is made up of all things. This is the one who fashioned man.[10] This is the God of Abraham and Isaac and Jacob,[11] above whom there is no other God, nor a Beginning, nor a Power, nor a Fullness. This is the Father of our Lord Jesus Christ,[12] as we shall demonstrate. If, therefore, we hold fast this Rule, we shall easily prove that they have strayed from the Truth, even though their statements are quite varied and numerous. It is true, nearly all the heretical sects, many as they are, speak of one God; but they alter Him by their evil-mindedness. They are thereby ungrateful to Him who made them, just as the pagans by idolatry. Moreover, they hold in contempt God's handiwork[13] by speaking against their own salvation; and they are thus their own most bitter accusers and false witnesses. Even though they do not wish to, they will surely rise again in the flesh in order to acknowledge the power of Him who raises them from the dead; they will, however, not be numbered with the righteous, because of their unbelief.[14]

2. Since, therefore, the exposé and refutation of all the heretical sects is different and multiform, and since we have resolved to give an answer to everyone according to its own standard, we have deemed it necessary first of all to give an account of their source and root, in order that you may know their most sublime Profundity,[15] and understand the tree from which such fruits came forth.

CHAPTER 23
THE TENETS AND PRACTICES OF SIMON MAGUS AND MENANDER.

1. Simon,[1] the Samaritan, was the famous magician of whom Luke, the disciple and follower of the apostles, said: *But there was a man named Simon, who had previously practiced magic in the city and seduced*

the people of Samaria, saying that he himself was somebody great. They all gave heed to him, from the least to the greatest, saying, "This man is that Power of God which is called Great." And they gave heed to him, because for a long time he had bewitched them with his magic.[2] This Simon, then, feigned faith; he thought that even the apostles themselves affected cures by magic and not by God's power. He suspected that, when by the imposition of hands the apostles filled with the Holy Spirit those who believed in God through Jesus Christ who was announced by them, they were doing this through some greater knowledge of magic. But when he offered the apostles some money so that he too might receive this power of bestowing the Holy Spirit on whomever he willed, he heard this from Peter: *Keep your money to yourself, to perish with you, because you thought you could obtain the gift of God with money. You have neither part nor lot in this matter, for your heart is not right before God. For I see that you are in the gall of bitterness and in the bond of iniquity.*[3] But he believed still less in God and greedily intended to rival the apostles so that he too might appear famous. So he made yet a deeper investigation into the entire art of magic to the amazement of the crowds of people. This happened during the reign of Emperor Claudius, who, so they say, also honored him with a statue because of his magic.[4] So this man was glorified by many as a god. He taught that he himself was the one who appeared among the Jews as the Son of God, while in Samaria he descended as the Father, and among the other nations he came as the Holy Spirit.[5] He also taught that he was the most sublime Power, that is, the Father who is above all things. He permitted himself to be called whatever people might call him.[6]

2. Now Simon, the Samaritan, from whom all heresies got their start, proposed the following sort of heretical doctrine. Having himself redeemed a certain Helen from being a prostitute in Tyre, a city of Phoenicia, he took her with him on his rounds, saying that she was the first Thought of his mind, the Mother of all things, through whom in the beginning he conceived in his mind to make the Angels and Archangels.[7] For he asserted that this Thought leaped forth from him, since she knew what her Father wanted, and descended to the lower regions and gave birth to Angels and Powers, by whom also this world was made.[8] But after she had given birth to them, she was detained by them out of envy, since they did not wish to be considered the off-

spring of anyone else. For he was entirely unknown to them. His Thought, however, who was detained by the Powers and Angels that had been emitted by her, also suffered all kinds of contumely at their hands, so that she could not return to her Father on high. [She suffered] even to the extent of being imprisoned in a human body and of transmigrating for ages into other female bodies, as from one vessel into another. For example, she was in the famous Helen on account of whom the Trojan war was fought; for that reason[9] Stesichorus who reviled her in his verses was struck blind, but after he repented and had written what are called palinodes, in which he sang her praises, his sight was restored.[10] Thus, passing from one body into another, and always suffering insults from the body, she was at last a prostitute in a public house. She was the lost sheep.[11]

3. He himself came for this reason that he might first take her to himself, free her from the bonds, and then bring salvation[12] to humankind by his own knowledge. The Angels governed the world badly, because each one desired to be sovereign. So he came, he said, to set matters right; having been transformed and made like the Principalities and Powers and Angels, he appeared in turn as a man, though he was not a man. He appeared to suffer in Judea, though he really did not suffer. Moreover, the Prophets uttered their prophecies by virtue of inspirations received from the Angels who made the world. Wherefore, those who put their trust in Simon and his Helen do not give heed to them, but do whatever they will, since they are free. For they say that men are saved through his grace, and not through holy deeds, because deeds are holy not by nature but by accident.[13] For example, the Angels who made the world laid down precepts and through these made slaves of people. He, therefore, promised that the world would be destroyed so that those who belong to him would be freed from the domain of those who made the world.

4. The mystic priests of these people live licentious lives and practice magic, each one in whatever way he can. They make use of exorcisms and incantations, love-potions too and philters, and the so-called familiars, and dream-senders.[14] They diligently practice whatever other magic arts there may be. They also have a statue of Simon patterned after Jupiter, and one of Helen patterned after Minerva. They worship these statues. They also have a name for them-

selves, the "Simonians" derived from Simon the author of this most impious doctrine,[15] from whom the falsely called knowledge[16] took its origin, as one can learn from their assertions.

5. The successor of Simon was Menander,[17] a Samaritan by birth. He too was most skillful in magic. He said that the first Power is unknown to all, but that he is the one who was sent as Savior by the invisible [regions] for the salvation of men. The world, however, was made by the Angels, who he too, just as Simon, claims were emitted by Thought. By the magic which he teaches he bestows upon them the knowledge to overcome the very Angels who made the world. For his disciples received the resurrection by being baptized into him and can no longer die, but will continue on without growing old; they are immortal.[18]

CHAPTER 24
THE ERRORS OF SATURNINUS AND BASILIDES.

1. Saturninus,[1] who was of Antioch near Daphne, and Basilides got their start from these heretics. Still they taught different doctrines, the one in Syria, the other in Alexandria. Saturninus, following Menander, assumed there is one Father who is unknown to all and who made the Angels and Archangels, Virtues and Powers. But the world and all that is in it was made by certain seven Angels. Man too is the work of Angels. When a shining image appeared from above from the sovereign Power and they were not able to hold fast to it because it immediately ascended again, he said that they exhorted each other, saying, "Let us make man after an image and likeness."[2] When this first-formed-man was made and was not able to stand erect because of the weakness of the Angels, but wriggled on the ground as a worm, then the Power on high had pity on him, because he was made after its likeness, and he sent a spark of life which raised him up and set him upright[3] and made him live. This spark of life, then, he claims, returns to its own kind after man's death, and the rest of the things out of which he was made are again resolved into these same things.

2. He assumed, furthermore, that Savior was unbegotten,[4] incor-

poreal, and formless; still he was believed to have appeared as man. He says the God of the Jews is one of the Angels. On this account, because his Father wished to destroy all the Principalities,[5] Christ came to destroy the God of the Jews and to bring salvation to those who believe in him. These are the ones who have in themselves the spark of life. In truth, he says[6] that two kinds of men were formed by the Angels, the one wicked, the other good. And since the demons aided the wicked, Savior came for the destruction of the evil people and the demons, but for the salvation of the good. Besides, he said that to marry and to beget children comes from Satan.[7] Most of his followers even abstain from animal food, misleading many by this false type of temperance. As for the prophecies, some were uttered by the Angels who made the world, others by Satan, whom he assumed to be the very Angel who opposes those who made the world, especially the God of the Jews.

3. Basilides[8] amplified his system indefinitely, that he might appear to have fabricated something more profound and plausible.[9] He states that Mind was born first of the ingenerate Father; then from Mind was born Word; from Word, Prudence; from Prudence, Wisdom and Power; from Power and Wisdom, the Powers and Rulers and Angels, which he also calls the first.[10] Then the first heaven was made by these. Next by an emission from these, other Angels were made. These in turn made another heaven similar to the first. In like manner, when still other [Angels] were formed by emission from these second, according to the pattern of those on high, they fashioned a third heaven. And from this third heaven was emitted, in downward direction, the fourth heaven of descending [Angels]. After that, in the same manner, many other Rulers and Angels were made, they say, and three hundred and sixty-five heavens. And for this reason there are as many days in the year as there are heavens.[11]

4. The Angels who rule[12] the lowest heaven, which can also be seen by us, made all the things which are in the world and portioned out for themselves the earth and the nations that are on it. The Ruler of these Angels is believed to be the God of the Jews. Now, when he wished to subject the rest of the nations to his people, that is, to the Jews, all the other nations resisted and opposed him.[13] Therefore, also the other nations rebelled against his nation. But when the ingenerate and unnameable Father saw the perversity of the Principalities,[14] he sent his

firstborn Mind, that is, him who is called Christ, to liberate from the power of the Angels who made the world those who believe in him. He thereupon appeared as a man on earth to the nations of these powers and worked wonders.[15] And so he did not suffer, but a certain Simon of Cyrene was compelled to carry the cross for him.[16] Through ignorance and error this Simon was crucified, having been transformed by Christ so that he was believed to be Jesus; while Jesus himself assumed the form of Simon and, standing by, ridiculed them. For, since he was an incorporeal Power and the ingenerate Father's Mind, he was transformed as he willed, and thus he ascended to him who had sent him, deriding them, since he could not be detained and was invisible to all. Those, then, who know these things are freed from the Princes who made the world. They are not obliged to acknowledge him who was crucified, but the one who came in the form of man, and was thought to have been crucified, was called Jesus, and was sent by Father in order to destroy through this Economy the works of those who made the world. Therefore, he asserts, if anyone acknowledges him who was crucified, he is still a slave and is under the power of those who made the bodies. He, however, who denies him is freed from them and has knowledge of the Economy of the ingenerate Father.

5. Salvation belongs to their soul alone, for the body is by nature corruptible. He asserts, too, that the prophecies themselves were uttered by the rulers who made the world, but the law was, strictly speaking, from that ruler of theirs who led the people out of the land of Egypt. The foods, too, offered in sacrifice one ought to despise[17] and consider food of no account, yet use them without hesitation. Moreover, other acts may be indulged in indifferently, as also all lust.[18] Likewise, they make use of magic and images and incantations and invocations and all the other curious arts. They also coin certain names as belonging to the Angels and declare that some are in the first heaven and some in the second. Finally, they strive to explain the names Rulers, Angels, and Powers of the three hundred and sixty-five false heavens; as for example, that Caulacau is the name by which Savior is said to have descended and ascended.[19]

6. He, therefore, who has learned these things and has known all the Angels and their causes becomes invisible and incomprehensible to all the Angels and Powers just as Caulacau was. And as Son was

unknown to all, so they too ought not to be known by anyone. On the contrary, since they know all the Angels and pass by all of them, they themselves remain invisible and unknown to all of them.[20] For they say: "You, know all of them, but let no one know you!" And so persons of such character are ready to recant; and what is more, they are not even able to suffer for the sake of a name, because they are like the Aeons.[21] The multitudes, however, cannot know these things, only one out of a thousand, or two out of ten thousand. They say that they are no longer Jews; but neither are they Christians.[22] In fact, their mysteries must by no means be spoken of in the open, but must be kept hidden by observing silence.

7. Just like the astrologers[23] they assign the locations of the three hundred and sixty-five heavens. They accept the theories of the astrologers and adapt them to their standard of doctrine. The ruler of these [heavens], they claim, is Abrasax, and because of this he possesses three hundred and sixty-five numbers in himself.[24]

CHAPTER 25
THE TENETS OF CARPOCRATES.

1. Carpocrates[1] and his disciples assert that the world and the things in it were made by Angels who are far inferior to the ingenerate Father, and that Jesus was begotten by Joseph and, though he was made like men, he was superior to the rest[2] of men. Moreover, since his soul was vigorous and innocent, he remembered what he had seen within the sphere which belongs to the ingenerate God. For this reason, a power was sent down upon him by God, that by means of it he could escape from the makers of the world and that this [soul], having passed through all their domains[3] and so remained free in all, might ascend to him [Father]. The souls that embrace things similar to it [Jesus' soul] will in like manner [ascend to him].[4] Furthermore, they say, the soul of Jesus, though trained according to the law in the practices of the Jews, despised[5] them, and for this reason received power by which he destroyed the passions which were in men as a punishment.

2. The soul, therefore, which is like that of Jesus, is able to hold in

contempt those Rulers and makers of the world, receiving like Jesus a power to perform the same things that he performed. Wherefore,[6] some of them advanced to such a pitch of pride that they claim to be like Jesus; others even claim that they are more powerful than Jesus; some again assert that they are superior to his disciples, as, for instance, Peter and Paul and the rest of the apostles. They claim that they are in no way inferior to Jesus. Really, their souls, they claim, descend from the same sphere, and because in like manner they hold in contempt the makers of the world, they have been deemed worthy of the same power and return again to the same place. If, however, anyone has despised the things here below[7] more than he did, such a one can be better than he.[8]

3. These men, too, practice magic and make use of incantations, philtres, spells, familiars, dream-senders, and the rest of the evil magic. They assert that they have power even now to exercise dominion over the Rulers and Makers of this world; not only over them, but also over all the creatures in it. So some of them have been sent forth by Satan to the pagans[9] to malign the holy name of the Church, so that when people, in one way or another, hear their tenets and imagine that we all are like them, they would turn their ears from the preaching of the Truth; or even as they see their conduct they would speak slander of us all. However, we have nothing in common with them in doctrine, morals, or daily conduct. On the contrary, they live licentious lives and hold godless doctrine. But they use the Name [of Jesus] only to veil their own wickedness.[10] *Their condemnation is just*.[11] They will be punished by God in keeping with the deserts of their deeds.

4. They have fallen into such unbridled madness that they boast of having in their power and of practicing every kind of impious and godless deed. For they claim that deeds are good or bad only because of human opinion. Therefore, they say that the souls must have experience in every kind of life and in every act by means of transmigration from one body to another, unless some soul would preoccupy itself once and for all, and in an equivalent manner do in one coming [into this world] all the deeds—deeds which it is not only wrong for to us to speak of and to listen to, but which we may not even think[12] or believe that such things are done among people who live in our cities. The purpose of this, according to their writings, is that the souls, having had every experience in life, may at their departure not be

wanting in anything; moreover, they must take care lest they be again
sent forth into a body because something was wanting to their libera-
tion.[13] For this reason they assert that Jesus uttered the following
parable: *And as you with an accuser, make an effort to settle with him lest
he drag you to the judge, and the judge hand you to the officer, and he put
you in prison. Amen, I tell you, you will never get out till you have paid the
very last copper.*[14] They say that the adversary is one of the Angels who
are in the world. They call him Devil. They claim that he was made in
order to lead from the world to the Ruler those souls that perished.
They also say he is the first of the Authors of this world and he hands
such souls over to another Angel, who is his minister, that he might
imprison them in other bodies; for the body is a prison, they assert.
And this clause: *You will never get out till you have paid the very last
copper,* they interpret to mean that no one will escape from the power
of the Angels who made the world, but[15] will always transmigrate from
one body to another until he has had experience in absolutely every
kind of action that exists in the world. And when nothing is wanting
to him, his soul, having been liberated, escapes to the God who is
above the Angels, the makers of the world. In this manner all souls are
saved—whether in one coming [into this world] they preoccupy
themselves in being mixed up in every kind of action, whether they
transmigrate from one body to another, or, what is the same, whether
they have been sent into every kind of life. And having fulfilled the
requirements and paid the debts, they are liberated, so that they no
longer have to operate in a body.[16]

5. Now,[17] whether these impious, unlawful, and forbidden acts are
really practiced by them, I would hardly believe.[18] But in their writings
it is so written, and they also explain it so. Jesus, they assert, spoke
privately in mystery to his disciples and apostles and commissioned
them to hand down privately these things to those who are worthy and
believe; for they are saved by faith and love. But the other things are
indifferent, some good, some bad, according to the view of men,
inasmuch as nothing is bad by nature.

6. Some of them put a mark on their disciples, branding them on the
underside of the lobe of the right ear.[19] Marcellina belonged to their
number. She came to Rome under Pope Anicetus and, since she
belonged to this school, she led multitudes astray.[20] They call themselves Gnostics and possess images, some of which are paintings,

some made of other materials. They said Christ's image was copied by Pilate at the time that Jesus lived among men. On these images they put a crown and exhibit them along with the images of the philosophers of the world, namely, with the image of Pythagoras, Plato, Aristotle, and the rest. Toward these [images] they observe other rites that are just like those of the pagans.

CHAPTER 26
TENETS OF CERINTHUS, OF THE EBIONITES,
AND OF THE NICOLAITANS.

1. A certain Cerinthus[1] taught in Asia that the world was not made by the first God, but by some Power which was separated and distant from the Authority that is above all things, and which was ignorant of the God who is above all things. He proposes Jesus, not as having been born of a Virgin—for this seemed impossible to him—but as having been born the son of Joseph and Mary like all other men, and[2] that he excelled over every person in justice, prudence, and wisdom.[3] After his baptism Christ descended on him in the shape of a dove from the Authority that is above all things. Then he preached the unknown Father and worked wonders. But at the end Christ again flew off from Jesus. Jesus indeed suffered and rose again from the dead, but Christ remained impassible, since he was spiritual.[4]

2. The so-called Ebionites[5] admit that the world was made by the true God,[6] but in regard to the Lord they hold the same opinion as Cerinthus and Carpocrates.[7] They use only the Gospel according to Matthew[8] and reject the Apostle Paul, saying that he is an apostate from the law.[9] The Prophetical Writings, however, they strive to interpret in a rather curious manner. They circumcise themselves and continue in the practices which are prescribed by the law and by the Judaic standard of living, so that they worship Jerusalem as the house of God.[10]

3. The Nicolaitans had as teacher Nicolas, one of the seven who were the first to be ordained deacons by the apostles.[11] They lived unbridled lives. What sort of people they are is fully exposed by the Apocalypse of John, for they assert that there is no difference between

committing fornication[12] and eating food sacrificed to idols.[13] For that reason the Word also spoke this of them: *Yet this you have, you hate the works of the Nicolaitans, which I also hate*.[14]

CHAPTER 27
TENETS OF CERDO AND MARCION.

1. A certain Cerdo also got his start from the disciples of Simon.[1] He settled in Rome under Hyginus, who held the ninth place of the episcopacy by succession from the apostles.[2] He taught that the God who had been proclaimed under the law and the prophets was not the Father of Our Lord Jesus Christ, for the former was known, but the latter was unknown; again, the former was just, whereas the latter was benevolent.[3]

2. Marcion of Pontus succeeded Cerdo and amplified his doctrine.[4] He uttered the impudent blasphemy that the God who was proclaimed by the law and the prophets was the author of evil,[5] and desirous of war. He was inconsistent in his teaching and contradicted himself. Jesus, however, who has his origin in the Father who is above the God who made the world, came to Judea at the time when Pontius Pilate presided as procurator of Tiberius Caesar. He was manifested in the form of a man to those who were in Judea.[6] He abolished the prophets and the law and all the works of the God who made the world, whom he also styled the World-Ruler. Besides all this, he mutilated the Gospel according to Luke, discarding all that is written about the birth of the Lord, and discarding also many of the Lord's discourses containing teaching[7] in which it is most clearly written that the Lord confessed His Father as the Maker of the universe. Marcion persuaded his disciples that he was more truthful than the apostles who handed down the Gospel, though he gave them not the Gospel, but only a portion of the Gospel.[8] In like manner, he mutilated the Letters of Paul, removing whatever was clearly said by the Apostle about the God who made the world inasmuch as he is the Father of Our Lord Jesus Christ; for the Apostle taught by quoting from the Prophetical Writings that foretold the Lord's coming.[9]

3. Only those souls that had learned his doctrine would attain salva-

tion. The body, on the contrary, since it was taken from the earth, is incapable of sharing in salvation.[10] Besides the blasphemy against God, he added this one (thus truly speaking with the devil's mouth and uttering all things contrary to the truth): Cain and those like him, the Sodomites and the Egyptians and those like them, and all the pagans who walked in every mess of wickedness were all saved by the Lord when he descended into the netherworld and they met him, and he took them into his kingdom. But Abel, Enoch, Noah, and the rest of the righteous and the patriarchs who came from Abraham, together with all the prophets and those who pleased God, did not share in salvation, as the Serpent that was in Marcion proclaimed. For, he says, since these people know that their God always tempted them, they had a suspicion that he was tempting them at that time, and they did not go to meet Jesus, nor did they believe in his preaching. As a result their souls remained in the netherworld.[11]

4. Now, since this man alone was openly so bold as to mutilate the Scriptures and to calumniate God more impudently than all others, we will answer him separately and expose him by his own writings, and also from the discourses of the Lord and the apostles which he himself kept and used; and thus with God's grace we shall overthrow him.[12] We have necessarily made mention of him at present that you might know that all those who in any way adulterate the truth and do injury to the preaching of the Church are the disciples and successors of Simon, the magician of Samaria.[13] For even though they do not acknowledge the name of their teacher in order to mislead others, yet it is his doctrine they teach. By proposing the name of Christ Jesus as a kind of incentive, they put many to death by wickedly disseminating their own teaching by means of the good Name [Jesus],[14] and by handing them the bitter and wicked poison of the Serpent, the author of the apostasy,[15] under the guise of the delight and beauty of this Name.

CHAPTER 28
TENETS OF THE ENCRATITES, TATIAN, AND OTHERS.

1. Already many offshoots of many heretical sects have been made from the ones we have mentioned, because many of these people, in

fact all, wish to be teachers and to forsake the heresy in which they had been. They insist on teaching in a novel manner, composing from one teaching another tenet, and then another from that. They declare themselves inventors of any opinion which they may have patched together.

To cite an example,[1] the so-called Encratites, who sprang from Saturninus and Marcion, preached abstinence from marriage and so made void God's pristine creation, and indirectly reprove him who made male and female for generating the human race.[2] They also introduced abstinence from what is called by them animal food, being thus ungrateful to the God who made all things.[3] They deny salvation to the first-formed-man. This was but recently fabricated by them. A certain Tatian was the first to introduce this blasphemy.[4] He had been a follower of Justin and, as long as he was with him, he did not express such a view. However, after Justin's martyrdom, he apostatized from the Church and as a teacher he was conceited and elated and puffed up as if he were superior to the rest. It was then that he composed his own standard of teaching. He related a myth about invisible Aeons similar to those of Valentinus. Like Marcion and Saturninus, he declared that marriage was corruption and fornication. The denial of salvation to Adam was his own invention.

2. Contrariwise, others who got their start from Basilides and Carpocrates introduced promiscuity and plurality of marriages and carelessly ate foods sacrificed to idols.[5] Their excuse is that God is not much concerned about such things. But enough of that! It is impossible to tell the number of those who have fallen away from the Truth[6] in various ways.

CHAPTER 29
THE BARBELIOTES.

1. Besides the Simonians already mentioned, a multitude of Gnostics have sprung up and shot out of the ground like mushrooms.[1] We will describe their main tenets.

Certain ones of them propose that there is a certain Aeon in a

virginal spirit who never grows old. They call her Barbelo.[2] There
also exists a certain unnameable Father who thought of[3] revealing
himself to this Barbelo. This Thought [Barbelo], however, came forward and stood before him and asked him for Foreknowledge. When
Foreknowledge had come forth, they again made a request, and Incorruption came forth; and after that, Eternal Life. While Barbelo
gloried in them and looked upon the Majesty and took delight in a
conception, she gave birth to a Light similar to the Majesty.[4] They say
she is the beginning of all light and generation, and that when Father
saw this Light, he anointed it with his kindness that it might be made
perfect. Furthermore, they maintain that this Light is Christ, who in
turn asked that Mind be given him as a helpmate. Thereupon Mind
came forth. In addition, Father produced Will and Word.[5] Then there
existed the conjugal couples of Thought and Word, of Incorruption
and Christ. Likewise, Eternal Life was added to Will, and Mind to
Foreknowledge. Thereupon these magnified the great Light and
Barbelo.

2. After this, they assert, Self-begotten was emitted by Thought
and Word and an image of the great Light.[6] He was greatly honored,
they say, and all things were made subject to him.[7] However, Truth
was emitted at the same time as he was, and Self-begotten and Truth
formed a conjugal couple. They also assert that from Light, that is,
from Christ, and Incorruption, four Lights were emitted as bodyguard
of Self-begotten. Again, from Will and Eternal Life other four emissions were made to minister to the four Lights. These they call Grace,
Volition, Understanding, and Prudence. Grace was given to the first
and great Light, who they hold is the Savior and is called Armozel;
Volition was given to the second Light, which they also call Raguel;
Understanding, to the third Light, which they call David; Prudence,
to the fourth, which they call Eleleth.

3. After all these things had been established, Self-begotten emitted
a perfect and true Man, whom they also call Untamable,[8] because
neither he nor those from whom he originated were tamed. He, too,
along with the first Light was separated from Armozel. Together with
this Man, Self-begotten emitted perfect Knowledge, which was wedded to Man. And because of this they say that Man, too, knew of the
one who is above all things. Likewise, an unconquerable power was
given to him from the virginal Spirit. Thereupon, as all were at rest,

they sang the praises of the great Aeon.[9] And so they claim were manifested Mother and Father and Son. Moreover, from Man and Knowledge was born tree, which they also call Knowledge.[10]

4. Next, Holy Spirit, whom they also style Wisdom and Prounikos,[11] was emitted from the first Angel who remains near to Only-begotten. When she saw that all the others belonged to a conjugal couple and she did not, she went in search of someone she might wed. When she was not able to find anyone, she struggled and strained forward and looked in the lower regions,[12] thinking she might find a consort there. When she found none, she leaped forward, but was seized with sudden sadness because she had made the leap without Father's approval. After that, moved by simplicity and kindness, she generated a work in which there were Ignorance and Boldness. They claim that this her work was the First-Ruler, the Maker of this creation. But they tell us that he took away a great Power from his Mother, departed from her to the lower regions, and made the firmament of the heavens, in which he also dwells. Since he is Ignorance, he made those Powers which are inferior to himself and the Angels and the firmament and all earthly things. Next, they say, he was wedded to Boldness and begot Wickedness, Jealousy, Envy, Discord,[13] and Lust. After these had been generated, Wisdom, the Mother, was grieved and fleeing withdrew to the upper regions. And so, counting downwards, there resulted the Ogdoad. After she had departed, he [First-Ruler] thought he was the only one in existence, and so he said: *I am a jealous God, there is no one besides me.*[14] Such are the lies that these people tell.

CHAPTER 30
TENETS OF THE OPHITES.

1. Others again[1] narrate prodigies. There exists a certain first Light in the power of Profundity, which is blessed, incorruptible, and infinite. This is Father of all things and is called First-Man. They likewise say that, when his Thought came forth, he emitted a son, and this is the Son of Man or Second-Man. Moreover, below these there exists

Holy Spirit, and under this superior Spirit exist the separated elements—water, darkness, abyss, and chaos—over which Spirit moved. This Spirit they call First-Woman. After that, First-Man, together with his son, took delight in the beauty of Spirit, who is the woman, and by illuminating her, generated from her an incorruptible Light, the Third-Man, whom they call Christ, the son of First-Man and Second-Man and of First-Woman.

In other words, both the Father and the Son were wedded to the Woman whom they call *the Mother of the living*.[2] 2. When she was not capable of enduring or receiving the greatness of the lights, they say that she was completely filled and then overflowed on the left side. Thus, their own son, Christ, as of the right side and elevated to the upper regions, was immediately caught up with his Mother into the incorruptible Aeon. So this is both the true and holy Church, which was the appellation, the meeting, and the union of Father of all things, the First-Man, and of his Son, the Second-Man, and of Christ, their Son, and of the Woman mentioned above.

3. The Power, on the other hand, which overflowed from the Woman, since it was endowed with moisture of light, fell downwards from her Progenitors, they teach, though she of her own will retained the moisture of light,[3] which they call Left-handed, Prounikos, Wisdom, and Bisexual. She simply descended into the waters which were in a state of calm and set them in motion by recklessly agitating them to their depths.[4] From them she took a body for herself. They relate that all things ran to meet this moisture of light and clung to it and embraced it. And unless she had possessed that [moisture], she would perhaps have been entirely absorbed by, and submerged in, matter. When, therefore, she was held bound by the body and weighed down very much, she regretted [what had happened] at one time and made an attempt to escape from the waters and ascend to her Mother. She could not accomplish this because of the weight of the body which surrounded her. She felt very bad and schemed to hide the light she had from above, fearing lest it too should suffer from the lower elements as she had. But when she had received power from her moisture of light, she leaped back and was lifted up on high. And having attained the heights, she spread herself out as a covering and thus made out of her body the heaven that is visible. She remained under the heaven that she had made, and still possesses the form of the watery body.[5] But

when she was seized by a longing for the higher light and had received power through all things, she put off the body and was freed from it. Now this body which she is said to have put off they style a female from a female.[6]

4. They affirm, furthermore, that her son also possessed a certain longing for incorruption which was left him by his Mother and by means of which he functions. Having become more powerful, he in turn emitted a son from the water without the aid of the Mother; for they hold that he had no knowledge of the Mother. His son, in turn, emitted a son in imitation of his father. And this third son generated a fourth son, and the fourth too generated a son; and from this fifth son a sixth son was generated, and the sixth generated a seventh. In this way Hebdomad was completed by them, and the Mother held the eighth place. They precede each other in dignity and power, just as they do in birth.

5. Likewise, in keeping with their manner of lying, they conferred names such as these: The first-born of the Mother is called Jaldabaoth; and his son, Jao; and this one's son, Sabaoth; the fourth, Adoneus; the fifth, Eloeus; the sixth, Horeus; the seventh and last, Astaphaeus.[7] They submit that these are the Heavens, Virtues, Powers, Angels, and Creators, and sit in heaven according to their rank of birth, and that while invisible they rule the heavenly and earthly things. The first one of them, Jaldabaoth, holds his Mother in contempt, in this that he produced sons and grandsons without any permission, even of the Angels, Archangels, Virtues, Powers, and Dominions.[8] After this his sons turned against him and fought and quarreled about the supreme rule. This made Jaldabaoth very sad and filled him with despair, so he looked down upon the mire of material substance that was lying below him and fixed his desire on it with the result that a son was born. This son is Mind itself, twisted into the shape of a serpent.[9] Then [he begot] spirit, the soul, and all mundane things. From him too were begotten all forgetfulness, wickedness, jealousy, envy, and death. They assert that this their serpentlike and distorted Mind upset the Father still more by its crookedness when he was with their Father in heaven and paradise.

6. On account of these things he exultantly boasted that he is above all the things which are below him, and said: "I am the Father and God, and there is no one above me."[10] But when his Mother heard this,

she shouted at him: "Do not lie, Jaldabaoth, for there is above you the Father of all things, who is First-Man, and so is that Man who is the Son of Man." At the unexpected proclamation of this new voice all were disturbed and made an inquiry as to the source of the shouting. Then Jaldabaoth, in order to draw them away and lead them to himself, is supposed to have said: "Come, let us make man to the image."[11] When six of the Powers had heard these words, their Mother gave them an idea of a man so that through him she might deprive them of their sovereign power. So they assembled and formed a man[12] immense in breadth and length.[13] But he was able only to wriggle;[14] so they carried him to their father [Jaldabaoth]. But Wisdom so managed things that she deprived Jaldabaoth of the moisture of light so that with the power which he possessed he was not able to raise himself up against those who were above him. When, then, he breathed the spirit of life into man,[15] he was secretly deprived of that power. On the other hand, man from then on had intelligence and intention. These are the things, they say, that are saved. This man at once gave thanks to First-Man, thus forsaking his makers.

7. Thereupon, Jaldabaoth was jealous and wanted to devise a way by which to deprive man [of power] with the aid of a woman. So he brought forth a woman from his Intention, but Prounikos took her to herself and invisibly deprived her of power. But the rest came and admired her beauty and called her Eve. They were filled with desire toward her and begot sons from her, who they claim are also angels.[16] Their Mother, however, tried to[17] mislead Adam and Eve through the serpent to transgress the precept of Jaldabaoth. Eve, thinking she was hearing this from the Son of God, easily believed and persuaded Adam to eat of the tree of which God had commanded them not to eat. But when they had eaten, they received knowledge[18] of that Power which is above all things and forsook those who made them. Now, when Prounikos saw that they were overcome by their own handiwork, she greatly rejoiced and again cried out that, since there was already incorruptible Father, he [Jaldabaoth] told a lie when he once called himself Father, and that, since Man and First-Woman [Spirit] existed of old, he sinned by making an adulterated copy.[19]

8. However, Jaldabaoth, because of the forgetfulness with which he was surrounded, did not even pay any attention to those things and threw Adam and Eve out of paradise, because they had transgressed

his command. For he had wanted to generate sons for himself by Eve; but he was not successful, because his Mother opposed him in all things and secretly deprived Adam and Eve of the moisture of light, in order that Spirit who originated from the Authority might not share in the curse or opprobrium. And so, according to their teaching, Adam and Eve, deprived of divine power, were cursed by him and cast out of heaven into this world; but the Serpent who worked against the Father was cast out by him into the lower world. The Serpent, however, brought under his power the Angels who were here below. He also generated six sons. He himself was the seventh in the Hebdomad, which was made after the pattern of the Hebdomad, that is, with Father. They say that these are the seven devils of the world, who are forever opposing and resisting the human race, since on their account their Father was cast down.[20]

9. Adam and Eve formerly had light and luminous and kind of spiritual bodies, just as they had been fashioned.[21] But when they came to this world, their bodies were changed to darker, fatter, and more sluggish ones. Even their soul became feeble and languid inasmuch as it had from its Maker only the mundane breath, until Prounikos had pity on them and gave them back the sweet fragrance of the moisture of light, by which they attained consciousness and recognized that they were naked[22] and had a body of material substance. They also realized that they carried death about with them. They practiced long-suffering when they realized that they would be clothed with the body only for a time. They also found food through the guidance of Wisdom, and when they were satiated, they had carnal knowledge of each other and begot Cain. But the Serpent who had been cast down, together with his sons, immediately laid hold of him and destroyed him and filled him with worldly forgetfulness by driving him into folly and boldness with the result that he killed his brother Abel, and thus was the first to manifest jealousy and death.[23] After these two, according to the foresight of Prounikos, Seth was begotten, they say, and then Norea.[24] From these two the rest of the multitude of people were begotten and driven into every wickedness by the lower Hebdomad, even into apostasy from the holy Hebdomad on high, and into idolatry, and contempt of everything, since their Mother was invisibly always against them, and since she saved [only] that which was proper to herself, that is, the moisture of light. But they hold that the holy

Hebdomad is the seven stars, which they style planets. Further, they say that the Serpent who was cast down has two names, Michael and Samuel.[25]

10. Jaldabaoth was angry with men, because they did not worship or honor him. So as their Father and God he sent the deluge on them that he might destroy all together. But even here Wisdom opposed him,[26] and those who were with Noah in the ark were saved because of the moisture of light which they had from her, through whom the world was again filled with people. From among these Jaldabaoth himself chose a certain Abraham and made a covenant with him, promising to give him the earth for an inheritance if his posterity would continue to serve him. Afterwards, through Moses, he led the descendants of Abraham out of Egypt and gave them the law and made them Jews.[27] From among these he chose seven Gods,[28] in order that, when the others would hear the praises, they too would serve the Gods which the prophets announced.

11. They arrange the prophets in the following order: To Jaladabaoth belong Moses, Joshua son of Nun, Amos, and Habakkuk; to the previously mentioned Jao belong Samuel, Nathan, Jonah, and Michah; to Sabaoth, Elijah, Joel, and Zechariah; to Adonai, Isaiah, Ezekiel, Jeremiah, and Daniel; to Eloi, Tobit and Haggai; to Horeus, Michah and Nahum; to Astaphaeus, Ezra and Zephaniah. Each one of these, then, glorified his own Father and God. Wisdom [Prounikos] herself spoke much through them about First-Man and the incorruptible Aeon and about Christ on high. She admonished and reminded them of the incorruptible light of First-Man and of the descent of Christ from on high. The Rulers were terrified by these things, and, while they were marveling at the novelty of the things announced by the Prophets, Prounikos functioned through Jaldabaoth—though he was ignorant of what she was doing—and emitted two men, the one from the sterile Elizabeth, the other from the Virgin Mary.

12. And since she herself [Prounikos] had no rest, neither in heaven nor on earth, in her distress she called upon her Mother to help her. Thereupon her Mother, First-Woman, had pity on her repentant daughter and requested First-Man to send Christ to help her. Christ was then sent forth and descended to his sister and to moisture of light. When, however, Wisdom [Prounikos], who was here below, realized that her brother was descending to her, she announced his

coming through John, and prepared the baptism of penance, and made Jesus ready beforehand so that when Christ would descend, he would find a clean vessel, and so that through Jaldabaoth, her son, the woman might be announced by Christ.[29] They assert that he descended through the seven heavens and was made like to their sons and gradually deprived them of power. For they claim that all the moisture of light went to meet Christ, and when he descended to this world, he first clothed himself with his sister, Wisdom. Both were exultant, resting against each other. These they hold are bridegroom and bride.[30] Now Jesus, inasmuch as he was begotten of the Virgin by God's action, was wiser and purer and holier than all men. On him Christ, united with Wisdom, descended; and thus was formed Jesus Christ.

13. Many of Jesus' disciples, they assert, did not realize that Christ had descended on him. Still, when Christ had descended on Jesus, Jesus began to work wonders, to heal, to announce the unknown Father, and publicly to acknowledge that he himself is the Son of First-Man. At these things the Rulers and the Father of Jesus [Jaldabaoth] were indignant and conspired to kill him. But when he was being brought for that purpose, they say, Christ himself, together with Wisdom, departed into the incorruptible Aeon, but Jesus was crucified. Christ, however, did not forget about him [Jesus] but sent down on him a certain power that raised him up again in his body. This body they call ensouled and spiritual, because he left the worldly elements [of the body] in the world. But when the disciples saw that he had risen from the dead, they did not recognize him; no, not even Jesus [did they recognize], namely, in what manner he rose from the dead. This they claim was a very great error among the disciples that they thought he had risen in a worldly body, since they were ignorant of the fact that *Flesh and blood do not inherit the kingdom of heaven*.[31]

14. They wish to prove that Christ descended on Jesus and again ascended from him by the fact that neither before nor after his resurrection from the dead did Jesus perform any great deeds according to the statements of his disciples, who however were ignorant of the fact that Jesus had been united with Christ, and the incorruptible Aeon with the Hebdomad.[32] They also say that the worldly body was that of animals. After this resurrection he tarried yet for eighteen months.[33] When sentient knowledge came upon him, he learned what the truth

was.[34] He taught these things to those few disciples of his who knew he could grasp such great mysteries. Then he was assumed into heaven, where Jesus sits at the right hand of his Father,[35] Jaldabaoth, in order to receive unto himself the souls of those who knew them, after they had put off the worldly flesh. This Jesus enriches himself while the Father remains ignorant of him; in fact, he does not even see him. And so, insofar as Jesus enriches himself with holy souls, in so far his Father suffers loss and becomes inferior, being emptied of his power by the souls. For he will no longer have souls which he might again send into the world; he has only those souls that were derived from his substance, that is, those who come from his breath. The consummation, however, will take place when all the moisture of the light of the Spirit is gathered together and is snatched away into the incorruptible Aeon.

15. Such are their doctrines. Doctrines by which was generated, like the Lernaean serpent,[36] a wild beast with many heads, [that is] the Valentinian school.[37] Some of them, however, claim that Wisdom herself was the Serpent,[38] that for this reason she was opposed to the Maker of Adam and implanted knowledge in men, and that this is why the Serpent was said to be wiser than all.[39] Moreover, they maintain that the position and shape of our intestines—by which food is conveyed—manifest the mother hidden in us, who had the shape of the Serpent.[40]

CHAPTER 31
TENETS OF THE CAINITES.

1. Others, again,[1] say that Cain comes from the Supreme Authority on high. They confess that Esau, Core, the Sodomites, and all such persons are their relatives. And so they indeed were attacked by the Maker; but none of them were injured; for Wisdom snatched to herself from them whatever they possessed that was proper to herself. Also Judas, the traitor, they say, had exact knowledge of these things, and since he alone knew the truth better than the other apostles, he accomplished the mystery of the betrayal. Through him all things in

heaven and on earth were destroyed. This fiction they adduce, and call it the Gospel of Judas.

2. I have also collected their writings in which they admonish to destroy the works of the Womb. This Womb they call the Maker of heaven and earth.[2] Like Carpocrates, they hold that they cannot be saved except they pass through all things.[3] At everyone of the sins and impure actions, they say, an Angel assists, and the one who acts, ventures impudence, and imputes the impurity to the name of the Angel which is present for the action, and says: "O Angel, I do your work. O Power, I perform your action!" It is perfect knowledge, they say, to rush without fear into actions such as one is not even allowed to mention.[4]

Conclusion

3. By such mothers and fathers and ancestors it was necessary to expose clearly the followers of Valentinus—such as their very doctrines and rules show them to be—and to bring their teachings out into the open.[5] Perhaps, some of them can be saved if they do penance and convert to the one and only Creator and God, the Maker of the universe. Moreover, others will no longer be misled by their malicious though specious persuasion, thinking that they will learn of some greater or more sublime mystery from them. On the other hand, if people learn well from us what was taught by these [heretics], they may, it is true, ridicule their doctrine, but will have pity on them, inasmuch as these are still so arrogant about such miserable and unfounded fables that they consider themselves better than all the rest on account of this knowledge—rather ignorance. That is their exposé. Indeed, the very manifestation of their doctrine is a victory against them.[6]

4. For this reason we have endeavored to bring out into the open the entire ill-formed body of this little fox and clearly make it manifest. So there is no longer any need for many words to overthrow their doctrine, since it has been made manifest to all. To illustrate, when some wild beast has hidden himself in a forest and from there makes

attacks on others and kills them, one who cuts down the forest, and so brings the wild beast itself in sight, does not strive to capture the beast because he sees that it is really a wild beast. For people can see its attacks, guard themselves against them, throw javelins at it from all sides, wound it, and thus kill that destructive wild beast. In like manner, since we have disclosed their hidden mysteries which they guard in silence, there is no longer any need for us to destroy their doctrine with many words. You, too, and all those who are with you, are now in a position to examine what has been said and to overthrow their wicked and unfounded doctrines and to demonstrate the teachings that do not harmonize with the Truth.[7] Since the case is such, in keeping with our promise and according to our competence, we shall answer every one of them in a subsequent book, and so overthrow them. The account [of their tenets] is long, as you can see. As we encounter all of them in the order in which they were narrated, we shall supply means for overthrowing them that we may not merely expose the beast, but may also wound it from all sides.

NOTES

LIST OF ABBREVIATIONS

ACW	Ancient Christian Writers (Westminster, Md.-London-New York-Paramus, N.J.-Mahwah, N.J. 1946–)
ANF	The Ante-Nicene Fathers (Buffalo, N.Y. 1885–96; repr. Grand Rapids, Mich. 1951–56)
Athanasius, *Ar.* 1–3	Athanasius, *Orationes tres adversus Arianos*
Augustine, *C. Jul.*	Augustine, *Contra Julianum libri* 6
Augustine, *Catech. rud.*	Augustine, *De catechizandis rudibus*
Augustine, *Civ.*	Augustine, *De civitate Dei*
Augustine, *Doct. christ.*	Augustine, *De doctrina christiana*
Augustine, *Haer.*	Augustine, *De haeresibus ad Quodvultdeum*
Basil, *Spirit.*	Basil, *Liber de Spiritu sancto*
Benoît	A. Benoît, *Saint Irénée: Introduction à l'étude de sa théologie* (Paris 1960)
Bibl. Stud.	Biblische Studien
BKV	Bibliothek der Kirchenväter² (Kempten and Munich 1911–31)
BLE	Bulletin de littérature ecclésiastique
Caesar, *Gall.*	Caesar, *De bello Gallico*
CBQ	Catholic Biblical Quarterly
CCL	Corpus christianorum, series latina
CE	Catholic Encyclopedia (New York 1907–14)
Cicero, *De orat.*	Cicero, *De oratore*
Cicero, *Rab. Post.*	Cicero, *Pro C. Rabiro Postumo oratio*
Cicero, *Tusc.*	Cicero, *Tusculanarum disputationum liber*
Clement of Alexandria, *Ecl.*	Clement of Alexandria, *Eclogae ex scripturis propheticis*

Clement of Alexandria, Exc. Thdot.	Clement of Alexandria, Excerpta Theodoti
Clement of Alexandria, Paed.	Clement of Alexandria, Paedagogus
Clement of Alexandria, Str.	Clement of Alexandria, Stromateis
Coll. Messina	The Origins of Gnosticism: Colloquium of Messina 13–18 April 1966, ed. U. Bianchi (Leiden 1970)
CPG I	Clavis Patrum Graecorum, vol. 1: Patres Antenicaeni, ed. M. Geerard (Turnhout 1983)
CSCO	Corpus scriptorum christianorum orientalium (Paris et alibi 1903–)
CSEL	Corpus scriptorum ecclesiasticorum latinorum (Vienna 1866–)
CW	The Classical World
Cyril of Jerusalem, Procatech.	Cyril of Jerusalem, Procatechesis
DACL	Dictionnaire d'archéologie chrétienne et de liturgie (Paris 1907–53)
DBS	Dictionnaire de la Bible, Supplément (Paris 1928–)
DCB	A Dictionary of Christian Biography, Literature, Sects, and Doctrines (London 1877–87)
DHGE	Dictionnaire d'histoire et de géographie ecclésiastiques (Paris 1912–)
DPAC	Dizionario patristico e di antichità cristiane (Casale Monferrato 1983–88)
DSp	Dictionnaire de spiritualité (Paris 1932–)
DTC	Dictionnaire de théologie catholique (Paris 1903–50)
Dufourcq Irénée	A. Dufourcq, Saint Irénée, Les Saints (Paris 1904)
Dufourcq Pensée	A. Dufourcq, La pensée chrétienne (Paris 1905)

Epiphanius, *Haer.*	Epiphanius, *Panarion* seu *Adversus lxxx haereses*
Eusebius, *H.e.*	Eusebius, *Historia ecclesiastica*
Eusebius, *P.e.*	Eusebius, *Praeparatio evangelica*
Filaster, *Haer.*	Filaster, *Diversarum haereseon liber*
GCS	Die griechischen christlichen Schrift-steller der ersten drei Jahrhunderte (Leipzig 1897–)
Gk. Epiph.	The Greek text of Irenaeus's *Adversus haereses* contained in Epiphanius (ed. K. Holl, GCS 25 [1915], 31 [1922], 37 [1933])
Goodspeed	*Die ältesten Apologeten: Texte mit kurzen Einleitungen,* ed. E. J. Goodspeed (Göttingen 1914)
Grabe	The edition of the *Adversus haereses* by J. E. Grabe (Oxford 1702)
Harvey	The edition of the *Adversus haereses* by W. W. Harvey (Cambridge 1857)
HERE	Encyclopedia of Religion and Ethics, ed. J. Hastings (New York and Edinburgh 1908–26)
Hermas, *Mand.*	Hermas, *Mandata pastoris*
Hippolytus, *Haer.*	Hippolytus, *Refutatio omnium haeresium sive philosophoumena*
Hippolytus, *Trad. ap.*	Hippolytus, *Traditio apostolica*
Homer, *Il.*	Homer, *Ilias*
Homer, *Od.*	Homer, *Odyssea*
HTR	Harvard Theological Review
Ignatius of Antioch, *Smyrn.*	Ignatius of Antioch, *Epistula ad Smyrnaeos*
JEH	Journal of Ecclesiastical History
Jerome, *Ad Jovin.*	Jerome, *Adversus Jovinianum libri 2*
Jerome, *Epist.*	Jerome, *Epistula*
Jerome, *In Tit.*	Jerome, *Commentarius in epistulam Pauli ad Titum*
Jerome, *Vir. ill.*	Jerome, *De viris illustribus*
JThS	Journal of Theological Studies

Justin, *Dial.*	Justin, *Dialogus cum Tryphone Judaeo*
Justin, 1, 2 *Apol.*	Justin, *Apologiae*
Klebba, BKV	*Des heiligen Irenäus Fünf Bücher gegen die Häresin*, trans. E. Klebba, BKV 3–4 (Kempten 1912)
Lampe, PGL	*A Patristic Greek Lexicon*, ed. G. W. H. Lampe (Oxford 1961)
Lat. Iren.	The Latin version of Irenaeus's *Adversus haereses*
Lebreton-Zeiller	J. Lebreton and J. Zeiller, *History of the Primitive Church*, trans. E. C. Messenger (New York 1942–47)
LSJ	*A Greek-English Lexicon* compiled by H. G. Liddell and R. Scott revised and augmented by H. Stuart Jones and R. McKenzie et al. (Oxford 1940)
LSJ Suppl.	H. G. Liddell, R. Scott, H. Stuart Jones, *Greek-English Lexicon: A Supplement*, ed. E. A. Barber et al. (Oxford 1968)
LTK	Lexikon für Theologie und Kirche (Freiburg 1930–38)
LTK²	Lexikon für Theologie und Kirche, 2d ed. (Freiburg 1957–67)
Lundström *Studien*	S. Lundström, *Studien zur lateinische Irenäusübersetzung* (Lund 1943)
Mannucci	*Irenaei Lugdunensis Episcopi Adversus Haereses Libri Quinque* (Rome 1907)
Marius Victorinus, *Adv. Arrium*	Marius Victorinus, *Adversus Arrium libri 4*
Marius Victorinus, *Gen. div. verb.*	Marius Victorinus, *De generatione divini verbi*
Maximus Confessor, *Schol. e.h.*	Maximus Confessor, *Scholia* in Pseudo-Dionysius Areopagita, *De ecclesiastica hierarchia*
MG	Patrologia graeca, ed. J. P. Migne (Paris 1857–66)

ML	Patrologia latina, ed. J. P. Migne (Paris 1844–64)
M. Polyc.	*Martyrium Polycarpi*
NCE	New Catholic Encyclopedia (New York 1967)
Nilus the Ascetic, *Ep.*	Nilus the Ascetic, *Epistula*
NJBC	*The New Jerome Biblical Commentary,* ed. R. E. Brown, J. A. Fitzmyer, and R. A. Murphy (Englewood Cliffs, N.J. 1990)
NRT	Nouvelle revue théologique
NTAbhand.	Neutestamentliche Abhandlungen
OCD²	The Oxford Classical Dictionary, 2d ed. (Oxford 1970)
ODCC²	The Oxford Dictionary of the Christian Church, 2d ed. (Oxford 1983)
Origen, *Cels.*	Origen, *Contra Celsum*
Photius, *Cod.*	Photius, *Bibliothecae codices*
Plautus, *Most.*	Plautus, *Mostellaria*
Pliny, *Nat.*	Pliny, *Naturalis historia libri 37*
PO	Patrologia orientalis (Paris 1904–)
Proof	*Saint Irenaeus: Proof of the Apostolic Preaching,* trans. J. Smith, ACW 16
Ps.-Tertullian, *Haer.*	Ps.-Tertullian, *Liber adversus omnes haereses*
Quasten *Patr.*	J. Quasten, *Patrology,* 3 vols. (Westminster, Md., Utrecht, and Antwerp 1950–60; repr. Westminster, Md. 1983)
RAC	Reallexikon für Antike und Christentum (Stuttgart 1950–)
RB	Revue bénédictine
RBibl	Revue biblique
RE	Real-Encyclopädie der classischen Altertumswissenschaft, ed. A. Pauly, G. Wissowa, W. Kroll (Stuttgart 1893–)
RGG	Die Religion in Geschichte und Gegenwart, 3d ed. (Tübingen 1957–65)
RHE	Revue d'histoire ecclésiastique
RPT	Realencyklopädie für protestantische

	Theologie und Kirche (Leipzig 1896–1913)
RSPT	Revue des sciences philosophiques et théologiques
RechSR	Recherches de science religieuse
RSRUS	Revue des sciences religieuses
RTAM	Recherches de théologie ancienne et médiévale
Rudolph *Gnosis*	K. Rudolph, *Gnosis: The Nature and History of Gnosticism*, tr. P. W. Coxon, K. H. Kuhn, R. McL. Wilson (Edinburgh 1984; also in paperback edition, San Francisco 1987)
Sagnard *Gnose*	F. Sagnard, *La gnose valentinienne et le témoinage de saint Irénée* (Paris 1947)
SC	Sources chrétiennes (Paris 1942–)
SCent	The Second Century
Stieren	The edition of the *Adversus haereses* by A. Stieren (Leipzig 1848–53)
Tacitus, *Ann.*	Tacitus, *Annales (ab excessu divi Augusti) libri 16*
TDNT	*Theological Dictionary of the New Testament*, ed. G. Kittel and G. Friedrich and trans. G. Bromiley (Grand Rapids, Mich. 1964–76)
Tertullian, *Adv. Marc.*	Tertullian, *Adversus Marcionem*
Tertullian, *Adv. Val.*	Tertullian, *Adversus Valentinianos*
Tertullian, *Anim.*	Tertullian, *De anima*
Tertullian, *Praescr.*	Tertullian, *De praescriptione haereticorum*
Tertullian, *Spec.*	Tertullian, *De spectaculis*
Theodoret, *Ep.*	Theodoret, *Epistula*
Theodoret, *Haer.*	Theodoret, *Haereticarum fabularum compendium*
Theophilus of Antioch, *Auto.*	Theophilus of Antioch, *Ad Autolycum*
ThRdschau	Theologische Rundschau
ThS	Theological Studies

TRE	Theologische Realenzyklopädie (Berlin 1976–)
TU	Texte und Untersuchungen zur Geschichte der altchristlichen Literatur (Leipzig-Berlin 1882–)
VC	Vigiliae christianae
VD	Verbum Domini
Vernet	F. Vernet, "Irénée (Saint)," in DTC 7.2.2394–2533
ZKT	Zeitschrift für katholische Theologie
ZNTW	Zeitschrift für die neutestamentliche Wissenschaft und die Kunde des Urchristentums
ZRGG	Zeitschrift für Religions- und Geistesgeschichte
ZTK	Zeitschrift für Theologie und Kirche

Abbreviations for books of the Old Testament and New Testament are those found in *The Chicago Manual of Style: The 13th Edition of A Manual of Style Revised and Expanded* (Chicago and London 1982) 388–89. Where a given book of the Bible is differently designated in the New American Bible (NAB) and in the LXX (and Vulgate), both forms are given. But the NAB designation is given first. For example, 2 Sam. (2 Kings), Sir. (Ecclus.), Rev. (Apoc.). When Psalms are cited, the Septuagint enumeration is given first. For example, Ps. 138(139).13.

Finally, a word about the citation of the justificative notes found in SC 263.167–316. There are often several justificative notes per page. To avoid confusion, the following system of citing these notes is used throughout this volume: SC 263.167 (SC 264.19 n. 1). This indicates which justificative note on p. 167 of SC 263 is meant (i.e., the first note on p. 19 of SC 264).

NOTES

INTRODUCTION

1. Translated by J. Smith, this volume (ACW 16) was published in 1952. Hereinafter the *Proof of the Apostolic Preaching* will be referred to as *Proof.*

2. Tertullian, *Adv. Val.* 5 (CCL 2.756). See also H. B. Swete, *Patristic Study* (London 1902) 36. For recent scholarship on Irenaeus see the following: C. Kannengiesser, "Bulletin de théologie patristique: Ignace d'Antioche et Irénée de Lyon," RechSR 67, no. 4 (1979) 610–23; T. P. Halton and R. D. Sider, "A Decade of Patristic Scholarship: Volume 1," CW 76, no. 2 (November–December 1982) 96–101; M. A. Donovan, "Irenaeus in Recent Scholarship," SCent 4, no. 4 (Winter 1984) 219–41. Donovan mentions several Irenaean works published after this article in "Alive to the Glory of God: A Key Insight in St. Irenaeus," ThS 49 (1988) 283. For very recent surveys on Irenaeus see H.-J. Jaschke, "Irenäus von Lyon," TRE 16.258–68; A. Orbe, "Ireneo," DPAC 2.1804–16. In addition, see recent issues of *Bibliographia patristica,* ed. W. Schneemelcher (Berlin [and later Bonn and New York] 1959–) and *L'année philologique.*

3. The following works can be consulted on Gnosticism: W. Bousset, *Hauptprobleme der Gnosis* (Göttingen 1907); idem, "Gnosis," RE 7.2.1503–33; idem, "Gnostiker," RE 7.2.1537–47; H. Leclercq, "Gnosticisme," DACL 6.1.1327–67; G. Bareille, "Gnosticisme," DTC 6.2.1437–67; "Gnostizismus," LTK² 4.1021–31 has five articles by as many authors: K. Prümm, K. Schubert, R. Schnackenberg, H. Rahner, K. Algermissen; P. T. Camelot, "Gnose chrétienne," DSp 6.509–23; E. Cornelis, "Le Gnosticisme," DSp 6.523–41; G. Quispel, "Gnosticism," *Encyclopedia Brittanica* 10.505–7; K. Berger, "Gnosis/Gnostizismus I," TRE 13.3–4. 519–35; R. McL. Wilson, "Gnosis/Gnostizis-

mus II," TRE 13.3–4. 535–50; J. Lebreton, *Histoire du dogme de la Trinité* 2 (Paris 1928) 81–121, treats both pre-Christian and Christian Gnosticism; Lebreton-Zeiller 1.355–59, 2.617–53; L. Cerfaux, "Gnose pré-chrétienne et biblique," DBS 3.659–701 is particularly valuable for the origins of Gnosticism; C. Colpe, "Gnosis II (Gnostizismus)," RAC 11.537–659; G. Filoramo, "Gnosi/Gnosticismo," DPAC 2.1642–50; Sagnard *Gnose,* passim; Quasten *Patr.* 1.254–77, gives a handy classified bibliography; Sagnard, SC 34.44–70; H. A. Wolfson, *The Philosophy of the Church Fathers,* 2d ed., *Structure and Growth of Philosophic Systems from Plato to Spinoza* 3 (Cambridge, Mass. 1964) 1.495–574; H. Jonas, *The Gnostic Religion: The Message of the Alien God and the Beginnings of Christianity,* 2d ed. (Boston 1963); G. Van Groningen, *First-Century Gnosticism: Its Origins and Motifs* (Leiden 1967); J. Pelikan, *The Emergence of the Catholic Tradition (100–600),* vol. 1 of *The Christian Tradition: A History of the Development of Doctrine* (Chicago 1971) 68–97; K. Rudolph, *Gnosis: The Nature and History of Gnosticism,* tr. P. W. Coxon, K. H. Kuhn, R. McL. Wilson (Edinburgh 1984; also in paperback edition, San Francisco 1987; hereinafter Rudolph, *Gnosis*). H.-M. Schenke, "The Problem of Gnosis," SCent 3, no. 2 (Summer 1983) 73–87.

4. See the following items on Nag Hammadi: J. M. Robinson, "The Coptic Gnostic Library Today," NTS 14 (1968) 356–401; M. Krause, "Der Stand der Veröffentlichung der Nag Hammadi Texte" in Coll. Messina 61–89; G. Filoramo, "Nag Hammadi (scritti di)," DPAC 2.2329–32; J. Doresse, *The Secret Books of the Egyptian Gnostics: An Introduction to the Gnostic Manuscripts Discovered at Chenoboskion,* trans. P. Mairet (London 1960); J. Dart, *The Laughing Savior* (New York 1976); F. Wisse, "The Nag Hammadi Library and the Heresiologists," VC 25 (1971) 205–23; J. M. Robinson, "The Jung Codex: The Rise and Fall of a Monopoly," *Religious Studies Review* 3 (1977) 17–30. An English translation of the documents can be found in *The Nag Hammadi Library,* ed. J. M. Robinson et al. (3d rev. ed. with an afterword by R. Smith, San Francisco 1988). Important information is also available in D. M. Scholer, *Nag Hammadi Bibliography 1948–69,* Nag Hammadi Studies 1 (Leiden 1971), which is updated in annual supplements in *Novum Testamentum.*

5. See Quasten *Patr.* 1.294.

6. See D. J. Unger, "Christ's Rôle in the Universe according to

St. Irenaeus," *Franciscan Studies* 5 (1945) 3–20, 114–37 (with bibliography); F. Beuzart, *Essai sur la théologie d'Irénée* (Paris 1908); A. M. Clerici, "Incontro tra la storia biblica e la storia profano in Ireneo," *Aevum* 43 (1969) 1–30. W. Widmann, "Irenaeus und seine theologischen Väter," ZTK 54 (1957) 156–73, examined what is proper to Irenaeus and not borrowed from predecessors, and correctly says it is his thought of a total economy of God for humankind, centered on Jesus Christ as the Beginning and the End, who recapitulates humankind's whole history and whole being. This same thought emerges from the study of G. Wingren, *Man and the Incarnation: A Study in the Biblical Theology of Irenaeus*, trans. R. MacKenzie (Edinburgh 1959) xiv, 26–27, 79–87, 122–28, 131, 170–75, 183, 191–202, 212, and J. Lawson, *The Biblical Theology of Saint Irenaeus* (London 1948) 140–98. Benoît 202–33 discusses the following as main themes in Irenaeus: the unity of God; the economy, which is universal and one; recapitulation; and gradual progress in salvation.

7. D. van den Eynde, *Les normes de l'enseignment chrétien dans la littérature patristique des trois premiers siècles* (Paris 1933) 163, writes as if there was no development in the doctrine of Irenaeus. A. Harnack was of the same mind; see his *History of Dogma*, trans. from the 3d German edition by N. Buchanan, 2 (Boston 1896) 312.

8. See Eusebius, *H.e.* 2.13.5; 3.28.6 (GCS 2.1.136, 258). St. Basil, *Spir.* 29.72 (SC 17².506). St. Jerome, *Vir. ill.* 35 (TU 14.1.a.25). St. Maximus Confessor, *Schol. e.h.* 7 (MG 4.176C). Photius, *Cod. 120* (MG 103.401), who placed this short title after the longer one. The definite article in the English translation is warranted by Eusebius and Basil and the contents. See Massuet, *Dissertatio* (hereinafter Diss.) 2.2.46 (MG 7.220–22).

9. Eusebius, *H.e.* 5.7.1 (GCS 2.1.440).

10. See A.H. 2 Prf. 2; 4 Prf. 1; 5 Prf. Irenaeus also alludes to it in A.H. 1.22.2; 1.31.3; and 2.24.4.

11. See *euersio huiusmodi aedificationis* (A.H. 2.27.3) with reference to doctrine.

12. Irenaean authorship is indicated particularly in view of the many citations and long quotations from this work, beginning with his contemporaries St. Hippolytus and Tertullian till St. John Damascene. J. S. Semler denied the Irenaean authorship in *Dissertatio I* from his edition of Tertullian (5 [Halle 1770–76; reprinted 1824–29] 245–90). He

was amply refuted by G. F. Walch, *Commentatio de authentia librorum Irenaei adversus haereses* (cf. MG 7.381–404).

13. Grabe, *Prolegomena* 1.2.6 (MG 7.1358), held that the work is incomplete. Cf. Massuet, Diss. 2.2.54 (MG 7.235). W. Bousset, *Jüdischchristlicher Schulbetrieb in Alexandria und Rom: Literarische Untersuchungen zu Philo und Clemens von Alexandria, Justin, und Irenäus* (Göttingen 1915) 272–82, claimed the following sections are not genuine: 4.20.8–12, 21, 25.2, 33.10–14, 37–39; 5.21–36.

14. Sagnard *Gnose* 84, n. 4.

15. See A. Vaccari, S.J., *Institutiones Biblicae*, 6th ed. (Rome 1951) 1.283.

16. See R. E. Brown, D. W. Johnson, K. G. O'Connell, "Texts and Versions," NJBC #68, nn. 70–74, 82.

17. A.H. 1 Prf. 2; 1.9.1; 1.31.4; 3 Prf.; 4 Prf. 1; 5 Prf.

18. A.H. 1 Prf. 3; 4 Prf. 1.

19. A.H. 1 Prf. 2–3.

20. A.H. 1.31.4.

21. 1 Prf. 3.

22. A.H. 1.31.3.

23. See Dufourcq *Irénée* 74.

24. A.H. 2.31.2; 2.35.2. See also A.H. 3.12.12.

25. For a more detailed breakdown of Book 1 see SC 263.113–64.

26. See A.H. 1.15.4–5. Sagnard *Gnose* 72–74 rightly praises his rhetorical ability.

27. See A.H. 1.4.4; 2.6.3; 2.14.7.

28. Jerome, *Epist.* 75.3 (CSEL 55.33).

29. See Bonaventura ab Andermatt, O.M.Cap., "Sancti Irenaei doctrina de Sacrae Scripturae inspiratione atque inerrantia," (S.T.D. diss., Gregorian University, Rome 1937) passim; W. S. Reilly, "L'inspiration de l'Ancient Testament chez Saint Irénée," RBibl 14 (1917) 489–507; he does not always have a correct evaluation of Irenaeus's thought. J. Hoh, *Die Lehre des hl. Irenäus über das Neue Testament* (NTAbhand 7.4–5 [1919] 62–75, 90–109).

30. A.H. 2.27.1; 2.35.4; 3.21.2.

31. A.H. 1.8.1; 2.2.5; 2.34.1; 5 Prf.; *Proof* 98.

32. A.H. 3.24.1.

33. A.H. 2.28.2; 3.1.1; also 3.5.1; 3.14.2–4.

34. A. Camerlynck, *St. Irénée et le canon du Nouveau Testament*

(Louvain 1896) 26–27; T. Zahn, "Kanon des Neuen Testaments," RPT 9.768–96; idem, *Introduction to the New Testament*, 3d ed., trans. M. W. Jacobus and J. M. Trout (Edinburgh 1909) 2.295, 301, 310 n. 9, 387, 393–94, 433–34; 3.201 n. 14, 205 n. 27, 254 n. 6, 445, 448 n. 5.

35. A.H. 1.30.11.

36. A.H. 4.17.3; 4.17.5.

37. See Vernet 2416; Camerlynck, *Saint Irénée* 38–39; Benoît 103–47.

38. A.H. 4.20.2.

39. Irenaeus uses *graphē* in reference to the letter of Pope Clement at A.H. 3.3.3. Benoît 146 agrees that Irenaeus does not consider Hermas as strict Scripture. See also SC 100.248–50 on the question of whether or not Irenaeus considered Hermas as canonical Scripture as indicated by his use of *graphē*.

40. Twice he ascribes it to Jeremiah (A.H. 4.22.1; *Proof* 78); once to Isaiah (A.H. 3.20.4); three times to the prophets (A.H. 4.33.1; 4.33.12; 5.31.1). In *Proof* 4 he quotes this passage also, but he does not refer it to Hermas. There he adds "the Father" after "God," and changes "brought everything into being out of what was not," to "brought being out of nothing." See ACW 16.137 and n. 28. See SC 100.255, 687 n. 2 for a different view on A.H. 4.33.1; 4.33.12 and 5.31.1.

41. A.H. 5.33.3–4; 5.36.2. See E. Jacquier, "Les sentences du Seigneur extracanoniques (les Agrapha)," RBibl 15 (1918) 129–31.

42. See J. Chapman, "Did the Translator of St. Irenaeus Use a Latin N.T.?" RB 36 (1924) 34–51. See also K. T. Schäfer, "Die Zitate in der lateinischen Irenäusübersetzung und ihr Wert für die Textgeschichte des Neuen Testaments," *Von Wort des Lebens: Festschrift für Max Meinertz zur Vollendung des 70. Lebensjahres 19. Dezember 1950,* ed. N. Adler (Münster 1951) 50–59.

43. See SC 100.89–92.

44. See F. G. Kenyon, *The Text of the Greek Bible*, 3d ed. rev. A. W. Adams (London 1975) 169, 182; idem, *Our Bible and the Ancient Manuscripts,* 5th ed. rev. A. W. Adams (London 1958) 166–78.

45. A.H. 4.6.1; 4.6.3; 4.6.7 are texts where Matt. 11.27 is cited three different ways. See H. J. Vogels, "Der Evangelientext des hl. Irenaeus," RB 36 (1924) 25 and A. Merk, "Der Text des Neuen Testamentes beim hl. Irenaeus," ZKT 49 (1925) 307.

46. Such is the contention of B. Hemmerdinger, "Les Hexaples et Saint Irénée," VC 16 (1962) 19–20.

47. J. R. Harris and V. Burch, *Testimonies* (Cambridge 1920). P. Prigent, *Les Testimonia dans le christianisme primitif: L'épître de Barnabé I-XVI et ses sources* (Paris 1961), made a detailed literary study to discover patterns of citation that show up in preexisting documents. J.-P. Audet, "L'hypothèse des Testimonia: Remarques autour d'un livre récent," RBibl 70 (1963) 381–405, disagrees with Prigent and sides with C. H. Dodd, *According to the Scriptures* (Welwyn 1952) 28–60, that the *Testimonia* were not collections of merely short proof texts but fairly extensive passages. R. A. Kraft, "Barnabas' Isaiah Text and the 'Testimony Book' Hypothesis," JBL 79 (1960) 336–50, argues that the matter is not as simple as Harris had presented it. In the late Jewish and early Christian period there was a *Schulbetrieb* which produced short and independent documents of a testimony page. Greek and Semitic communities handed down similar note pages which were eventually gathered into larger units that resulted in various recensions of the same testimony. A. Benoît, "Irénée *Adversus haereses* IV 17, 1–5 et les Testimonia," *Studia patristica* 4 (TU 79 [1961], 20–27), makes a good case that Irenaeus used *Testimonia* for this section of A.H.

48. Thus Hemmerdinger, "Les Hexaples," 19–20; see also idem, "Remarques sur l'ecdotique de Saint Irénée," *Studia patristica* 3 (TU 78 [1961] 70). Hemmerdinger incorrectly assigns the false attribution of Isaiah to A.H. 3.9.3; it should be 3.9.2.

49. A.H. 1.9.4.

50. A.H. 2.28.1.

51. A.H. 3.7.1–2.

52. A.H. 2.10.1; 2.27.

53. A.H. 2.28.3.

54. A.H. 3.1.1; 3.4.1–2; see A. J. Coan, "The Rule of Faith in the Ecclesiastical Writings of the First Two Centuries: An Historico-apologetical Investigation" (S.T.D. diss., The Catholic University of America, Washington, D.C. 1924) 69–93. N. Brox, in his careful introductory study of Irenaeus, *Offenbarung: Gnosis und gnostiker Mythos bei Irenäus von Lyon: Zur Charakteristik der Systeme* (Munich and Salzburg 1966) 69–103, holds that, according to Irenaeus, the Scriptures are perfect and complete, namely, as a source of revelation. But he must then modify somewhat his theory.

55. A.H. 3.1.1; 3.2.1–2; and passim.

56. See van den Eynde, *Normes de l'enseignment* 159–87.

57. A.H. 3.2.2; 3.3.1–3; and passim.

58. A.H. 1.9.4; 1.10.1–2; 3.1.1; 3.4.1–2; 3.24.1.

59. See Book 3 for a full discussion of A.H. 3.3.2., a justly famous passage.

60. A.H. 3.1.1.

61. A.H. 3.5.1; see van den Eynde, *Normes de l'enseignement* 261–80.

62. For a detailed study of the Greek for Books 1 to 5, see SC 263.61–100, SC 293.83–100, SC 210.49–132, SC 100.51–87, SC 152.64–157.

63. See SC 100.15 and L. Doutreleau, "Saint Irénée de Lyon," DSp 7.2.1934.

64. See SC 263.9–59, SC 293.17–82, SC 210.11–48, SC 100.15–50, SC 152.27–63. The following studies on the Latin text may be consulted: F. Loofs, *Die Handscriften des lateinischen Übersetzung des Irenäus und ihre Kapitelteilung*, Kirchengeschichtliche Studien H. Reuter gewidmet (Leipzig 1888) 1–93 (printed separately Leipzig 1890); O. Bardenhewer, *Geschichte der altkirchlichen Literatur* 1 (2d ed. Freiburg 1913) 500; *Nouum Testamentum Sancti Irenaei Episcopi Lugdunensis*, ed. W. Sanday, C. H. Turner, A. Souter et al., Old-Latin Biblical Texts 7 (Oxford 1923) xxv–xxxv; W. Sanday, "The MSS of Irenaeus," *Journal of Philology* 17 (1888) 81–94; F. C. Burkitt, "Dr. Sanday's New Testament, With a Note on Valentinian Terms in Irenaeus and Tertullian," JThS 25 (1923) 56–67; E. Köstermann, Neue Beiträge zur Geschichte der lateinischen Handschriften des Irenäus, ZNTW 36 (1937) 1–34; Sagnard *Gnose* 12–15; J. S. A. Cunningham, *Irenaeus: Adversus haereses I: A New Edition of the Latin Text* (Ann Arbor, Michigan 1968) xvii–xix (Microfilm).

65. For an attempt to discover the identity of one of Erasmus's MSS see J. Ruysschaert, "Le manuscrit '*Romae descriptum*' de l'édition Érasmienne de Irénée de Lyon," *Scrinium Erasmianum*, ed. J. Coppens, 1 (Leiden 1969) 263–76. Cunningham (*Irenaeus* xxi) believes that the *editio princeps* by Erasmus should have a claim on our attention as a witness to the tradition as his variants are just as valuable as those in the other *recentiores*.

66. See M. L. Guillaumin, *A la recherche des manuscrits d'Irénée* (Studia patristica 7.1 [TU 92, 1966] 65–70). For Doutreleau's views, see SC 263.319–27.

67. See SC 263.319–27 and SC 152.55–57 n. 1. I have not listed the Mercier MSS, because they are really not independent MSS.

68. See B. Botte, "Notes de critique textuelle sur l'*Adversus haereses* de saint Irénée," RTAM 21 (1954) 165–78. Cunningham (*Irenaeus* xxiv) also believes that C should be the MS against which the others should be compared.

69. Chap. 9 (ML 104.85). G. Mercati first held that there was a second translation, but later changed his mind. On this see G. Mercati, *Note di letteratura biblica e cristiana antica,* Studi e Testi 5 (Rome 1901) 241–43. C. H. Turner, "Mercati on Cyprian and Irenaeus," JThS 2 (1901) 143–48, holds that there is no second translation.

70. Sagnard *Gnose* 18. Burkitt, "Sanday's New Testament of Irenaeus," 63: "The more I study the Latin Irenaeus the more I feel that its importance lies chiefly in what it tells us about the original Greek text of St. Irenaeus." The Armenian version of Books 4 and 5 prove that the Latin is in general a faithful translation of the Greek original. S. Lundström has made four helpful studies on the Latin version: *Studien zur lateinischen Irenäusübersetzung* (Lund 1943) (hereinafter Lundström *Studien*); "Textkritischen Beiträge zur lateinischen Irenäusübersetzung," *Eranos Löfstedianus: Opuscula philologica Einaro Löfstedt A.D. XVII Kal. Iul. Anno MCMXLV dedicata* (Uppsala 1945) 285–300; *Neue Studien zur lateinischen Irenäusübersetzung* (Lund 1948); *Übersetzungstechnische Untersuchungen auf dem Gebiete der christlichen Latinität,* (Lund 1955).

71. Feuardent, *Commonitio ad lectores de sua quinque librorum D. Irenaei editione* (MG 7.1340C-D).

72. See Massuet, Diss. 2.2.53 (MG 7.233–34).

73. A. Merk, "Der Text des Neuen Testamentes beim hl. Irenaeus," 304, claims that the dependence of Tertullian on the Latin of Irenaeus is not proved, but that the end of the fourth century for the Latin translation is too late.

74. See Grabe, *Prolegomena,* 1.2.3 (MG 7.1356); Massuet, Diss. 2.2.53 (MG 7.234); W. Sanday, "The Date of the Latin Irenaeus: A Fragment," in *Nouum Testamentum Sancti Irenaei,* ed. W. Sanday et al., lvii–lxiv; Harvey l. clxiv. See also A. D. Alès, "La date de la version latine de saint Irénée," RechSR 6 (1916) 133–37; F. R. M. Hitchcock,

Irenaeus of Lugdunum: A Study of His Teaching (Cambridge 1914) 44, 347–48; Sagnard *Gnose* 12. P. T. Camelot, "Eirenaios," LTK² 3.774, admits that it saw the light of day perhaps around the year 200, but certainly before 396. It is difficult to admit Henry Dodwell's idea that the Latin translator made use of Tertullian. See H. Dodwell, *Dissertationes in Irenaeum* (Oxford 1689) 397–400.

75. Augustine seems to have used Irenaeus, or at least was influenced by him, for a number of years. See B. Altaner, "Augustinus und Irenäus: Eine quellenkritische Untersuchung," ThQ 129 (1949) 162–72. This was published again in the author's *Kleine patristische Schriften*, TU 83 (1967) 194–203. Augustine quotes A.H. 4.2.7 and 5.19.1 in *C. Iul.* 1.3.5 (ML 44.644). He mentions Irenaeus by name when he sums this up again in 1.7.32 (ML 44.662). Augustine wrote this work in A.D. 422. So the Latin of Irenaeus had to exist then, at least. But Augustine might have used Irenaeus in earlier works. He might have used A.H. 1.23.1 in *Haer.* 1 (ML 42.25); and A.H. 4.33.10 in *Catech. rud.* 3.6 (CCL 46.125). But it is more certain that he used A.H. 4.30.1 in *Doctr. christ.* 2.40.60 (CCL 32.73–74). This last work was written for the greater part in 396–97 and so Altaner infers that the Latin translation of Irenaeus was made shortly before this, since it had not been quoted by anyone else. See Altaner, "Augustinus und Irenäus" 172, which is also reprinted in TU 83 (1967) 203. Dodwell, *Dissertationes in Irenaeum* 400–401, seems to have been the first to present this later date for Lat. Iren. It was accepted also by H. Jordan, "Das Alter und die Herkunft der lateinischen Übersetzung des Hauptwerkes des Irenäus," *Theologische Studien: Theodor Zahn zum 10. Oktober 1908 dargebracht*, ed. N. Bonwetsch et al. (Leipzig 1908) 133–92; also by F. J. A. Hort, in "Did Tertullian Use the Latin Irenaeus?" *Nouum Testamentum Sancti Irenaei*, ed. Sanday et al. xliv, and Burkitt, "Sanday's New Testament of Irenaeus" 56–67. Lundström (Lundström *Studien* 90–109) reexamined the data for both sides, and concluded that the arguments for the early date were scarcely convincing. Yet he rejects Souter's claim that the translator was the same person who made the Latin translation of Origen's commentary on Matthew, which was made between A.D. 370–420. Dodwell also suggested that the occasion for the translation was the refutation of Priscillianism. See Dodwell, *Dissertationes in Irenaeum* 405–7. B. Hemmerdinger (SC 100.16)

is of the opinion that Dodwell's view has not received sufficient attention. He refers to his own review article, "Saint Irénée évêque en Gaule ou en Galatie?" REG 77 (1964) 291–92. In his translation with notes of Firmicus Maternus's *The Error of Pagan Religions* (ACW 37), C. A. Forbes calls attention to some parallels in Firmicus to Irenaeus and remarks: "The passages cited in this and the preceding notes argue for the probability that Firmicus knew the writings or at least the views of Irenaeus" (ACW 37.213, n. 470). He cited A.H. 3.18.1; 5.16.3; 5.17.4; 5.18.3 as parallels to *The Error* chap. 25.2 (ACW 37.101) and chap. 27.3 (ACW 37.105). He might have cited also A.H. 3.19.1; 3.19.3; 3.21.10; 3.22.3; 5.19.1; 5.21.1. Possibly there is a borrowing in chap. 21.2, where Firmicus speaks of the Lernean Hydra, from Irenaeus, A.H. 1.30.15. To be noted also is that, according to Forbes (ACW 37.31–32): "Vecchi sees a clear proof of Firmicus' discipleship to Irenaeus in his invariable attribution of the authorship of the Old Testament to the Holy Spirit.' " See A. Vecchi, "Guilio Firmico Materno e la 'Lettera agli Ebrei,' " *Convivium* 25 (1957) 641–51 (in particular, 650 n. 1). The ideas are certainly Irenaeus's; but the parallels in phrasing are not so strong that one can be certain that Firmicus used Lat. Iren. If his use of Lat. Iren. were proved, since Firmicus's work was written in A.D. 346–47, we would have an argument for a somewhat earlier date for Lat. Iren.

76. The text was discovered in 1904 by K. Ter-Mekerttschian and published by E. Ter-Minassiantz in TU 35.2 (1910) viii–264.

77. See also on this J. B. Pitra, *Analecta sacra* 4 (Paris 1883) 33, 304. H. Jordan, *Armenische Irenaeusfragmente mit deutscher Übersetzung nach Dr. W. Lüdtke zum Teil erstmalig herausgegeben und untersucht* (TU 36.3 [1913] viii–222), gives twenty-nine Armenian fragments with a German version.

78. See Vernet 2403. Harvey 1. clxiv, following Massuet (Diss. 2.2 [MG 7.237A]), believes that there was no complete Syrian version. The fragments referred to are in Harvey 2.431–53 and Pitra, *Analecta sacra* 17–25, 292–99. A. Houssiau, "Vers une édition critique de S. Irénée," RHE 48 (1953) 143, agrees that the Syriac fragments do not come from a full translation of A.H., but from Syriac works, such as Severus of Antioch and Timothy Aelurus.

79. Cf. SC 100.39–40.

80. Cf. SC 100.39.

81. Cunningham (*Irenaeus* xxvii) contends that Harvey's debt to Stieren is much greater than is generally realized.

82. The chronology of publication is set forth by A. Rousseau in SC 293.7–14, which is summarized in Donovan, "Irenaeus in Recent Scholarship" 220. M. Geerard, CPG i.110, refers to the SC edition as an "*editionis laudatae.*"

83. Before the Reverend Dominic J. Unger died in July, 1982, he asked me to update and complete the work that still remained before this translation could be published. He regretted that he had not able to compare his translation with the text published by A. Rousseau and L. Doutreleau in SC 263–64 in 1974. His translation has been checked against the SC text and modified where this was deemed necessary. I want to thank the Capuchin Province of Mid-America for the opportunity to work on this translation and also thank three of his confreres: the Reverend Blaine Burkey, O.F.M.Cap.; the Reverend Thomas Weinandy, O.F.M.Cap.; and the Reverend Ronald Lawler, O.F.M. Cap., for helping me on numerous occasions. Thanks are also owed to the Reverend Gerald O'Collins, S.J.; Doctor Margaret Schatkin; the Reverend Daniel Mindling, O.F.M. Cap.; and the Reverend Paul Watson for bibliographical assistance. Finally, I am grateful to the members of the Mother of God Community, Gaithersburg, Maryland, for their support and assistance (Ed. Note).

84. On this problem see SC 100.186–91 and SC 152.31–34. See also SC 210.47–48 where L. Doutreleau takes issue with what F. Sagnard had written in SC 34.77–78.

85. D. J. Unger was not able to review *Irenäus: Gott im Fleisch und Blut ausgewählt und übertragen von Hans Urs Von Balthasar* (Einsiedeln 1981). This work is a translation of selected passages of the *Adversus haereses* and the *Proof of the Apostolic Preaching* organized around six themes: the Sign of the Son of Man, the True God and the False God, Faith and Gnosis, Salvation History, Incarnation as Recapitulation, and Fulfillment in God. Von Balthasar's introduction to this volume presents a perceptive and sympathetic overview of Irenaeus's theological concerns. This volume is now available in English: *The Scandal of the Incarnation: Irenaeus Against the Heresies*, introduced

and selected by H. U. von Balthasar, trans. J. Saward (San Francisco 1990) (Ed. Note).

PREFACE

1. For Book 1, from the Preface till 11.2, the Greek is preserved by Epiphanius, *Haer.* 31.9–32 (GCS 25.398–435), which though good is not absolutely reliable because it is an excerpt and was also liable to scribal errors. Rousseau and Doutreleau edit the Greek as their first Greek fragment. See SC 263.83–85 on this.

2. "Discarding," for *parapempomenoi.* Obviously *refutantes* was meant as a good translation of the word in that meaning. *Refutare* has that meaning in 2.12.6 (rejecting either Silence or the Word), in 3.14.3 (rejecting Luke's Gospel), in 3.14.4 (twice, as opposed to receiving), in 5.3.2 (rejecting God's power). *Refutare* has this meaning also in classical Latin; e.g. in Cicero, *Rab. Post.* 16.44: *bonitatem . . . aspernari ac refutari;* and Cicero, *Tusc.* 2.23.55: *refutetur ac reiciatur Philoctetus clamor.*

3. 1 Tim. 1.4. Tertullian also wrote about the Valentinian *fabulas et genealogias indeterminatas* (*Adv. Val.* 3.4 [CCL 2.755]), an obvious use of 1 Tim. 1.4 and possibly also of Irenaeus. By quoting Paul, Irenaeus seems to indicate that Paul, by anticipation, condemned full-blown Gnosticism, the seeds of which were beginning to sprout already in Paul's day.

4. "Patch together" for *sugkrotein,* which means to beat, hammer, weld together, compose. The Latin *exercitata,* which can mean "having been thought out," seems here to mean "worked out," and so is equivalent to the Greek in the sense of "composed." There is then no need to assume, with Grabe or Massuet (MG 7.438 n. 7), that the original Latin was *excitata* or *excita.*

5. The phrase *ta logia Kuriou,* or elsewhere often *kuriaka logia,* has been hotly disputed by critics. Cf. J. Donovan, *The Logia in Ancient and Recent Literature* (Cambridge 1924) 21–27, and G. Kittel, "*logion,*"

TDNT 4.139–41. Some scholars would restrict *logia* to sayings. But others, rightly, claim that it can be the equivalent of Gospel, including deeds as well as discourses. In A.H. 1.8.1 the context clearly includes deeds in *kuriakōn logiōn*. It must have the same meaning in our present passage. For some reason the Latin translator, though very slavish generally, was given to variant versions for the same Greek phrase. In our passage of 1 Prf. 1 it is *uerba Domini*, but in 1.8.1 it is *dominicis eloquiis;* the Greek is the same for both. Elsewhere, where the Greek is not extant, *Domini sermones* is used a number of times, which seems to suppose the same Greek expression as here. Cf. 3.11.9; 3.25.7; 4 Prf. 1; 4.36.5; 4.41.4. A. Rousseau, L. Doutreleau, et al. do not quite agree with this last statement as is evidenced by their Greek retroversion for 3.11.9: *tous tou Kuriou logous* (SC 211.177); 3.25.7: *tous tou Kuriou . . . logous* (SC 211.491); 4 Prf. 1: *dia tōn Kuriou logiōn* (SC 100.383); 4.36.5: *ek tōn logōn tou Kuriou* (SC 100.901); 4.41.4: *ta logia tou Kuriou* (SC 100.993).

6. These heretics called themselves Gnostics because they claimed to possess true knowledge (*gnōsis*); For more information on the Gnostics, see n. 3 to the Introduction.

7. Cf. Gen. 1.1; Exod. 20.11; Ps. 145(146).6; Acts 4.24, 14.15. Time and again we shall have occasion to note that the Gnostics assert that they know of a god, whom they style Profundity, who is far superior to the god who created the universe. Rousseau notes that this text is a fundamental one for Irenaeus which will be echoed in the first article of the Rule of Truth (A.H. 1.10.1) and which Irenaeus will cite many times in A.H. From the first page of A.H., Irenaeus is not content to base upon the Scripture the faith of the Church in God the Creator, but he likes to illustrate in a concrete manner the unity of the two Testaments attacked by heresy (SC 263.167–68 [SC 264.19 n. 2]). In his other work, *Proof* 99, Irenaeus refers to his refutation of the godless and blasphemous heretics who claim to have found a Father of their own who is superior to the Creator. He is there referring to the present *Adversus haereses.*

8. Rousseau proposes the translation "without being further troubled concerning probability" here. He draws attention to the intentional opposition in the Greek *pithanōs men . . . apithanōs de.* He

feels Irenaeus wants to stigmatize the duplicity of the Gnostics. This reading of the Greek is confirmed by A.H. 2.13.10 and 2.14.8 where the same opposition is indicated by the Latin *uerisimiliter . . . non ueri-similiter*. This characterizes the strategem of the Gnostic teachers who begin by luring certain souls who are credulous in departing from notions which are familiar to them and in maintaining a discourse for them which offers some appearance of truth. Later, when the teachers have succeeded in making themselves accepted, they demand these simple souls admit the worst absurdities without the least proof or any concern for probability. See SC 263.168–69 (SC 264.21 n. 1).

9. Whenever *Dēmiourgos* refers to the Gnostic creator-god, I translate it *Demiurge*. But when Irenaeus uses it for the true Creator, I translate *Creator* to avoid ambiguity. The Demiurge is the god who made the material world and is the author of wickedness, quite inferior to the supreme deity.

10. Holl (GCS 25.399) prints *mēde en tōi diakrinein dunamenōn to pseudos apo tou alēthous*, which is scarcely translatable, though Harvey (1.2 n. 5) suggested that nothing need be changed if *en tōi* is taken in the sense of *en toutōi*, namely, in regard to the matter discussed. But the Latin *non discernere ualentium falsum a uero* suggests a different approach, as Massuet (MG 7.440 n. 10) already noted. The Greek, he felt, was originally *mēden ti*, "in no way whatever." That could easily have been changed by a scribe to the reading of Epiphanius. There is a parallel for the simple *mēden* with the infinitive in A.H. 1.6.2; 1.6.3; 1.7.1; and *mē* alone in 1.15.1. *Ti*, which the Latin skipped, would merely emphasize the negation. I accepted this suggestion in the translation. Rousseau and Doutreleau, however, emend the Greek in the following manner: *mē diakrinein dunamenōn to pseudos apo tou alēthous*. They feel that *mēde en tōi* is an accidental corruption for *mē*. They further note that Holl proposed *mēde en tōi* to save at all costs the reading of the Greek MSS, but this is neither natural nor in Irenaeus's manner of expression. It is not, then, the reading the Latin translator had before his eyes. See SC 263.169 (SC 264.21 n. 2).

11. Harvey has nothing corresponding to *ridiculum est et dicere* in the Greek text which he prints, although he felt that *ho kai eipein geloion* was missed by the Latin translator (Harvey 1.3 n. 4). Yet the

Latin seems genuine, because there appears no reason for having added it in Latin if it was not in the Greek copy. A. Rousseau and L. Doutreleau print ⟨*geloin to kai eipein*⟩ in their version of the Greek text (SC 264.21), following Holl's suggestion (GCS 25.399), and Rousseau suggests (SC 263.169 [SC 264.21 n. 3]) that there is no reason to doubt the primitive character of the Latin. They also point out an analogous passage in A.H. 4.30.2: *dicetur enim quod uerum est, licet ridiculum quibusdam esse uideatur.* Tertullian reports that the Gnostics care for nothing more than to hide what they preach, if indeed they preach what they hide, and that in this they are like the votaries of the Eleusinian mysteries (*Adv. Val.* 1.1–4 [CCL 2.753–54]).

12. The authority referred to could be Bishop Pothinus, Irenaeus's predecessor in the see of Lyons. On Pothinus see ODCC[2] 1113.

13. The Latin adjective *rudis* supposes *akeraios*. This seems to be correct and was adopted by Holl (*Haer.* 31.9.6 [GCS 25.399]) as well as Rousseau and Doutreleau (SC 264.21).

14. "Treachery" follows the Greek *epiboulēn*. Massuet (MG 7.441 n. 2) and Harvey (1.4) accept that, and Harvey claims that the Latin (*propter exterius ovilis pellis superindumentum*) is tautological, since the overcoat cannot be other than external. Yet Stieren (1.6, n. d) preferred the Latin, supposing *epibolēn*. Rousseau and Doutreleau also prefer *epibolēn* (SC 264.22). Tertullian accuses Valentinus of perverting the Scriptures by interpolation and interpretation; and Marcion, of mutilating them (*Praescr.* 38.1–10 [CCL 1.218–19]).

15. Cf. Matt. 7.15.

16. Matt. 19.11.

17. Rousseau and Doutreleau (SC 264.22) have *exeptukasin*, which means "to spit out" (e.g. salt water) for the purpose of cleansing the mouth; hence, "to purge." Irenaeus uses the verb again in 5.5.2 of Jonah's being vomited up (*exeptusthē, exsputus est*) by the sea monster. The idea of purging the brain occurs in Plautus: *lmmo etiam cerebrum quoque omne e capite emunx'ti meo* (*Most.* 1110). Harvey (1.4 n. 5) thought that the translator might have read *ekhontes tetukhēkasi, cerebrum habent*, which Klebba (Klebba BKV 3.2) translated: "*Ihren Verstand verloren haben.*" Klebba preferred the Latin on the ground that it is difficult to explain the corruption from the simple reading supposed

by the Latin to the complicated reading in the Greek as preserved by Epiphanius. Yet the Latin could be a scribe's simplification of what was unintelligible to him in Greek. Rousseau (SC 263.170 [SC 264.23 n. 1]) points out that Irenaeus's language here is ironic. If not all are capable of admitting without any conditions the extravagant assertions of the heretics, it is because they have not "purged their brains." In other words, they have rejected what makes them intelligent beings.

18. "Against God." Holl (GCS 25.400) emended the Greek to *theon* which Rousseau and Doutreleau accept (SC 264.23). The expression "profundity of nonsense" seems an ironical play on the name of the Gnostic supreme Being, called Profundity. On this see also SC 263.170 (SC 264.23 n. 2).

19. That Ptolemaeus's doctrine was Valentinian is brought out in other places: see A.H. 1.12.1; 2.4.1. See also Hippolytus, *Haer.* 6.29.1; 6.35.6; 6.38.5 (GCS 26.155, 165, 169). Rousseau (SC 263.171 [SC 264.23 n. 3]), however, argues that this might be better translated "of Ptolemaeus and the people of his circle." The Greek expression *hoi peri tina* customarily designates the circle of a person with this person himself or herself. It is a matter, then, of Ptolemaeus and his school. See also there Rousseau's remarks about Ptolemaeus and his disciples as the most telling representatives or "flower" of the tradition descended from Valentinus.

20. The Gnostics insisted that their doctrines be kept secret; see A.H. 4.32.1. Simon Magus is said to have given the following order in regard to a treatise of his: "So let it be sealed, hidden, concealed, and let it repose in the dwelling where the root of all things is grounded" (Hippolytus, *Haer.* 6.9.4 [GCS 26.136]).

21. Matt. 10.26; see also Luke 8.17, 12.2; Mark 4.22.

22. As Harvey (1.6 n. 1) points out, we know from Caesar *Gall.* 1.1 and Pliny *Nat.* 4.17.105 that Gaul was divided into three parts: the region north of the Seine, where the Belgae lived; that south of the Garonne, where the Aquitani were; that between the two rivers, where the Celts dwelt. The Celts' principal city was Lyons. On Irenaeus's apology for his style see Intro. par. 18–20.

23. Rousseau (SC 263.171 [SC 264.27 n. 1]) notes that the words

"seeds" and "beginnings" and the phrase "reap abundant fruit" belong to the quasi-technical vocabulary of the Gnostics. Irenaeus gathers them together at this place for a clearly ironic purpose.

CHAPTER I

1. In 1.11.1 the Bishop of Lyons treats of Valentinus himself. There some notes will be found on him. In these first eight chapters he treats of Ptolemaeus's brand of Valentinianism. Valentinus first taught at Alexandria. Later he went to Rome. Ptolemaeus became one of his chief disciples in the West. He developed his master's doctrine and made it more elaborate. The account of his system given in 1.1.8 by Irenaeus is substantially reliable; see n. 1 to chap. 11. Irenaeus's account is not a conglomeration of several schools that were even contradictory, as C.F.G. Heinrici propounded in *Die Valentinianische Gnosis und die heilige Schrift* (Berlin 1871). See Sagnard *Gnose* 200–208 on Heinrici's thought. Neither is it an account of an elaboration that was made in the third century, as if the heresiarch Valentinus had a rather simple system, which Ptolemaeus followed faithfully, making only small emendations, but on which others elaborated later. E. de Faye, *Gnostiques et gnosticisme: Etude critique des documents du gnosticisme chrétien aux IIe et IIIe siècles,* 2d ed. (Paris 1925) 107–8, 114, 501–2, tried to defend this view. See a discussion and refutation in Sagnard *Gnose* 208–20. Tertullian borrowed heavily from these chapters of Irenaeus for his *Adv. Val.* (CCL 2.753–78). On this see Quasten *Patr.* 2.277. See also Ps.-Tertullian, *Haer.* 4 (CCL 2.1406–7). Hippolytus treats Valentinian opinions in *Haer.* 6.21–37; 10.13 (GCS 26.148–68, 273–74). He evidently used Irenaeus as a source, though at times he adds material which differs from Irenaeus. Hippolytus, *Haer.* 29.6.5–30.5 (GCS 26.156–57), is parallel to A.H. 1.1–2; and Tertullian, *Adv. Val.* 7 (CCL 2.757–59), is parallel to A.H. 1.1.1. We should note here that Ptolemaeus wrote the *Letter to Flora* (an apostate woman), in which the Mosaic Law is ascribed to the evil god. This letter is preserved by Epiphanius, *Haer.* 33.3–7 (GCS 25.450–57). A new edition was published by G. Quispel, *Ptolemée: Lettre à Flora* (SC 24bis [Paris 1966]). According to

Irenaeus (1.8.5) Ptolemaeus also wrote a commentary on John's prologue. The terms and ideas given by Irenaeus agree with the content of the *Letter to Flora*, showing that Irenaeus is reliable as a historian of Gnosticism. See also Sagnard *Gnose* 476–79 and Quasten *Patr.* 1.261–62. A. Orbe, *La teología del Espíritu Santo* (Rome 1966) passim, provides notes which are excellent in explaining the material found in A.H. 1.1–8.

2. We meet here for the first time the word Aeon, which plays such a large role in the Gnostic systems. Its etymology is disputed, whether it comes from *aeiōn* ("ever-existing") or from some other root. Actually, among the Greek philosophers from Heraclitus and Empedocles on, it meant "time" in relation to being. Plato restricted its use to endless time in itself, that is, to absolute eternity. Aristotle went back to the original meaning and reserved it to created being; but since for him the world was eternal, the "aeon" of the world was really indefinite in time. During the Hellenistic era "aeon" took on a religious meaning, being used, already about 200 B.C., to designate the deities of the mystery religions at Alexandria, where the Aeon was identified with Osiris and Serapis. (Cf. J. P. Steffes, "*Äon,*" LTK 1.527.) It should be noted that Endless Time (*Zrvan Akarana*) was used in Persian theology for the highest principle. This personified aeon also held an important position in the later Persian, particularly in the Mithraic, cult. "Aeon" was used very frequently in the Old and the New Testament, but never in a personified sense, except perhaps in Eph. 2.2 of demons. So the Gnostics simply borrowed this term, as other elements, from the pagan mystery religions to designate the various divine beings in their Fullness. On all this see H. Sasse, "*aiōn,*" TDNT 1.197–209. The Valentinian Aeon was certainly a god. Tertullian, *Adv. Val.* 7.3 (CCL 2.758), notes that the Valentinian god was called "the perfect Aeon" by reason of his essence (*substantialiter*), but "First-Father and First-Beginning" by reason of his person (*personaliter*).

3. "First-Beginning" was supplied from the Latin version. According to Holl it is also in Codex Vaticanus of Epiphanius (GCS 25.401). Already Tertullian was puzzled about what to do with these names: the meaning of some would not be equally obvious in translation, the genders of others would not fit, still others were more familiar in Greek. So for most of them he kept the Greek names; see *Adv.*

Val. 6.1–2 (CCL 2.757). We have given translated names to the Aeons and other emissions. The names occur so often that the Greek names would make clumsy reading and would be meaningless to most people. We had to make an exception for *Sophia* (Greek) and *Achamoth* (Hebrew), both of which mean wisdom. To keep all the names of the Aeons in the Fullness in English, we gave Wisdom to *Sophia* of the Fullness, and kept *Achamoth* for her counterpart on earth. In Greek all these names have the definite article. In English the article could not be used with names from abstract nouns, or with some concrete nouns (e.g. Man). So we have omitted the article before all the names of the Aeons and other emissions when these belong to the Gnostic system. This will help to set them apart from any Christian realities using the same names, and to give the impression that they are names of personal beings. For Rousseau's rationale for his rendering of the names of the Aeons in his French translation see SC 363.171–72. In the sentence on which we are commenting, "perfect Aeon" is called Profundity, and the three other names with the prefix *pro* in Greek: *Pro-Archē, Pro-Patōr,* and *Pro-On.* These titles are used frequently in Irenaeus. What is the force of the prefix in them? It has generally been taken for granted that it means "first." Profundity is Beginning, Father, and Being; but he is the first in point of time and cause of all others who are a beginning, or father, or being. In recent years, A. Orbe has made several lengthy studies on this problem. Aided by an explanation in Marius Victorinus, *Gen. div. verb.* 3 (SC 68.134–36) and *Adv. Arrium* 1.39 and 4.23 (SC 68.302–4, 566–70), he holds that the prefix means *pre-* and not *first.* In other words, the title expresses something that existed prior to what the noun or participle implies: prior to being principle or beginning, prior to being father, prior to being "being." Pre-Being would then be practically equivalent to another description of this Aeon, namely, that he is "Non-Being" in the sense that he is above all "being" as we know it. See A. Orbe, "A propósito de un nombre personal del 1. eon valentiniano," *Gregorianum* 34 (1953) 262–70; and *Hacia la primera teología de la procesión del Verbo* (Rome 1958) 6–23. But in spite of Orbe's scholarly study I am not convinced that he has proved his point. True, the perfect Aeon is utterly ineffable; yet he is Being, he is Beginning, and he is Father. Precisely because he is these things first and superior to all others he is First-Beginning, First-Father, and First-Being. The supreme God is

"Non-Being" as described, but that does not say that this is a necessary interpretation of *Pro-On* and *Pro-Archē;* in other words, that *pro* has the same meaning as *non.* The prefix *pro* is definitely used in the sense of "first" in the title *proanennoētos* (first-unthinkable), which is used four times in A.H. 1.11.3, 1.11.4, and 1.12.4. A positive adjective with the prefix *pro* in the sense of *pre-* can make sense; namely, *pre-thinkable* could be one prior to our being able to think of him. But I fail to see what sense there can be in a negative adjective with *pro* as a prefix in the sense of prior to; namely, pre-unthinkable, that is, prior to being unthinkable. Unthinkable is ultimate and absolute, prior to which there can be nothing. He certainly could not be thinkable prior to unthinkable. But, if *pro* has the meaning of "first" with this title, it does so also with the other titles used in the same series; namely, *Pro-Archē* and *Pro-Patōr* and *Pro-On* in 1.11.3; 1.11.4; 1.12.5; and in the passage under discussion (1.1.1). This is supported by the fact Irenaeus adds to *Pro-Archē* the explanation "before all things" both in 1.11.3 and 1.11.4. Once more, *Pro-Archē* is modified by the adjective *Prōtos* (first) in 1.11.5; namely, it is the first First-Beginning of all other things. First Pre-Beginning would make no sense. Hippolytus, who in *Haer.* 6.38 (GCS 26.168) has a parallel to our passage, has only "Beginning," without the prefix, but he modifies it with "first," and so he is clearly in favor of First-Beginning, and not Pre-Beginning. All this adds up to great probability, if not certainty, that the commonly accepted view of the past is correct.

4. This clause is from Lat. Iren.; it is not in Gk. Epiph. Holl thinks it got into the Latin through dittography (GCS 25.401). Yet it seems necessary for the complete thought. *Cum autem a nullo caperetur et esset inuisibilis,* which is in Lat. Iren. and Gk. Epiph., seems certainly to presume something was said about that in the preceding sentence. The Lat. Iren. has that in the clause: *esse autem illum inuisibilem et quem nulla res capere possit.* Gk. Epiph. dropped it, so we conjecture, by haplography, as Grabe (7 n. 5 on the Greek text; cf. Harvey 1.8 n. 3), Massuet (MG 7.445 n. 3), and Mannucci (76 n. 3) suggested. Rousseau, however, disagrees with this in SC 263.172 (SC 264.29 n. 2). There he argues that *esse autem illum inuisibilem et quem nulla res capere possit* is a gloss unduly entered into the text.

5. Some scribe must have added *khronōn* in Gk. Epiph. to avoid taking *aiōsi* for the Gnostic Aeons. Rousseau and Doutreleau (SC

264.29) place *khronōn* in brackets following Holl (GCS 25.401). It is
not translated in Lat. Iren. or Tertullian (*Adv. Val.* 7.4 [CCL 2.758]). It
is not needed, because Irenaeus uses *aiōsi* here in its original meaning
of "ages," as he certainly does in 4.38.3 ("for many ages"). Tertullian
understood it so: *Infinitis retro aeuis.*

6. Rousseau (SC 263.173 [SC 264.29 n. 3]) feels that neither the
Greek nor the Latin are fully satisfactory here and one must be recti-
fied by the other. The Latin seems to have read *probalesthai* unduly for
hēn probalesthai. The Latin *eius quae cum eo erat Sige* gives the impression that the original Greek was *tēs sunuparousēs . . . Sigēs* rather than
tēi sunuparousēi . . . Sigēi. Doutreleau and Rousseau, then, emend the
Greek participial phrase to the genitive rather than the dative case (SC
264.29). Finally, Rousseau would eliminate the *kai* before *katathesthai.*

7. Only-begotten's father, Profundity, was called First-Beginning
and First-Father, while Only-begotten himself was merely Beginning
and Father. See n. 3.

8. This Tetrad has intelligence; it is not merely a combination of
irrational numbers. Because numbers were considered of all things the
most immaterial, the Pythagoreans used them to symbolize the spiritual nature of the divine intellect. This Ptolemaean Tetrad seems to
have been the first four numbers (1, 2, 3, 4), which when added together equal ten, the perfect number. See Sagnard *Gnose* 337–48.

9. These are not Man and Church of the earth, but the Aeons of
the Fullness by those names, archetypes of those on earth.

10. Rousseau and Doutreleau (SC 264.31) add ⟨*hēn kai kharin kai
Sigēn kalousin*⟩ to the Greek text as preserved by Epiphanius.
Rousseau (SC 263.173 [SC 264.33 n. 1]) notes that these words seemed
to render well a phrase that somehow slipped out of the Latin
translation.

11. For A.H. 1.1.2 and 1.1.3, compare Tertullian, *Adv. Val.* 8 (CCL
2.759–60).

12. What a progeny the First-Father had! Tertullian observed that
Valentinus dared to conceive of Profundity and Silence as gods who
produced thirty aeons as a litter of the divinity, like the sow of Aeneas
(Virgil *Aen.* 8.43). See Tertullian, *Adv. Marc.* 1.5.1 (CCL 1.446). These
names in English are self-explanatory and show how ridiculous their
system is. Who would be the male and who the female in these couples was decided by the gender of the words in Greek, and a few times

in Hebrew; e.g., spirit (*pneuma*) is neuter in Greek, but feminine (*ruach*) in Hebrew; so Spirit is fated to be female. "Self-producing" (*autophuēs*) could have active or passive meaning: self-producing or self-produced. He is self-producing in the sense that he produces by his own power. In 2.14.8 the Lat. Iren. attempted an interpretation with *naturalem*, seemingly "self-grown." "Maternal" is *mētrikos*. The second letter makes it certain that it has some relation to mother (*mētēr*), not to metrical (*metrikos*). Hippolytus expressly explains this adjectival noun as derived from *mētēr*, just as *patrikos* derives from *patēr* (*Haer.* 5.26.4,5,6 [GCS 26.127]). So Hippolytus must have understood Irenaeus to mean "maternal" also in *Haer.* 6.29.5 (GCS 26.157), which is parallel to the Irenaean passage under discussion. The fact that it has the masculine ending, and so is the male of this couple, though derived from "mother," is a tolerable inconsistency in the intolerably inconsistent system of the Gnostics. "Praise" stands for the Latin *Aenos*, which seems to be a transliteration of *ainos;* for in 2.14.8 the Latin is *Ainon*. Tertullian, *Adv. Val.* 8.2 (CCL 2.759), has according to the MSS *aenos,* or *aenus;* yet Kroymann corrected it to *aeinus,* in keeping with *aeinous* ("ever-mind") of Gk. Epiph., which Massuet (MG 7.449) had suggested already. Epiphanius has the same in the Letter from a Valentinian Book in *Haer.* 31.5.8, 31.6.1 (GCS 25.392). However, *aeinous* seems a corruption of *ainos,* since the other names of these male Aeons are adjectival nouns, which *aeinous* is not; and it would be strange that they should give the title Ever-Mind to one inferior to Mind. When P. Wendland completed his edition of Hippolytus, *Haer.* 6.30.5 (GCS 26.157) he wrote *Aeinous,* following Gk. Epiph. The Codex Parisinus Suppl. gr. 464 had *aiōnos.* However, *aiōnos* seems rather a corruption of *ainos,* than *aeinous,* a mistake that was easily made. So, hesitatingly, I keep *ainos* (Praise).

13. Tertullian says that the Gnostics claim that the thirty Aeons are known only to themselves and unknown to everyone else (*Adv. Val.* 9.1. [CCL 2.760]). See also Theodoret, *Haer.* 1.7 (MG 83.353C).

14. There is disagreement among the Valentinians as to the manner in which the number thirty is obtained. According to the earlier system, Profundity was a unity and really had no consort; Silence was a mere negation. Christ and Spirit were added to make up the thirty. In the later Ptolemaean system Profundity and Silence were the first couple (Harvey 1. cxix–cxx). In the Ptolemaean system the Decad was

produced by Word and Life; the Dodecad, by Man and Church. In the earlier system the Decad was produced by Mind and Truth; the Dodecad, by Word and Life. See Hippolytus, *Haer.* 6.31 (GCS 26.158).

15. Cf. Luke 3.23.

16. Cf. Matt. 20.1–7.

17. The Greek construction has been a puzzle to translators. The Latin version does not have anything for *en plēthei,* but Grabe (cf. Harvey 1.13 n. 3) thinks it fell out through a scribe's carelessness. Rousseau and Doutreleau would remove *en plēthei;* on this see SC 264.35. In ANF (1.317 n. 3) the clause is translated: "And if there is anything else in Scripture which is referred to by a definite number . . ." which follows Petavius's suggestion (cf. MG 7.451 n. 3). That embodies a possible meaning of *en plēthei* when taken by itself; but in the present combination the translation of Klebba BKV (3.5), which I have adopted, seems to be more accurate. Already Desgallards (cf. MG 7.451 n. 3) read it that way. Literally, "of the things mentioned in large numbers in the Scriptures."

18. Since neither the Greek nor the Latin construction is clear, Holl (GCS 25.402) rightly thinks some words fell out between *dunētheiē* and *prosarmosai;* perhaps *helkesthai eis tauta boulontai.* We accept that. See 1.3.6: *eis polla helkesthai dunamenōn.* Rousseau prefers *dunētheiēsan* over *dunētheiē.* He would also remove *en plēthei.* See SC 263.174 (SC 264.35 n. 1).

CHAPTER 2

1. For A.H. 1.2.1–1.2.2 see Tertullian, *Adv. Val.* 9 (CCL 2.760); for A.H. 1.2.1–1.2.4 see Hippolytus, *Haer.* 6.30.6–9 (GCS 26.157–58).

2. How can it be said that this passion began in Mind and Truth? The passion was Intention, the emission of Wisdom; but this Intention has its archetype in the Intention of Profundity, whereby Profundity begot Mind and Truth, as is explained in Clement of Alexandria, *Exc. Thdot.* 7 (GCS 17².108). See also Rousseau, SC 263.175 (SC 264.39 n. 1).

3. "By infection." The Greek has *apeskēpse.* Medical writers used

that verb for determining the humors of the body. Cf. LSJ, s.v. "*aposkēptō.*" Grabe (cf. Harvey 1.14) notes that Galen, *ad Glauconem de medendi methodo* 2.9 (*Medicorum Graecorum opera quae exstant* 11, ed. C. G. Kühn [Leipzig 1826] 116), explained the noun *aposkēmmata* as the feelings one has when some humors infect a part of the body and then spread to another. So Irenaeus could well have used the verb to express the fact that passion passed in a contagious manner from one Aeon to another. Tertullian brought out the correct sense by: *et genus contrahit uitii, quod exorsum quidem fuerat in illis aliis* (*Adv. Val.* 9.2 [CCL 2.760]). Erasmus et al. (SC 264.38) have read *deriuauit* at 1.2.2, which means "spreads itself out"; on this see A.H. 2.17.7: *deriuauit autem in Sophiam.* Tertullian, *Adv. Val.* 9.2 (CCL 2.760), has also this idea: *in hunc autem, id est in Sophiam, deriuarat.* Rousseau and Doutreleau (SC 264.38), however, read *diriuauit* at A.H. 1.2.2. According to Hippolytus, *Haer.* 6.29.5 (GCS 26.156), Father "was love, but love is not love unless there is something to love." See also Rousseau SC 263.175–76 (SC 264.39 n. 3) on *apeskēpse* and *eis touton paratrapenta.* See also D. Good, "Sophia in Valentinianism," SCent 4, no. 4 (1984) 200.

4. Rousseau and Doutreleau emend the Greek to *tolmēi;* for their reasons, see SC 263.176 (SC 264.39 n. 4).

5. Rousseau (SC 263.176 [SC 264.39 n. 5]) translates this "he had not been united," stating Doutreleau's and his preference for *kekoinōsthai* over *kekoinōnēsthai,* the reading of the Codex Vaticanus gr. 503 which was adopted by Holl (GCS 25.403). Rousseau and Doutreleau also note that, as far as they can determine, *koinōneō* is only used in the active voice.

6. Rousseau (SC 263.176 [SC 264.39 n. 6]) notes that this is the only time in Irenaeus's exposition of Gnostic theses and indeed in all of A.H. that the "Abyss" is designated under the term *Bathos.* Elsewhere it is under the name *Buthos.*

7. That seems an evident allusion to Phil. 3.13, which the heretics must have misused for their own system.

8. By her desire to see Profundity, she almost lost her individuality by being absorbed into the substance that was common to all in the Fullness. Tertullian's *in reliquam substantiam dissolui* (*Adv. Val.* 9.3 [CCL 2.760]) means the same thing.

9. Rousseau (SC 263.176 [SC 264.41 n. 1]) notes that *ta hola* is an

expression which the Gnostics use to denote the Aeons, and thus they
translate this by "the Aeons."

10. "Restrained" follows the Latin *abstentum,* supposing *apeskhēsthai,* though Tertullian's *periculo exempta et tarde persuasa* (*Adv.
Val.* 9.4 [CCL 2.760]) agrees with Gk. Epiph. *epeskhēsthai* (GCS
25.403). Rousseau and Doutreleau (SC 264.40) have retained
epeskhēsthai but note (SC 263.176 [SC 264.41 n. 2]) that the Latin does
indeed seem to presume *apeskhēsthai,* as Harvey (1.16) had also noted.

11. The Greek is *enthumēsis,* which the Latin translator gave by
intentio, excogitatio, concupiscentia, and many times by the transliterated *enthumesis.* There seems to be in it an element of intellection and
of volition or passion. In fact, the Enthymesis of the Fullness is the
emission of Thought and gives birth to Word. But its use in specific
contexts often connotes passion. Tertullian called it *animatio* (*Adv.
Val.* 9.4 [CCL 2.761]). "Intention" seemed to be the more serviceable
English equivalent. See also Rousseau, SC 263.177 (SC 264.41 n. 3).

12. This paragraph was practically taken over by Tertullian, *Adv.
Val.* 10 (CCL 2.761–62).

13. Holl (GCS 25.403) has emended *pōs* of Codex Vaticanus and
Codex Marcianus to *houtōs.* This is adopted by Rousseau and Doutreleau (SC 263.177 [SC 264.41 n. 4]).

14. According to the Gnostics the male aeon gave the form, the
female gave the substance. Since Profundity was bisexual, he gave
both. Wisdom, being female, could give only substance; consequently
her offspring was formless. Cf. Hippolytus, *Haer.* 6.30.8–9 (GCS
26.158). Lat. Iren. has "female" in the nominative, as subject of *habe-
bat;* and this verb has a potential meaning ("could"). The clause reads:
"such a nature as she, a female, could bring forth." This makes good
sense, namely, expressly stating that the parent is female and implying
that the offspring is such too. But Codex Vaticanus and Codex Marcianus have "female" in the accusative, modifying "nature." The
clause reads: "such a female nature as she could bring forth." Massuet
(MG 7.455–56, nn. 5, 10) insisted that this Greek is the original of
Irenaeus. This is confirmed by the fact that twice later (1.2.4; 2.20.3)
there is a similar idea, and in both cases the offspring, not the parent, is
said to be female. Holl (GCS 25.404), however, felt that "female"
should be in the nominative. Rousseau and Doutreleau (SC 264.41)
follow Holl.

15. I give the translation according to the Codex Vaticanus and the Codex Marcianus: *auto to einai teleios ekhein*. Lat. Iren. missed the meaning by *ne hoc ipsum finem habeat*. Massuet (MG 7.455–56 n. 6) following the Latin wrongly interprets the passage thus: She feared that this incomplete offspring of hers should not have the perfection due it. Tertullian (*Adv. Val.* 10.2 [CCL 2.761]) caught that meaning in *ne finis quoque insisteret,* namely, for her. In A.H. 1.4.1 Achamoth is in fear of losing her life as she had lost light; and in 1.3.1 Irenaeus himself says she "nearly perished." Again, according to Hippolytus (*Haer.* 6.31.1 [GCS 26.158]), because of what happened to Wisdom, the Fullness itself was confused and feared lest "in like manner the emissions of the Aeons might become formless and unfinished, and that some corruption would overtake the Aeons in a short time." Clement of Alexandria (*Exc. Thdot.* 31 [GCS 17^2.117]) has the same idea of Wisdom becoming ignorant and formless. In keeping with this, Holl (GCS 25.404) corrected the Greek by changing *teleiōs* to *telos,* and *ekhein* to *ekhēi.* But these changes seem unnecessary since *teleiōs ekhein* can mean "to come to an end," as *dunatōs ekhein* means "to be able." Rousseau and Doutreleau prefer *touto* to *to einai.* For their reasons see SC 263.177–78 (SC 264.41 n. 5).

16. Neither the Greek nor the Latin has a genitive modifier of "cause." Obviously, however, Intention seeks the cause of that which she immediately afterwards tries to conceal. Furthermore, *to gegonos* could mean either "what was born" or "what happened." Lat. Iren. has the first meaning in *quod erat natum.* Tertullian (*Adv. Val.* 10.2 [CCL 2.761]) has *ratione casus. Casus* here seems to mean misfortune, namely, of begetting an unfinished offspring. If so, he has the second meaning, "what happened." Harvey (1.16) suggests that Intention was seeking the reason of "that which she begot without a father." So he too refers it to her offspring; but the manner of begetting, namely, without a father, does not seem to have been her quandary.

17. Hippolytus (*Haer.* 6.31.2 [GCS 26.158]) has the same idea.

18. Clement of Alexandria (*Str.* 2.8.36.2–2.8.38.5 [GCS 52{15}.132–33]) notes that, according to Valentinus, all things originated from fear.

19. Hippolytus treats of Limit's emission in *Haer.* 6.31 (GCS 26.159). The accusative *asuzugon, athēlunton* of Gk. Epiph., and *feminam marem* of Tertullian (*Adv. Val.* 10.3 [CCL 2.761]) refer to Limit, so that

Father, who himself has no consort, emitted Limit as bisexual and without forming a conjugal couple, namely, according to his own image. However, the Lat. Iren. *sine coniuge* and *masculo-femina*, in the ablative, modify *in imagine sua*, namely, in the image of Father who brings forth without consort, being bisexual. This supposes, as Harvey (1.18 n. 1) notes, that the Greek was originally in the dative. But since both Tertullian and the Gk. Epiph. have the accusative, the Lat. Iren. seems to have missed the construction. For additional remarks on *athēlunton* see SC 263.178 (SC 264.43 n. 1).

20. Rousseau and Doutreleau (SC 264.42) read *suzugou* here. For their reasons see SC 263.178 (SC 264.43 n. 2).

21. Rousseau (SC 263.178 [SC 264.43 n. 3]) is puzzled why *huper arren kai huper thēlu* is what is found in Gk. Epiph., while Lat. Iren. is *pro masculo et pro femina?* He wonders if it is a translation error in that Lat. Iren. has confused two senses of *huper* or if the original Latin was *super masculum et super feminam.*

22. *Stauron et Lytroten* of Lat. Iren. is evidently correct, and so *Sullutrōtēn* of the Codex Vaticanus and the Codex Marcianus is a corruption of *Stauron kai Lutrōtēn* as Holl (GCS 25.404) has suggested. Originally *stauros* meant a stake. It has that meaning here as is clear from its function of fencing off. "Reaper" is *Karpistēn*, which has been variously interpreted. Grabe (cf. MG 7.459 n. 8) has Emancipator; Massuet (MG 7.458 n. 8), Judge and Arbiter; Stieren (24–25 n. c), Reaper. The word occurs in Arrian, *Epict.* 3.24.76; 4.1.113, in the sense of emancipator. However, the Gnostics applied Luke 3.17 to Limit as the reaper who *separates* the wheat from the chaff: see A.H. 1.3.5. According to Clement of Alexandria (*Exc. Thdot.* 42 [GCS 7² 120]), Theodotus taught that Stake and Limit have this task of separating. So "Reaper" would seem to be the best translation. A. Orbe, *La teología del Espíritu Santo* 613–14, makes a probable cause for "offerer" or "sanctifier" because of the relation between reaping (*karpoun*) and offering (*holokaustoun*) in the LXX, and because Horos, who bears these names, is also Cross, which is, of course, related to sacrifice. "Limiter" is *Horothetēn*, that is, one who sets boundaries or puts a limit to something. "Restorer" is *Metagogēa*, because of his function of bringing back, restoring all to that grade of being for which they were destined. Tertullian (*Adv. Val.* 10.3 [CCL 2.761]) interprets it "that is, one who leads about" (*circumductorem*). It is interesting to

note that Hippolytus (*Haer.* 6.31.6 [GCS 26.159]) has a different word, *Metokheus* ("Partaker"), and an explanation in keeping with that word: "Because he partakes of Degeneracy," that is, Wisdom. Cf. Orbe, *La teologia del Espíritu Santo* 614–16, who has an interesting note on this difficult name. "Restorer" still seems as good as any.

23. Rousseau (SC 263.179 [SC 264.43 n. 5]) suggests it might be better to translate these words "reinstated in her syzygy." He also feels that *coniugi* is either a corruption of *coniugationi* or possibly of *coniugio*. But he also notes that *coniugium* is not otherwise used in A.H.

24. We correct *einai* of MSS of Gk. Epiph. to *meinai* according to Lat. Iren. *perseuerasse* and Tertullian's *remansisse* (*Adv. Val.* 10.4 [CCL 2.762]). Holl too made this correction in his edition of Epiphanius (GCS 25.404). "Subsequent" stands for *epigenomenōi*. The Latin has *appendice*, that is, something that is added. See also 1.2.2, where the Latin has *ea quae acciderat passione* for *epigenomenōi pathei*.

25. Codex Vaticanus and Codex Marcianus have *aposterēthēnai* ("was deprived of"), but Lat. Iren. and Tertullian (*Adv. Val.* 10.4 [CCL 2.762]) have *crucifixam*, supposing *apostaurōthēnai* which is certainly the original reading and was restored by Holl (GCS 25.104). However, here it does not mean "crucified" but "staked off" according to the original idea of *stauros* (see n. 22). It has this meaning in Thucydides, 4.69; 6.101; and elsewhere. But F. C. Burkitt, "Dr. Sanday's New Testament of Irenaeus, with a Note on Valentinian Terms in Irenaeus and Tertullian," JThS 25 (1924) 65–66, claims *stauros* as a palisade, but from the symbolism of the cross as a dividing principle between right and left. See Gal. 5.24. Even so, Lat. Iren. and Tertullian would be correct with *crucifixam*. See the summary of Grabe's and Sagnard's positions on this along with Rousseau's remarks in SC 263.179–80 (SC 264.43 n. 6).

26. She "received nothing" by way of form through conception from Wisdom, who could not give form, but only substance; cf. n. 14.

27. "Fruit." Because of their preoccupation with sex the Gnostics thought of the emissions as fructifications.

28. Cf. Tertullian, *Adv. Val.* 11.1 (CCL 2.762), and Hippolytus, *Haer.* 6.31.2–4 (GCS 26.158–59).

29. Lat. Iren. lost some words here. Tertullian (*Adv. Val.* 11.1 [CCL 2.762]) has the equivalent of the Greek: *Solidandis rebus et Pleromati*

muniendo iamque figendo, ne qua eiusmodi rursus concussio incurreret.
On this see also SC 263.181 (SC 264.45 n. 1).

30. The "comprehension of Ingenerate" is Only-begotten, as
Grabe (cf. MG 7.460–61 n. 1) remarked. But Massuet (MG 7.460 n. 1)
claimed "ingenerate" is an error that crept into the text already prior
to the Latin version; instead of *agennētou* it should be *genētou*, namely,
"comprehension of (Only-) begotten." Moreover, Massuet said that
the "comprehension of Ingenerate" as Only-begotten is possible, but
it is not indicated anywhere in the context. That is not true, because at
the end of this very paragraph Irenaeus tells us what can be comprehended of Father is Son, who alone comprehends Father. That seems
to be a certain key to the interpretation of the "comprehension of
Ingenerate," namely, that it is Only-begotten Son, who comprehends
the ingenerate Father. All that the other Aeons can ever know is
Only-begotten, but since they know him who comprehends Father,
they are said to know the comprehension of Father, the Ingenerate.
That knowledge is sufficient for them and is all they are ever allowed.
In fact, the Gnostics claim that Christ announced: "Don't look for
God; he is unknown; you will not find him" (A.H. 4.6.4). Moreover,
precisely because Wisdom tried to fathom Father she was nearly annihilated. All this is amply confirmed by Clement of Alexandria: "The
face of Father is Son, through whom Father is known" (*Exc. Thdot.*
10.6 [GCS 17².110]). Again, "the face of Father is Son, since the face is
whatever is comprehensible of Father (*katalēpton tou Patros*), which
they see who have been taught by Son" (*Exc. Thdot.* 23.5 [GCS 17².114]).
On the other hand, since Ingenerate is incomprehensible to all except
to Only-begotten, by knowing Only-begotten they can be said to
know what is incomprehensible of Ingenerate. Clement of Alexandria
again gives a parallel: "Silence kept silence what she was not able to
say about the Unspeakable, but she narrated the incomprehensible
which she comprehended" (*Exc. Thdot.* 29 [GCS 17².116]). So Holl's
changes and interpolations in Epiphanius's text (GCS 25.405) are not
necessary. Klebba (Klebba BKV 3.7) translated the passage quite differently: *Dass es hinreiche, wenn sie die Natur der Paarung als einen
Denkakt des Urvaters erkennen.* This combination of phrases is not
necessary, and it is hardly probable that the comprehension is here an
act of Ingenerate. On the other hand, Rousseau (SC 263.181 [SC 264.45
n. 2]) notes that every editor and translator of Irenaeus has striven to

make sense out of *agennētou to katalēpsin ginōskontas hikanous einai* and none have been satisfied with the efforts of their predecessors. They suggest that these words simply be bracketed, for the phrase makes good sense without them.

31. Cf. Matt. 11.27. Rousseau and Doutreleau emend the Greek text to ⟨*all'*⟩ *ē dia monou tou Monogenous* [*gignōsketai*] and suggest the translation be similar to this: "No one can either see or hear him except through the Only-begotten alone." See SC 264.45.

32. Codex Vaticanus and Codex Marcianus have *katalēpton*, which should certainly be *akatalēpton*, according to the Latin and Tertullian (*Adv. Val.* 11.3 [CCL 2.763]). It is demanded by the sense. Holl prints *akatalēpton* in GCS 25.405. Rousseau and Doutreleau (SC 264.46) adopt Holl's reading and themselves emend *loipois* to *holois*. See SC 263.181–82 (SC 264.47 n. 1) for their reasons for this.

33. "His Son" follows the Latin: *quod quidem filius est;* it is strongly confirmed by Tertullian (*Adv. Val.* 11.3–4 [CCL 2.762–63]). Holl (GCS 25.405) corrected the Gk. Epiph. accordingly.

34. Tertullian used this paragraph in *Adv. Val.* 12 (CCL 2.763–64), but he embellished it with his clever irony. Hippolytus has nearly the same in *Haer.* 6.32 (GCS 26.159–61).

35. "Thereupon" translated the Greek *epi toutōi*, and also the Lat. Iren. *in hoc*, though this is in a queer position, owing no doubt to a very literal translation of the Greek. There is a parallel construction in 1.29.3: *Confirmatis igitur sic omnibus, . . . Et refrigerantia in hoc omnia hymnizare. . . .* The Greek is not extant for this passage, but *refrigerantia* here must stand for the same Greek as *requiescentia* (*anapausamena*).

36. An alternative translation based on suggestions made by Rousseau in SC 263.182: "They sang hymns amid much rejoicing to First-Father, all taking part in the great exultation." Rousseau puts forth his questions about *metaskhonta* in SC 263.182 (SC 264.47 n. 3). He thinks that the Latin *participantem* is possibly a corruption of *participantes*. If *participantem* is the primitive reading, this only proves the Latin translator considered *metaskhonta* as a masculine accusative singular aorist participle modifying *Propatora*. In that case a proper translation would be what is printed in the body of the text: "First-Father who himself took part in the great exulation." Rousseau feels, however, that, owing to the movement of thought in this pas-

sage, it is better to take *metaskhonta* as neuter nominative plural aorist participle which agrees with *hola*.

37. Rousseau (SC 263.182 [SC 264.47 n. 4]) points out that, even though the words *tou de Patros autōn sunepisphragizomenou* appear only in the Greek, there is no reason to question their primitive character.

38. Grabe's edition of Lat. Iren. has *Bythi* based on an ancient MS in which this reading is alleged by Feuardent (cf. Harvey 1.23 n. 2). Tertullian (*Adv. Val.* 12.4 [CCL 2.763]) has *patris*, which also seems to refer to Bythos, the First-Father. However, Harvey (1.23 n. 2) reports that the extant MSS of Gk. Epiph. have either *Hori* or *Orthi*, which seems out of context altogether. Hippolytus (*Haer.* 6.32.1 [GCS 26.160]) has Son (*huion*), which Harvey (1.23 n. 2) considers the original reading that corrupted into *Horos* or *Orthos*. But that would not explain *Bythos* in Lat. Iren. and *Pater* in Tertullian. Besides, the context seems to demand that the reference be to First-Father, Bythos, for whose glory the rest of the Aeons existed.

39. To whom are the angels equal? Tertullian (*Adv. Val.* 12.5 [CCL 2.764]) thought the term *par genus*, as he translated *homogeneis* "ambiguous": if the angels were equal among themselves, the term would be good; but if they were consubstantial with Savior, it would be ambiguous, because what superiority would he then have over his co-equal bodyguard? So some consider the term synonymous with *hēlikiōtōn* ("peers"), used in A.H. 1.8.4. These appeal to St. Athanasius, who evidently uses this passage of Irenaeus when he says that the angels, according to Valentinus and other heretics, are *homogeneis* with Christ (*Ar.* 1.56 [MG 26.129]). However, immediately before this clause Athanasius clearly interprets the word as equality in nature: "The things compared are *homogenē*, so that the Son is of the same nature as the angels." Harvey (1.23–24 n. 5) tries to solve the difficulty by saying the angels are co-equal in time (*hēlikiōtai*) with Savior, but co-equal in nature (*homogeneis*) with each other. But the text plainly says they are co-equal with Savior in nature (*homogeneis*). According to the heretics the angels are of the same nature as Savior; both are created and not increate. This is confirmed by A.H. 2.4.1., where Irenaeus speaks of the emission of Silence and says: "But if it is not emitted, it must have sprung from and been generated by itself, and must be equal in time to

their Profundity, the Father of all. Then void would be of the same nature and have the same honor as their Father of All." Here we have both equality in time and identity of nature. The Greek is not extant for this passage. But his argument seems to be: If contemporary, then also of like nature.

CHAPTER 3

1. Rousseau (SC 263.182–83 [SC 264.49 n. 1]) points out that instead of *hup' autōn* the Latin translator must have read *autōn*. The Greek reading is confirmed by A.H. 2.24.1: *non erga uera est illa quae* ab eis *in Pleromate dicitur negotiatio.* The use of *pragmateia* is noteworthy, for this shows that *pragmateia*, which Irenaeus used here in an ironic sense, was used by the Gnostics themselves to indicate the "production" of their Pleroma.

2. "Material substance." The Greek MSS of Epiphanius have *hulēi*, agreeing with the Latin *materia*, which I kept in the translation. Yet Holl (GCS 25.406) proposed the correction *lupēi;* if that is the correct reading, the mistake was made already before the Latin version. Both versions fit the Gnostic context. Rousseau and Doutreleau (SC 264.49) read *hulēi* here.

3. In Greek and Latin "stabilization" is governed by a genitive, obviously a subjective genitive, because in the preceding paragraph Wisdom is stabilized by Limit, so I translate "by Limit" etc. *"After her agony"* is in Greek and Latin *ex.* Massuet (MG 7.467–68 n. 5) lists many attempts of editors to correct this. There is no need. Rousseau (SC 264.49) would disagree with this last statement and would propose *hexagōnos* instead of *exagōnos* (following Codex Vaticanus) or *ex agōnos* (the reading of Codex Marcianus). He would suggest "hexagonal assemblage" as an alternative translation for "stabilization after her agony" and feels (SC 263.183 [SC 264.49 n. 2]) that the burlesque presentation this phrase would make fits in well with the irony Irenaeus intends in the whole scene.

4. Cf. Matt. 19.11.

5. Cf. A.H. 1.1.3.

6. Cf. Luke 3.23.

7. Cf. Matt. 20.1–7.

8. Eph. 3.21. See also SC 263.183 (SC 264.51 n. 1).

9. Because Christ gave thanks at the Last Supper, "to give thanks" (*eukharistein*) very early meant to celebrate the Eucharistic Sacrifice, and even to consecrate; and Eucharist (*eukharistia*) meant the Sacrifice of the New Law. See A.H. 4.18.5. In the present passage the Greek has the singular, while the Latin has the plural, *in gratiarum actionibus*. Hence it is doubtful whether there is reference here to the Eucharist, as Massuet (MG 7.469 n. 1) holds, or to some other thanksgiving prayer, as Harvey (1.25 n. 1) maintains.

10. To include such phrases in the doxologies of the liturgy was a very ancient custom.

11. Cf. Luke 2.42–46.

12. Cf. Matt. 10.2, Luke 6.13.

13. The same error was held by the Ophites; see A.H. 1.30.14. It is clearly against Acts 1.13. Perhaps it was in some apocryphal work. Moreover, the eighteen Aeons are strikingly pointed out by the first two letters of his name [Jesus], namely, iota and eta. The iota has the numeric value of 10, the eta 8; the sum of the two is 18.

14. Cf. Matt. 5.18.

15. The Gk. Epiph. text is corrupt. To understand the discussion we must quote it in full, as reported in Harvey (1.26): *to de peri ton dōdekaton Aiōna gegonos pathos huposēmainesthai legousi dia tēs apostasias [dia Ioudan] ⟨tou Iouda⟩, hōs dōdekatos ēn tōn Apostolōn, genomenēs prodosias [deiknusthai legousi]*. Words in square brackets should be omitted; those in angle brackets should be added as correct. The Latin is simple and correct, which we translated, adding only the last phrase from the Greek. That Judas is the type of the Aeon is expressed also in 2.20.2: *Aeonis passionem per Iudam demonstrari*, that is, by Judas's apostasy. Grabe (cf. Harvey 1.26 n. 2) would drop the first "is pointed out," and have "passion" control the genitive "of the apostasy." But that is impossible because the passion is ascribed to the Aeon, of which Judas's apostasy is the type. Since Lat. Iren. has *significari dicunt* at this point, we retain it here and drop the duplicate at the end, where the Latin does not have it. Holl (GCS 25.407) and Rousseau and Doutreleau (SC 264.53) also have omitted *deiknusthai legousi*. And so we reject Grabe's suggestion (cf. Harvey 1.26 n. 2) that

huposēmainesthai legousi was a marginal correction for the faulty *sēmainousi legesthai* a few lines earlier, which crept into the text here. *Per apostasiam Iudae* is certainly correct, and the Greek *tēs apostasias*, since it cannot be governed by any noun, needs a preposition. A simple correction is the transposition of *dia*, which Holl has suggested (GCS 25.407). We hesitatingly retain the Greek genitive absolute ("when the betrayal took place"), as an explanation of the apostasy of Judas, though it is not in the Latin and is really not needed. Holl (GCS 25.407) as well as Rousseau and Doutreleau (SC 264.53) exclude this genitive absolute.

16. Rousseau (SC 263.184 [SC 264.53 n. 1]) points out that the subject of *epathen* is not explicit. There are two possible interpretations. The simpler is "by the fact that he whom we call the Lord suffered in the twelfth month." This is the interpretation adopted here. The other is that he who suffered could not be the "Savior" in an absolute sense, for, since he was an Aeon of pneumatic essence, he could not suffer. He who suffered, according to the Gnostics, would be of a physical essence—the physical "Christ" or "Jesus (sprung) from the 'economy' " in whom the "Savior" descended under the form of a dove when he was baptized in the Jordan and from whom he flew away before the Passion.

17. Cf. Luke 4.19, Isa. 61.2. This error in regard to the length of Christ's public ministry seems to have been the prevailing opinion, not only among the heretics, but also among some orthodox writers. It was held by Clement of Alexandria, Julius Africanus, Tertullian, and others. They were misled by Isa. 61.2. See U. Holzmeister, *Chronologia vitae Christi* (Rome 1933) 114–17.

18. Mark 5.31.

19. We follow the Latin construction. The Greek says more directly: "She who suffered . . . is that power." At the end of the paragraph it is said that the power came from Limit to Wisdom. So here the power came from Christ into the woman. Still she herself is pointed out as the power because she possessed it. "Touched the Son's cloak" is in all the Latin MSS. Codex Vaticanus gr. 503 and Codex Marcianus 125 omit "Son." Holl (GCS 25.407) and Sagnard *Gnose* 37 restored it, but omitted "that." "Son's" is testified too in the Latin. The Greek verb *epsause* governs the genitive (*tou phorēmatos*). But *tēs alētheias* is also genitive and seemingly governed

by the same verb. That would put Truth in apposition to cloak: Truth would be the cloak. In touching the cloak of Christ she would have touched Truth. If that is correct, as we assume in the translation, then Lat. Iren. missed the Greek syntax and should have written *Veritatem*, because *tetigisset* governs the accusative. Lat. Iren. took Truth in apposition to Son. Lundström (Lundström *Studien* 50) follows Grabe (cf. Lundström *Studien* 50) and Mannucci (93 n. 4) in keeping *Veritatis* in apposition to *illius filii*. Rousseau (SC 263.185 [SC 264.55 n. 4]) believes this is one of several occasions in which the Latin translator has wrongly construed the Greek text. In this instance the Latin translator did not see in *Alētheias* the apposition to *phorēmatos*, and thus translated it by an accusative (*Veritatem*) as Latin syntax would demand. A.H. 2.20.1 has a parallel clause, from which it is certain that Tetrad is the hem, and Truth is the cloak. So the woman (Wisdom) touched the hem (Tetrad) of the cloak (Truth) of that Son (Christ), who was interested in her recovery. In the last phrase Gk. Epiph. omits "universal." But it is unquestionably original because it is in the Latin and is supposed in Tertullian's *in reliquam substantiam* (*Adv. Val.* 9.3 [CCL 2.760]). Compare also A.H. 1.2.2: *uniuersam substantiam*. In a parallel in 2.20.1, Irenaeus has the same expression as here. In explanation of this phrase it should be noted with Harvey (1.27 n. 3) that Wisdom would not have been annihilated completely; she was constituted of form and substance; she would have lost form, and so also individuality. But her substance would have been resolved into the substance common to all the Aeons, in which she herself participated. See also Rousseau's remarks at SC 263.185 (SC 264.55 n. 5).

20. Cf. Exod. 13.2; Luke 2.23. "Every" is neuter in the Greek Bible in the distributive sense. But the Gnostics used it in the collective sense of "All."

21. This translation is based on the suggestion of Rousseau (SC 263.186 [SC 264.57 n. 1]) that *kai* before *exoristheisēs* be suppressed. He also accepts Massuet's suggestion (MG 7.474–75 n. 10) that *separat ea* (C V) and *separata ea* (A Q S), may be corruptions of *separatae*, a participle that exactly translates *exoristheisēs*.

22. Cf. Col. 3.11.

23. Cf. Rom. 11.36.

24. Col. 2.9.

25. Eph. 1.10. Irenaeus often used this Pauline text throughout, especially in Book 5. For our translation of the key words "recapitulate" and "recapitulation" see n. 11 to chap. 10. Both Holl (GCS 25.408) in his edition of Epiphanius and Lat. Iren. have "through God," which is not in Paul's text, and which necessitates taking the verb in the passive voice, though in Paul it is middle voice. S. Lundström (Lundström *Studien* 69) suggests that *dia theou* should be *dia touto,* which would leave the verb in the middle voice. But we fail to see what sense that would have here. Rousseau and Doutreleau (SC 264.57) would also remove *dia tou theou.*

26. "Likewise . . . sword." There is an Armenian fragment, which Rousseau and Doutreleau designate as Fr. arm. 1 from the Galata 54 MS, that covers these lines as well as the extant Latin and Greek texts. For more information on this Armenian fragment see SC 263.101–5.

27. Cf. Luke 14.27; Matt. 10.38.

28. Cf. Mark 10.21. It is not indicated here just how the cross is supportive. Of course, it makes one a follower of Savior, and in that sense links with him and does not separate. "Having taken up the cross" is not in several manuscripts of Mark. On this see SC 263.187 (SC 264.59 n. 1).

29. Matt. 10.34.

30. Cf. Matt. 3.12; Luke 3.17. Rousseau and Doutreleau (SC 264.59) read *diakatharai* over *diakathariei* of V and M. Rousseau also notes (SC 263.187 [SC 264.59 n. 2]) that the New Testament knows both readings. He feels, then, that it is impossible to know with certainty which of the two was the reading in the original text of Irenaeus.

31. Cf. 1 Cor. 1.18.

32. Cf. Gal. 6.14. "By whom" is in Lat. Iren. *per quem,* and so cannot refer to the cross (*crucem,* which is feminine) and must refer to Christ. But the Greek relative (masculine) could refer to either Jesus or *stauros,* both of which are masculine. We have the same problem in the Bible itself.

33. Rousseau (SC 263.188 [SC 264.61 n. 2]) remarks that in Gnostic terminology *ta hola* and *ta panta* often denote the Aeons. Thus Rousseau and Doutreleau translate *pantōn* and *uniuersorum* by *Eons* (SC 264.61).

34. Rousseau (SC 263.188 [SC 264.61 n. 4]) does not believe that

when Irenaeus mentions "the law and the prophets" Irenaeus is referring to texts beyond what he has already mentioned.

35. This sentence is obviously corrupt. Gk. Epiph. defies translation as transmitted in the MSS. But neither is the Latin without difficulties. We must quote it, because one can scarcely follow the discussion without seeing the whole sentence. The text here is cited according to Harvey (1.31) with some slight editing: *hate pollōn parabolōn kai allēgoriōn eirēmenōn kai eis polla helkein dunamenōn, to amphibolon dia tēs exēgeseōs. Heteroi de deinōs tōi plasmati kai doliōs epharmozontes—cum multae parabolae et allegoriae sint dictae, et in multa trahi possint; ambiguum per expositionem, propensius ad figmentum suum dolose adaptantes.* Let us eliminate what seem certain mistakes. The active *helkein* cannot be translated in context. It must be passive, *helkesthai,* which agrees with Latin *trahi* and was accepted by Holl (GCS 25.409). Again, the Latin has nothing corresponding to *heteroi de deinōs;* and really the phrase seems foreign to the context, in which there is question of only one class of heretics, not "others." Besides, *heteroi* as subject would have to begin a new clause and then its transitive verb would have no object, namely, without joining this clause to the preceding. For this phrase the Latin has only *propensius.* That supposes the comparative *deinoterōs* and this suggested to some that the comparative is original and corrupted into *heteroi de deinōs.* Holl (GCS 25.409) adopted the comparative. Yet, though that would not be impossible, it would involve too much change. Harvey (1.31), who accepts *deinoterōs,* suggests that maybe *heteroi de* was *heteroias* ("unusual"), modifying the preceding "explanation." In that case, maybe *deinōs* is correct, since *doliōs,* the second adverb in the pair, is not comparative. Besides, it is rather odd to have two adverbs so close but not in the same degree. The Latin translator could have misread *heteroias deinōs* as *heteroi deinoterōs. Dunamena* with a passive verb, indicating that a Scriptural passage can be drawn to some other meaning, occurs also in 1.18.2 and 1.18.3. But what is the subject of this participle in our passage? The Greek genitive plural supposes the subject to be "parables and allegories," namely, a genitive absolute, parallel to "have spoken." That is grammatically possible and agrees with the Latin *possint* transmitted by two MSS, the Arundel and Voss. (The Clermont MS has *possit.*) *Possint* is thus parallel to *sint dictae.*

The only other possible subject for *possint* (*dunamenōn*) would be *ambiguum;* but since this is singular and nominative, the Greek would have to be changed to *dunamenon*. Massuet (MG 7.477 n. 4) accepted this construction, and so he had to cancel *kai* before *eis polla*. But in this construction "adapt" would be without an object. So I think the only solution, and that rather simple, is to place a punctuation mark after *possint* (*dunamenōn*), reading what precedes as a genitive absolute, and removing the punctuation after *expositionem* as was done in this translation. See A.H. 2.22.1, where Irenaeus reports that "the prophets spoke many things in parables and allegories, and not according to the literal meaning of the words themselves." In 2.10.1 he reports: "It is manifest that they now generate another god who was not sought after before, inasmuch as parables, which themselves need to be studied for their meaning, they adapt incorrectly to the god whom they invented." Then he continues explaining about "ambiguous Scriptural passages." Rousseau also (SC 263.188–89 [SC 264.63 n. 1]) does not find either the Latin or the Greek text satisfactory here and so proposes a number of emendations. On the Latin side he prefers *possint* to *possit*. On the Greek side he accepts Holl's (GCS 25.409) correction of *helkesthai* over *helkein* of the Codex Vaticanus and Codex Marcianus. He also suggests that *heteroi de* be omitted and proposes to attach *to amphibolon* to *epharmozontes*. With these and one other change the phrase not only becomes coherent but also provides the framework for Irenaeus to develop in 1.8–9. See also his discussion on Irenaeus's use of *parabolē* in this paragraph. Rousseau notes that Justin Martyr used *parabolē* in a similar sense in *Dial.* 36.2, 52.1, 63.2, 68.6, 77.4, 78.10.

36. Here we follow Rousseau who prefers "in one Jesus Christ alone, Son of God" (SC 264.63). He gives his reasons for omitting *Kurion* here at SC 263.189–90 (SC 264.63 n. 2).

37. We have here the two main beliefs of the Creed.

CHAPTER 4

1. This number was used by Tertullian in *Adv. Val.* 14 (CCL 2.764–65) and by Hippolytus in *Haer.* 6.32 (GCS 26.159–61).

2. Achamoth is not so inexplicable as Tertullian thought (*Adv. Val.* 14.1 [CCL 2.764]). It could easily stem from the Hebrew word for wisdom (*ḥokmah*), which in the plural is *ḥokmôth*. A variant spelling of the plural (*ḥakmôth*) occurs in Prov. 14.1.

3. Rousseau (SC 263.190 [SC 264.63 n. 3]) notes that Lat. Iren. certainly has *a superiore Pleromate* but the adjective *superiore* is a useless redundancy without doubt introduced by a scribe or the translator. This is also true a few lines down in the expression *superiorem Christum*. Very different is *superioris Sophiae* which is a translation of *tēs anō Sophias*. The word *anō* has good reason to exist as it distinguishes "Wisdom from on high" (the thirtieth aeon of the Pleroma) from "Wisdom" outside of the Pleroma (Achamoth).

4. *Skēnōmatos* (tent) of the Greek MSS should certainly be *kenōmatos* (emptiness) according to the Latin *uacuitatis*, with which Tertullian (*Adv. Val.* 14.1 [CCL 2.764] and Theodoret, *Haer.* 1.7 (MG 83.356C) agree. Holl (GCS 25.409) as well as Rousseau and Doutreleau (SC 264.63) read *kenōmatos*. Irenaeus himself (A.H. 1.4.2) has "in the darkness and emptiness," and these are supposed to be the opposites of "light and Fullness." See also A.H. 2.8.3: *neque uacuum esse, aut umbram capiet . . . de umbra cenomatis.*

5. Because she came from Wisdom alone she had only substance, but no form; see nn. 14, 26 to chap. 2.

6. Stake was also called Limit; he was the boundary fence of the Fullness, over which Christ extended himself to assist Achamoth.

7. So she had existence, which included intelligence, as we are told later, but not the special kind of knowledge which the other Aeons received from Mind. See D. Good, "Sophia in Valentinianism," SCent 4, no. 4 (1984) 200, where she points out that Doutreleau and Rousseau have added "Achamoth" in the French translation at least four times in A.H. 1.4.1–2 where the word is absent from the Greek and Latin texts.

8. Rousseau (SC 263.190 [SC 264.65 n. 1]) prefers "a sure odor of incorruptibility" here.

9. "Thus" is according to the Latin *sic*, which supposes *houtōs*. Gk. Epiph. has *entautha* here.

10. Tertullian says more explicitly *inclamauerit in eam* (*Adv. Val.* 14.3 [CCL 2.765]). Various derivations are given for *Jao*. Commonly it is said that it is some kind of shortened form of the Hebrew name for

God, Yahweh, as are also *Yahu* and *Ya'hu*. But Harvey (1.33–34 n. 8) advanced the opinion that it may be a combination of symbolic letters from the Hellenistic synagogues: iota is for Yahweh; alpha and omega, as symbolic of eternity, being the first and last letters of the Greek alphabet. Whatever truth there might be in that explanation, it seems farfetched to say that in the Apocalypse St. John had in mind this name Yaho, when he called Christ the Alpha and the Omega.

11. Tertullian, *Adv. Val.* 14.4 (CCL 2.765): *coepit adfigi maerore . . . metu . . . consternatione . . . ignorantia.* See A.H. 1.5.4.

12. Literally the Greek would be: "She had no change in the passions, as her Mother, but a contradiction." The meaning is that Wisdom had received the special knowledge from Mind like the other Aeons, but because of her apostasy from the Fullness she degraded herself; she was changed. Her offspring Achamoth never had this knowledge, and so a change for the worse was not possible in her. Tertullian confirms this when he says that Wisdom was an Aeon, but Achamoth was by nature inferior: *pro condicione deterius* (Tertullian, *Adv. Val.* 14.4 [CCL 2.765]).

13. The matter of 4.2.2–4.2.4 was used by Tertullian in *Adv. Val.* 15 (CCL 2.765–66), but he again developed it in his own ironical style. Holl (GCS 25.410) and Sagnard *Gnose* 39 prefer *suntaxin* (the reading of the Codex Marcianus) to *sustasin* (the reading of the Codex Vaticanus). Rousseau (SC 263.191 [SC 264.67 n. 1]) prefers *sustasin* and notes that in this context *sustasin* means "origin."

14. We follow Lundström's (Lundström *Studien* 45) suggestion that a comma be placed after "phantasy," and the rest be read as a genitive absolute. Holl (GCS 25.410) has the same.

15. Matt. 10.8.

16. We follow Holl (GCS 25.411) as well as Rousseau and Doutreleau (SC 264.71) who read *hidrōtōn* here. Harvey (1.37) explains the *mē* as the prefix of the verb. Rousseau and Doutreleau (SC 264.71) put square brackets around *mē* and print *eskhēkenai*. In this they follow Holl (GCS 25.411). St. Nilus the Ascetic, *Ep.* 234 (MG 79.168D), has a reference to this idea.

17. A.H. 1.4.5 furnished Tertullian with material for *Adv. Val.* 16 (CCL 2.766–67) and Theodoret for *Haer.* 1.7 (MG 83.356). In Clement of Alexandria, *Exc. Thdot.* 23.2 (GCS 17².114), the account is varied: Christ enters the Fullness, leaving Achamoth outside, but he prays for

help for her; then by the will of the Aeons Jesus is sent to her as Advocate. This is really the doctrine of Valentinus, which Ptolemaeus had modified. See below A.H. 1.11.1 and SC 23.105 n. 4.

18. Cf. Matt. 11.27, 28.18; Luke 10.22.

19. Cf. Col. 1.16. The Valentinians added the word "Divinities." According to Clement of Alexandria (*Exc. Thdot.* 43.3 [GCS 17².120]) they read it thus: "Thrones, Dominions, Kingdoms, Divinities, Liturgies." This is a case of their interpolating the Scripture. On this see also SC 263.191–92 (SC 264.73 n. 1).

20. Cf. Clement of Alexandria, *Exc. Thdot.* 21.1 (GCS 17².113): the male "seeds" were the angels; the female "seeds" of Wisdom were the Valentinians.

21. Clement of Alexandria, *Exc. Thdot.* 44.1 (GCS 17².120–21), has a variation of this: Wisdom saw him who was like the light that had left her, she recognized him, ran to him, rejoiced, and adored him. When, however, she saw the male angels who were sent with him, she blushed and veiled herself.

22. "Prolific retinue" is *karpophoria.* Harvey (1.39 n. 3) thinks this means all the excellencies or endowments derived from the Aeons. But Tertullian (*Adv. Val.* 16.2 [CCL 2.767]) translates *fructiferumque suggestum,* which ANF 3.512 gives as "prolific equipage." Irenaeus himself (1.4.5) says that Achamoth had contemplated the lights, that is, the angels, that were with Savior. And from Clement of Alexandria (*Exc. Thdot.* 44.1 [GCS 17².120–21]), it is certain that there is reference to the angels who accompanied Savior.

23. Christ had formed her according to substance; Savior now grants the formation according to knowledge. See Clement of Alexandria, *Exc. Thdot.* 45.1 (GCS 17².121).

24. Clement of Alexandria, *Exc. Thdot.* 45.2 (GCS 17².121). He separated the passions from her, but he did not destroy them; he made them into the material creation.

25. That seems to be the meaning of *hektika ēdē kai dunata einai.* The literal Latin version, *eo quod iam habilia et possibilia essent,* gives the same sense, as does Tertullian's *indita habilitate atque natura* (*Adv. Val.* 16.3 [CCL 2.767]). Massuet (MG 7.487 n. 6) too explains the Greek thus: *eo quod in habitum jam cessissent, ac robur contraxissent.*

26. Both the Greek and the Latin are difficult. In Clement's *Exc. Thdot.* 46 (GCS 17².121) there is a parallel, which though it has a few

extra words gives the same idea: *ex asōmatou pathous kai sumbebēkotos eis asōmaton eti tēn hulēn:* (He changed them) "from incorporeal and accidental passion to material substance as yet incorporeal." The words "and accidental" might have been dropped by a scribe from Irenaeus before the Latin version was made, or Irenaeus may never have had them. Thus there are two steps: from incorporeal passion to incorporeal substance, then from this to composite bodies. In A.H. 1.5.2. St. Irenaeus says that Demiurge "made corporeal things out of incorporeal." Tertullian's vague *in materiae corporalem* (*Adv. Val.* 16.3 [CCL 2.767]) shows that he had difficulty with the phrase. Harvey (1.40 n. 3) shows that the idea of an "incorporeal body" is Platonic (an observation already made by Massuet [MG 7.488–89 n. 12]) and that Clement of Alexandria clearly admits of bodies that are incorporeal, though not like our bodies (*Exc. Thdot.* 10.6; 11.3; 14 [GCS 17².110, 111]).

27. The "substantial essences" are really qualities of the same being; compare Hippolytus, *Haer.* 6.32.6 (GCS 26.160) and Tertullian (*Adv. Val.* 16.3 [CCL 2.767]), *duplex substantiarum condicio.*

28. Rousseau and Doutreleau (SC 264.75) prefer to translate the sentence something like this: "It is because of all this that they say that Savior has done virtually the work of Demiurge." They note (SC 263.193 [SC 264.75 n. 2]) that in the eyes of the Gnostics the first and in one sense true "Demiurge" is "Savior" himself. That "Savior" would be the "first Demiurge" gives in advance a clue to a passage in A.H. 2.7.2.

29. Rousseau (SC 263.193–94 [SC 264.75 n. 3]) sees an allusion to Gen. 30.38–39 here and wishes to correct the Greek of the MSS to *egkissēsasan eis autous.* To support this he compares this text to A.H. 1.29.1 and 2.19.6.

30. Gk. Epiph. and Lat. Iren. are in this sentence fairly close, and yet some adjustment must be made for a correct reading. First, the *kai* before *sullabousan* seems original and calls for *et* before *concepisse.* Rousseau and Doutreleau (SC 264.74–75) would solve this differently. They do not print *et* before *concepisse* and would place square brackets around the *kai* before *sullabousan*, following Holl (GCS 25.412). The participle *sullabousan* is in a context of conception, and so one might say with Harvey (1.41 n. 2) that it has that meaning, namely, that Achamoth "conceived the contemplation of the lights"; but since conception is implied below in *egkissēsasan*, it seems preferable to hold (with

Grabe [p. 24 n. 2 in the Greek; cf. Harvey 1.41 n. 2], Massuet [MG 7.490 n. 7] and Stieren 1.56–57 n. 5) that *sullabousan theōrian* simply means that she received the vision of the lights, and in virtue of that conceived, since the reception of the contemplation itself is not identical with conception. However, because of the context there may be a play on the verb that would connote conception. That agrees with Irenaeus A.H. 1.5.6, that her offspring "was conceived by virtue of her contemplation of the angels who surround Savior." Tertullian (*Adv. Val.* 17.1 [CCL 2.767]) is rather blunt about the same matter: *Abhinc Achamoth . . . in opera maiora frugescit. Prae gaudio enim tanti ex infelicitate successus concalefacta simulque contemplatione ipsa angelicorum luminum, uta ita dixerim, subfermentata—pudet, sed aliter exprimere non est—quodammodo subsuriit intra et ipsa in illos et conceptu statim intumuit spiritali ad imaginem ipsam.* The verb *egkissēsasan* means to yearn after a mate for conceiving. The Latin expressed this in a toned-down and condensed fashion by *delectationem in conspectu eorum*, still governed by *concepisse* above, without a new verb as in Greek: "After she received . . . the contemplation of the lights . . . and pleasure in their sight." The Greek seems to have the original wording. In fact, it is possible, as Harvey (1.41) suggests, that *conspectu* is a scribal error for *conceptu*. With that correction the Latin would be still closer to the Greek: "After she received . . . pleasure in their conception." "Their image" in place of the Latin "his image" is according to the correction (*kata tēn eikona ⟨autōn⟩*) made by Holl (GCS 25.412) and Sagnard *Gnose* 40, which is confirmed by what follows: "after the likeness of Savior's bodyguard." Rousseau (SC 263.194 [SC 264.75 n. 4]) would argue that the correct reading of the Greek is *kata tēn ekeinōn eikona*.

CHAPTER 5

1. All of chap. 5 was used by Hippolytus in *Haer.* 6.32.7–9 and 6.33 (GCS 26.161–62). The first sentence of par. 1 is the last of Tertullian's in *Adv. Val.* 17.2 (CCL 2.767); the rest of Irenaeus's paragraph he expanded in *Adv. Val.* 18–19 (CCL 2.767–68).

2. "Ensouled" seemed, everything considered, the most suitable

translation for *psukhikos* in the Gnostic system. Originally it meant pertaining to life or to soul, either of which might be animal in opposition to rational, or carnal as opposed to spiritual or glorified. Now, for the Gnostics the earthly or material was that which could not receive knowledge and be saved: the spiritual was that which had to receive knowledge and be saved. The *psukhikos* was between these two: it could receive knowledge and be saved if it inclined that way (see A.H. 1.6.1). So it really was not carnal; nor was it merely "animal" in the usual sense of that word. It was both natural and rational. On the other hand, all three classes of men (material, ensouled, spiritual) could be, in fact they had to be, morally carnal to be saved. See Lampe PGL, s.v. "*psukhikos*," E. Jacob, TDNT 9.611–17, s.v. "*psukhē*," A. Dihle, TDNT 9.656–58, s.v. "*psukhē*," and K.-W. Tröger, TDNT 9.658–60, s.v. "*psukhē*." Some authors use "psychic"; but that does not convey the correct meaning in the Gnostic system. Where *psukhikos* is used for animal in the physical or moral sense, I have translated it "animal."

3. These instructions make the formation of the offspring of Achamoth not merely according to substance, but also according to knowledge as Grabe (cf. Harvey 1.42 n. 1) noted. Rousseau (SC 263.194 [SC 264.77 n. 1]) notes that the immediately preceding coordinate clause really says nothing else than what Irenaeus wrote at the end of this paragraph: "For when Intention wished to make all things to the honor of the Aeons, she, or rather the Savior through her, made images of them [the Aeons]."

4. Rousseau and Doutreleau (SC 264.76) add *theon kai* here, following Holl's suggestion (GCS 25.413) in the critical apparatus of his text. Rousseau (SC 263.194 [SC 264.77 n. 2]) comments that the Latin *et Saluatorem* is perhaps an aberrant reading. He believes that the reading *Deum* can be retained even if nothing corresponds to it in the Greek. To support this contention he refers to Theodoret, *Haer.* 1.7: *ton theon kai Patera* and the beginning of A.H. 1.5.2: *Patera oun kai Theon legousin auton gegonenai tōn ektos tou Plerōmatos . . .*

5. Cf. Matt. 25.33.

6. The Latin has *post eum*, so Harvey (1.42) suggests *met' auton* instead of *kat' auton* of Codex Vaticanus gr. 503, namely, all things that were made after him in time were formed by him. Holl has adopted this (GCS 25.413), as have Rousseau and Doutreleau (SC

264.77). But the Greek "according to him" also makes sense here, because all things that were made, temporally, after Demiurge were also made "according" to him. The Latin translator might have misread or mistranslated the Greek.

7. "Mother-Parent," because he was emitted by Achamoth as the sole source of his existence. "Fatherless," because he did not proceed from a male parent. The origin of this Demiurge idea, namely, of a lower god who is the maker of the world and is responsible for all the evil in it, is disputed. H. Jonas, "Response to G. Quispel's 'Gnosticism and the New Testament,'" in *The Bible in Modern Scholarship: Papers Read at the 100th Meeting of the Society of Biblical Literature. December 28–30, 1964,* ed. J. P. Hyatt (Nashville and New York 1965) 286–93, opposed the theory that Gnosticism had any roots in Judaism. But G. Quispel, "The Origins of the Gnostic Demiurge," *Kyriakon: Festschrift Johannes Quasten,* ed. P. Granfield and J. A. Jungmann, 1 (Münster 1970) 271–76, shows how the conflict between the good and the evil as found in Jewish literature, canonical and non-canonical, could have led to the opinion of a lower god, by way of Jewish sectarians, especially the Magharians. The general relation between Gnosticism and Judaism is, of course, firmly established among scholars today. Among others see B. A. Pearson, "The Problem of 'Jewish Gnostic' Literature," in *Nag Hammadi, Gnosticism and Early Christianity,* ed. C. W. Hedrick and R. Hodgson (Peabody, Mass. 1986) 15–35, and Rudolph *Gnosis* 52, 227, 277–82.

8. Inasmuch as Savior was an aggregate of all the perfections of the Aeons, Achamoth, when she beheld Savior and conceived, gave birth to reproductions of the perfections of the Aeons.

9. Since Intention gave the formation through Savior, it is doubtful, according to some scholars, what the subject is in this sentence. Massuet (MG 7. 493 n. 1) and Harvey (1.43) think that Intention, of the preceding sentence, is the subject and change "her" to "herself" as object. But since "Savior" can be subject, and since both the Greek and the Latin have the simple "her," a change of the text is neither necessary nor desirable. Holl (GCS 25.413) claims that "in the image" is an old error for "the image" in the accusative. But that accusative seems impossible grammatically, because *men* and *de* make *autēn* parallel to *touton,* and since *touton* is accusative of "preserved," "image" would be a second accusative of the same verb. Of course, this would

be possible if "image" were in apposition to "her," but then the meaning would be exactly the same as for "in the image," and there would be no need to change the text. Rousseau and Doutreleau, however, prefer *tēn eikona*. An alternate translation based on this is "She herself offered the image of the invisible Father. . . ." For their reasons see Rousseau's remarks in SC 263.195 (SC 264.79 n. 1).

10. This paragraph is chap. 20 of Tertullian's *Adv. Val.* (CCL 2.769). Hippolytus used it in *Haer.* 6.34 (GCS 26.164). See also Clement of Alexandria, *Exc. Thdot.* 47.1–3 (GCS 17².121).

11. Valentinus's idea of the seven heavens is found also in the Jewish Cabbala, which in turn seems to have had its origin in the Zoroastrian Amashaspands, according to Harvey (1.44 n. 1). Harvey frequently refers to the influence of the Jewish Cabbala on Gnosticism. The Jewish Cabbala was written down after A.D. 500. But it has its beginnings before Christ, possibly in the thirteenth and fourteenth centuries, and later it came under the influence of the philosophers and, during the Babylonian captivity, especially of Zoroastrianism. Hence, we do not know whether Gnosticism was influenced by the Cabbala or vice versa in a given case, or whether both borrowed from the mystery religions. Cf. J. S. Minkin, "Cabala," *The Universal Jewish Encyclopedia*, ed. I. Landman et al., 2 (New York 1948) 614–20. At most we can simply state the parallels. In *Proof* 9, Irenaeus accepts in a Catholic sense that "the earth is encompassed by seven heavens," which he most likely got from Jewish traditions. See ACW 16.53, 146 and "The Testament of Levi 3.1–9," ed. R. H. Charles in *The Apocrypha and Pseudepigrapha of the Old Testament in English*, vol. 2: *Pseudepigrapha*, ed. R. H. Charles (Oxford 1913) 305–6.

12. Rousseau (SC 263.195–96 [SC 264.81 n. 1]) follows Harvey (1.44) and Sagnard *Gnose* 41 in correcting *noētous* (the reading of Codex Vaticanus gr. 503 and Codex Marcianus 125) to *noerous*. See also his remarks there regarding the assimilation *topos = theos*.

13. Tertullian (*Adv. Val.* 20.1–2 [CCL 2.769]) has the same thought. He agrees with Lat. Iren. in calling Paradise an Archangel, and not merely an Angel, as in Gk. Epiph. But in saying that Adam received something from the Archangel's power, he disagrees with both Lat. Iren. and Gk. Epiph., which have Adam receive something from the Angel himself. Clement of Alexandria (*Exc. Thdot.* 51.1 [GCS 17².123]) speaks of Adam being created in paradise, which is in the fourth

heaven. That paradise was in the fourth heaven came from the rabbinical Haggadah. See L. Ginzberg, "Die Haggada bei den Kirchenvätern
und in der apokryphischen Litteratur," *Monatschrift für Geschichte
und Wissenschaft des Judentums* 42 (1893) 550, as noted by Sagnard in
SC 23.165, n. 2. In *Proof* 12 (ACW 16.55), Irenaeus himself says "a place
was prepared for him better than this world . . . and its name is the
Garden."

14. See Clement of Alexandria, *Exc. Thdot.* 49, 53.4 (GCS 17².123–
24). Tertullian treats this matter in *Adv. Val.* 21 (CCL 2.769).

15. Rousseau points out the double divergence between the Latin
and the Greek here. On this see SC 263.196 (SC 264.81 n. 2).

16. "False notion" follows Gk. Epiph. *oiēseōs*, for which Lat. Iren.
has *operationis*, supposing *poiēseōs*. We follow the Greek as more in
keeping with the immediate context, supposing with Massuet (MG
7.496 n. 7) that Lat. Iren. had written *opinationis*, which corrupted into
operationis. It is possible, however, that Lat. Iren. wrote *operationis*
misreading *poiēseōs* for *oiēseōs*. De Billy (cf. MG 7.496 n. 7) and Sagnard *Gnose* 42 and 42 n. 2 follow the Latin. Hippolytus (*Haer.* 6.34.8
[GCS 26.164]) seems to indicate that "false notion" is correct when he
speaks of Demiurge thinking that he created the world and being
ignorant that Wisdom (Achamoth) made all things for him. The same
can be inferred from Clement of Alexandria, who even uses the verb
oiomenos: "He (Demiurge) did not know her who created through
him, *believing* that he created by his own power" (*Exc. Thdot.* 49 [GCS
17².123]). See also SC 263.197–98 (SC 264.83 n. 1).

17. The male parent is Profundity. The mother, Achamoth, had no
consort; still she is given a name of masculine gender since she functioned also as father.

18. Then she will return into the Fullness. See A.H. 1.7.1.

19. The ideas of this paragraph are found also in Tertullian, *Adv.
Val.* 21–22 (CCL 2.769–70), and in Hippolytus, *Haer.* 6.34 (GCS
26.162–64).

20. Hippolytus, *Haer.* 6.32.5 (GCS 26.160), gives "supplication" as
a fourth element. This, it seems, is to be identified with "amendment"
in the next line of Irenaeus, as Harvey (1.46 n. 2) pointed out.

21. Rousseau (SC 263.198–99 [SC 264.83 n. 3]) is amazed by this
statement. Irenaeus states that material substance consists of three
passions: fear, grief, and perplexity. At the same time Irenaeus states

that the ensouled substance come forth from fear and amendment. From sadness come spirits of evil, and corporal or material substance come from perplexity or despair. The fact that the Latin and Greek texts are in nearly complete accord rules out textual alteration. Finally, Rousseau notes that the hesitation noticeable in Irenaeus's text may reflect a hesitation he found in his source(s) for this material.

22. For *atonōteron* ("too weak") the Latin has *superiorem*, supposing *anōteron*, which is clearly incorrect, because shortly afterward Demiurge is said to be wholly ignorant of spiritual things. Tertullian confirms this by his *inualitudine spiritalia accedere* (*Adv. Val.* 22.1 [CCL 2.769]). See also Rousseau's remarks on this in SC 263.199 (SC 264.83 n. 4).

23. Cf. Isa. 45.5, 46.9. See also Hippolytus, *Haer.* 6.33 (GCS 26.162).

24. Cf. Eph. 6.12.

25. This title is found in Eph. 6.12. In the sense of "universal monarch" it is well known in the commentary of the rabbis. Compare the title "Prince of this world" which was given to Satan since the Babylonian captivity, and which Jesus used in John 12.31. See Harvey 1.47, n. 3.

26. The translation here follows the text as proposed by Rousseau and Doutreleau (SC 264.85). Rousseau (SC 263.199–200 [SC 264.85 n. 1]) writes that *kai tous aggelous* do not correspond to any words in the Latin and do not seem to be authentic.

27. Hippolytus has the same material in *Haer.* 6.32.6 (GCS 26.160). See also Clement of Alexandria, *Exc. Thdot.* 48 (GCS 17².122).

28. Rousseau (SC 263.200 [SC 264.85 n. 2]) feels that the Latin reading is not correct. In their critical apparatus Rousseau and Doutreleau (SC 264.84) suggest that the Latin should perhaps be *supercaelestis*.

29. Achamoth dwelt above the heavens though outside the Fullness, but Demiurge dwelt in a lower region, hence not above the heavens, but in the heavens. So *huperouranion* should be *epouranion*. The Lat. Iren. *qui sit in caelo locus* and Tertullian, *Adv. Val.* 23.1 (CCL 2.770) *in Hebdomade sua* agree with that change.

30. Gk. Epiph. is somewhat corrupt here, but it can be easily adjusted. Gk. Epiph. has *amēkhanias*, but the Latin has *aporia*, which often translates *aporia*, and so Harvey (1.48) would substitute it here. But *amēkhania* and *aporia* are synonyms, and Lat. Iren.

could easily have used *aporia* as a translation for *amēkhania.* "More ignoble" follows Lat. Iren. *de uesaniori.* Codex Vaticanus gr. 503 has *hōs ek tou asēmoterou,* which can mean "from more insignificant," and so would not differ much from the sense of the Latin. Tertullian in a similar context speaks of the world as consolidated *ex Sophiae utilissimis casibus,* literally "on occasion of (or, out of) Sophia's very useful misfortunes" (*Adv. Val.* 23.2 [CCL 2.770]). There is no good reason, except to adjust Tertullian to Irenaeus, for Massuet (MG 7.499 n. 1) to have suggested that *utilissimis* should be *vilissimis.* Holl (GCS 25.415) and Sagnard *Gnose* 42 as well as Rousseau and Doutreleau (SC 264.85) follow the reading of Codex Marcianus 125: *stasimōterou* ("more steadfast"), but that does not seem to fit the context at all.

31. Codex Vaticanus gr. 503 (after correction) added *tōn dakruōn* after *tou phobou.* Harvey (1.48) suggests dropping it. Actually the two genitives are awkward. But maybe Lat. Iren. dropped "of tears" because it was not easily intelligible and not needed. Still it would explain how water came from fear, namely, from tears caused by fear. However, Holl (GCS 25.415) and Rousseau and Doutreleau (SC 264.86) follow Codex Vaticanus gr. 503 (before correction) and do not include *tōn dakruōn.*

32. See SC 263.200 (SC 264.87 n. 1).

33. This paragraph was copied by Tertullian in *Adv. Val.* 24 (CCL 2.770–71). See also Clement of Alexandria, *Exc. Thdot.* 50 (GCS 17².123).

34. Cf. Gen. 2.7, 1 Cor. 15.47. Rousseau (SC 263.200 [SC 264.87 n. 2]) notes in the Gnostic system set forth by Irenaeus that *khoikos* is nearly a synonym of *hulikos.* The only difference between them is that *khoikos* has a Biblical and Christian origin while *hulikos* has a philosophical origin.

35. Cf. Gen. 2.7.

36. Cf. Gen. 1.26.

37. Rousseau (SC 263.201 [SC 264.87 n. 4]) thinks this refers to the ensouled Demiurge. He feels this term issues from the Gnostic source Irenaeus is using.

38. Cf. Gen. 2.7.

39. Cf. Gen. 3.21. The same is noted by Clement of Alexandria, *Exc. Thdot.* 55 (GCS 17².125).

40. Tertullian explains this matter in *Adv. Val.* 25 (CCL 2.771).

41. The spiritual "seed" could have been infused into Demiurge, because being of ensouled substance, he could not perceive it. But he was doubly ignorant of it because according to Clement of Alexandria (*Exc. Thdot.* 17².105–6) it was infused while he slept.

42. Gk. Epiph. has only "perfect," but the Latin has *perfectae rationis*, and Tertullian (*Adv. Val.* 25.2 [CCL 2.771]), *sermoni perfecto.* Both *ratio* and *sermo* suppose *logos* ("word") which in the present case means knowledge. Holl (GCS 25.416) as well as Rousseau and Doutreleau (SC 264.89) add *Logou.* Rousseau gives their reasons for including *Logou* in SC 263.201 (SC 264.89 n. 1).

43. Cf. Gen. 2.7.

CHAPTER 6

1. For this paragraph consult Tertullian, *Adv. Val.* 26 (CCL 2.771–72), and also Hippolytus, *Haer.* 6.35 (GCS 26.164–65). M. A. Donovan notes that R. Berthouzoz thinks L. Schottrof and E. H. Pagels read accounts in A.H. 1.6.1 and 1.7.5 as if they were equivalent. See M. A. Donovan, "Irenaeus in Recent Scholarship," SCent 4, no. 4 (Winter 1984) 234, and R. Berthouzoz, *Liberté et grâce suivant la théologie d'Irénée de Lyon: Le débat avec la gnose aux origines de la théologie chrétienne* (Fribourg and Paris 1980) 127.

2. Cf. Matt. 5.13–14.

3. According to the Latin *animali* and Tertullian, *Adv. Val.* 26.1 (CCL 2.771) and the singular "ensouled element" below, the genitive plural of Gk. Epiph. should be singular and in the dative, *tōi psukhikōi*, which Holl (GCS 25.416) and Rousseau and Doutreleau (SC 264.91) adopted. See SC 263.201–4 (SC 264.91 n. 1) for Rousseau's comments on this.

4. In regard to the formation of Savior consult also Theodoret, *Haer.* 1.7 (MG 83.356–57). "Self-determining power" is for *autexousion*, which Lat. Iren. translated by *suae potestatis.* It means having free will or the power freely to choose or determine. See Lampe PGL, s.vv. "*autexousios, autexousiōs.*" But since there are other terms for this idea, and sometimes several are used in the same clause or sentence, "free will" could not be used.

5. "Economy" for *oikonomia*, which was a favorite term with the Gnostics and the Christians. It was used in classical Greek from Xenophon and Plato on. The primary meaning is management of the affairs of a house (*oikos*). From this it was applied to any management, office, arrangement, plan. In the New Testament Paul adopted it to designate especially God's plan and administration of salvation through Jesus Christ (Eph. 1.10; 3.9), and so the office of a minister of this Economy was called an economy (Eph. 3.2; 1 Cor. 1.25). Irenaeus used the word in its various meanings; e.g., for the arrangement between Sarah and Abraham (1.18.3), for God's arrangement in regard to the ark (1.18.3), but most frequently for God's plan and administration of salvation, both for the Christian and for the Gnostic systems. By further extension, the Incarnation itself and even the Savior was called Economy, as in our present passage. In Latin it was translated by *dispensatio* and *dispositio*. Yet when the Greek text is not extant, one cannot always be sure that these words stand for *oikonomia*, because they also translate *diathesis* and *pragmateia*. Tertullian used also *administratio* for this idea; e.g., *Adv. Val.* 26.2 (CCL 2.772). We have chosen to translate this word by Economy, capitalizing it when it refers to the Incarnation or the whole plan of salvation, and it seemed more satisfactory than "dispensation," which in English has too much of a juridical ring. For "economy" in Scripture see O. Michel, TDNT 5.151–53, s.v. "*oikonomia*"; and for the Fathers see G. L. Prestige, *God in Patristic Thought*, 2d ed. (London 1952) 57–67. For Irenaeus in particular see A. D'Alès, "Le mot *oikonomia* dans la langue théologique de Saint Irénée," REG 12 (1919) 1–9. We were not able to use M. Widmann, "Der Begriff *oikonomia* im Werk des Irenäus und seine Vorgeschichte" (Ph.D. diss., Tübingen University 1956).

6. "Visible and tangible" is according to Lat. Iren., which receives confirmation from Tertullian, *Adv. Val.* 26.2 (CCL 2.772): *quo congressui et conspectui et contactui . . . subiaceret;* and also Theodoret, *Haer.* 1.7 (MG 83.357C). Holl (GCS 25.416) accepted this correction in place of the evidently faulty "invisible and intangible" of the Greek MSS. Irenaeus repeated the same idea in 1.9.3. Valentinianism was essentially Docetic; see Tertullian, *Adv. Val.* 27.1 (CCL 2.772).

7. Cf. Clement of Alexandria, *Exc. Thdot.* 62 (GCS 17².128). In *Exc. Thdot.* 59 (GCS 17².126) he explains that Jesus had put on Christ who

was ensouled and so was invisible. Hence Jesus was given a body from the invisible and ensouled substance.

8. "Perfected." The notion of being perfected and consequently saved was prominent in the Gnostic systems. We shall see in the other Books that Irenaeus himself made capital of this idea in the Christian sense. The notion and even the word was, of course, frequent in the New Testament, where it meant to justify (Heb. 10.1, 14), to attain spiritual maturity or perfection (Heb. 11.40; 12.23), and to glorify (Heb. 2.10). See F. Zorell, S.J., *Lexicon Graecum Novi Testamenti*, 3d ed., s.v. "*teleioō*." So Christ was called the "perfecter" (Heb. 12.2); Christians were to be "perfected" (Heb. 5.13–14; 1 Cor. 2.6; 14.20). The "spiritual" and the "perfect" were the same; compare 1 Cor. 2.6 and 3.1. Perfection in Irenaeus in its highest form was the glory of man and woman in body and soul, but this began already through the first graces of baptism. The Incarnate Word was willed by God as the Mediator of this gradual process of perfection. For more on this see D. J. Unger, "Christ's Rôle in the Universe According to St. Irenaeus," *Franciscan Studies*, n. s., 5 (1945) 9–14. Since the initial step toward perfection was by initiation into the mysteries, "to perfect" is used at times for that act of initiation. Some would, therefore, translate *teleioō* by "initiate." However, the two words are never entirely synonymous. In this very paragraph Irenaeus carefully distinguishes the two, and in the Preface to Book 2 he explains: "They initiate those who are being made perfect."

9. We have followed the Greek as arranged by Holl (GCS 25.417), Sagnard *Gnose* 44 (as well as Rousseau and Doutreleau [SC 264.92–93]).

10. See Rousseau's remarks on this at SC 263.204 (SC 264.93 n. 1).

11. Absolute salvation is spoken of in Clement of Alexandria, *Exc. Thdot.* 56.1–3 (GCS 17².125). This principle was first held by Simon Magus or his followers, according to Hippolytus, *Haer.* 6.19.5 (GCS 26.146), and Clement of Alexandria, *Str.* 3.1–4 (GCS 52 [15].195–97). St. Augustine informs us that Eunomius held it too (*Haer.* 54 [CCL 46.324]).

12. Paragraphs 3–4 furnished matter for Tertullian, *Adv. Val.* 30 (CCL 2.774).

13. Cf. Gal. 5.21.

14. The council of the apostles prescribed that the Gentile converts had to abstain from food sacrificed to idols (Acts 15.20). Abuses continued to exist. St. Paul had to correct some people at Corinth (1 Cor. 8.10); John condemned some in the churches of Pergamum (Rev. [Apoc.] 2.14) and of Thyatira (Rev. [Apoc.] 2.20). Ecclesiastical writers continued to denounce it; e.g., Tertullian, *Spect.* 13 (CCL 1.239).

15. Gk. Epiph. and Lat. Iren. differ in this clause and neither has the correct reading. Rousseau (SC 263.204–5 [SC 264.97 n. 1]) however feels the sense of the Greek here is excellent. In Latin *diem festum* is controlled by *factum*. Seemingly in Greek it is the pleasure that is held in honor of the idols. But *genomenēn* is feminine, not because it modifies *terpsin*, but because it modifies *heortasimon*, which is also feminine (an adjective supposing *hēmera*), as is certain from the other adjective *pasan*. In Lat. Iren. *uoluntate* is certainly a scribe's error for *uoluptate* (in those days often written *uolumptate*), as the Greek *terpsin* and the logic of ideas demand. See also Rousseau SC 263.205 (SC 264.97 n. 1) on this. But the Greek scribe omitted a preposition corresponding to *pro*, possibly *dia*. But there is little probability to Harvey's (1.55 n. 2) suggestion, followed by Sagnard *Gnose* 45 n. 1, that *dia* is a corruption for *kai*, which was already present before the Latin translation was made, as if the phrase would read "at every festival *and* pleasure." The Latin reading and the logic are against that change. Harvey (1.55 n. 3) prefers *deorum*, noting that the Arundel MS and some others have *eorum*, which is obviously not correct; but the Greek has *eidōlon*. The context is about eating food offered to idols, and so "idols" might be original, and the Latin scribe, possibly as an interpretation, wrote *deorum*. We follow Rousseau and Doutreleau (SC 264.96) who prefer *idolorum*, agreeing with Grabe's emendation (Harvey 1.55 n. 3).

16. See the remarks by Rousseau (SC 263.205 [SC 264.97 n. 2]) on this.

17. Rousseau (SC 263.205 [SC 264.97 n. 3]) notes that *apodidosthai* here means "to give (to someone what he or she has a right to)." He also thinks that this phrase seems in a curiously twisted way to echo Matt. 22.21.

18. For a brief survey on the discipline of penance in Irenaeus see

H. Vorgrimler, *Busse und Krankensalbung,* vol. 4 fasc. 3 of *Handbuch der Dogmengeschichte,* ed. M. Schmaus, A. Grillmeier, L. Scheffczyk (Freiburg 1978) 41–42.

19. The Greek *apokalein* has a note of irony: to give something a disparaging name, to stigmatize. See LSJ, s.v. "*apokaleō.*"

20. Cf. Luke 19.26.

21. "Put into practice" is *meletan,* which means to think about, to attend to, to study, to practice or train (used for speakers and actors). See LSJ, s.v. "*meletaō.*" In Ireneaus it means to practice. The Latin *meditari* bears that meaning, as it did even in classical Latin. Cicero, for instance, says of Demosthenes, *perfecit meditando, ut nemo planius esse locutus putaretur (De orat.* 1.61). In Pliny it is used as a synonym for *exerceri (Nat.* 8.50 [32].113). See *Oxford Latin Dictionary,* s.v. "*meditor.*"

22. Cf. John 17.11.

23. Cf. John 18.37.

24. Cf. John 17.14–16.

25. In the context it is clear that the Gnostics claimed they, possessing as they do the spiritual seed, could not be defiled by lust or overcome by concupiscence, which could not keep them from attaining the truth; they were never of the world, though in the world (cf. John 17.16), an idea of Christ's that they distorted to their foul purpose. Non-Gnostics, however, as only ensouled and devoid of the spiritual seed, were of the world always, and are overcome by concupiscence if they have conjugal relations; they can therefore never attain to the Truth. For these, then, it was necessary to strive for continence and other good actions. In this context we must say that the two negatives (*mē . . . mē*) give the opposite meaning, contrary to what follows immediately in Irenaeus. Lat. Iren. gives the correct sense. So the two negatives must have been added. Harvey (1.57, 1.57 n. 3), followed by Sagnard *Gnose* 45, thinks they crept into the text as a corruption of other particles. But their suggestion that the first *mē* represents an original *kai,* which makes good sense, is not necessary. The Greek and Latin participles are simply circumstantial temporal participles. Maybe the second *mē* plus *en* came from an original *en tēi.* Massuet (MG 7.510 n. 9) suggested that *kratēthēnai* and *kratētheis* be changed to *kerasthēnai* and *kerastheis.* But we are following Harvey (1.57 n. 2),

Sagnard *Gnose* 45 n. 3, as well as Rousseau and Doutreleau (SC 264.99) who amend the text to *krathēnai* and *kratheis*. It should be noted that we read this infinitive and participle as gnomic aorists, which are generally translated in English by the present.

26. I followed the Latin: *Quapropter nobis quidem, quos psychicos uocant*. Gk. Epiph. *kalous* does not agree with the Latin or the context. Judging by the Latin, the Greek was either *hēmin hous* (Holl, GCS 25.419) or *hēmin hous kai* (Harvey 1.57 n. 4 and Sagnard *Gnose* 45) or *hēmin men hous* (de Billy; cf. Harvey 1.57 n. 4, Massuet, MG 7.511–12 n. 5, Stieren [1.78 n. a], also Rousseau and Doutreleau, SC 264.100). Irenaeus uses very much *men . . . de* for contrasts, and since Lat. Iren. has *quidem quos* (*men hous*), the last suggestion seems best. Merely cancelling *kalous* would not explain *quidem quos*.

CHAPTER 7

1. Tertullian, *Adv. Val.* 31–32 (CCL 2.774–76). E. H. Pagels believes that Irenaeus has twisted Gnostic teaching in this chapter from what is more faithfully preserved in Clement of Alexandria, *Exc. Thdot*. R. M. Grant disagrees with Pagels on this point, as he feels that the differences are slight and Irenaeus's account of Gnostic teaching here is accurate. See E. H. Pagels, "Conflicting Versions of Valentinian Eschatology: Irenaeus' Treatise vs. the Excerpts of Theodotus," HThR 67 (1974) 35–53, and R. M. Grant, "Review of Elaine Hiesey Pagels," *The Johannine Gospel in Gnostic Exegesis* and *The Gnostic Paul*," *Religious Studies Review* 3 (1977) 30–34. M. A. Donovan notes that "the consensus of scholarship favors the reliability of the Irenaean presentation of the teaching of his Gnostic opponents." See M. A. Donovan, "Alive to the Glory of God: A Key Insight in St. Irenaeus," ThS 49 (1988) 284.

2. Cf. John 3.29.

3. Cf. Matt. 9.15.

4. Cf. Tertullian, *Adv. Val.* 31 (CCL 2.775), who also notes that this is the bridegroom of the Scriptures (cf. Matt. 25.6, and perhaps 9.15, for "bridal chamber"). Here too the Gnostics would have misused Scriptures.

5. The soul (in humans) was made by Demiurge, but the spirit was secretly deposited in humans by Achamoth, as explained previously. At the consummation a separation will take place: the spirit will ascend into the Fullness, whereas the soul will remain in heaven, the intermediate region. Nothing merely "ensouled" can enter the Fullness; so the spirituals discard their "souls" and then enter. See Clement of Alexandria, *Exc. Thdot.* 64 (GCS 17².128).

6. As Harvey (1.59 n. 4) observes, material fire has no prototype in the Fullness, and so it must burn itself out. "Be aflame" is *exaphthen*, but Lat. Iren. has *comprehendens*. *Exaptō* has two rather different meanings. First "I fasten" and in the middle voice "I hang on to"; and second, "I enkindle." On this see LSJ, s.v. "*exaptō*." The text obviously calls for the second meaning, whereas the Latin read the first meaning into the word, as Massuet (MG 7.514 n. 6) noted. Or, maybe the Latin read correctly (*econtra* Rousseau SC 263.206–7 [SC 264.103 n. 2]) and originally the translator wrote *comburens*, which was corrupted into *comprehendens* (cf. Harvey [1.59 n. 3]). Rousseau does not think that *comprehendens* makes any sense here. So he suggests that the Latin translator might have read *eklambanon* instead of *eklampsan*. The second verb in Lat. Iren. is *consumit*, which agrees with *sunanalōthēsesthai* of Gk. Epiph. Gk. Epiph. has two different verbs: *katergasamenon . . . sunanalōthēsesthai*, while the Latin has *consumit . . . consumptum*, in the sense of destroying. The first Greek verb can mean "to put an end to," "to kill," or it can mean "to work up," e.g., in digestion, for consuming. On this see LSJ, s.v. "*katergazomai*." Perhaps that is the meaning here, which the Latin *consumit* rendered correctly. Tertullian confirms this by his parallel line: *Tunc, credo, ille ignis erumpet, et uniuersam substantiam depopulatus* (*Adv. Val.* 32 [CCL 2.776]). The deponent *depopulor* means to waste or to destroy. So the Greek reading seems correct, and should not be changed to *katakausamenon* (*comburens*), as Harvey (1.59 n. 3) suggested, even though in 1.3.5 Irenaeus quotes Luke 3.17, where the Greek is *katakausei* and the Latin *comburet*, which Irenaeus interprets with *analiskein* (*consumit*). The passages are not parallel. In 1.3.5 one verb (*consumit*) interprets the other (*comburet*), while here they are successive acts. In conclusion let us note that the original meaning "working out" seems out of context, against de Billy and Massuet (cf. MG 7.514 n. 6) who translated it *confectaque*.

7. Tertullian treats this in *Adv. Val.* 27 (CCL 2.772–73). Cf. also Clement of Alexandria, who in *Exc. Thdot.* 47.3 (GCS 17².121) speaks of Demiurge making Christ of an ensouled substance according to the image of Son, and the archangels according to the image of the Aeons.

8. From the beginning of this paragraph to this point there also exists a Syriac fragment in addition to the Greek and Latin and Armenian versions. For more on this Syriac fragment see SC 263.109–10. On the Armenian fragment here see n. 9. Theodoret, *Ep.* 146(145) (SC III.180), gives a summary of the heretics on this matter: Simon, Menander, Cerdo, and Marcion denied the Incarnation and called the nativity from the Virgin a fable. Valentinus, Basilides, Bardesanes, and others admitted the conception and birth from the Virgin but said that the Word passed through her as through a channel and took nothing from her, as he was a man only in appearance.

9. Cf. Matt. 3.16; Luke 3.22. From the beginning of this paragraph up to this point there exists an Armenian fragment from the Galata 54 MS. For more on this fragment which Rousseau and Doutreleau designate Fr. arm. 2 see SC 263.101–5.

10. He preserved the primary Tetrad by the fact that the fourfold element of which he consisted was patterned on the Tetrad on high. Cf. Tertullian, *Adv. Val.* 27.2 (CCL 2.772).

11. According to Clement of Alexandria, *Exc. Thdot.* 61.6 (GCS 17².127), Theodotus spoke of Christ's forsaking Jesus at the Passion. For more on this see SC 263.207–8 (SC 264.105 n. 1).

12. Rousseau (SC 263.209 [SC 264.107 n. 1]) comments that the phrase "by way of mystery" may well be understood in this way: "in the conditions such that this passion makes up a mystery, that is a visible symbol of an invisible reality."

13. The sense of this cryptic sentence is that Christ on high, in extending himself beyond and over Stake-Limit in order to give form to Achamoth, is the type of Christ who stretched himself out on the cross. Tertullian's parallel (*Adv. Val.* 27.3 [CCL 2.773]) makes this plain: "However, the sensuous and fleshy Christ suffered in imitation of the Christ on high."

14. Gk. Epiph. says the Gnostics explain that the many things were spoken "by" (*hupo*) the offspring "through" (*dia*) the prophets. Lat. Iren. says that they explain that the many things were spoken "of" (*de*) the offspring "through" (*per*) the prophets. Now, from what follows

below it is certain that the offspring did some of the speaking through the prophets. So the Greek must be correct here too. Petavius, de Billy, and Desgallards (cf. MG 7.516 n. 11) were wrong, then, in suggesting *huper* for *hupo* to adjust to the Latin.

15. Rousseau (SC 263.209 [SC 264.107 n. 2]) notes that a problem of interpretation exists here: first, Irenaeus speaks of a twofold source of prophecies, then immediately afterward he speaks of a threefold source of prophecies. Although he does not feel that Sagnard's solution in Sagnard *Gnose* 411 n. 1 satisfies all grammatical difficulties, Rousseau adopts Sagnard's solution as the most satisfactory way to interpret the passage. Sagnard had noted the interplay of conjunctions (*kai polla ... polla de kai ... alla kai*) and thus distinguished three sources of prophecies.

16. Harvey (1.63–64 n. 5) thinks that *prosplokē* ("admixture") is an unknown word, and that it has the same meaning as *diaplokē* (*simultas*, strife, encounter). But the word is given in LSJ, s.v. "*prosplokē.*" It means admixture or embrace. See A.H. 2.12.3, where *permixtio* equals *perplexio*, for conjugal union. In this case Lat. Iren. *perplexio* agrees with the Greek. However, *tōn kheirōn* ("of the hands") in Gk. Epiph. does not agree with Lat. Iren. *peiorum*, which supposes *tōn kheironōn* ("of baser things"), the correction adopted by Holl (GCS 25.421), Rousseau and Doutreleau (SC 264.108), and in this translation. The authors seem to refer to three classes of people: the spiritual, the ensouled, and the material. Some of the prophecies are due even to material persons. Hence the Latin is correct. A scribe of Gk. Epiph. could have taken *prosplokē* in the sense of an embrace, and since hands are used for that, he could have misread *kheironōn* as *kheirōn*.

17. "He remained" translates *diatetelekenai*. This verb can mean persevere or remain. The Latin translator most likely read it in that meaning but did not choose the best word in *conseruasse*. It would have to have an intransitive meaning, or the reflexive *se* could have fallen out. And so, though normally *conseruare* translates *tērein* or *suntērein*, it does not have to suppose that verb in our passage. Similarly, Rousseau (SC 263.210 [SC 264.109 n. 2]) suggests that the Latin translator could have read improperly *diatetērēkenai* for *diatetelekenai*.

18. Cf. Matt. 8.9; Luke 7.8.

19. "Economy," as in Gk. Epiph., which is confirmed by Tertullian (*Adv. Val.* 28.2 [CCL 2.773]), *dispensationem*. Lat. Iren. has *creationem*,

which is certainly faulty. Harvey (1.64 n. 3) thinks the Latin may originally have read *procurationem* or *curationem*.

20. See Tertullian, *Adv. Val.* 29 (CCL 2.773–74), and Clement of Alexandria, *Exc. Thdot.* 54 (GCS 17².124–25).

21. Rousseau (SC 263.210–11 [SC 264.111 n. 1]) notes that the last two adjectives in this series are inverted in the Greek of Epiphanius. The Latin seems to have preserved the original order. Further, he notes that the three adjectives and the three proper names that follow are in a chiastic arrangement which would be quite in line with Irenaeus's style.

22. In Adam all three elements are present; but here each individual represents a different class of the three elements. The Greek phrase has no verb; the Latin has *ut ostendant*. So either the Greek implied a verb and the Latin translator supplied it (cf. Harvey 1.65 n. 1) or the Greek text lost the verb. See 1.8.1 where there is a similar construction. See Hippolytus, *Haer.* 10.9.12 (GCS 26.268), and Clement of Alexandria, *Exc. Thdot.* 54 (GCS 17².124–25).

23. Cf. Clement of Alexandria, *Exc. Thdot.* 56 (GCS 17².125).

CHAPTER 8

1. This translation follows the Latin *abundantius* which supposes *perissōterōs;* this correction was adopted by Holl (GCS 25.422) and Rousseau and Doutreleau (SC 264.112) in place of *peri tōn holōn* of the Greek MSS. A Greek version of nearly all this paragraph also exists in the *Peri tēs aretēs* of Ps.-Ephraem as well as what has been preserved in Epiphanius. For more on this see SC 263.78–80.

2. "Non-scriptural" is *agraphōn*, which are here not the oral sayings of Jesus that are "unwritten," but the written words that are really not Scripture. We call them apocryphal. Rousseau (SC 263.211 [SC 264.113 n. 1]) thinks that here *agraphōn* is practically synonymous with the Apocrypha.

3. Rousseau (SC 263.211 [SC 264.113 n. 2]) notes that Epiphanius and the so-called Irish family of MSS (C, V) favor *axiopistōs* while Ps.-Ephraem, the so-called Lyonnaise family (A, Q, S), and the

editio princeps of Irenaeus prepared by Erasmus in 1526 favor *axiopista*. Rousseau prefers, along with Massuet (MG 7.520), *axiopistos*, but mentions that, if the reading *axiopista* were adopted, the sense would be fundamentally the same.

4. See n. 3 to 1 Prf. "Phantasy" is according to the Latin. Gk. Epiph. has *sophia*, no doubt a copyist's error. *Phantasia* is used a few times below. "Lord's words" is *kuriakon logion*. See n. 5 to 1 Prf.

5. This is a good example of how Irenaeus could confound his adversaries by drawing an apt and concrete parallel that made them look ridiculous. "By way of illustration . . . fables" also exists in a Syriac fragment. For more on this fragment designated by Rousseau and Doutreleau as Fr. syr. 2 see SC 263.109–10.

6. Cf. 1 Tim. 4.7.

7. Note that the Scripture is God's Word. Just below it is called *ton graphon*.

8. Rousseau (SC 263.212 [SC 264.117 n. 1]) notes that *prosoikeoun* is practically synonymous with *epharmozein, prosarmozein,* and *proseika-zein*. He finds Lat. Iren. *ad suos insinuare* puzzling.

9. Cf. 1 Pet. 1.20.

10. Rousseau (SC 263.212 [SC 264.117 n. 2]) notes that *pragmateias* here is used in an ironic sense by Irenaeus similar to his use of it against the Gnostics in 1.3.1.

11. Cf. Matt. 9.18–19, 23–26; Luke 8.41–42. "Visited" is *epistas* which was translated by *insistens*. In the Gospel account no verb used fits in clearly with *epistas*. Christ was asked to come and put his hand on her. *Epistas* has such a varied meaning that it is difficult to determine what it means here and how the Latin translator understood it. Massuet's *accedens* (MG 7.523 n. 8) is not satisfactory. *Insistere* is used three other times in Irenaeus (1.28.1; 2.12.4; 3.5.2; cf. B. Reynders, *Lexique comparé du texte grec et des versions latine, arménienne, et syriaque de l' "Adversus haereses" de saint Irénée*, vol. 2: *Index des mots latins*, CSCO 142 [Louvain 1954] 164). But since the translator was at times quite fickle in giving a new meaning to the same word, *insistere* can here very well be synonymous with *adsistere*, and this as well as the Greek can mean to pay attention to, and so to *visit*.

12. 1 Cor. 15.8.

13. Cf. 1 Cor. 11.10. Paul had written *exousian*, but Irenaeus has *ka-lumma* (veil), which is also in several Vulgate MSS (*velamen*) and in

the Bohairic translation. Some, notably Grabe (cf. Harvey 1.69 n. 3), explain "veil" in Irenaeus by saying that he wrote from memory. Harvey (1.69 n. 3) thinks he used the Syriac N. T., because in Syriac the world for "authority" is *shuṭonoh*, which also means a headdress, the meaning that Irenaeus then took out of it, because a woman's veil is the symbol of man's authority over her. But apart from the fact that Irenaeus did not retranslate from Syriac, such a change seems far-fetched. The word must have been in the Western text that the Gnostics used, or they changed from power to veil according to the sense of the symbol to fit their purpose. For "coeval" see n. 39 to chap. 2.

14. "Over her face" is missing in Gk. Epiph.; it was supplied according to the Latin as necessary in the context. Holl (GCS 25.423) added *epi to prosōpon autēs* in the text of Epiphanius. Rousseau (SC 263.212–13 [SC 264.119 n. 1]) feels that Holl's change was not proper. The verb *epitithemai* makes *epi to prosōpon autēs* superfluous. "On the other hand, Moses clearly manifested" is from the Greek; it was skipped in the Latin probably by haplography. Cf. Exod. 34.33–35; 2 Cor. 3.13.

15. Cf. Matt. 27.46; Ps. 21(22).2. Rousseau (SC 263.213 [SC 264.119 n. 2]) places *derelicta est a lumine in eo cum* in square brackets at 1.53 as it seems a doublet of the text at 1.55 and follows Holl (GCS 25.423) in inserting *kai* before *en men tōi eipein en tōi staurōi* at 1.824.

16. Matt. 26.38.

17. Rousseau (SC 263.213–14 [SC 264.121 n. 1]) points out that Irenaeus uses Matt. 26.38 again in 3.22.2 and suggests that *quam* may be a corruption of *perquam*. *Perquam tristis*, furthermore, would make a good translation of *perilupos*. Owing to his philological critique here, he does not agree with the views expressed by A. Orbe in *Cristología Gnóstica: Introducción a la soteriología de los siglos II y III* 2 (Madrid 1976) 190–91.

18. Cf. Matt. 26.39.

19. Cf. John 12.27. The words "I do not know" are not authentic in John. The Valentinians may have added them as the passage would then more completely express the idea of perplexity.

20. Cf. Matt. 8.19–20; Luke 9.57–58.

21. Cf. Luke 9.61–62.

22. Cf. Matt. 19.16–22. Rousseau (SC 263.214 [SC 264.123 n. 1]) notes the explicit opposition made by the Gnostics between the "just" iden-

tified with the ensouled and the "perfect" identified with the spiritual class.

23. Cf. Matt. 8.22; Luke 9.60.

24. Cf. Luke 19.5. The sentence that follows this quotation is missing from Lat. Iren., but it is in Gk. Epiph. and is demanded by the parallelism of the construction. On this see also SC 263.214 (SC 264.123 n. 2).

25. Cf. Matt. 13.33; Luke 13.20–21.

26. 1 Cor. 15.48.

27. Cf. 1 Cor. 2.14.

28. 1 Cor. 2.15.

29. Cf. Rom. 11.16.

30. Since the Latin has *cum*, *sun* is no doubt the correct prepositional prefix. *Erexisse* indicates the correct stem, which is also in keeping with the idea of dough rising up through fermentation. Hence the original word might have been either *sunanestēkenai* (Grabe [cf. Harvey 1.73. n. 1]), *sunanestakenai* (Holl [GCS 25.424]), or *sunestēkenai* (Harvey [1.73 n. 1]). Rousseau (SC 263.125 n. 1 [SC 264.125 n. 1]), however, prefers *sunanestalkenai*, the reading of Codex Vaticanus gr. 503.

31. Cf. Matt. 18.12–13; Luke 15.4–7.

32. Cf. Luke 15.8–10.

33. Luke 2.29.

34. Cf. Luke 2.36–38.

35. Cf. n. 39 to chap. 2.

36. Cf. Luke 7.35.

37. 1 Cor. 2.6.

38. "By the one passage" translates *epi henos*. Though "by the one name" in the next paragraph (5) might be a kind of illustration of the present statement, it is not a perfect parallel. Rather, Mark 12.26, *epi tou batou*, that is, "in the passage about the bush" (Exod. 3), seems to be a parallel use of *epi*. The Latin *in uno ostendentem* is capable of the same interpretation.

39. Cf. Eph. 5.32.

40. I followed Gk. Epiph. The Latin has *et omnium generationem* in the preceding sentence, but in the present sentence it omits all the words between "John" and "produced all things." It is hard to explain

that difference between the Greek and the Latin. Though one would hold that "the origin of all things" was originally in both places, namely, where the Latin has it and also where the Greek has it, haplography would still not explain the omissions, because not all the words in the supposed haplographic phrase are omitted, and a phrase is omitted after the haplographic phrase. Rousseau (SC 263.215 [SC 264.129 n. 2]) also follows Gk. Epiph. and believes that a careful reading of the Latin and Greek indicates only the Greek offers a satisfactorily coherent sense here.

41. Holl (GCS 25.426) corrected "whom" to "which" in Gk. Epiph. The Latin *quod* would seem to favor that. But it seems just as likely that Irenaeus wrote "whom" making it agree with its predicate (Only-begotten), instead of with its antecedent (*to prōton*), while Lat. Iren., following Latin syntax, wrote *Principium . . . quod*.

42. Cf. John 1.34, 49; 3.18.

43. This seems to be an allusion to John 1.18, which differs here in Gk. Epiph. and Lat. Iren. In A.H. 3.11.6, where only the Latin is extant, it is *Vnigenitus Filius Dei* (SC 211.154). But in 4.20.6, the Latin version gives it thus: *unigenitus Filius* (SC 100.646), while the Armenian has *unigenitus Deus* (SC 100.646), the reading that both the Latin and Armenian have in 4.20.11 (SC 100.660). This agreement makes it quite clear that Irenaeus read in his Bible *Unigenitus Deus*, and the reading in 3.11.6 must be judged as an adjustment to the Latin Bible. In our present passage he is not quoting on his own; in fact he is just describing the Gnostic system, and must be using their version. We may therefore not correct it to agree with the other passages. But since Gk. Epiph. and Lat. Iren. differ here, what did Irenaeus write originally? In Latin the repetition of *uocat* in such close succession is suspect, and it is missing in the Greek. So it is rather probable that *Mind* with the first *uocat* is not original, but an interpretation, and the text should read *et Filium et Unigenitum Domini uocat*. Rousseau (SC 263.215–16 [SC 264.129 n. 3]) likewise feels that the first *uocat* is not necessary and it is not at all likely that Ptolemaeus would have used the word *Noun* (*Nun*). But *Domini* is most likely a false reading for the abbreviation of *Theon*. The Latin would suggest a Greek scribe would have misplaced *kai* before, instead of after, "Only-begotten," and the original was *Huion kai Monogenē Theon*, which would then agree with the Latin as corrected, and with the quotations in Book 4. That is also the

reading of the best Greek MSS of the Bible (B, S, C) and the Bodmer papyri and is accepted in most modern critical editions. It is interesting to note, however, that Clement of Alexandria, *Exc. Thdot.* 6–7 (GCS 17².107–8), has both readings.

44. John 1.1–2.

45. John 1.3. Irenaeus here describes the Gnostic views and quotes Scripture according to them. The Ptolemaeans closed the clause with "nothing" or "not a thing," and then began the next clause with "What was made," joining it to 4a as subject. That is the ancient reading of these verses. It was read so also by other Gnostics: Heracleon, Theodotus, the Naasenes. But contrary to E. Haenchen, "Probleme des johanneischen '*Prologs*,'" ZTK 60 (1963) 305–34, this did not originate with the Gnostics. It is consistently the reading of Irenaeus himself, namely in 1.22.1; 2.2.5; 3.8.3; 3.11.8; 5.18.2; *Proof* 43. That must have been the reading in his Bible. All the Church writers prior to the end of the fourth century have the same. Later writers changed to what became the Vulgate reading (. . . *quod factum est; in ipso vita erat*). They did so because the Arians were trying to defend their view about the Word having been created by the older reading of the Gospel. There is here another problem. If that earlier reading is accepted, should "in him" be controlled by "what was made," or should it be joined with "is life"? In our present passage, when explaining the Gnostic view, Irenaeus makes known that they held the first combination: "What was made in him." In the other places where Irenaeus is on his own, he does not explain this matter, and one has no positive clue at all as to how he joined the phrases. He only explains the *per ipsum* of the preceding clause. Maybe one can conclude that he holds the same phrasing as the Gnostics, but interprets the *in ipso* as instrumental, with the same meaning as *per ipsum*. But I would not say that we can list Irenaeus with authors who probably joined *in ipso* with *vita erat*, as does I. de la Potterie, "De interpunctione et interpretatione versuum Joh. 1, 3.4," VD 33 (1955) 193–208. This article may be consulted for a modern study on the problem, and so can M. E. Boismard, *St. John's Prologue*, trans. Carisbrooke Dominicans (Westminster, Md. 1957) 10–18; and B. Vawter, "What Came To Be in Him Was Life (Jn 1, 3b–4a)," CBQ 25 (1963) 401–6.

46. Rousseau and Doutreleau (SC 264.132) read *morphōseōs* here in place of *morphēs* of the Codex Vaticanus gr. 503 and the Codex Mar-

cianus 125. Rousseau (SC 263.216 [SC 264.133 n. 1]) notes that apart from the fact *morphōseōs* corresponds to the Latin *formationis*, there is a good parallel for the change in A.H. 1.2.5.

47. Cf. John 1.3–4. "Is" in place of "was" is found also in other writers.

48. The singular, as in Greek, not the plural, as in Latin, is correct. Irenaeus is writing of Word and Life only. See Clement of Alexandria, *Exc. Thdot.* 6 (GCS 17².107).

49. John 1.4.

50. Rousseau (SC 263.217 [SC 264.133 n. 2]) remarks that here "men" denotes the Aeons "Man" and "Church" in the system of Ptolemaeus.

51. Cf. Eph. 5.13.

52. Lat. Iren. makes "him" the fruit *within* the Fullness, obviously reading *entos*, in place of *pantos*, as in Gk. Epiph., which we prefer, because Irenaeus repeatedly tells us that Savior is the fruit of the *whole* Fullness. Because of a supposed contrast to *ektos*, *pantos* was easily misread as *entos*. See also SC 263.217 (SC 264.135 n. 1).

53. It is interesting to note that from the explanation given about being ignorant, it is clear that the Gnostics took John 1.5, *katelaben*, as intellectual comprehension, and not as "overcoming."

54. Cf. John 1.14. That is the way John wrote it according to the heretics. They changed *hōs* ("as") to *hoia* ("like"). This change implies their heretical notion that Jesus, Savior of the earth, of whom John wrote, is only similar to, not identical with, the Only-begotten of the Fullness. However, we should also mention that Rousseau (SC 263.217 [SC 264.135 n. 2]) thinks that Irenaeus is reproducing here the work of a Valentinian exegete. In the preceding sentence the exegete presented a paraphrase of John's thought followed by the actual text. Had Irenaeus wished to interject a personal comment on this, they feel he would have written a much stronger and less ambiguous one than what is here. The heretics referred "full" to "glory." "Full" is in later Greek an indeclinable adjective, which occurs very often in the papyri. Hence, since the words to which it might refer here are either in the genitive or the accusative case, it is no doubt indeclinable here. On this see also SC 263.218 (SC 264.137 n. 1). It may refer to "glory," but more probably to "his." It is really the incarnate Word that has the fullness of grace and truth; see v. 16. According to Clement of Alexandria, *Exc. Thdot.* 7.3 (GCS 17².108), the heretics argued that in the

Fullness Only-begotten Son was in the bosom of Father announcing Intention to the Aeons by means of knowledge (cf. John 1.18). But he who appeared on earth is no longer called Only-begotten, but Quasi-Only-begotten.

55. John 1.14. When, in the preceding sentence, Irenaeus gave the Ptolemaean version of John 1.14, he introduced it with *phēsi* ("he asserted"); now, when he gives the genuine version, he introduced it with *Legei de houtōs* ("But John put it thus"). Tertullian referred to such patchwork in his *Praescr.* 39.5 (CCL 1.219–20): *Homerocentones etiam uocari solent qui de carminibus Homeri propria opera more centonario ex multis hinc compositis in unum sarciunt corpus.*

56. "Father" is Profundity and "Grace" is Silence; cf. 1.1.1. From this it seems evident that the Ptolemaean Valentinians, whose system Irenaeus is describing, counted Profundity and Silence in their system of thirty Aeons. See n. 14 to chap. 1.

57. Rousseau and Doutreleau (SC 264.137) add *Kai ho Ptolemaios houtōs* to the text. For Rousseau's rationale see SC 263.218 (SC 264.137 n. 2).

CHAPTER 9

1. The Latin *constare*, for *sunistēmi*, as it is in 1.28.1, in the sense of establishing a doctrinal system.

2. Lat. Iren. has *astutias et dictiones*. Gk. Epiph. has only one term, *tas lexeis*. Harvey (1.81 n. 1) suggests that the Greek was *tas tekhnas kai lexeis;* and that is possible. Yet in two other places in this chapter (1.9.4) Irenaeus paired *lexeis* with *onomata* (*dictiones et nomina*); and a little later in this same paragraph *ta . . . onomata kai tas lexeis kai tas parabolas—nomina et dictiones et parabolas.* Irenaeus used *astutia*, in the singular, only in two other places (4.41.3; 5.23.1) of deceitful action. Since, however, Irenaeus speaks in the introduction two times of the Gnostic deceitful manner of acting (*panourgōs—subdole*), one might argue that *astutias* is correct here. However, we prefer to follow here Rousseau (SC 263.219 [SC 264.137 n. 3]) who does not consider *astutias et dictiones* to be original and notes that *astutia* is the most common

translation of *panourgia*, a word that occurs a few lines below. So he wonders if the placement of *astutias* besides *dictiones* is owing to a displacement of the word or some other accident that occurred in transmitting the text.

3. Cf. Eph. 4.14.

4. Cf. John 1.3.

5. Cf. John 1.1.

6. Cf. John 1.18.

7. Cf. John 1.9.

8. Cf. John 1.10.

9. Cf. John 1.11.

10. Cf. John 1.14.

11. Cf. John 1.1. Rousseau (SC 263.219 [SC 264.143 n. 1]) notes that Irenaeus gives the substance here of the exegesis that he will develop at greater length in 3.11.1–3.

12. John 1.14.

13. Rousseau (SC 263.219–20 [SC 264.143 n. 2]) notes that the MSS of Epiphanius have *tēs oikonomias* in place of *pantōn gegonōs kai* which Holl (GCS 25.429) had suggested. Rousseau feels the reading *tēs oikonomias* of Codex Vaticanus gr. 503 and Codex Marcianus 125 is not acceptable and the reading of Lat. Iren. is strengthened by these parallel passages: 1.7.1; 2.14.5; 2.20.5; and 3.11.3.

14. "Learn . . . us" is also extant in Armenian in the Galata 54 MS. For more on this fragment designated by Rousseau and Doutreleau as Fr. arm. 3 see SC 263.101–5.

15. Cf. Eph. 4.10; John 3.13. I cannot agree with Harvey (1.84 n. 1) that the Latin *descendit . . . ab uno Vnigenitus Filius* gives a heretical cast to the thought. It does no more than the Creed which professes *qui descendit de caelo*. The Son remained God even while He descended.

16. Though ensouled, his body was not material. This is the view of the later Ptolemaeans, whereas the earlier Valentinians held that his body was spiritual. See Hippolytus, *Haer.* 6.35 (GCS 26.165).

17. "Flesh . . . broken up" is also extant in Syriac. For more on this fragment designated by Rousseau and Doutreleau as Fr. syr. 3 see SC 263.109–10.

18. Our English translation for the phrase "this empty . . . which" is based on the French translation by Rousseau in SC 264.147.

19. Rousseau believes that very early a scribe neglected to transcribe *gar* between *idian* and *hupothesin* with the result that *idian ⟨gar⟩ hupothesin anaplasamenoi* was wrongly attached to the previous sentence. For his rationale in adding *gar* and his account of Irenaeus's argument at the end of 1.9.3 and the beginning of 1.9.4 see SC 263.220–22 (SC 264.147 n. 1).

20. See n. 21 to chap. 6 for "put them to verse."

21. These lines are respectively from Homer's *Od.* 10.76; *Od.* 21.26; *Il.* 19.123; *Il.* 8.368; *Od.* 6.130; *Il.* 24.327; *Od.* 11.38; *Il.* 24.328; *Od.* 11.626; *Il.*, 2.409. This manner of quoting from all sections of Homer's two works is thought by some to indicate that Irenaeus had a personal and rather close acquaintance with Homer. And really Irenaeus does not say that he is copying from someone else. His construction clearly supposes that he is the composer of the cento. He uses a present participle (*scribens*) in a conditional sense, "if one would write," just as in a previous sentence he wrote "like those who would propose": *similia facientes*. The construction is the same in the Greek. Further, his remarks after the poem also betray competence in Homer. Irenaeus knew the classics. He refers to and quotes Homer in A.H. 1.12.2; 1.13.6; 2.5.4; 2.14.2; 2.22.6; 4.33.3. Other poets to whom Irenaeus also refers include Anaxilas, Hesiod, Pindar, Antiphanes, Menander, Sophocles, Stesichorus, and the Comic poets in general. On this see A.H. 1.13.1; 1.23.2; 2.14.1; 2.14.2; 2.14.4; 2.14.5; 2.18.5; 2.21.2; 5.13.2; cf. W. R. Schoedel, "Philosophy and Rhetoric in the *Adversus haereses* of Irenaeus," VC 13 (1959) 22–32, and M. Clark, "Builders of the Christian Culture: A Study of Irenaeus of Lugdunum and Clement of Alexandria," Ph.D. diss., Harvard University, 1970, passim. Homer was the backbone of Hellenistic education, and, among the early Christians, Homer was a topic of discussion and controversy. But the Gnostics also used him; he was the prophet of the Valentinians (cf. A.H. 4.33.3). Hippolytus accuses them of falsifying Homer (cf. *Haer.* 6.19.1 [GCS 26.145]). Rousseau (SC 263.222 [SC 264.149 n. 1]) also notes that some have thought Irenaeus himself wrote this cento, notably H. Ziegler, *Irenäus der Bischof von Lyon* (Berlin 1871) 17. J. Daniélou, *The Gospel Message and Hellenistic Culture,* vol. 2 of *A History of Early Christian Doctrine before the Council of Nicaea,* trans. J. A. Baker (London and Philadelphia 1973) 85, thinks that Valentinus himself composed this cento and that he gave it an allegorical meaning in reference to the

Gnostic tenets, particularly in regard to the sending of Savior who is surrounded by angels and accompanied by Christ and the Holy Spirit. R. L. Wilken, "The Homeric Cento in Irenaeus, 'Adversus haereses' I,9,4," VC 21 (1967) 25–33, doubts that Valentinus wrote it and gave it this alleged allegorical meaning, since Irenaeus gives no such indication, and he quickly forgets about the cento. He wished merely to show how the Gnostics misinterpret Scripture by distorting the passages when lifting them from their context. Benoît 60–61, flatly denies that Irenaeus wrote this cento.

22. The Greek has no noun with *idiāi* ("own"). The Latin added *libro*, supposing *biblioī*. De Billy (cf. Harvey 1.87 n. 5), Massuet (MG 7.545 n. 7), Stieren (1.116 n. b), Holl (GCS 25.431), following the Latin, added "book." Rousseau (SC 264.151) in his French translation also adds "book." But since theme (*hupothesis*) was spoken of, the simpler solution seems to take this noun as the antecedent of "own," as in my translation, according to the suggestion of Harvey (1.87 n. 5). Grabe (cf. Harvey 1.87 n. 5) would substitute "order" since shortly after this phrase there occurs *tēi idiai taxei*. However, in that sentence there is question of arranging jewels in order; here, of passages to their theme.

23. In A.H. Irenaeus speaks of Tradition as "the Rule of the Truth," but in *Proof* 3 he calls it "the Rule of the Faith." So these terms are used as synonyms for Christian Tradition. In the concrete, Irenaeus applies "Rule of the Truth" to the Sacred Scriptures (2.25.1; 2.28.1; 4.35.4) and to the preaching of the Church (*Proof* 3), which is also known as the body of the Truth (2.27.1; *Proof* 1). This Rule of the Truth forms a harmonious picture (1.8.1). It also serves as a criterion of Truth (1.9.4; 1.10.1). N. Brox, *Offenbarung: Gnosis und gnostiker Mythos bei Irenäus von Lyon: Zur Charakteristik der Systeme* (Munich and Salzburg 1966) 105–12, also holds that the Rule of the Truth is in Irenaeus not a Creed, but is the entire faith believed and preached by the Church. It is *ipsa veritas*.

24. "Body" is for *sōmation—corpusculum*, which is really a little body. But the word has a varied meaning. It is used, for example, for volume or structure (of a poem). See LSJ, s.v. "*sōmation*." Because of the context it seems this last would be a good translation, which brings out the well-planned structure of Truth, over against the patchwork of the heretics. But because of the term "body" used elsewhere in Irenaeus, we retained that in our translation. F. Kattenbusch, "Das

Sōmation tēs alētheīas bei Irenäus," ZNTW 10 (1909) 331–32, rightly argues against Zahn that Irenaeus does not refer this term to the Creed, but to the genuine picture of the entire Catholic System of the Truth. This is confirmed from *Proof* 1, where Irenaeus speaks of the book he is about to write as "comprehending in a few details all the members of the body of truth."

25. The Greek *apolutrōsis* (redemption) is considered by some (Massuet [MG 7.547 n. 2]) to have here the meaning of *apolusis*, which is a dramatic term meaning the ending or dismissal. However, according to Harvey's (1.89 n. 1) observation, it is more probable that Irenaeus had actually written *apolusis* and some scribe wrongly wrote *apolutrōsis*, a word that occurred very frequently in Irenaeus. Rousseau (SC 263.222–23 [SC 264.151 n. 1]) agrees with Harvey's observations. Certainly this latter word would here have nothing to do with the true redemption as Irenaeus treats it passim. *Sic* Massuet against de Billy and Desgallards (cf. MG 7.547 n. 2.).

26. "Before" is for *pro* and is certainly the correct reading. Lat. Iren. has *ex ostensione*, that is, even from the demonstration, which does not make good sense in this context. The universally accepted body of the Truth in the Church is itself a proof of its authenticity in contrast to the different and dissonant systems of the Gnostics, even before adducing Scriptural arguments. See also the comments by Rousseau on this at SC 263.223 (SC 264.153 n. 1).

27. Rousseau (SC 263.223 [SC 264.153 n. 2]) notes that Lat. Iren. *eam firmam* provides surety that the original Greek would have been *tēn babaian* and not *bebaian tēn* of Codex Vaticanus gr. 503 and Codex Marcianus 125.

CHAPTER 10

1. As a Rule of Truth this form is probably not a previously composed and used Creed, as Harvey (1.90 n. 1) notes, because Irenaeus must have added some terms to a standard Rule, which would more specifically reject Valentinian tenets. As a matter of fact, we have here a number of terms and expressions that are truly Irenaean: en-

fleshed . . . who through the prophets preached the Economies, the
coming . . . the Passion . . . the bodily ascension into heaven . . . His
coming from heaven in the glory of the Father to recapitulate all
things . . . to raise up all flesh . . . just judgment . . . send into everlasting fire the spiritual forces of wickedness . . . after repentance . . . He
might confer on him the gift of incorruption and clothe them with
everlasting glory. This chapter is truly a gem of ancient Christian
literature. See SC 263.133–34 on the Rule of Truth. "The Church . . .
confess Him" is also extant in Armenian in the Galata 54 MS. For
more on this Armenian fragment designated by Rousseau and Doutreleau as Fr. arm. 4 see SC 263.101–4.

2. "Indeed" renders *kaiper*, which was omitted in Latin. In this
chapter the Bishop of Lyons insists that the Church is catholic or
universal. He knew of the adjective *katholikos* (see 3.11.8) where it is
used two times in the sense of "principal" ("four principal winds . . .
four principal covenants"); but he does not use it for the Church,
though the term "Catholic Church" had been used already by St.
Ignatius of Antioch in his *Smyrn*. Cf. J. A. Kleist, *The Apostolic Fathers*
(ACW 1.93, 141–42) and four times in the martyrdom of Polycarp (*M.
Polyc.*): in the inscription; 8.1; 16.2; 19.2 (cf. ACW 6.90, 93, 98, 99). See
also Kleist's comments on this at ACW 6.202, n. 46, and G. Bardy, *La
théologie de l'église de saint Clément de Rome à saint Irénée* (Paris 1945)
64–67. Irenaeus, however, uses the phrase from which that adjective
was derived: *kath' holēs tēs oikoumenēs* ("throughout the whole
world"). See also 1.10.2, 3. See also 1.10.2, he describes more in detail
how "universal" the Church is geographically. Often St. Irenaeus
speaks of the whole Church throughout the world, or of the Church
in many nations: cf. 2.9.1; 2.31.2; 3.3.1; 3.11.8; 3.15.1; 4.33.8, 9; 4.36.2; 5 Prf.;
5.20.1; *Proof* 98. He knows of the Church as catholic in territory
(1.10.1–3) and in time (4.8.1; 4.36.2; 5.34.1).

3. Cf. Exod. 20.11; Ps. 145 (146).6; Acts 4.24; 14.5.

4. Cf. John 1.14. These two statements are a direct rejection of the
two main tenets of Gnosticism. There is only one God who is supreme and who is also Creator of all things; there is only one Son of
God, the Only-begotten, the Word, Jesus Christ. This Son did not
become man in appearance only, but in reality. He assumed flesh, and
so all flesh is capable of salvation.

5. H.-J. Jaschke investigates the third article of the Creed as it

appears in A.H. 4.33.7; 4.33.15; 5.20.1; *Proof* 6, as well as in this chapter. After he has analyzed it in other nearly contemporary writings which witness to the tradition, he studies what Irenaeus taught about the Holy Spirit. See H.-J. Jaschke, *Der heilige Geist im Bekentniss der Kirche: Eine Studie zur Pneumatologie der Irenäus von Lyon im Ausgang von altchristlichen Glaubensbekentniss* (Münster 1976) passim.

6. "Economies," namely, the Economy of the Old and the New Testaments. For more on this see SC 263.223–24 (SC 264. 155 n. 1). Our translation "coming" follows *tēn eleusin*, which Massuet (MG 7.550 n. 4) had felt was the correct reading here and which Rousseau and Doutreleau (SC 264.155) chose as well. Harvey (1.90 n. 3) had preferred *tas eleuseis* ("comings") because he reasoned that Irenaeus was referring to both of Christ's comings (at the Incarnation and the end of the world) as they were foretold by the Prophets (A.H. 4.34.1–3).

7. Cf. Luke 9.51.

8. Cf. Eph. 1.6. Although E. Lanne, "Le nom de Jésus-Christ et son invocation chez saint Irénée de Lyon," *Irénikon* 48 (1975) 454, feels that Irenaeus makes an allusion to 1 Pet. 1.8 here with *tou ēgapēmenou*. Rousseau (SC 263.224–25 [SC 264.157 n. 1]) believes that Irenaeus's allusion is to Eph. 1.6.

9. Here again Irenaeus rejects Docetism of the Incarnation and of the Redemption. The Word really took flesh from Mary, and so Christ is truly God and Man. He really suffered and rose again and ascended into heaven, to God who is the only true Fullness.

10. Matt. 16.27.

11. Eph. 1.10. The word *anakephalaiōsis* expressed a capital idea in Irenaean theology. It is used so often and is so characteristic that, at the risk of seeming archaic, we retain the one word "recapitulate" (for the noun, "recapitulation"), in order not to lose the force of the one Greek word and Irenaeus's argumentation based on it. It must convey the idea of being brought to a head as a unifying principle and of somehow resuming all things. This process of recapitulation of all things begins with the Incarnation and will be completed with the glorification of the body, yet because the Word preexisted creation and was in the planning, and was operative from creation on, the Incarnate Word recapitulates all things. He summarizes in Himself all creation and unites all people and angels too to Himself as under one Head, and in so doing He duplicates, or resumes, the acts of Adam

either by similarity or by opposition. For a fuller treatment and a bibliography see D. J. Unger, "Christ's Rôle in the Universe according to St. Irenaeus," *Franciscan Studies* 5 (1945) 128–34.

12. "All flesh," with the implication that the "spiritual" Gnostics will not be the only ones who will rise.

13. Cf. Col. 1.15.

14. Cf. Eph. 1.9.

15. Phil. 2.10–11. Irenaeus likes to emphasize the glory that came to Christ, the God Man, through the resurrection and ascension.

16. Cf. Rom. 2.5.

17. Cf. Matt. 18.8; 25.41.

18. Cf. Eph. 6.12. The various names for wicked men that follow were obviously added for the benefit of the Gnostics.

19. Cf. Titus 1.8.

20. Cf. John 14.15.

21. Cf. John 15.10.

22. Cf. John 15.27.

23. Cf. 2 Tim. 2.10; 1 Pet. 5.10. This is against the base and abominably immoral principle of the Gnostics that good works are not necessary for salvation, that sin is even a necessity, that those who are saved are saved merely because they have the spiritual "seed" and "knowledge." "Bestow on them as a gift of grace" is an attempt to catch the full meaning of the gratuity of the gift contained in the double *kharisamenos . . . dōrēsētai* (also in the Latin *donans . . . loco muneris conferat*). However, since the idea of penance precedes, it is not impossible that the first verb (*donans*) means "having forgiven," a meaning both the Greek and Latin can have, or at least this connotation can be present.

24. Cf. Acts 4.32.

25. An Armenian translation of Timothy Aelurus's *Refutation of the Doctrine Defined at the Council of Chalcedon* contains an Irenaean excerpt that begins at A.H. 1.10.1 and ends at this point. For more on this Armenian fragment designated by Rousseau and Doutreleau as Fr. arm. 4 bis see SC 263.105–6. We have here a wonderfully simple expression of the Catholic unity in the Church, and that in a beautifully balanced construction. St. Irenaeus does not treat of the Mystical Body *ex professo*, but the idea of the Church as a Mystical Body was in his blood. About this he wrote beautiful passages every once in a while. The doctrine on "recapitulation" is his expression of the mar-

velous unity between Christ and the Church. See E. Mersch, *The Whole Christ: The Historical Development of the Doctrine of the Mystical Body in Scripture and Tradition,* trans. J. R. Kelly (Milwaukee, 1938) 227–43.

26. *Dunamis* could have a stronger meaning than "meaning" in this passage, including also the fact that tradition is something "dynamic." Rousseau (SC 263.225 [SC 264.159 n. 1]) notes that, in opposition to the words *dialektoi anomoiai,* which call to mind the diversity of vocabularies and languages that translate the faith, the words *dunamis . . . mia kai hē autē* express the unique and identical content of meaning that exists under this diversity of languages and expressions.

27. They do not hand down anything else than the universal Church does. For Catholicity see n. 2. Lat. Iren. used the singular for "Germany," which is also found in Caesar. The Greek has the plural, which is found in Tacitus, *Ann.* 2.73, and Tertullian, *Adv. Iud.* 7 (CCL 2.1354–55). The plural refers to the entire Germany made up of various sections. See R. Kereszty, "The Unity of the Church in the Theology of Irenaeus," SCent 4, no. 4 (1984) 207, where he notes that Irenaeus uses *themelioō* when he refers to the establishment of a church by an apostle. He further notes that Irenaeus, however, uses *hidruō* (as in this case) when he discusses the founding of churches in general.

28. "The Light" is added from the Latin, since it was missing in the Greek MSS. Holl (GCS 25.432) added it in his critical edition of Epiphanius, but he thought that an adjective like *noēton* (intellectual) dropped out already before the Latin translation was made. Hardly, because light was used for mind and no such adjective was necessary. Massuet (MG 7.554 n. 5) and Harvey (1.94 n. 5) thought that light was a marginal note that crept into the text. Of course, the clause would have the same meaning without "light," because if "preaching the Truth shines and enlightens," it is functioning as light. This sentence is a kind of mosaic of ideas and words from John 1.5, 9; 1 Tim. 2.4. "Light" shining is in John 1.5, 9 (with "shines" in v. 5 and "enlightens" in v. 9). Irenaeus joins both verbs here. In John 1.9 the light is designated as "true"; that becomes "preaching of the Truth." John 1.9 speaks of the Word enlightening "every man," but 1 Tim. 2.4 has the plural: "all people" come to the knowledge of truth. Irenaeus may have chosen the plural from 1 Tim. to stress against the Gnostics that

all men and women have a chance to be saved, not merely a few chosen souls. Note the parallel and difference in the last phrase of Irenaeus and 1 Tim. Irenaeus has "enlightens all people who wished to come to the knowledge of the Truth"; but Paul has "He [God] wishes all people to be saved and come to the knowledge of truth."

29. Cf. Matt. 10.24; Luke 6.40. In this last part Irenaeus borrowed the phrases from 2 Cor. 8.15 and/or Exod. 16.18 (LXX). Paul was speaking of collections. Harvey (1.94 n. 2) incorrectly observes that this paragraph is against any theory of development of doctrine in Irenaeus. But one must interpret the statements of the bishop in the light of his own practice. He opposed any development that was against the revealed truth; he was not against development that was in keeping with revealed truth. He himself developed doctrines, for instance, that of recapitulation of all things in Christ and the New Eve doctrine about Mary. See Introduction, par. 3.

30. See SC 263.225–26 (SC 264.161 n. 1) for Rousseau's remarks about how Irenaeus had applied the analogy of the manna to the Christian Creed and their observation that this passage hits head-on the whole of Gnostic ideology where faith is only as a last resource, totally appropriate for those who cannot raise themselves up to "gnosis."

31. See on this chapter W. C. van Unnik, "An Interesting Document of Second Century Theological Discussion (Irenaeus, Adv. haer. 1.10.3)," VC 31 (1977) 196–228. Van Unnik suggests on p. 203 an alternate translation for this phrase: "The fact that some people know more or less by insight."

32. Codex Vaticanus gr. 503 and Codex Marcianus 125 have "of the faith" and this is accepted as correct by Massuet (MG 7.555 n. 3) and Harvey (1.95 n. 4). But it seems "of the Truth" according to the Latin is correct in the context. The Greek scribe copied it incorrectly. Rousseau and Doutreleau (SC 264.162) agree with this and change the reading of the Greek to *alētheias*. Rousseau believes (SC 263.226–27 [SC 264.163 n. 1]) that there is a parallel passage in A.H. 2.25.1 that enables them to make this change.

33. Gk. Epiph. has *pragmateian kai tēn oikonomian*. The Latin is *instrumentum et dispositionem*. Normally the Latin translator used *dispositio* for *oikonomia*. Though sometimes he used *dispositio* for *pragmateia*, in this case we think it matches *oikonomia*, since each is the

second noun. But how does *instrumentum* fit *pragmateia?* Harvey
(1.95 n. 5) thinks it does not; and he would match *dispositio* with *prag-mateia*, and then correct *oikonomian* to *oikodomian*, which would be
translated by *instrumentum*. True, *instrumentum*, like its Greek origi-
nal, can mean to build up. In A.H. 3.3.3 *instruentes* translates *oiko-
domēsantes*. But such an inversion does not seem likely. Rather, *instrumentum* translates *pragmateia*, which are God's dealings.
Instrumentum is used in A.H. 4.35.1 in "as if He did not have His own
means" for announcing without adulteration what is in the Fullness.
So God used *instrumenta* for His dealings with humans, and the *instrumenta* could have stood for the dealings themselves, as in Greek.
Rousseau (SC 263.227 [SC 264.163 n. 2]) argues, on the other hand, that
pragmateia and *oikonomia* constitute a hendiadys designating the work
of salvation performed by God to aid all men and women. See the
following studies which discuss theologizing by Irenaeus in this
chapter and elsewhere in A.H.: R. Kereszty, "The Unity of the
Church in the Theology of Irenaeus," SCent 4, no. 4 (1984) 206;
W. R. Schoedel, "Theological Method in Irenaeus," JThS, n. s., 35
(1984) 31–49. Schoedel's arguments are summarized by M. A. Donovan, "Irenaeus in Recent Scholarship," SCent 4, no. 4 (1984) 223–26,
who also mentions the following studies on theological questions
posed by Irenaeus in A.H. 1.10.3.: A. Harnack, *Lehrbuch der Dogmengeschichte* 1 (Tübingen 1909) 565; A. Bengsch, *Heilsgeschichte und
Heilswissen: Eine Untersuchung zur Struktur und Entfaltung des theologischen Denkens im Werk "Adversus haereses" des hl. Irenäus von Lyon*
(Leipzig 1957) 51–55; A. Houssiau, *La christologie de saint Irénée* (Louvain 1955) 100.

34. Many of the Fathers thought, erroneously, that the "sons of
God" in Gen. 6.2 were bad angels. On this subject see G. E. Closen,
Die Sünden der Söhne Gottes (Rome 1937) passim. Since Irenaeus
speaks of God's long-suffering with them, he holds that opinion here,
as he certainly does in A.H. 4.16.2; 4.36.4; *Proof* 18.

35. An Armenian fragment from the Galata 54 MS begins here and
ends at "appeared at the end." For more on this fragment designated
by Rousseau and Doutreleau as Fr. arm. 5 see SC 263.101–5.

36. Cf. Rom. 11.32.

37. Harvey (1.96 n. 2), because "It is so difficult to make a satisfac-

tory sense with this word," wants to change *eukharistein* to *paristan* ("show"). However, that change is not necessary. The Latin, too, has *gratias agere*. *Gratia* may mean an acknowledgement; so we could translate the Latin "acknowledge with gratitude," which is also the meaning of the Greek. Massuet (MG 7.556 n. 15) suggests a similar translation, "embrace with grateful mind" or "recall." Perhaps there is an allusion to the Eucharist as a memorial. Van Unnik, "An Interesting Document" 211, has proposed that the correct reading must have been *(an)euriskein* ("to find out"). Van Unnik believes that this is in line with the rest of the phrase and not very far from the transmitted text. But Rousseau (SC 263.227–28 [SC 264.165 n. 1]) argues that Irenaeus discusses here an action which one performs to thank God because God has given His Son as Savior and Redeemer. He also thinks that Irenaeus may mean indeed the Eucharist itself here and compares this text to A.H. 4.33.7–8.

38. John 1.14.

39. See the rationale presented by Rousseau (SC 263.228–29 [SC 264.165 n. 2]) as to why he prefers the Greek reading here over the Latin.

40. Cf. Eph. 2.12.

41. Eph. 3.6. Cf. Eph. 2.19.

42. Cf. 1 Cor. 15.53, 54.

43. Hos. 2.23; Rom. 9.25.

44. Cf. Isa. 54.1; Gal. 4.27.

45. Rom. 11.33.

46. For knowledge here, see remarks by Rousseau (SC 263.229 [SC 264.167 n. 1]) who argues that *suneseōs* here forms an inclusion with *sunesin* at the beginning of 1.10.3, which is devoted to the exploration of what constitutes true knowledge of God. He also notes that the Lat. Iren. has *sententia* which could well be a corruption of *scientia*.

CHAPTER II

1. Irenaeus gave an exposé of the Ptolemaean Valentinianism in the first nine chapters. In chap. 10 he penned a neat summary of the

Catholic Rule of Truth. Now he returns to an exposé of the various Gnostic systems in particular. First he will treat Valentinus's system. Valentinus, the celebrated leader of the school of Gnosticism that bears his name, was perhaps the most influential of all the Gnostics. In him Gnosticism reached a peak. He was born in lower Egypt (the date is unknown) and studied at Alexandria. He learned Platonic philosophy and became acquainted with all the ancient Egyptian doctrines. See also C. Gianotto, "Valentino gnostico," DPAC 2.3542–44. According to Tertullian, *Adv. Val.* 4.1 (CCL 2.755), he was a convert to Christianity, but turned heretic when his ambition to be a bishop was frustrated. He was acquainted with earlier Gnosticism and knew Basilides' system in particular. After teaching at Alexandria for a while, he went to Rome while Hyginus was Pope (ca. A.D. 137–40). He lived there for a long time and made many disciples. Irenaeus, A.H. 3.4.3, says that he remained in Rome till the reign of Anicetus (ca. A.D. 154–66). Some claim that Irenaeus implies that Valentinus died in Rome; see Holl, GCS 25.396. However, that is not a necessary conclusion. In fact, Epiphanius, *Haer.* 31.7 (GCS 25.396), writes that Valentinus went to Cyprus and was active there spreading his errors. There he died. The Bishop of Lyons informs us that Valentinus had written many works (A.H. 3.11.9). Of these only a few fragments have reached us. Seven are preserved by Clement of Alexandria and one by Hippolytus (cf. Sagnard *Gnose* 121–26). He composed a commentary on St. John's Gospel, of which fragments are extant in Origen. Irenaeus says that he used John's Gospel very much (A.H. 3.11.7), but only to distort it, as well as the other Scriptures (cf. A.H. 3.12.12), and Tertullian, *Praescr.* 38.10 (CCL 1.219). Descriptions of this heresiarch's doctrines are meagre. Irenaeus has only the present short account. Hippolytus proposed to speak of it but after saying that it is basically Pythagorean and Platonic, he wrote about the Ptolemaean brand of Valentinus's school (*Haer.* 6.21–29 [GCS 26.148–56]). It may be that he confused the doctrine of the master and of his disciple Ptolemaeus into one system and added his own philosophizing. So Valentinus's teachings must be culled by comparison with his disciples. But they formed two schools, the earlier and the later, which some scholars have less correctly called the Oriental and the Italian. His doctrine was basically arithmetical; see Hippolytus, *Haer.* 6.24 (GCS 26.150–51). As to his sources, there are two schools of thought. One stresses his borrowing from the philosophers; the other, his use of mythological materials from Oriental religions. There were, of course, also Christian elements, which were distorted. Cf. Sagnard *Gnose* 575–609. For a long while it was commonly held that Valentinus set up one system of thought while teaching at Alexandria, and when he moved to Rome he taught a somewhat different system. The Eastern system is what Hippolytus is thought to describe. Theodotus is a later exponent of that system, which is described by Clement of Alexandria in *Exc. Thdot.* The system that he taught at Rome was later developed by his disciples Ptolemaeus and Heracleon. This is the system that Irenaeus describes in A.H. 1.1–8. Thus there would have been almost two contemporary systems of Valentinianism. Sagnard (Sagnard *Gnose* 7, 208–20) notes that De Faye in *Gnostique et gnosticisme* even tried to prove that the two systems were contradictory, and that Irenaeus 1.1–8 is mostly a work of a third generation Gnostic, with only slight traces of influence from Ptolemaeus and Heracleon, whose system was much simpler. Sagnard also writes that P. Hendrix, *De Alexandrijnsche Haeresiarch Basilides: Een bijdrage tot de geschiedenis der gnosis* (Amsterdam 1926) passim, proved quite conclusively that this contradiction is a chimera. G. Quispel, "The Original Doctrine of Valentine," VC 1 (1947) 43–73, has tried to reestablish the system of Valentinus as follows. He assumed that there must have been very few occasions of exchange of ideas between the Valentinians of the East and those of the West. Furthermore, Irenaeus and Clement have their information from a common source that describes events outside the *plērōma*. Hippolytus, he said, gives us the later Italic development. A similar solution was given earlier by W. Foerster, *Von Valentin zu Herakleon: Untersuchungen über die Quellen und Entwicklung der valentinianischen Gnosis* (Giessen 1928) 100–101. This was a step in the right direction, but it seems the principle used has a loophole. What is common to both is no doubt Valentinus's doctrine. But when the matter is not common, one of the two may have at least at times retained the master's doctrine, and only the other would have departed from it. Already O. Dibelius, "Studien zur Geschichte der Valentinianer," ZNTW 9 (1908) 230–47, held that the fact that there is so much in common in Irenaeus A.H. 1.1–8 and in the *Exc. Thdot.* 43–65 shows that they had a common source, which, however, he claimed was not the work of the heresiarch. F. Wisse has argued that Irenaeus had borrowed material from an already existing catalog of heresies for this and the next chapter of A.H. 1. See F. Wisse, "The Nag Hammadi Library and the Heresiologists," VC 25 (1971) 205–23. P. Perkins, however, takes issue with Wisse and argues that A.H. 1.11–12 are rightly ascribed to Irenaeus. See P. Perkins, "Irenaeus and the Gnostics: Rhetoric and Composition in *Adversus haereses* Book One," VC 30 (1976) 193–200. In his work on Valentinian Gnosticism, Sagnard (Sagnard *Gnose* 224–27), who followed up the work of Foerester, but improved on him by using more documents, tried to show that there was no Eastern and Western Valentinianism, but an earlier and a later development. A comparison of the various documents shows that there are only accidental differences. Hippolytus's account is substantially the same as that given by Irenaeus in 1.1–8, which is the Ptolemaean school. Hippolytus, though he pretends to speak of Valentinus's system, seems to have had no more information on it that Irenaeus 1.11.1, which he puffed up with material from Ptolemaeus's system in 1.1–8, and expanded it still more by relating it to the ancient philosophers. So Hippolytus is not so reliable as Irenaeus. Clement, *Exc. Thdot.* 29–68, and several other paragraphs agree very closely with Irenaeus 1.1–8 (Sagnard *Gnose* 220–32). Again, the Letter of Ptolemaeus to Flora (cf. Epiphanius, *Haer.* 33.3–7 [GCS 25.450–57]), agrees in terms and ideas with what these two heresiologists related. See Sagnard *Gnose* 452–79, and G. Quispel, "La lettre de Ptolémée à Flora," VC 2 (1948) 17–56. Lastly, the fragments of Heracleon that we possess are quite similar in doctrine to Irenaeus A.H. 1.1–8 and to the Letter of Ptolemaeus to Flora (cf. Sagnard *Gnose* 480–520). So, since these men all describe substantially the same system, it is the same system that developed with accidental changes from Valentinus to Theodotus to Heracleon. We should, therefore, not speak of an Eastern and a Western, but of an earlier and a later Valentinianism. A. J. Visser, "Der Lehrbrief der Valentinianer," VC 12 (1958) 27–36, has advanced the opinion that in Egypt there were at first various groups of popular Gnosticism in a complex form. Valentinus by his strong personality branched off from that popular Gnosticism, which however returned again later. The doctrinal letter "from a Valentinian book" spoken of in Epiphanius, *Haer.* 31.5–6 (GCS 25.390–95), is said to be a witness of that popular Gnosticism, as also the many documents from the Cheonoboskion discovery. For a summary of Valentinianism see G. Bareille, "Gnosticisme," DTC 6.1447–53; Quasten 1.260–61. For parallels to this section see Hippolytus, *Haer.* 6.21; 10.13 (GCS 26.148–49, 273–74); Tertullian, *Adv. Val.* 1–39 (CCL 2.753–78); Ps.-Tertullian, *Haer.* 4 (CCL 2.1406–7); Filaster, *Diversarum haereseon liber* (hereinafter *Haer.*) 38 (CCL 9.234–35). Irenaeus called Valentinus "foremost" (*prōtos*) in relation to the two or three referred to. There is no need to correct this adjective to an adverb (e.g., "first of all"), as Holl (GCS 25.434) does.

2. We base the translation on the Greek text as emended by Rousseau and Doutreleau in SC 264.167. See SC 263.230 (SC 264.167 n. 3) for Rousseau's reasoning behind the emendation.

3. Gk. Epiph. has *tas arkhas eis idion kharaktēra didaskaleiou*, which can be translated thus: "(having applied) the principles of the so-called Gnostic heresy to the peculiar character of his own school." The MSS of Lat. Iren. are unanimous in support of this: *antiquas in suum characterem doctrinas transferens:* "he transferred the ancient doctrines to his own system." There is a similar clause in regard to Tatian in 1.28.1: *idion kharaktēra didaskaleiou sunestēsato:* "he set up his own system of doctrine." Here too the Latin has *proprium characterem doctrinae constituit.* Again, in the two following cases the Greek is not extant, but the Latin has *doctrina* (not school). In 1.24.7: *Illorum enim theoremata accipientes, in suum characterem doctrinae transtulerunt.* This is very close to our passage in construction, namely, theorems or principles were transferred to fit his own system of doctrine. In 2.31.1: . . . *ea quae sunt extra ueritatem transferentes ad characterem suae doctrinae.* In the first two cases in Greek and in the Latin three cases in Latin, *kharaktēra* or *characterem* governs a genitive (*didaskaleiou* or *doctrinae*). It would seem certain then that in the first case *doctrinas* is a scribe's error for *doctrinae,* a genitive as in Greek. But then *antiquas* must be wrong too. It can however not be genitive, modifying *doctrinae,* because that would make no sense. It must be accusative but changed to *principia,* according to the Greek *tas arkhas,* which the Latin translator misread as *arkhaias.* As we saw in 1.24.7 there is a parallel to this where *theoremata* (here *principia*) were adapted to his own system. Thus, should the word *doctrinae* be "doctrine" or "school"? In all four cases noted above the Latin has *doctrina,* but in two cases where the Greek is extant it is *didaskaleion.* An easy solution is that the word *didas-*

kaleion is used here for doctrine, as it may be: see Lampe, PGL, s.v.
"*didaskaleion.*" Also in Iren. 1.27.2, as Lampe notes in PGL, *didaskaleion* cannot mean school. Marcion could only have amplified
Cerdo's doctrine, not the school. Further, it is worth noting that Lat.
Iren. knew of *schools* of heretics, for which he uses *scolae:* 1 Prf. 2;
1.30.15. The Greek is extant only in the last case, where it is *skholēs.*
Even in 1.28.1 "school" does not fit well: he does not really establish
his own system of school, but of doctrine.

4. This Father is Mind, because he is the consort of Truth. He is
not Profundity, who was also called Father as well as First-Father. See
Hippolytus, *Haer.* 6.29 (GCS 26.156).

5. "Become degenerate" is *husterēsasan* from *husterein*, which
means to be defective, to deteriorate, to degenerate. *Husterēma* is
the act of becoming or the state of being degenerate. And because this
Aeon became defective and degenerate she is often called Degeneracy.
It was difficult to chose from the various possible translations of
husterēma. In our present passage Lat. Iren. has *destitutam.* In 1.4.1
Irenaeus spoke of a *heteroiōsis* (*demutatio*) of this Aeon, and in 1.2.2 he
says the Aeon was estranged or changed (*paratrapenta*). So the idea is
that this Aeon changed, and that, for the worse; her act was a defection. However, since the defection was one who had been emitted by
generation, it seemed that Degeneracy would be the most fitting English name for her. This Degeneracy was Wisdom. Whether in the
original teaching of Valentinus there was only one Sophia or two is
disputed. G. C. Stead, "The Valentinian Myth of Sophia," JThS, n. s.,
20 (1969) 75–104, opts for one original Sophia, in the Fullness. This
gradually developed into an Upper and a Lower Sophia.

6. "Affairs" is *pragmateian;* in English the plural fits better. All
things that happened outside the Fullness, especially the formation of
Demiurge and through him the creation of the world, were ultimately
the result of Wisdom's straying from the Fullness.

7. Codex Vaticanus gr. 503 and Codex Marcianus 125 read *gnōmēn*
(knowledge). So Harvey (1.100, 100 n. 2) and Massuet (MG 7.561). We
follow, however, Holl (GCS 25.434), as well as Rousseau and Doutreleau (SC 264.169), who read *mnēnēn* here. Wisdom's memory is of
the things she experienced in the Fullness before she apostatized.
Massuet (MG 7.562 n. 5) followed the Greek of Codex Vaticanus and

the Codex Marcianus but admitted the sense was the same. "Shadow," because of the sorrow or because of the obscurity that set in through her separation.

8. Irenaeus uses *Gnōstikois* here to designate a well-defined group of heretics. On this see SC 263.230–31 (SC 264.171 n. 1) and SC 263.299–300 (SC 264.359 n. 1). So the epithet was not first used in the eighteenth century by Church historians. Cf. N. Brox, "*Gnōstikoi* als häresiologischer Terminus," ZNTW 57 (1966) 105–14.

9. The Greek has *phuta* (plants), which seems the better reading; the Latin has *folia* (leaves) supposing *phulla*. Neither word occurs elsewhere in Irenaeus. Note in 1.30.15 *multiplex capitibus fera [de] Valentini scola generata est*, which is merely a change of figure from plant life to wild animal life. Note also 1 Prf. 2, where he calls the Ptolemaean Gnosticism a *flosculum* of the Valentinian (*apanthisma*). The very last sentence of this paragraph is not in Gk. Epiph., possibly because it did not serve his purpose of excerpting. Rousseau and Doutreleau (SC 264.171) restore conjecturally *tauta men ekeinos.* Rousseau (SC 263.231 [SC 264.171 n. 3]) justifies the conjecture as being in accordance with the Latin which he believes is authentically Irenaean.

10. This paragraph is preserved by Epiphanius, *Haer.* 32.1.5–6 (GCS 25.439). But Hippolytus's account (*Haer.* 6.38 [GCS 26.168]) is more literally like the Latin of Irenaeus. Epiphanius may have condensed Irenaeus's thought here. Rousseau and Doutreleau discuss the Greek fragment (Fragment 2) in SC 263.85–86. Tertullian gives us the same information in *Adv. Val.* 38 (CCL 2.778). See also Theodoret, *Haer.* 1.8 (MG 83.358D); Filaster, *Haer.* 40 (CCL 9.234f.); Ps.-Tertullian, *Haer.* 4.7 (CCL 2.1407), notes that Secundus and Ptolemaeus agree with Valentinus except that they added eight more Aeons and, as also Irenaeus states, the apostate Wisdom was not part of the original Triacontad.

11. Epiphanius used this paragraph in *Haer.* 32.5 (GCS 25.445), Hippolytus made use of it in *Haer.* 6.38 (GCS 26.168–69), and Tertullian used it in *Adv. Val.* 37 (CCL 2.777–78). For Rousseau's and Doutreleau's discussion on the Greek fragment (Fragment 3) see SC 283.86. Who was this renowned teacher? The Alexandrian Gnostic Carpocrates (see below 1.25.1–6) had a son Epiphanes, who learned the

sciences and Platonic philosophy from his father, and wrote a very immoral treatise called *On Justice* (cf. Clement of Alexandria, *Str.* 3.2.5.3 [GCS 52{15} 197]). He is said to have died at the early age of seventeen, after having astonished the world with his precocious mind and immoral conduct. After his death Cephalonia, the native island of his mother, built a temple to his honor and offered divine cult, chanting hymns to him and offering sacrifices at new-moon festivities. According to Clement, *Str.* 3.2.5.2–3 (GCS 52[15].197), he was the originator of monadic Gnosticism. That information would fit in with what Irenaeus tells us here about this renowned teacher. However, it seems that Clement's only source was Irenaeus, and he mistook the Greek "renowned" as the proper name of the teacher. That it should, however, be an adjective, modifying teacher, seems certain from the Latin *clarus*, and from Tertullian's *insignioris . . . magistri*. Epiphanius also adds Epiphanes and identifies this person with the son of Carpocrates. For more on this see SC 263.232 (SC 264.173 n. 2). In Hippolytus, too, "renowned" most likely should modify "teacher." The identity of this renowned teacher would then not be known. A. Neander, *Genetische Entwickelung der vornehmsten gnostischen Systeme* (Berlin 1818) 356, thought it was Marcus. But more probably, as Harvey (1.102–3 n. 2) thought, it was Colorbasus, who is mentioned in 1.14.1. Irenaeus says this renowned teacher is among those who are "more perfect than the perfect," and "who have more knowledge than those who have the 'knowledge' " (1.11.5). In our paragraph he is said to be extending himself toward a greater height and more profound knowledge. Now, Hippolytus classes Colorbasus among the "prescient" (*prognōstikous*), who also did much trifling with numbers (*Haer.* 4.13 [GCS 26.45]). See also *Haer.* 4.14, 43 [GCS 26.45–48, 64–66]). Ps.-Tertullian mentions him as a fellow heretic of Marcus, holding the same nonsense about numbers as he (*Haer.* 5 [CCL 2.1407–8]). His name, variously spelled as Colarbasus, Colorbasus, Kolarbasos, or Kolorbasos, baffles scholars. Its meaning is equally baffling. Cf. G. Bareille, "Colorbasus," DTC 3.1.378. He was an Egyptian by birth but also lived in Rome, and there he became the originator of the "Western" Valentinianism. More is not known about him. However, Rudolph *Gnosis* 324, 388 n. 148, states that Kolarbasos (or Kolorbasos) is fictitious. The name is actually derived from the Hebrew name of the "tetrad" (*kol-'arba'* "all is four") which Marcus placed before the thirty Aeons. Cf. Quasten *Patr.* 1.267–68 on Epiphanes.

12. "A First-unthinkable." We follow Gk. Epiph., with which the Lat. Iren. agrees. The word occurs again below in par. 4. But Hippolytus has "a certain unthinkable First-Beginning, who is both. . . ." Tertullian, *Adv. Val.* 37.1 (CCL 2.778), has *inexcogitable*, which agrees with Hippolytus.

13. "Without bringing forth." As object of "bringing forth" the Latin has "nothing," which supposes *mēden*. But Gk. Epiph. has the simple *mē* ("not"), which agrees with Tertullian's *protulerunt non proferentes* (*Adv. Val.* 37.2 [CCL 2.778]). Massuet (MG 7.586 n. 11) and Harvey (1.104 n. 1) accept the simple negative. This is confirmed too by 1.11.4, where the Latin has *emiserunt, cum non emisissent.* The Greek is not extant here, but Irenaeus's ironical parallel supposes the same Greek construction as in our present passage. We follow the Greek. Neander, *Genetische Entwickelung* 169, explains Oneness and Unity begot Beginning, but in such wise that Beginning was eternally inseparable from Unity. See also Harvey 1.104 n. 1.

14. The simpler Latin seemed more correct than the Greek of Codex Vaticanus gr. 503 and Codex Marcianus 125 which inserted "made by those who wrote such ridiculous things for such a nomenclature. . . ." Rousseau and Doutreleau agree with this assessment in their remarks on this fragment (Fragment 4) in SC 263.86–87.

15. Epiphanius gives us merely an abstract of the rest of this paragraph in *Haer.* 33.1.1 (GCS 25.448).

16. See Rousseau's remarks (SC 263.232–33 [SC 264.177 n. 1]) concerning how their reconstructed Greek text is based partially on the Latin translation and partially on the citation from Epiphanius and, as is often the case, how the Latin and Greek both complement and correct each other here.

17. "First-nonsubstantial" is *proanypostatos* in Latin. No Greek is extant here, but that Latin is obviously a transliteration. Klebba (Klebba BKV 3.37) translated it "*vorunpersönliche*." It was called such because it existed *before* every other substance; and it was "non-substantial" because the Gnostics considered the deity before the creation of material substance as not having substance, as nothing. Cf. n.

24, n. 3 to chap. 1, n. 9 to chap. 24. "First-ever-forward-rolling" is *proprocylindomene,* which is again a mere transliteration. Klebba (Klebba BKV 3.37) translated this as *"vorwärtsfortrollende."* Prokulindesthai means to roll forward. Massuet (MG 7.567) would drop the first *pro,* but that seems necessary: the simple *procylindomeme* expresses the forward-rolling action. The *pro* added to it, moreover, in the style of Irenaeus with other such words, indicates that this is the *first,* in the long line of an indefinite number of future emissions. Rousseau (SC 263.233–34 [SC 264.177 n. 2]) points out the rhetorical effect of *proprocylindomene,* which Irenaeus uses here to ridicule the Gnostic position.

18. The Latin *potestatis* supposes *ousios.* The Greek is not extant, but it seems that it should be *homoousios* (of the same substance), which was misread by Lat. Iren. as *exousias* (of power). See also the remarks by Rousseau on this at SC 263.234 (SC 264.177 n. 4).

19. Cf. Num. 11.5.

20. Rousseau and Doutreleau (SC 264.176) see in *utique* (C V) and *ut* (A Q S) a corruption of the infinitive *uti,* which is a correction they also make to the Latin text.

21. Cf. Epiphanius, *Haer.* 32.7 (GCS 25.446–47), and Hippolytus, *Haer.* 6.38 (GCS 26.169). Tertullian follows Irenaeus rather closely in *Adv. Val.* 35 (CCL 2.777). Rousseau and Doutreleau discuss this Greek fragment (Fragment 5) at SC 263.87–88.

22. The Greek is *gnōstikōteroi.* Lat. Iren. rendered the Greek he read by *magis gnostici veri.* Harvey (1.107) would read *viri* for *veri.* But *veri* seems better, adding the object for the greater knowledge, namely, truth. Rousseau and Doutreleau, however, put square brackets around *veri* at SC 264.178. Irenaeus is obviously playing on the name of these heretics. In all the other systems Profundity was the first principle and prior to him there was nothing. In the system being described there was a Tetrad (four attributes: First-Beginning, Unthinkable, Unutterable, Invisible), which was considered to have existed prior to Profundity, and still somehow existed in him. From this first Tetrad there proceeded a second Tetrad (Beginning, Incomprehensible, Unnameable, Ingenerate). These, too, were coeval with Profundity.

23. Even among the pagans it was the accepted notion that the Supreme Being is without sex. Eusebius, *P.e.* 1.9.13–14 (GCS 43^i.37–38), remarks that the Greeks knew nothing of the nonsense of denominating masculine and feminine gods. Augustine too says: "The true God does not have sex or age" (*Civ.* 4.27 [CCL 47.121]). Hence, even the general run of Gnostics, whose entire system was one of reproduction by conjugal couples, did not ascribe sex to Profundity, as did these to whom Irenaeus is now referring.

24. For the Basilidians the Supreme Being was different before the creation of other beings than after. Before, he was simply "nothing," because "being" and "essence" were thought of as belonging only to material and active existence. Before the existence of other beings, he was an unthinkable and incomprehensible something, and so "nothing." Cf. n. 17, n. 13 to chap. 1, n. 9 to chap. 24. The Marcosians also spoke of the Supreme Being as without substance (*anousios*). For more on this see Harvey 1.108 n. 2 and A.H. 1.14.

CHAPTER 12

1. Epiphanius has preserved this number in *Haer.* 33.3–7 (GCS 25.448–49). The Greek seems to have been tampered with in the excerpting. Hippolytus agrees better with the Latin in *Haer.* 6.38 (GCS 26.168–70). Rousseau and Doutreleau discuss this Greek fragment (Fragment 6) in SC 263.88–89. Tertullian, *Adv. Val.* 33 (CCL 2.776–77) certainly had Irenaeus in mind. See also Tertullian, *Adv. Val.* 38 (CCL 2.778). Theodoret merely mentions Ptolemaeus in *Haer.* 1.8 (MG 83.358D). Ps.-Tertullian, *Haer.* 4 (CCL 2.1406–7), who does not distinguish between the doctrine of Secundus and Ptolemaeus; Filaster, *Haer.* 39, 43 (CCL 9.234, 235). For Ptolemaeus see n. 1 to chap. 1, and for his relation to Valentinus see n. 1 to chap. 11. On the expression *hoi peri ton Ptolemaion duo suzugous auton ekhein legousin* see SC 263.235–36 (SC 264.181 n. 1).

2. "Dispositions" is *dispositiones* in Lat. Iren. and *diatheseis* in the Greek text as edited by Rousseau and Doutreleau (SC 264.181). Mas-

suet (MG 7.570 n. 14) suggested that *affectiones* would have been a better translation; in fact *adfectibus* and *adfectuum* occur later in the paragraph. It is often difficult to distinguish the two words, though it seems *dispositio* (*diathesis*) was an active emotion, while *passio* was passively endured emotion.

3. Cf. Homer, *Il.* 2.1–4.

4. Lat. Iren. has *sensus*, supposing *nous*. We prefer that to "light" according to the Greek. Irenaeus has a similar sentence in three other places (2.13.3; 2.28.4; 4.11.2) with a variation in the number of terms and their order. B. Hemmerdinger, "Observations critiques sur Irénée, IV (*Sources Chrétiennes* 100) ou les mésaventures d'un philologue," JThS 17, n. s. (1966) 308, thinks that Irenaeus is using a passage from the Greek philosopher and poet Xenophanes. From his work *On Nature* this fragment is extant: *houlos horai, houlos de noei, houlos de t'akouei*. See H. Diels, *Die Fragmente der Vorsokratiker*, 8th ed. edited by W. Kranz, 1 (Berlin 1956 [1952]) 135. One notices two obvious differences. Xenophanes has verbs (sees), while Irenaeus has nouns (sight). Xenophanes has only three terms, while Irenaeus has a varying number in the several passages. Especially the final phrase ("the whole fountain of all good things"), which is in every one of the passages of Irenaeus, is missing in the fragment of Xenophanes, though Epiphanius has the Greek for it in *Haer.* 33.2.5 (GCS 25.450). So, while it seems possible that Irenaeus used Xenophanes, maybe through a secondary source, we think he is more likely using another more immediate source, which possibly is an adaptation of Xenophanes. See also the remarks by Rousseau on this in SC 263.237–38 (SC 264.185 n. 1) and SC 263.90 where Rousseau and Doutreleau discuss the last five lines of 1.12.2 in their discussion of Fragment 7.

5. Paragraphs 3–4 are in Epiphanius, *Haer.* 35.1 (GCS 31.39). See SC 263.90–91 for more on the Greek fragment (Fragment 8) here.

6. For Rousseau's resolution of the textual difficulties here see SC 263.238 (SC 264.185 n. 2).

7. See Tertullian, *Adv. Val.* 39 (CCL 2.778).

8. The last phrase is in the Latin version and Theodoret, *Haer.* 1.12 (MG 83.361). This is an evident corruption of the true doctrine that Christ Jesus exists for the glory of God the Father; see John 17.

9. See SC 263.238 (SC 264.187 n. 1) for information on the Latin and Greek text here.

10. Cf. Eph. 3.9; Col. 1.26.

CHAPTER 13

1. The text for chap. 13 is preserved by Epiphanius, *Haer.* 34.1–3 (GCS 31.5–10). Hippolytus, *Haer.* 6.39 (GCS 26.170–71), has a parallel; at times he is closer to the Latin than Epiphanius, but at times he too condenses. See also Ps.-Tertullian, *Haer.* 5 (CCL 2.1407–8); Theodoret, *Haer.* 1.9 (MG 83.359A–B); and Filaster, *Haer.* 42 (CCL 9.235). Doutreleau also cites Eusebius, *H.e.* 4.11.4 (GCS 9¹.322), as a source for this paragraph. For more on this Greek fragment (Fragment 9) see Rousseau's and Doutreleau's remarks at SC 263.91–92. Hippolytus teaches that Marcus as well as Colorbasus belonged to the Valentinian school. Cf. Hippolytus, *Haer.* 6.55.3 (GCS 26.189); still he deviated much from the Ptolemaean school. On Marcus and Colorbasus see also Rudolph *Gnosis* 324 and C. Gianotto, "Marco," DPAC 2.2099.

2. Rousseau (SC 263.240 [SC 264.189 n. 2]) considers this teacher to be Valentinus.

3. Harvey (1.114) brackets *et perfectissimum* for omission as neither Epiphanius nor Hippolytus has an equivalent expression. However, we follow Rousseau and Doutreleau (SC 264.190) who introduce *teleiotatōi* into the Greek influenced by the late Latin. For their reasons see SC 263.240 (SC 264.191 n. 1).

4. Grabe (cf. Harvey 1.115 n. 2) notes that Pliny refers to this Anaxilaus's recreations in magic.

5. That was a feigned consecration, a distortion of the true Eucharist; cf. n. 9 to chap. 3. See *econtra* Rudolph *Gnosis* 242. Gk. Epiph. has the plural; but the singular "cup mixed with wine" is according to the Latin and Tertullian. From the very beginning a little water was mixed with the wine in the true Eucharist. See A.H. 5.1.3, one element of the true Eucharist is the "mixture," and in 5.2.3 it "has been mixed." Justin, when speaking of the rite of the Eucharist, says that "bread and a cup of water and of mixture" were brought. See Justin, *1 Apol.* 65 (*Die ältesten Apologeten: Texte mit kurzen Einleitungen*, ed. E. J.

Goodspeed [Göttingen 1914] 74 [hereinafter referred to as Good-speed]). The extra cup of water was given to the newly baptized. See J. Quasten, *Monumenta eucharistica et liturgica vetustissima,* Florilegium patristicum, no. 7, pt. 1 (Bonn 1935) 16–17, n. 3. In *1 Apol.* 67.5 (Goodspeed 75), Justin describes a Sunday liturgy and says that wine and water were brought. Hippolytus (*Trad. ap.* 21 [SC 11bis.92]) omits mention of the wine, but that does not seem to be a valid argument, as Harvey (1.116 n. 4) thinks that Marcus, and later the followers of Tatian, used only water. At A.H. 1.13.2 begins the tenth Greek fragment as edited by Rousseau and Doutreleau which will continue to the end of 1.21.4. This is for the most part based on Epiphanius, but Rousseau and Doutreleau weave in relevant material from Hippolytus in 1.14–1.17. They also weave in material from Eusebius at 1.21.3. For more on this fragment see SC 263.92–95.

6. An epiclesis is an invocation. In the ancient liturgies the epiclesis was the prayer in which God was called upon to send down the Word or the Holy Spirit to effect the consecration of the bread and the wine and/or to make the Eucharistic Sacrifice and/or Communion fruitful for the faithful. The later epicleses are quite commonly of the Holy Spirit. See F. Cabrol, "Épiclèse," DACL 5.1.142–44, 177–78. The earlier epicleses seem to have been of the Word. Though denied by some scholars, it seems certain that Justin refers to such an epiclesis of the Word in *1 Apol. 66* (cf. Quasten, *Monumenta eucharistica,* 18, 18 n. 1). Irenaeus has the idea of an epiclesis of the Word in 5.2.3. In 4.18.5 he uses the term "epiclesis" for the invocation of God to change the bread and wine. On this see also SC 152.213 and D. van den Eynde, "Eucharistia ex duabus rebus constans: S. Irénée, *Adv. haereses,* IV, 18, 5," Antonianum 15 (1940) 26–27. In St. John of Damascus's Greek fragment of this passage the MSS have *ekklēsis,* but since Lat. Iren. has *inuocatio,* the original evidently had *epiklēsis.* See A. Harnack, "Die Pfaff'schen Irenäus-Fragmente als Fälschungen Pfaffs: Nachgewiesen," TU, n. s. 5.3 (Leipzig 1909) 56; Lampe, PGL, s.v. "*ekklēsis*"; and SC 100.69. In the present passage Irenaeus certainly refers to a mock imitation of the Eucharistic Sacrifice, and "the prayer of invocation" is the mock consecratory invocation. However, this might not refer to a particular prayer of invocation, but to the entire Eucharistic prayer or Canon. Cf. Cabrol, "Épiclèse," 142–44; S. Salaville, "Épiclèse," DTC 5.1.233; E. Lingens, "Die eucharistische Consecrations-

form: Ein dogmengeschichtlicher Überblick zur Epiklesenfrage," ZKT 21 (1897) 79–82. See also SC 263.240–41 (SC 264.191 n. 2).

7. Cf. Eph. 3.16.

8. Cf. Matt. 13.31, Mark 4.31. For more on this formula see Sagnard *Gnose* 416–17.

9. Hippolytus, *Haer.* 6.41 (GCS 26.172–73), gives the same information.

10. Cf. Matt. 18.10.

11. That "Greatness" is an angel is clear from 1.13.6, where Matt. 18.10 is applied to Greatness.

12. Rousseau (SC 263.242 [SC 264.195 n. 1]) notes that in late Greek the sense of *khōreō* is often "to give in oneself a place to" or "to receive in oneself."

13. For more on this formula see Sagnard *Gnose* 417–18 and J.-M. Sevrin, "Les noces spirituelles dans l'Évangile selon Philippe," Muséon 87 (1974) 144–51.

14. This is most likely Bishop Pothinus; cf. n. 12 to 1 Prf.

15. For more on this see SC 263.242 (SC 264.199 n. 1).

16. Grabe (cf. Harvey 1.120 n. 1) notes that Horace has a few lines that refer to this custom: *nec regna vini sortiere talis,* and . . . *quem Venus arbitrum/ dicet bibendi? (Carm.* 1.4.18; 2.7.25–26).

17. Jerome alludes to this passage in his *Epist.* 75.3 (CSEL 55.32).

18. The followers of Simon Magus (1.23.1) and of Carpocrates (1.25.1) indulged in the same practices.

19. Irenaeus indicates a vivid memory of his stay in Asia Minor and the close relation between the Churches of Asia and Gaul. From other sources we know that this is a fact. The Churches of Vienne and Lyons wrote their famous letter to the Churches in Asia Minor. For more on this letter see Quasten *Patr.* 1.180.

20. Cf. n. 18 to chap. 6.

21. St. Paul describes such errors in advance in 2 Tim. 3.6.

22. Grabe (cf. Harvey 1.123–24 n. 3) and others hold that this "redemption" of the Marcosians consisted merely in an imprecatory formula, similar to that of the Jews for their redemption from Egypt, called Geulah, which was offered up every morning and evening. However, Harvey (1.123–24 n. 3) rightly claims that it was a second baptism. Like the baptism of Jesus in the Jordan, their first baptism was material; it effected the remission of sins. Their second baptism

was like the descent of Christ upon Jesus in the form of a dove; it was spiritual and effected the redemption. See 1.21.1–5. Hippolytus, *Haer.* 6.42 (GCS 26.173), explicitly referring to Irenaeus, mentions this two-fold baptism.

23. See SC 263.243 (SC 264.203 n. 1) for the reasons for which we translate "through whom" here.

24. Cf. Matt. 18.10.

25. This Coadjutor is Wisdom.

26. Homer (*Il.* 5.844–45) sings of Pallas as putting on the helmet of Hades that the mighty Mars would not see her. On this see also SC 263.243 (SC 264.205 n. 1).

27. The angels accompanying Savior are the consorts of the Gnostics, whom Achamoth made according to their image. To them the Gnostics will be restored after death. Cf. 1.5.6 for the similar tenet of Ptolemaeus.

28. According to Jerome, *Epist.* 75.3 (CSEL 55.32) and *In Is.* 17.64 (ML 24.623), Marcus preached his heresy in the Rhone valley and later also in Spain. It has generally been accepted by scholars (cf. Sagnard *Gnose* 82–83, 358) that Marcus himself had been in the Rhone valley. But Irenaeus does not say so expressly; he says that Marcus's disciples were operative there (cf. 1.13.6–7). Because of that E. Griffe, "Le gnostique Markos est-il venu en Gaule?" BLE 54 (1953) 243–45, holds that the heresiarch himself did not visit the Rhone valley.

29. Cf. 1 Tim. 4.2.

30. Cf. n. 18 to chap. 6.

31. "Life of God" is a beautiful expression for the life of grace in the soul. This life is a sharing in God's own life; it is not merely a life given by God. That is all the more true of the sharing in God's life in glory, which Irenaeus seems to have more directly in mind here. Irenaeus may be alluding to Eph. 4.18, "estranged from the life of God."

CHAPTER 14

1. Epiphanius, *Haer.* 34.4.1–7 (GCS 31.10–11), is a parallel to this. Hippolytus, *Haer.* 6.42 (GCS 26.173–75), follows Irenaeus rather closely in this section. On these arithmetical adventures of Marcus, see Sagnard *Gnose* 358–86.

2. We have reconstructed the Greek according to Lat. Iren. Rousseau and Doutreleau have felt the need to do the same in this paragraph. For their remarks on the Greek fragment see SC 263.92–95. As for the meaning, Marcus professed to improve on his teacher's doctrines and considered himself the greatest Power of the Fullness. Moreover, he borrowed from Colorbasus, also a follower of Valentinus, the notion about an unutterable Monad prior to Profundity and Silence from which all other Aeons were emitted. Since he claimed to be so great, he identified himself with this Monad and thought of himself as the matrix and receptacle of Silence according to Colorbasus's teaching. For a different view on Colorbasus see Rudolph *Gnosis* 324. In Ps.-Tertullian, *Haer.* 5 (CCL 2.1407–8), Colorbasus is mentioned as a fellow heretic of Marcus, holding the same nonsense about numbers.

3. We base our translation on the textual emendation of Rousseau and Doutreleau (SC 264.206). Rousseau (SC 263.244 [SC 264.207 n. 1]) believes that *tou hustērmatos* of the Codex Vaticanus gr. 503 and the Codex Marcianus 125 is only a corruption of *sperma to* and the solution to the textual problem is to reestablish the original Greek so that it agrees with the Latin.

4. Lat. Iren. seems to have the correct reading, of which the Gk. Epiph. ("the Father was in travail") is a corruption. On this see also SC 263.244 (SC 264.207 n. 2).

5. Compare Valentinus's pretense of having a revelation of the Word in the form of an infant in Hippolytus, *Haer.* 6.42.2 (GCS 26.173).

6. Combination is *sullabē*, but that is not to be taken in the sense of our syllable. Actually the first combination has two of our syllables. In the following descriptions Irenaeus uses two words to designate the letters of our alphabet: *stoikheion* and *gramma*. Though it is difficult to see the precise distinction between the two, according to 1.14.2 he uses them as follows: the *stoikheion* is the letter of the alphabet inasmuch as it is the name and symbol of the letter. We would refer to the *stoikheia* as the ABC's. The *gramma* is the letter of the alphabet inasmuch as it is used to spell out the *stoikheia* of a word. We have translated *stoikheion* by character and *gramma* by letter. See also SC 263.244–45 (SC 264.209 n. 1) on this.

7. Rousseau and Doutreleau (SC 264.209) would suggest a differ-

ent translation. They would prefer something like this: "Finally he uttered the last which had twelve characters." An English translation of what they consider a more literal rendering of the text would be "he uttered that which [came] after [everything] that [has been spoken about] which had twelve characters."

8. This last phrase is from Epiphanius, *Haer.* 34.4.5 (GCS 31.11), and Hippolytus, *Haer.* 6.42.6 (GCS 26.174). Rousseau (SC 263.245 [SC 264.209 n. 3]) notes that the MS of Hippolytus reads *auto*—in his judgment the correct reading here—while the MSS of Epiphanius have *autos*. Holl (GCS 31.11) had emended the text to *auto*. Instead of this last phrase Lat. Iren. has *neque ipsum super elementum est.* That is evidently incorrect because it leaves the preceding phrase without its complement.

9. Both Hippolytus and Lat. Iren. have "know." Gk. Epiph. has *poliorkei,* which Holl (GCS 31.11) corrected to *ginōskein,* according to the Latin.

10. The Greek has *monoglōssēsanta.* What does it mean? At the end of 1.14.2 we are told that First-Father gave to each of the characters the power to utter its own pronunciation only, and not the whole name. So it seems to mean that each character has the power of *voicing* its name *only.* See also Lampe, PGL, s.v. *"monoglōsseō."*

11. See SC 263.245–46 (SC 264.211 n. 1) on *apokatastasin* here and also A. Méhat, *"Apokatastasis* chez Basilide," in *Mélanges d'histoire des religions offerts à Henri-Charles Puech* (Paris 1974) 365–73.

12. Cf. Matt. 18.10.

13. Cf. Epiphanius, *Haer.* 34.4.8–5.4 (GCS 31.11–12). Hippolytus describes this Marcosian system of letters in *Haer.* 6.43 (GCS 26.175–76).

14. This sound corresponds to Achamoth in the other systems.

15. Rousseau and Doutreleau (SC 264.213) translate this participial phrase in a different manner. An English equivalent would be "going from the All, begot some suitable characters after the image of the characters of this All. . . ." For the reasons for this translation see SC 263.246 (SC 264.213 n. 1).

16. These things correspond to the seven heavens and Demiurge in the other systems.

17. Rousseau (SC 263.246 [SC 264.213 n. 2]) notes that here it is an issue of the "All" or the "Pleroma" as the context so shows. He also feels this exemplifies the strange fluidity of the Gnostic terminology.

18. Rousseau (SC 263.246 [SC 264.213 n. 3]) remarks that this seems to be an author intrusion by Irenaeus into this discourse by the Tetrad.

19. For example, epsilon of the delta is made up of epsilon, psi, iota, lambda, omicron, and nu. The same process can be repeated for the other letters.

20. Cf. Epiphanius, *Haer.* 34.5.5–8 (GCS 31.12–13). Hippolytus used this paragraph, but he has a different anatomical description of Truth in *Haer.* 6.44 (GCS 26.176–77).

21. Cf. Epiphanius, *Haer.* 34.6.1–4 (GCS 31.13–14). Hippolytus made use of this paragraph in *Haer.* 6.45 (GCS 26.177). It deals with the formation of Jesus Christ explained by alphabetical nonsense.

22. "Symbolical name," because it contained the symbolical number six (cf. 1.14.4; 1.15.2; 2.24.2). Six was represented by the archaic Greek letter digamma. Cf. Sagnard *Gnose* 366.

23. Cf. Matt. 20.16. Literally, "known by all of those of the calling," that is, of the Church on earth. According to Hippolytus, *Haer.* 10.9 (GCS 26.268), the Church was threefold—angelic, ensouled, and earthly—and the names were respectively "chosen, called, and captive."

24. Cf. Epiphanius, *Haer.* 34.6.5–13 (GCS 31.14–15). Hippolytus made use of this paragraph in *Haer.* 6.46 (GCS 26.177–78).

25. On this see SC 263.247–48 (SC 264.221 n. 2).

26. These are beta, gamma, delta, theta, kappa, pi, tau, phi, and chi.

27. These are zeta, lambda, mu, nu, xi, rho, sigma, and psi.

28. That clause is somewhat enigmatic. That the semivowels are intermediate between the vowels and the consonants is clear enough. Now, in the illustration, Word and Life hold a middle place in the sense that they were emitted by higher Aeons, but are themselves the source of lower Aeons, which are referred to them as their cause. That seems to be the meaning of the phrase that they receive "an ascent from those below," as de Billy (cf. MG 7.603C) indicates by his translation.

29. For an explanation of the text of the previous six lines see SC 263.248 (SC 264.223 n. 1).

30. That is, the three feminine Aeons: Truth, Life, and Church joined respectively to Father, Word, and Man.

31. Rousseau and Doutreleau (SC 263.249 [SC 264.223 n. 3]) would add here "which Marcus asserts."

32. These are zeta (ds), xi (ks), and psi (ps).

33. See on this SC 263.249 (SC 264.223 n. 4).

34. Cf. Epiphanius, *Haer.* 34.7.1–4 (GCS 31.15–16). Hippolytus copied this section in *Haer.* 6.47 (GCS 26.179). For "arrangement" he has "analogy"; but Epiphanius, with whom Lat. Iren. agrees, has the correct reading.

35. Cf. Rom. 1.23.

36. Cf. Matt. 17.1 and Mark 9.2. Peter, James, and John were the other three. See Sagnard *Gnose* 376–82.

37. When Moses and Elijah appeared on the Mount there were six. The Transfiguration symbolized the descent of Savior to visit Achamoth. Together with Limit and Demiurge and the conjugal couple of Christ and Spirit there were six.

38. Hebdomad means seven. Luke indicated this by saying "the next day" (9.37), namely, plus the six days. By Hebdomad he probably understood the dwelling of Demiurge, that is, the seven heavens. Above these dwelt Achamoth, but outside the Fullness (cf. 1.5.2, 4). Savior was detained in this Hebdomad only for a while.

39. Savior contained in himself "the entire number of the characters," that is, thirty, because he was thirty years old when he was baptized. Moreover, the dove symbolized him who was the alpha and the omega. But the numeric value of alpha is one and of omega 800; so, of both 801. This is also the numeric value of the Greek for dove (*peristera*); see n. 3 to chap. 15, SC 263.249–50 (SC 264.225 n. 1), and Sagnard *Gnose* 373–74.

40. Cf. Gen. 1.26, 31.

41. Lat. Iren. has *cena pura*, a name that was given to the Parasceve because the Jews had to be clean in garments, food, body, and soul for the celebration of the Pasch.

42. We follow what Rousseau (SC 263.250 [SC 264.225 n. 2]) indicates is the better of two solutions to sort out the various textual difficulties here.

43. Cf. Luke 16.8; John 12.36; Eph. 5.8; 1 Thess. 5.5.

44. Our translation is based on suggestions made by Rousseau and

Doutreleau (SC 264.227). For Rousseau's reasoning on this see SC 263.250–51 (SC 264.227 n. 1).

45. This symbolical number is six, and, as Harvey (1.141 n. 1) notes, it is contained in the three double letters inasmuch as the sum of the single letters is six.

46. Cf. Epiphanius, *Haer.* 34.7.5–34.8.2 (GCS 31.16–17), for par. 7–9. Par. 7 was also used by Hippolytus in *Haer.* 6.48 (GCS 26.179–81).

47. We follow Gk. Epiph. and Lat. Iren. and not Hippolytus, who has *ta di' eikonōn* in place of *diakonei*, which would read: "But those that are by the images of the Mother's Intention, being in imitation of the inimitable." Still Harvey (1.142 n. 1) thinks this suggests the true reading as *alla tade* ("others that are by the images of the Mother's Intention . . ."). See SC 263.251–52 (SC 264.229 n. 1) for a careful commentary on this paragraph.

48. This information is interesting in view of the fact that the Gnostics most certainly had some kind of musical system in which they chanted the vowels, which represented the seven notes on the heptachord. Likewise, the seven planets were symbolized by the seven vowels and each planet was represented by one of the seven tones. According to one explanation Kronos is omega (mi, on the scale), Zeus is upsilon (fa), Ares is omicron (sol), Helios is iota (la), Aphrodite is eta (si), Hermes is epsilon (ut), Selenes is alpha (re). Cf. H. Leclercq, "Alphabet vocalique des Gnostiques," DACL 1.1.1268–88.

49. Ps. 8.3.

50. Ps. 18(19).2.

51. "For its own purgation" is *eis diulismon.* The verb *diulizein* means to strain out, to purge. Irenaeus uses it in 4.33.7, when quoting Matt. 23.24. Clement of Alexandria, *Paed.* 1.6.32 (GCS 12.108), when speaking of the Gnostics, says that some held that the memory of the better things is a purging (*diulismon*) of Spirit, and that the purging is the separation of the worse things by the remembrance of the better. Again in *Exc. Thdot.* 42 (GCS 17².119), the seeds are said to have been purged together with (*sundiulisthē*) Christ as far as possible on entering the Fullness. So Harvey's (1.143 n. 2) suggestion to correct the word to *di' alusmou* ("because of anguish") is unnecessary.

52. The soul on earth was made after the image of the angel on high, and so these are kin.

53. Rousseau and Doutreleau (SC 264.232) emend the Greek to

conform to the Latin ("their Tetrad . . . their words") noting (SC 263.252–53 [SC 264.233 n. 1]) that their Tetrad is a rather natural expression and also Irenaeus's friend would not be interested in the teaching of Marcus alone but in all the teachings of the heretics in order to refute them properly.

CHAPTER 15

1. Chap. 15 is in Epiphanius, *Haer.* 34.8.3–12 (GCS 31.17–23). Rousseau and Doutreleau (SC 263.95) point out that Hippolytus has made use of and thus preserved Irenaeus's Greek text near the end of this paragraph that contains an explanation of the Marcosian arithmology.

2. The name of Savior, *Iēsous*, has six letters, and when only the sound that each letter represents is pronounced, the name is unutterable. But how is it unutterable, and how does it have twenty-four letters? Irenaeus suggests the solution in 1.14.2 when speaking about delta; namely, when the names of the letters that make up that name delta are spelled out, and again the names of each one of those letters in turn, it cannot be pronounced; e.g., Deltaepsilonlambdataualpha, etc. So with Jesus, it would be Iotaetasigmaomicronupsilonsigma, and then the names of each of these letters in turn *ad infinitum*. But how did he arrive at the number twenty-four? Hippolytus, *Haer.* 6.49.4 (GCS 26.182) suggests the answer when for *Khreistos*, the other name of Jesus, he got the numeric value twenty-four. See n. 3. So, for *Iēsous* it would be: four for iota, two for eta (written ei), five for sigma, two for omicron (written ou), six for upsilon, five for sigma. For more on this see Harvey 1.145 n. 3. But in 1.15.2 Irenaeus says that *Iēsous* has thirty letters. He no doubt counted the six letters of *Iēsous* and added them to the twenty-four above.

3. The expression "Christ the Son" is in Greek *Huios Khreistos.* There are twelve letters, and the name is utterable. But when the letters of the names of these letters of *Khreistos* are summed up, one gets thirty. Cf. 1.15.2. As was observed in n. 2, Hippolytus (*Haer.* 6.49 [GCS 26.182]) attempted a solution, but his count actually amounts to

only twenty-four and not thirty: chi is three, rho is two, epsilon (ei) is two, iota is four, sigma is five, tau is three, omicron (ou) is two, san (a different name for sigma) is three. Sagnard (Sagnard *Gnose* 371–72) thinks that perhaps his count of twenty-four is correct and was taken as totality, which symbolized the Fullness, and so thirty. Harvey (1.146 n. 1) suggests this calculation: chi is two, rho is two, epsilon is seven, iota is four, sigma is five, tau is three, omicron is two, sigma is five. He claims that in those days epsilon was written out, but not omicron.

4. Cf. Matt. 3.16.

5. See n. 39 to chap. 4.

6. Hippolytus copied part of this paragraph in *Haer.* 6.50 (GCS 26.182–83). For Rousseau's and Doutreleau's remarks on this see SC 263.94.

7. Lat. Iren. is *A Matre enim universorum, id est primae quaternationis.* Already Massuet (MG 7.615 n. 2), and Lundström (Lundström *Studien* 50) who follows him, thought the Latin translator faultily wrote *primae quaternationis,* simply imitating the Greek construction, unaware that in Greek it must be a genitive governed by *apo,* but in Latin it must be an ablative governed by *a.* The "first Tetrad" is the "Mother of all things"; cf. 1.13.6; 1.14.1; 1.14.4; 1.14.5. So "first Tetrad" is in apposition to "Mother of all things."

8. Lat. Iren. has: "the origin of the supercelestial Jesus." For more on this see SC 263.253 (SC 264.239 n. 1).

9. Lundström (Lundström *Studien* 53) wants *ostendentia* changed to *ostendens;* but it is neuter plural, agreeing with "A B" as a neuter plural in a Greek accusative with infinitive construction.

10. Rousseau (SC 263.254 [SC 264.241 n. 2]) argues that the Greek *tois huiois* should be read here, adding that the sons mentioned here are the same as the "sons of light" mentioned in 1.14.6.

11. In 1.15.1 it was said that the utterable name of Jesus has six letters, but the unutterable twenty-four. The two together make thirty. Cf. n. 2.

12. This is an allusion to John 14.6, if Gk. Epiph. *hodou* is correct, as seems likely. Lat. Iren. has *ducatore* supposing *hodēgou,* which he misread for *hodou.* See also Harvey (1.149 n. 1) as well as Rousseau (SC 263.254–55 [SC 264.241 n. 3]). Yet we would not rule "leader" out altogether. It occurs in 1.13.6 and 2.18.7.

13. Cf. Luke 9.35.

14. Lat. Iren. *dictum* should obviously be *electum*. See the next paragraph with *elegit*. See also on this SC 263.255 (SC 264.241 n. 4).

15. For more on the Marcosian exegesis of Luke 1.35 which follows, see Orbe, *Cristología Gnóstica* 1.337–38.

16. Cf. Luke 1.26, 35. Lat. Iren. and Hippolytus have "Most High"; Gk. Epiph. has "Son." Rousseau and Doutreleau (SC 264.242) amend the text of Gk. Epiph. to *Huphistou* following Hippolytus and Lat. Iren.

17. Cf. Luke 9.35.

18. Cf. Matt. 3.16.

19. Codex Vaticanus gr. 503 before correction has *sunsparentōn* ("contemporaries"). We follow Lat. Iren. *conseminati*, which is confirmed by Hippolytus's *sugkatasparentōn*, a word that Gk. Epiph. has in 1.5.6.

20. On this sentence see SC 263.255–56 (SC 264.243 n. 2).

21. The sense is that Jesus made known his Father, who was the Christ on high. Grabe (cf. Harvey 1.151 n. 1), not understanding this, proposed to change "Christ" to the nominative so the clause would read "But Christ made known the Father." That is a tenet of some Gnostics, but is not expressed here. Harvey's suggestion (1.151 n. 1) of putting a period after Father and drawing Christ Jesus to the next clause involves too much of an unnecessary change. See also SC 263.256 (SC 264.245 n. 1).

22. In translating *kakosunthenton* by deplorable, we have been influenced by Rousseau's rationale (SC 263.256 [SC 264.245 n. 2]) for his choice of *déplorable* in his French translation.

23. Cf. Gen. 31.2.

24. Irenaeus states that Palamedes added the long letters and that the aspirates and double letters had been introduced separately prior to this. There were various traditions about the origin of the Greek alphabet. According to Greek and Roman traditions Cadmus lived a long time in Phoenicia and on his return brought back the alphabet, or rather, according to one tradition, introduced the sixteen letters (ca. 1313 B.C.). During the Trojan War (ca. 1183 B.C.) Palamedes added the double letters (theta, xi, phi, chi) and Simonides of Ceos later added zeta, eta, and omega. Cf. D. Diringer, *The Alphabet: A Key to the History of Mankind*, 3d ed. rev. R. Regensburger, 1 (New York 1968) 358. In that case, Irenaeus followed a different tradition of his day.

25. Lat. Iren. has the additional words *temporis quam Palamedes,* which were dropped already by Feuardent (cf. SC 264.246). Massuet (MG 7.623–24 n. 2) and Harvey (1.153 n. 1) try to defend them. They are, however, unnecessary. They are in an awkward position and construction, since *Palamedes* is singular but *addiderunt* plural, and *addiderunt* already has its plural subject. Rousseau (SC 263.257 [SC 264.247 n. 1]) considers *temporis quam Palamedes* a marginal gloss entered into the text by a scribe influenced by *tempore quam Cadmus* which occurs earlier in the paragraph.

26. Cf. Ps. 32(33).6.

27. Cf. Hermas, *Mand.* 1.1 (SC 53bis.145). For more on this phrase which occurs often in Irenaeus see SC 100.249–50.

28. According to Harvey (1.155 n. 1), "Daedalus [was] the first fabricator of the Cretan labyrinth," and so he was an apt figure for the mystical maze of the Marcosians. See also G. M. A. Hanfmann, "Daedalus," OCD² 309–10.

29. This is most likely Bishop Pothinus; cf. ODCC² 1113. Gk. Epiph. has *theios* ("saintly"); but Lat. Iren. has *divinae adspirationis senior,* supposing, it seems, *theopneustos.*

30. Azazel and Asa were in Jewish demonology the two angels who quarrelled at the creation of man and woman, and so were punished by being detained on earth. On this see ODCC² 118 and the remarks by Harvey (1.156 n. 2) and Rudolph *Gnosis* 324–25.

31. Lat. Iren. has two verbs: *facile argui et conuinci* for the one Greek word *euelegkta,* unless another Greek word fell out.

CHAPTER 16

1. Cf. Luke 15.4–7.

2. Since this sentence is missing in Hippolytus, and *ap' autēs* of the following sentence has "Monad" of the preceding sentence as its antecedent, Harvey (1.157 n. 1) thinks this sentence is an interpolation. However, Hippolytus has the same calculation in *Haer.* 6.23.5 (GCS

26.150). It seems certain that *ap' autēs* does not refer to the Monad but to the Dyad of this same sentence and should really be *aph' heautēs;* otherwise the count would not be twelve but thirteen, since according to the method of calculating, the Decad above the Monad itself would have to be counted. Klebba (3.54) in BKV translated correctly: *von sich ausging.* The verbs conceiving and generating might sound queer here, but they are used because of the Marcosian preoccupation with the generation of Aeons.

3. Namely, two plus four plus six plus eight plus ten is thirty.

4. Rousseau (SC 263.257–58 [SC 264.255 n. 2]) notes that the number twelve can be obtained by adding together two, four, and six. These numbers are arranged in an arithmetic progression ending in six. Thus the Dodecad is ended by the symbolical number or the digamma. It would be highly appropriate, then, to have the defection or the passion of the Aeon symbolized by a sign that had vanished from the alphabet.

5. Cf. Luke 15.3–7.

6. Cf. Luke 15.8–10.

7. This point is not in Luke's parable. It could have been in the Valentinian version of it.

8. The numerical value of the letters of Amen is ninety-nine; namely, one plus forty plus eight plus fifty. This idea seems to derive from the Jewish Cabbala, in which Amen is said to sum up Yahweh Adonai. On this see Harvey 1.159 n. 2. Rousseau (SC 263.258 [SC 264.255 n. 3]), on the other hand, points out that ninety-nine, the result of multiplying nine by eleven, is the preeminent number of the deficiency.

9. *Tupon,* which is found in Gk. Epiph., Hippolytus, and Lat. Iren. (*typum*), is undoubtedly genuine. Harvey's (1.160 n. 1) suggestion of *topos* is unwarranted. Harvey (1.160 n. 1) thinks that *skhēmati tou logou* (*figura Logi*) means "method of calculation," and Klebba (3.55) in BKV has *Schema der Rechnung.* Our translation here is based on the work of Rousseau (SC 263.258–60 [SC 264.259 n. 1]) who argues that if Gk. Epiph. is corrected by the Lat. Iren., the sense becomes very clear. He restores the Greek to *en skhēmati tou Logou* and then explains that the letters lambda and mu evoke the "economy" of on high and the Logos.

10. Grabe (cf. Harvey 1.161 n. 3) notes that the ancients enumerated up to ninety-nine with gestures of the left hand, but from one hundred and over with the right hand.

11. Cf. 1 Tim. 4.7.

12. Cf. Titus 3.11.

13. Cf. Titus 3.10.

14. Cf. 2 John 11. This passage of Irenaeus is a valuable witness to the authenticity of 2 John.

15. Isa. 48.22, according to the LXX. The Vulgate has "peace." For more on this see SC 263.260 (SC 264.263 n. 1).

16. Demiurge was the creator according to the Gnostics; but he was the product of Achamoth's passion, and Achamoth herself was the product of Wisdom who had apostatized from the Fullness.

17. At baptism part of the rite of exorcism consists in exhaling on the one to be baptized, symbolic of driving out the wicked spirit. This ceremony is very ancient. St. Cyril of Jerusalem, *Procatech.* 9 (*St. Cyril of Jerusalem's Lectures on the Christian Sacraments: The Procatechesis and the Five Mystagogical Catecheses*, ed. F. L. Cross [London 1951] 5–6), has the earliest mention of the ceremony; but the fact that these heretics already had exorcisms (cf. 1.23.4) seems proof that it existed earlier. See G. Bareille, "Catéchumenat," DTC 2.2.1984. Irenaeus clearly is witness to the fact that the Church of his day practiced official and charismatic driving out of demons; cf. 2.32.4, *Proof* 96–97 (ACW 16.106–7). This practice was inherited from the Jews (cf. 2.6.2). But in no case is there any reference to such a practice at baptism itself.

18. See SC 263.260 (SC 264.265 n. 1) on this.

19. Cf. Matt. 12.43–45.

20. "Prepared." In keeping with the Greek (aorist active participle) the Latin should be *componens*, not *compositam*. "For expulsion." The Greek is *huperekkrousin*. Cf. Lampe, PGL, s.v. *"huperekkrousis,"* where the only example cited for this word is the present passage. Massuet (MG 7.636 n. 13) interprets it as a vehement agitation which he thinks would fit this context well. Actually *ekkrousis* does exist and is a driving away. Cf. LSJ, s.v. *"ekkrousis."* As in other cases Irenaeus may have made up a word to indicate an excessive (*huper*) or vehement expelling. This would agree tolerably well with Lat. Iren. *exclusionem.* In 2.32.4 *excludunt* means to expel; but there the extant Greek has

elaunousin. But are they prepared to expel someone or to be themselves expelled? It seems the latter is likely. By their foolishness they were fittingly prepared by the wicked spirits for being expelled from divine knowledge by the imposition of the Ogdoad of wicked spirits. De Billy's (cf. Harvey 1.164 n. 2) correction to *hupekkrousin* (deceit) is neither necessary nor suitable.

CHAPTER 17

1. Chap. 17 is in Epiphanius, *Haer.* 34.14 (GCS 31.27–29). Hippolytus copied par. 1 in *Haer.* 6.53 (GCS 26.187–88).

2. According to Hippolytus the Gnostics borrowed this notion from the Pythagoreans (*Haer.* 6.28 [GCS 26.154–55]), as also their idea of a fiery Demiurge who presides over the seven heavens (*Haer.* 6.32.7–8 [GCS 31.161]).

3. Gk. Epiph. has *hexēs* ("next" or "in continuation"), but Lat. Iren. has *ex qua* (supposing *ex hēs*), which is correct, because, as Harvey (1.165 n. 1) observes: "The seven heavens were considered to derive their substance and properties from the lower ogdoad." Rousseau and Doutreleau (SC 264.266), however, prefer *hexēs*.

4. This passage is difficult because the reading is uncertain and the sense obscure. For "linked to" Gk. Epiph. has *antepezeukhthē,* which agrees with Lat. Iren. *superiunctum*. That should be preferred to the reading of the Codex Parisinus Suppl. gr. 464 of Hippolytus: *antezeukhthē* ("join again"). Wendland (Hippolytus, *Haer.* 6.53.4 [GCS 26.187]) would amend the text to *antepezeukhthē*. "Movement" is according to Hippolytus's *anaphora*, which is an astronomical term for the ascent of the sign measured in degrees of the equator. Cf. LSJ, s.v. "*anaphora*." That makes better sense than *phora* ("weight") of Gk. Epiph. and the Latin *oneri*. However, the dative case in the Latin assures us that the dative in Hippolytus is correct, against the accusative of Gk. Epiph. Rousseau and Doutreleau (SC 264.267) prefer *phorāi* here with Holl (GCS 31.28). The Latin causal clause *cum sit uelocissimum,* modifying "highest heaven," is not a correct translation

of the Greek participle. It is contradictory in the context, because later he says that the slowness of the highest heaven acts as a counter-balance to the others. "Highest heaven" is the reading of Hippolytus and Lat. Iren. Gk. Epiph. *houper ho khronos* ("of which the time") does not make sense and is a corruption of *ho huperthen ouranos*, the reading of the Codex Parisinus Suppl. gr. 464 of Hippolytus, and as supposed by the Latin. Rousseau (SC 263.261 [SC 264.267 n. 1]) notes that there are quite a number of translation mistakes here in the Latin, particularly *et e contrario superiunctum ... quod superpositum est caelum.*

5. The Marcosian division of a day was according to the ancient custom. The Roman day, which began with sunrise and ended with sunset, was divided into twelve equal "hours." Naturally such an "hour" was shorter in winter than in summer, and an "hour" of the day was not always the same as an "hour" of the night. See Harvey 1.167 n. 1.

6. How is the relation between twelve and thirty preserved here? Massuet (MG 7.640 n. 9) explains that the sun each day describes a circle of three hundred and sixty degrees, which are made up of twelve parts of thirty degrees each. Now when the days are as long as the nights, each hour has fifteen degrees, so that in two hours, one-twelfth of a day, the sun completes thirty degrees.

7. "Perpendicularly," the reading of Gk. Epiph. seems correct, against the Latin *demissionem* ("sending down"). These zones were parallel to the equator and decreased in breadth as they approached the poles. Each zone marked the difference of half an hour. See Harvey 1.167 n. 3.

8. The accusative *dunamin* of Gk. Epiph. was corrected to a dative according to Hippolytus, *Haer.* 6.53.7 (GCS 26.188). Holl (GCS 31.188) makes this change to the dative in his edition of Epiphanius which Rousseau and Doutreleau adopt in SC 264.270. The ancients thought an "influence," an etherial fluid, flowed from the stars and affected the actions of men and women; later this influence was supposed to be an emanation of some occult power from the stars.

9. Hippolytus copied this paragraph in *Haer.* 6.54 (GCS 26.188–89).

10. According to Harvey (1.168 n. 2), even Plato's notion of infinitude amounted to only indefinite duration; and Aristotle's notion of it

was that of a numerical sum that could always be added to, however great it might be.

11. On this see SC 263.261–62 (SC 264.271 n. 1) and H. C. Puech, "La Gnose et le temps," in *En quête de la Gnose*, vol. 1: *La Gnose et le temps et autres essais* (Paris 1978) 255–56.

CHAPTER 18

1. This is in Epiphanius, *Haer.* 34.15–17 (GCS 31.29–32). Hippolytus does not give all of chap. 18–20 of Irenaeus. He has adapted the first three sentences and then makes a summary statement about the misuse of Scripture by the Marcosians, and that Irenaeus, to whom he is indebted for information, has forcefully and elaborately refuted them (*Haer.* 6.55 [GCS 26.189]).

2. "Thinks up" is *aduenit* in Lat. Iren., which supposes something like *epinoei*. This Latin verb is customary in Irenaeus in that sense. Gk. Epiph. has *epigennāi*. "More novel" is according to Gk. Epiph. *kainoteron*. The Latin has simply *aliquid noui*.

3. Gen. 1.1.

4. Simon Magus, according to Hippolytus, *Haer.* 6.13 (GCS 26.138), was the first to equate heaven and earth with Mind and Truth.

5. Gen. 1.2, according to LXX. Lat. Iren. differs from the Vulgate, being a literal translation of the LXX. The Gnostics' play on the word "invisible" is possible only in the LXX version.

6. Gen. 1.2. In this second Tetrad Simon Magus, too, put air in the third place and water in the fourth. See Hippolytus, *Haer.* 6.14 (GCS 26.139), and Harvey (1.170 n. 1).

7. Cf. Gen. 1.3–12.

8. Gen. 1.14–27.

9. Cf. Gen. 1.26.

10. They omitted the fifth sense, because their system called for a Tetrad. This fantastic idea was suggested by Gen. 2.7–14. According to Hippolytus, *Haer.* 5.9.15–18 (GCS 26.101), the ancient Ophites compared Eden to the brain and the four rivers to the four senses.

11. Cf. 1.14.3.

12. Cf. Gen. 1.14–19.

13. Here and in the next paragraph we follow the reading of Rousseau and Doutreleau (SC 264.277) who prefer *aulaiai* ("curtains") to *aulai* ("courts"). For Rousseau's explanation see SC 263.262 (SC 264.277 n. 1).

14. Cf. Exod. 26.1; 36.8.

15. Exod. 28.17.

16. Cf. Gen. 2.7.

17. Cf. Gen. 1.26.

18. Cf. Gen. 2.7.

19. Cf. Gen. 7.7, 13, 23; 1 Pet. 3.20. The last words are literally "the saving Ogdoad."

20. Cf. 1 Sam. (1 Kings) 16.10–11.

21. Cf. Gen. 17.12.

22. Cf. Gen. 15.19–20.

23. Cf. Gen. 16.2–3.

24. Cf. Gen. 24.22.

25. Cf. Gen. 24.55.

26. Cf. 1 Kings (3 Kings) 11.31.

27. Cf. Exod. 26.1; 36.8.

28. Cf. Exod. 26.16.

29. Cf. Gen. 42.3.

30. John 20.24.

31. Gen. 35.22–26.

32. Gen. 49.28.

33. Cf. Exod. 28.21; 36.21. But the number of the bells is not in Scripture. Since Justin, *Dial.* 42.1 (Goodspeed 138–39), agrees with Irenaeus, the information may have been taken from the practice of the synagogue.

34. Cf. Exod. 24.4.

35. Josh. 4.3, 8, 9.

36. Cf. Josh. 4.20.

37. Cf. Josh. 3.12.

38. Cf. 1 Kings (3 Kings) 18.31.

39. Cf. Gen. 6.15.

40. Cf. 1 Sam. (1 Kings) 9.22. The LXX has seventy men, but the Hebrew and Vulgate have thirty. So the Marcosians must have had a Greek text different from the LXX.

41. Cf. 1 Sam. (1 Kings) 20. 1-42; 2 Sam. (2 Kings) 23.13. These are not cited correctly by the Marcosians. The biblical text says that David remained only until the third day. And only three of the thirty men came to David in the cave of Adullam.

42. Cf. Exod. 26.8.

43. Gk. Epiph. has *dia tōn toioutōn epideiknusai phileristousin:* "by them they earnestly strive to demonstrate . . . ." This was also accepted by Massuet (MG 7.649). Lat. Iren. has *per huiusmodi ostendunt adseuerationes:* "by such earnest strivings they demonstrate." In A.H. 5.13.2 Irenaeus uses the adverb *phileristikōs*, which Lat. Iren. translated *contentiose:* "earnestly."

CHAPTER 19

1. Chap. 19 is in Epiphanius, *Haer.* 34.18.1–6 (GCS 31.32–33).

2. Isa. 1.3.

3. Cf. Hos. 4.1.

4. Cf. Ps. 13(14).2–3; Rom. 3.11–12.

5. Cf. Exod. 33.20.

6. Cf. Exod. 33.20.

7. Cf. Dan. 12.9–10. In the Hebrew text and the Greek of Theodotion this passage reads: *Go, Daniel, because the words are shut up and sealed [until the appointed time. Many shall be chosen and made white, and shall be tried as fire]: the wicked shall deal wickedly, and none of the wicked shall understand, but the learned shall understand.* The words enclosed in brackets are given thus in the LXX: *Until many shall be tried and sanctified.* For the rest, at times the words of the LXX differ from Theodotion, but the ideas are the same. So we can see the Marcosians followed a reading that was a combination of the LXX and Theodotion, but even then they willfully distorted the last part. In

place of *many shall be chosen* they put *the learned will understand,* which they took from the end, and then made a parallel construction out of *making white.*

CHAPTER 20

1. Chap. 20 is in Epiphanius, *Haer.* 34.18.7–17 (GCS 31.33–34).

2. This myth was a favorite in the apocryphal writings. Irenaeus agrees closely with the version of it in the apocryphal Arabic Gospel of the Infancy of the Savior chap. 48, 49 (ANF 8.414). The same story is repeated in different words in the Gospel of Thomas, chap. 6, 14 (ANF 8.396, 397). For more on this see SC 263.263 (SC 264.289 n. 1) and Orbe, *Cristología Gnóstica* 1.467–69.

3. Cf. Luke 2.49.

4. Cf. Luke 10.5–6.

5. Matt. 19.16; Mark 10.17; Luke 18.18.

6. Cf. Matt. 19.17; Mark 10.18; Luke 18.19. The Marcosian text does not agree with any of these individually. And the words "Father in the heavens," for which Mark and Luke have simply "God," are in none of the genuine Gospels, though some of the Fathers added them. The Ophites, too, added them (cf. Hippolytus, *Haer.* 5.7.26 [GCS 26.84–85]).

7. Cf. Matt. 21.23; Mark 11.28; Luke 20.2. All these have "authority" instead of "power."

8. Cf. Matt. 21.24–27.

9. For solutions to the difficulties caused by the shortcomings in both the Greek and Latin texts see SC 263.264 (SC 264.291 n. 2).

10. This is not in the canonical Gospels. It is evidently from some apocryphal work. We base our translation of "they have often . . . they had no one" on the textual emendations of Rousseau and Doutreleau (SC 264.291). For Rousseau's explanation for these emendations see SC 263.264–65 (SC 264.291 n. 3).

11. Cf. Luke 19.42. This was not quoted correctly, and it seems to have been used merely because of the word "hidden."

12. Matt. 11.28–29.

13. Lat. Iren. is *ostensionem autem superiorum.* Gk. Epiph. lost the word corresponding to *ostensionem,* and it has *tēn anōtatō,* which was used as an adjective modifying the noun that was lost, possibly *apodeixin.* Cf. Harvey (1.179), Holl (GCS 31.34), and Rousseau and Doutreleau (SC 264.293). See also SC 263.265 (SC 264.293 n. 1). *Superiorum* supposes *tōn anōtatō,* namely, "proof of the beings above." Harvey (1.179) inserts this as the correct reading for the Greek; but ANF (1.345 n. 8) and BKV (3.63) followed Gk. Epiph. De Billy (cf. MG 7.655) too followed the Greek. That seems correct because in the following sentence it is clear that this text is considered a very strong proof for a being above, but only for one, namely, Profundity.

14. Cf. Matt. 11.25–27; Luke 10.21–22.

15. Rousseau (SC 263.266 [SC 264.293 n. 2]) argues that "heavens" here refer to the Aeons and the "earth" to Achamoth (as in 1.5.3).

16. Rousseau (SC 263.266–69 [SC 264.293 n. 3]) notes that this is the first time we encounter this text under a heretical form. See also SC 100.206–7.

17. "Whom they have falsely invented" is from Gk. Epiph.; it was lost in Lat. Iren.

CHAPTER 21

1. Chap. 21.1–4 is extant in Epiphanius, *Haer.* 34.19–20 (GCS 32.34–37). Cf. Hippolytus, *Haer.* 6.41 (GCS 26.172–73). On "Redemption," see 1.13.6. Rousseau (SC 263.269–70 [SC 264.295 n. 1]) feels that Irenaeus wants to underscore the difficulty of expressing clearly what each sect means when it speaks of "Redemption."

2. We accept Lat. Iren. as correct. Gk. Epiph. has "discarding (*apothesin*) of faith." Lat. Iren. has "destroying of faith," which supposes *apōleian.* Harvey (1.181 n. 2) thinks maybe the Latin translator wrote *destitutionem,* which corrupted into *destructionem,* since in 5.12.4, after quoting Col. 3.9: *spoliantes vos,* he remarks: *sed spoliantem pristinae nostrae conversationis.* But the idea of "destroying faith" fits

in well here, especially as a parallel to "denying the baptism of re-birth," and the expression "the discarding of faith" is not apt and was not in vogue. The *apothesin* of Gk. Epiph. could easily be a corruption of *apōleian*. "Injected." Gk. Epiph. has *hupobeblētai*, which would call for *submissa*, not *remissa* as in Lat. Iren. Feuardent and Massuet (MG 7.657–58 n. 12) would allow *immissa* as a substitute, in the sense of inject. Rousseau (SC 263.270 [SC 264.295 n. 2]), however, prefers to base his translation of *"envoyée en sous-main"* on *hupobeblētai*, which he feels makes good sense in this context.

3. The antecedent of "this" seems certainly to be "redemption," not "rebirth" (of the preceding paragraph) or "power." Note the pun on "depth" and "Profundity."

4. Cf. Luke 12.50. But only the first part is in Luke; the Gnostics probably corrupted the text as cited.

5. Cf. Matt. 20.22; Mark 10.38. Gk. Epiph. differs from the N.T. text.

6. Cf. Rom. 3.24; Eph. 1.7; Col. 1.14.

7. Cf. n. 8 to chap. 6. In regard to these invocations, Hippolytus (*Haer.* 6.41 [GCS 26.173]) informs us that the Gnostics say something in a secret voice and impose hands.

8. Except for the phrase "into the union and redemption and par-ticipation of the powers," and the Hebrew formula below, this para-graph is preserved also by Eusebius, *H.e.* 4.11.5 (GCS 9.1.322). It seems evident from this paragraph that the Marcosian heresy had a baptismal formula that was a travesty on the Catholic one. See also SC 263.270 (SC 264.299 n. 1) on this.

9. The formula of Hebrew words in the Greek differs consider-ably from that of Lat. Iren. It is evidently corrupt in both. The scribes most likely did not know Hebrew and substituted wrong letters and interchanged others. The Greek and Latin explanations agree verba-tim except that the Greek has "good Spirit," while the Latin omits "good." Many attempts have been made in the past to restore this formula, so that Massuet (MG 7.661–62 n. 6) declined to attempt an-other. For the reconstruction proposed by F. Graffin see SC 263.270–71 (SC 264.299 n. 2).

10. Since an ointment, not merely juice, was used, the Latin reading is correct, not the Greek "with the juice of balsam."

11. On the meaning of this expression see n. 9 to chap. 2, SC 263.176 (SC 264.41 n. 1) and SC 263.271 (SC 264.303 n. 1).

12. On the state of the Greek and Latin text here see SC 263.271 (SC 264.303 n. 2).

13. Epiphanius (GCS 31.37) concluded here with "thus far the words by Irenaeus." But in the thirty-sixth heresy he again gives us fragments (GCS 32.46–47). Some are merely paraphrases, others are closer transcriptions. So from now on we are almost exclusively dependent on the Latin version. On the eleventh Greek fragment of Rousseau and Doutreleau see SC 263.96.

14. The Greek is not extant here. Lat. Iren. *mortuos* ("dead") is inaccurate, because a few lines farther on it is said that they were capable of receiving instruction. Yet Theodoret, *Haer.* i.ii (MG 83.361B), uses *teleutōntōn* to describe these people and says the rite was performed "after death."

15. Owing to many points of conflict in the sense of the passage Rousseau (SC 263.272–75 [SC 264.307 n. 1]) compares this quotation to a parallel passage in the *(First) Apocalypse of James* (V,3) from Nag Hammadi. For the English translation of the *(First) Apocalypse of James* (V,3) see *The (First) Apocalypse of James* (V,3), introduced and trans. W. R. Schoedel and ed. D. M. Parrott in *The Nag Hammadi Library in English,* general ed. J. M. Robinson, 3d ed. (San Francisco 1988) 265–66. Epiphanius preserves the Greek text of "I am a son of Father . . . concerning the 'redemption.' For more on this fragment (Fragment 11) as edited by Rousseau and Doutreleau see SC 263.96.

16. "First being" is in Lat. Iren. *qui ante fuit,* and in Greek the participle *proonti.* We take that here as the name of the Profundity, as earlier, and not as a description of his having "preceded in existence."

17. Cf. Rom. 9.21.

18. Achamoth sprang from Wisdom, who had no consort, and so Achamoth had no father, nor did she have a consort for her own emissions. See A.H. 1.4.1–2.

19. Rousseau (SC 263.275–76 [SC 264.307 n. 2]) draws attention to a passage in the *(First) Apocalypse of James* (V,3) to clarify this passage. See Schoedel and Parrott, *(First) Apocalypse of James* 266.

20. Rousseau (SC 264.307) would translate this sentence somewhat differently: "The one initiated, however, breaks his bonds, that is, the

soul, and goes into his own possessions." He argues (SC 263.276 [SC 264.307 n. 3]) the Latin translator erred in using the plural for the singular in this sentence.

CHAPTER 22

1. We broke down the long Latin construction, which begins with a causal construction as protasis (*cum teneamus*), but does not give the apodosis until after a number of lines (*facile . . . arguimus*), though just before the apodosis the protasis is briefly repeated. A list of the main texts in which Irenaeus discusses the Rule of Truth can be found in R. Kereszty, "The Unity of the Church in the Theology of Irenaeus," SCent 4, no. 4 (1984) 205. What follows is an implicit partial citation of Hermas, *Mand.* 1.1 (SC 53bis .144). Cf. 2 Macc. 7.28; Wisd. of Sol. 1.14. Theophilus of Antioch has similar ideas in *Auto.* 1.4; 1.7; 2.10; 3.9; see R. M. Grant's edition (*Theophilus of Antioch Ad Autolycum: Text and Translation*) in Oxford Early Christian Texts (New York 1970) 6, 10, 38–40, 110–12.

2. For the significance of this phrase in Irenaeus's anti-Gnostic polemic see SC 263.276–78 (SC 264.309 n. 1).

3. Cf. Ps. 32(33).6. He uses this text also in A.H. 3.8.3 and *Proof* 5. In this last place, however, he omits "of his mouth" and "all the power of them" to better fit his argument, as Smith (ACW 16.50, 139 n. 31) notes.

4. John 1.3.

5. Cf. Col. 1.16.

6. Cf. 2 Cor. 4.18.

7. Rousseau (SC 263.278–80 [SC 264.309 n. 2]) feels that *per quandam dispositionem* is a translation of *dia tina oikonomian*. He believes that one question that Irenaeus begins to address here is why has our world not received directly a perfect and definitive pattern of existence instead of the precarious pattern it has presently. See also idem, "L'éternité des peines de l'enfer et l'immortalité naturelle de l'âme selon saint Irénée," NRT 99 (1977) 834–64.

8. Rousseau (SC 263.280 [SC 264.309 n. 3]) would compare this to A.H. 2.2.1.

9. Rousseau (SC 263.280–81 [SC 264.309 n. 4]) suggests an alternate translation here: "For God has no need of anything." He argues that the expression *Deus omnium* does not seem to appear in the A.H. except at A.H. 2.10.4, where it could well be *eius qui est omnium D<omin>us*. The underlying Greek could well be *aprosdeēs gar tōn hapantōn ho Theos*.

10. Cf. Gen. 2.7.

11. Cf. Exod. 3.6; Matt. 22.32.

12. Cf. Eph. 1.3.

13. The handiwork is their own body "fashioned" by God and destined for the resurrection, which the heretics deny. Irenaeus will treat this especially in Book 5.

14. This is a clear statement of the doctrine of the resurrection and of the eternal lot of humankind, against the immoral principle that people can do what they like.

15. There is irony in the combination "most sublime Profundity."

CHAPTER 23

1. In *Haer.* 6.7–20 (GCS 26.134–48), Hippolytus gives portions which are taken more or less loosely from the lost Greek text of Irenaeus. His summary in *Haer.* 10.12 (GCS 26.272–73) does not agree altogether with his own longer account. The first ecclesiastical writer on record to give us information on Simon, apart from Acts, is Justin, *1 Apol.* 26, 56 (Goodspeed 43, 67) and *Dial.* 120 (Goodspeed 240). Irenaeus could have used Justin for this matter. Cf. also Tertullian, *Anim.* 34.2–4 (CCL 2.835–36); Ps.-Tertullian, *Haer.* 1.2 (CCL 2.1401); Epiphanius, *Haer.* 21.1–6 (GCS 25.238–45); Theodoret, *Haer.* 1.1 (MG 83.342–45); Filaster, *Haer.* 29 [1] (CCL 9.228–29). The later Ps.-Clementine *Recognitions*, books 2–3, have much fantastic matter about Simon; cf. ANF 8.97–134. Except for what is narrated in Acts we know very little for certain about the life of Simon. Hippolytus (*Haer.* 6.20 [GCS 26.148]) tells us that Simon went to Rome and there met Peter, who refuted him. But Hippolytus's information on that is very doubtful; cf. E. Amann, "Simon le Magicien," DTC 14.2.2135. The Fathers

all regard this Simon of Acts as the arch-heretic; all other heresies had
some relation to his system; cf. A.H. 1.23.2; 1.27.4; 2 Prf. 1. However,
there is a big difficulty here. Simon of Acts must have been at least in
his twenties in Acts 8. But the type of Gnosticism he is supposed to
have taught did not exist until the second quarter of the second century, when he certainly was not alive any more. E. Amann, "Simon le
Magicien" 2137, solves the difficulty by admitting that Simon Magus of
Acts is the Simon who in popular tradition was deified, together with
Helen, but that occurred after his death. Later on, in the second century, when Gnosticism began to flourish, this Simon became the object of their mythical speculations. A system was built around him,
which was known by his name, although he did not originate it. But in
answer to that, Simon, even before his attempt to buy the power of the
Holy Spirit, was considered *as someone great, as having the power of
God, which is called great* (cf. Acts 8.9–10). After his defection he
certainly had immediate followers who admired him. As for his doctrines, allowing for some additions in Irenaeus's description that
really belong to his followers, it is not so impossible for him to have
held them. Moreover, full-blown Gnosticism did not crop up over-
night in the middle of the second-century. It was a gradual development, with roots that reach into pre-Christian times. In any case, his
connection with second-century Gnosticism remains a mystery. Perhaps the heresiarch designated by Justin as Simon of Gitta in Samaria
actually lived in the second century and is in fact a different person
from Simon Magus of Acts 8. On this see ODCC², s.v. "Simon
Magus." See also Rudolph *Gnosis* 294–98; W. Foerster, *Die "ersten
Gnostiker" Simon und Menander*, Coll. Messina 190–96; and M.
Schlier, "Das Denken der früchristlichen Gnosis (Irenäus Adv. Haer.
I 23. 24)," *Neutestamentliche Studien für Rudolf Bultmann zu seinem
siebzigsten Geburtstag am 20. August 1954* (Berlin 1954) 67–82. Other
valuable studies on Simon are G. Bareille, "Gnosticisme," DTC
6.2.1434–67; L. Cerfaux, "Gnose préchrétienne et Biblique," DBS
3.659–701; idem, "La Gnose simonienne: Nos sources principales,"
RechSR 15 (1925) 489–511 and 16 (1926) 5–20, 265–85, 481–503; G. Salmon, "Simon (1) Magus," DCB 4.681–88; G. N. L. Hall, "Simon
Magus," HERE 11.514–25; H. Lietzmann, "Simon Magus," RE, 2d
ser., 3.1.180–84; E. Peretto, "Simone Mago-Simoniani," DPAC

2.3209–10; Quasten *Patr.* 1.255. On the state of research on Simon Magus see K. Rudolph, "Gnosis und Gnostizismus, ein Forschungsbericht," ThRdschau 37 (1972) 322–47, and idem, "Simon—Magus oder Gnosticus? Zum Stand der Debatte," ThRdschau 42 (1977) 279–359.

2. Acts 8.9–11.

3. Acts 8.20–21, 23.

4. Irenaeus here takes his material from Justin, *1 Apol.* 26 (Goodspeed 43–44). Claudius Caesar reigned from A.D. 41 to 54.

5. Hippolytus gives the same information in *Haer.* 6.19.6 (GCS 26.147).

6. Cf. A.H. 2.9.2 for the data that Simon was the first to claim he was a god. Hippolytus (*Haer.* 6.19.6 [GCS 26.147]) has "what men wish to call him," that is, he accepted even the greatest titles.

7. Cf. Hippolytus, *Haer.* 6.19.3–4 (GCS 26.146), and Theodoret, *Haer.* 1.1 (MG 83.344).

8. Tertullian, *Anim.* 34.3 (CCL 2.835).

9. Rousseau and Doutreleau (SC 264.316) list as their twelfth Irenaean Greek fragment (edited in this case from Hippolytus, *Haer.* 6.19 [GCS 26.145–46]) material that encompasses "for that reason . . . passing from one body into another." For a discussion of this fragment see SC 263.96–97.

10. This Stesichorus was a Sicilian poet. He was struck blind according to legend by Castor and Pollux because of the offense mentioned by Irenaeus, but later his sight was restored. Cf. Harvey 1.192 n. 1 and Hippolytus, *Haer.* 6.18.19 (GCS 26.145).

11. Cf. Luke 15.6.

12. Rousseau and Doutreleau (SC 264.317–19) list as their thirteenth Irenaean Greek fragment (edited from Hippolytus, *Haer.* 6.19 [GCS 26.146–47]), material that encompasses "salvation to humankind . . . through His grace." For a discussion of the fragment see SC 263.96–97.

13. These antinomian principles were rather common to all the Gnostics, as we shall be able to observe.

14. Lat. Iren. did not understand all the Greek terms and so merely transliterated them, or perhaps these foreign terms were used in his language. The Paredri were familiars, as for instance those of Soc-

rates. Cf. Tertullian, *Anim.* 28.5 (CCL 2.825): *per catabolicos et paredros et pythonicos spiritus.* Eusebius, *H.e.* 2.13.3 (GCS 9.1.134), writes of Simon's operating "through the art of the demons possessing him."

15. Eusebius, *H.e.* 2.13.6 (GCS 9.1.136), admits that he depends on Irenaeus for this information.

16. Rousseau (SC 263.283 [SC 264.321 n. 2]) points out that Irenaeus uses the term *hē pseudōnumos gnōsis* to designate the Gnostics in a strict sense already in A.H. 1.11.1. From these people as his teachers Valentinus has borrowed the main lines of his system. Irenaeus discusses them at greater length in A.H. 1.29–30.

17. Writers who used Irenaeus on Menander include Hippolytus, *Haer.* 7.4, 28 (GCS 26.190, 208); Ps.-Tertullian, *Haer.* 1.3 (CCL 2.1401); Eusebius, *H.e.* 3.26.3 (GCS 9.1.254); Theodoret, *Haer.* 1.2 (MG 83.345); Filaster, *Haer.* 30 [2] (CCL 9.229). On Menander see Quasten *Patr.* 1.255–26; A. Monaci Castagno, "Menandro," DPAC 2.2218–19; and Rudolph *Gnosis* 106, 150, 276, 298.

18. Tertullian, *Anim.* 50.2–5 (CCL 2.856), speaks of Menander's profane conceits about being immortal.

CHAPTER 24

1. There is some doubt about the spelling of this heretic's name. Hippolytus, *Haer.* 7.28 (GCS 26.208), gives it as Satorneilos, which modern authors often prefer. See Rudolph *Gnosis* 298. In this translation we follow the preferred spelling of this name as given in ODCC² 1238. Hippolytus (*Haer.* 7.28 [GCS 26.208–10]) has preserved the Greek text on Saturninus which Rousseau and Doutreleau (SC 264.321–25) have edited slightly as their fourteenth Greek fragment. For their discussion on this fourteenth Greek fragment see SC 263.97–98. Others who have borrowed from Irenaeus are: Tertullian, *Anim.* 23 (CCL 2.815); Ps.-Tertullian, *Haer.* 1.4 (CCL 2.1401–2); Epiphanius, *Haer.* 23–24 (GCS 25.247–56); Eusebius, *H.e.* 4.7.3–4 (GCS 9.1.308–10); Theodoret, *Haer.* 1.3 (MG 83.348); Filaster, *Haer.* 31 [3] (CCL 9.230). See modern studies by G. Salmon, "Saturninus (1)," DCB 4.587–88; R. Liechtenhan, "Satornil," RPT 17.491–92; G. Bardy, "Satornil," DTC 14.1.1210–11; G. Bareille, "Gnosticisme," DTC

6.2.1443–44; A. Monaci Castagno, "Satornilo (o Saturnino)," DPAC
2.3106–7. Satornilians are mentioned by Justin, *Dial.* 35 (Goodspeed
131), and Hegesippus (cf. Eusebius, *H.e.* 4.22 [GCS 9.1.370]). Saturninus was a disciple of Menander. He taught at Antioch and was the
chief Gnostic in Syria (cf. Hippolytus, *Haer.* 7.28 [GCS 26.208–10]).
His doctrine was substantially that of Simon and Menander, but he
added points of his own. K. Rudolph (Rudolph *Gnosis* 298), however,
maintains that Saturninus is dependent on Menander for his views on
the creation of the world by inferior angels but not on Menander for
other aspects of his teaching. These would include the fact that the
female figure *Ennoia* seems to be lacking in Saturninus's teaching.
Another distinction is that the followers of Saturninus distinguished
clearly good from evil men and women and followed an ascetical
manner of living.

2. Cf. Gen. 1.26. The notion that the angels created the world was
borrowed from Simon and Menander. It was a common teaching of
other heretics; e.g., Basilides (cf. A.H. 1.24.4; 2.2.1, 3; 3.1; 3.11.1; 3.12.1;
3.11.2). Simone Pétrement, "Le mythe des sept archontes créateurs
peut-il s'expliquer à partir du christianisme," *Coll. Messina* 460–87),
discusses the origin of the myth of creator angels and their number
seven. "Our" before "image" seems to have been omitted by Saturninus, because he held that the image and likeness were of someone
else than the angels who made the world.

3. We base this translation on the Greek text of Hippolytus as
emended by Rousseau and Doutreleau (SC 264.322). For their reasons
for the emendation see SC 263.284–85 (SC 264.323 n. 1).

4. "Unbegotten" may here mean only that he was not born of a
woman. So Harvey (1.197 n. 2) understands it.

5. We base our translation here on remarks by Rousseau (SC
263.285 [SC 264.325 n. 1]) that the Greeks would naturally assume that
patera was the subject of *katalusai*. He believes that the correctness of
their interpretation is confirmed by Theodoret, *Haer.* 1.3 (MG 83.348).

6. We follow Rousseau (SC 263.285–86 [SC 264.325 n. 2]) in preferring the Greek of Hippolytus to the text in Lat. Iren. and in considering *hic primus* as an unwarranted marginal gloss that has been
introduced into the text.

7. This error was repeated by the Montanists and the Albigenses.
Already St. Paul forewarned Timothy against this abominable heresy

(1 Tim. 4.3). Clement of Alexandria, *Str.* 3.1 (GCS 52[15].195–97), tells how the Basilidians objected to marriage but lived licentious lives.

8. On Basilides, see Hippolytus, *Haer.* 7.2, 13–27; 10.14 (GCS 26.189, 190–208, 274–76), who differs in some respects from Irenaeus. For other patristic sources see Clement of Alexandria, *Str.* 1–8, passim (GCS 52[15] and 17²); Ps.-Tertullian, *Haer.* 1.5 (CCL 2.1402); Epiphanius, *Haer.* 24 (GCS 25.256–67); Theodoret, *Haer.* 1.4 (MG 83.348–49); Eusebius, *H.e.* 4.7.3–7 (GCS 9.1.308–10); Filaster, *Haer.* 32 [4] (CCL 9.230–31). See modern studies by F. J. A. Hort, "Basilides," DCB 1.268–81; A. S. Peake, "Basilides, Basilidians," HERE 2.426–33; G. Bareille, "Basilide," DTC 2.1.465–75; idem, "Gnosticisme," DTC 6.2.1444–46; P. Hendrix, *De alexandrijnsche Haeresiarch Basilides: Een bijdrage tot de geschiedenis der gnosis* (Amsterdam 1926) passim; J. H. Waszink, "Basilides," RAC 1. 1217–25; Quasten *Patr.* 1.257–59; W. Foerster, "Das System des Basilides," NTS 9 (1963) 233–55; E. Mühlenberg, "Basilides," TRE 5.296–301; A. Monaci Castagno, "Basilide gnostico," DPAC 1.487–89; Rudolph *Gnosis* 309–12. For the state of research on Basilides see K. Rudolph, "Gnosis und Gnostizismus, ein Forschungsbericht," ThRdschau 38 (1973) 2–6. Basilides was one of the principal leaders of Gnosticism. His life and system are enveloped in mystery. The date and place of his birth are unknown. K. Rudolph (Rudolph *Gnosis* 309) does not think very probable the view expressed in the Fathers that Basilides was a disciple of Menander. From Antioch he went to Alexandria and is the first known Egyptian Gnostic. He flourished during the first half of the second century, under the Emperors Hadrian (A.D. 117–38) and Antoninus Pius (A.D. 138–61), and under the pontificate of Hyginus (ca. A.D. 137–ca. 140). According to Hippolytus he drew some of his ideas from Aristotle. But he saw the importance of Christian tradition, so he claimed to have received his doctrine from St. Matthias through secret discoveries. He retained some Catholic terms but distorted their meaning, just as he disfigured the Scriptures that he retained in order to deceive the simple. Basilides wrote his own Gospel, which was mentioned by various ecclesiastical writers. He composed a commentary (*Exegetika*) in twenty-four books on it (cf. Eusebius, *H.e.* 4.7.7 [GCS 9.1.310]). Clement of Alexandria cites a long passage from Book 23 in *Str.* 4.12 (GCS 52[15].284–85). He accepts only some letters of the N.T. The Letter to the Hebrews he rejected emphatically (cf. Jerome, *In Tit.*

prologue [ML 26.555]). He also composed some Gnostic psalms and a Prophecy of Cham (cf. *Str.* 6.6 [GCS 52{15}.459]). In doctrine he did not break altogether with his predecessors: Simon, Menander, and Saturninus; but he thought up new angles that make his system quite complicated and abstract. According to Foerster, "Das System des Basilides" 233–55, the churchmen have two different versions of Basilidian Gnosticism. Hippolytus plus a few fragments from Clement of Alexandria and Origen give the purer form; all the others, including Irenaeus, give a later form which is really from his followers.

9. Eusebius, *H.e.* 4.7.4 (GCS 9.1.230), refers to Irenaeus's refutation of "interminable mystic doctrines." Basilides amplified the system of trying to give names to all the angels of the 365 heavens; cf. Hippolytus, *Haer.* 7.26.6 (GCS 26.205). Irenaeus does not touch upon Basilides' doctrine on the absolute ineffability of God, who cannot be expressed in human terms, so that he cannot be called even "nothing" or "being" or "unutterable." See Foerster, "Das System des Basilides" 236. By calling him "Nonbeing" he means that he cannot be grasped by categories of being as we know them. J. Whittaker, "Basilides on the Ineffability of God," HTR 62 (1969) 367–71, thinks that Basilides called God *oude arrēton* not because of any Aristotelian distinction between negative and privative prepositions, but simply to outdo predecessors in the field of negative theology. Cf. n. 3 to chap. 1, n. 17 to chap. 11, and n. 24 to chap. 11.

10. In his account of Basilides, Hippolytus distinguishes more clearly between three worlds. At the head of the first world is God, who is called Nonbeing God (*Haer.* 7.21 [GCS 26.196–97]), because nothing existed prior to his creating, and so we are unable to have any positive concept of God before the existence of other beings; cf. n. 17 to chap. 11, n. 24 to chap. 11, and n. 9. Irenaeus refers to this Basilidian God when, in *Proof* 99 (ACW 16.108), he says the heretics "make an idol out of some unreal one [God]." This God willed to create a cosmical "seed" and by a triple generation or sonship through this "seed" he passed from nothingness or potency to actuality (cf. Hippolytus, *Haer.* 7.22.7 [GCS 26.198]; cf. also Hippolytus, *Haer.* 10.14 [GCS 26.274–75]). But in reality this cosmic "seed" was more an emission than a creation.

11. As Irenaeus notes, the intermediate world was made by the Angels. It consisted of 365 heavens, each of which was ruled by a ruler

(*arkhōn*) and was peopled by aeons (Angels) who proceeded one from the other by emissions. The name of the highest heaven was Ogdoad, and that of the lowest, Hebdomad; another was called Caulacau (cf. Hippolytus, *Haer.* 7.27 [GCS 26.205–7]). Abrasax was the name of the ruler of Ogdoad, but he was really the ruler of the entire second world, somewhat as the Nonbeing God was the ruler of the first world. The correct spelling, as given by all the Greek churchmen, is Abrasax. The Latin churchmen interchanged sigma and xi and wrote Abraxas. Various attempts have been made to discover the etymology of the name, with little satisfaction. Possibly the simple explanation that a name was chosen which expressed the numerical value 365, the number of the heavens in the intermediate world, is correct. Cf. H. Leclercq, "Abrasax," DACL 1.1.129–34. However, K. Rudolph (Rudolph *Gnosis* 311) feels that even though Abrasax does have the numerical value 365 for its basis, it was probably a secret paraphrase of the Jewish God Yahweh written in four consonants (tetragram). Abrasax was ignorant of the triple sonship and thought he was the first of all beings. He needed to be redeemed from this ignorance and pride (cf. Hippolytus, *Haer.* 7.23 [GCS 26.201]). From the "seed" he emitted a son greater than himself (Hippolytus, *Haer.* 7.23.7; 7.26 [GCS 26.201, 204]). The Basilidian Gnostics had numerous medals or amulets on which there were symbols, namely, prayers expressive of their religious tenets. They are known as Abrasax, because this proper name of their Supreme Being is frequent on their amulets. These seem to have been used as a means of propagating their sect. Cf. Leclercq, "Abrasax" 127–55. The Ruler of the Hebdomad erred just as Abrasax had; so it seems all the Rulers erred in like manner. Cf. G. Bareille, "Gnosticisme," DTC 6.2.1445.

12. Lat. Iren. has *continent*, which supposes *kratountas*, and so with the meaning of "rule." But Theodoret, *Haer.* 1.4 (MG 83.349), has *oikountas*. "Rule" fits into the context about the Angels who rule the various heavens. The Ruler of Hebdomad of the second world was Demiurge of the third world, that is, ours (cf. Hippolytus, *Haer.* 7.25 [GCS 26.203]). Basilides identifies him with the God of the Jews. There was a question of a bad rule of the Angels already in the system of Simon (A.H. 1.23.3). J. Daniélou, "Le mauvais gouvernement du monde d'après le gnosticisme," Coll. Messina 448–59, shows that the myth of the Creator Angels and their bad governing of the world is

radically anti-Jewish, and specifically Gnostic in origin (neither pagan nor Christian); though elements were borrowed from the O.T., this tenet is actually a parody of the O.T.

13. Man and woman were made of body and soul; the body must necessarily perish. The soul preexisted in one of the heavens of the second world, where it had sinned and so, in punishment, was sent into our world; see Clement of Alexandria, *Str.* 4.12 (GCS 52[15].284–87). Basilides distinguished between three classes of souls: the rational, the ensouled, and the spiritual (Clement of Alexandria, *Str.* 2.20.112 [GCS 52{15}.174]; Hippolytus, *Haer.* 7.27.5 [GCS 26.206–7]). The spiritual souls can see God naturally and are by nature elect (Clement of Alexandria, *Str.* 5.1; 4.26 [GCS 52{15}.327, 321]). They have faith naturally and receive all doctrines by one intuition (Clement of Alexandria, *Str.* 2.3 [GCS 52{15}.118–19]). We have here a form of absolute predestination and fatalism.

14. We base our translation on remarks made by Rousseau in SC 263.286 (SC 264.327 n. 1).

15. Basilides laid great stress in his system on redemption, but he distorted it beyond all recognition. Cf. Harvey 1.cii–civ. Even the Aeons of the second world had to be redeemed from their ignorance about the triple sonship and pride. This was done through a savior called Gospel, who really belongs to the first world and is the first sonship. He descended into the Ogdoad and wrought salvation by bringing knowledge about the Nonbeing God and the triple sonship. He made this manifestation first to the son of Abrasax, and only through this son did he enlighten the Father, Abrasax, who then realized his ignorance, admitted it, and was consequently redeemed. In like manner were all the Aeons of the Ogdoad redeemed, as well as the rest of the heavens (Hippolytus, *Haer.* 7.26; 10.14 [GCS 26.204–5, 276]). As was noted above, the souls preexisted in the second world, where they sinned by wishing to rise above their level and rule over all others. The first who so fell was Abrasax himself, but in like manner all the rulers of all the heavens fell. The only beings, then, who never sinned were the supreme God and his first two sons. All others needed redemption. This was accomplished by a new Aeon called Jesus, who belonged to the heaven of the second world named Caulacau (Theodoret, *Haer.* 1.4 [MG 83.349]). He became incarnate through Mary. At baptism the light which had enlightened the rulers of the

Ogdoad and Hebdomad, descended on him (Hippolytus, *Haer.* 7.26.8 [GCS 26.205]). It was then that the third sonship, having been purified, attached itself to Jesus and was redeemed and elevated by God and thus the disorder in the "seed" was at an end (cf. Hippolytus, *Haer.* 7.26.10 [GCS 26.205], and idem, *Haer.* 7.27.11 [GCS 26.207]). According to the account of Irenaeus and Epiphanius (*Haer.* 24.3.2 [GCS 25.260]) Jesus did not suffer, but Simon of Cyrene did. Jesus redeemed us by illumination. However, according to Hippolytus, *Haer.* 7.27.12 [GCS 26.207-8]), Jesus did suffer. All those who do not belong to the sonship will be lost. Those who belong to it will quit the earth and be saved; these are the spiritual souls. They kept the feast day of Jesus' birth and also his baptism as an illumination (cf. Clement of Alexandria, *Str.* 1.21.146 [GCS 52{15}.90]). Some have misinterpreted Clement's account as if the Basilidians observed only the one feast of baptism. But before this Clement talks about those who keep his birthday, and then adds: "And the followers of Basilides celebrate *also* his day of baptism."

16. Cf. Matt. 27.32; Luke 23.26.

17. Our translation is based on remarks of Rousseau at SC 263.286 (SC 264.329 n. 1).

18. Basilides is said to have taught that a person must sin each time an occasion presents itself, else he or she has no right to glory (Clement of Alexandria, *Str.* 4.12 [GCS 52{15}.284-87]). And the predestined, spiritual souls can sin with impunity (idem, *Str.* 3.1.3 [GCS 52{15}.196]). Marriage, he held, is not really an evil but a simple remedy for concupiscence (idem, *Str.* 3.1.3 [GCS 52{15}.197]). The Fathers reproved Basilides severely for the immoral principles that he spread abroad. See Epiphanius, *Haer.* 24.3.7-8 (GCS 25.261), who does not even wish to speak of it; Jerome, *Ad Iovin.* 2.37 (ML 23.335), who calls him a teacher of debauchery. Maybe he himself did not merit the severe criticisms, but merely laid down the foundation that led to such immorality, already in his disciple Isidore. Although Isidore is called Basilides' "real son," K. Rudolph (Rudolph *Gnosis* 312) doubts that Isidore was necessarily the son of Basilides.

19. "Rulers" is *principia,* which, as it is used together here with "Angels and Powers," seems to be a synonym for *principes,* which occurs often with "Angels and Powers." The Latin as it stands in this

sentence is unintelligible: *Quemadmodum et [mundus] nomen [esse], in quo dicunt descendisse et ascendisse Saluatorem, esse Caulacau. Mundus* can certainly not be correct; at least it should be in the accusative with the infinitive. Rousseau (SC 264.330) would exclude it. Hippolytus, *Haer.* 5.8.3–4 (GCS 26.89), calls it, together with other similar names, a difficult name. The first or second *esse* must be dropped. Rousseau (SC 264.330) agrees with this statement and would exclude the first *esse.* Massuet (MG 7.678) and Klebba (3.74) retained *mundus,* namely, its name is Caulacau. But in 1.24.6 Irenaeus treats Caulacau as a person, as does also Theodoret, *Haer.* 1.4 (MG 83.349). Besides, Irenaeus is speaking of naming the heavens, and he would not call it world. Lastly *in* for *in quo* would hardly be the correct preposition if there were question of ascending and descending into and from that world. What is the meaning of Caulacau? In this translation we have it refer to Savior. Hippolytus, *Haer.* 5.8.3–4 (GCS 26.89), claims it is the heavenly Man, Savior; so does Theodoret, *Haer.* 1.4 (MG 83.349). Grabe is altogether wrong in holding that it is a name for our own world. Rousseau (SC 263.286 [SC 264.331 n. 1]) agrees that Grabe is mistaken here. Neander says it is the name of the world above in which Savior dwelt (cf. Harvey 1.201 n. 4) and that is the interpretation adopted by Klebba (3.74). However, that does not seem to fit the context. Perhaps the solution to this seeming confusion is provided by Rousseau in SC 263.286–87 (SC 264.331 n. 1) who comments that the name of Caulacau cannot be that of the world but only that of the "Savior." Epiphanius, *Haer.* 25.3.6 (GCS 25.270), writes that the Nicolaitans called a certain ruler by this name. Hippolytus says that the Ophites used this title, and he interprets it as "Adamas, who is the one from above" (*Haer.* 5.8.3–4 [GCS 26.89]). Authors dispute about the etymology of the word. Harvey (1.201 n. 4) suggests that it comes from the Hebrew "*Qau laqau,*" which would mean "line upon line"; cf. Isa. 28.10. That would seem to agree with Hippolytus's explanation.

20. Since the souls preexisted in the upper world, salvation is nothing but a restoration (*apokatastasis*) to the primitive state (Hippolytus, *Haer.* 7.27.4–5 [GCS 26.206–7]). See also n. 11 to chap. 14 and A. Méhat, "*Apokatastasis* chez Basilide" 365–73.

21. They do not demand loyalty to any truth. Besides, there is a big difference between the doctrines of the various Gnostics; so it matters

little what one holds. With them there can be no such thing as defending one definite creed. On the reasons for the translation of *omnibus similes* as "like the Aeons," see SC 263.215 (SC 264.129 n. 2).

22. Because of its immorality the Basilidian sect drew its members from the lower strata of society, though Basilides dared call the non-Basilidians pigs and dogs. His followers were not so numerous as those of Valentinus. The sect seems to have been confined to Egypt. Epiphanius, about the middle of the fourth century, still found some in the delta of the Nile. Jerome speaks of their infiltration among the Priscillianists of Spain. Cf. G. Bareille, "Basilide," DTC 2.1.474–75. That they were neither Jews nor Christians is true, but neither were they pagans. They were Basilidians, who could recant under persecution and could conform to the demands of the state. That explains why they escaped persecution and execution, while the Christians in the same area did not. See W. H. C. Frend, "The Gnostic Sects and the Roman Empire," JEH 5 (1954) 25–37.

23. Harvey (1.203 n. 4) notes that to these astrologers belong all who were versed in geometry, music, and other higher studies.

24. There is disagreement among the translators and interpreters on whether the antecedent of Abrasax is astrologers or heavens. Harvey (1.203 n. 5) and Klebba (3.74) refer it to astrologers, and translate *principem* as "chief." However, this noun seems to translate the Greek *arkhōn*, "ruler." So Abrasax was the name of the ruler of the highest heavens. And Irenaeus is saying the same as Hippolytus, who writes that the ruler of the Ogdoad had this name (*Haer.* 7.26.6 [GCS 26.205]). The numeric value of the name in Greek letters is 365, namely, 1 plus 2 plus 100 plus 1 plus 200 plus 1 plus 60.

CHAPTER 25

1. Cf. Hippolytus, *Haer.* 7.32 (GCS 26.218–20), and SC 263.98 for Rousseau's and Doutreleau's discussion of their fifteenth Greek fragment. See also Tertullian, *Anim.* 23–25 (CCL 2.815–21); Ps.-Tertullian, *Haer.* 3 (CCL 2.1405–6); Eusebius, *H.e.* 4.7.9 (GCS 9.1.310); Epiphanius, *Haer.* 27.2–3 (GCS 25.301–4); Theodoret, *Haer.* 1.5 (MG 83.349–

52); Clement of Alexandria, *Str.* 3.2 (GCS 52[15].197–200); Filaster, *Haer.* 35 [7] (CCL 9.232–33). See G. Bareille, "Carpocrate," DTC 2.2.1800–3; idem, "Gnosticisme," DTC 6.2.1447; A. Monaci Castagno, "Carpocrate," DPAC 1.597–98; Quasten 1.266–67. Little is known of his life except that he lived in Alexandria, as had his predecessor Cerinthus, and his contemporaries Basilides and Valentinus. So it was during the first half of the second century under Hadrian (Theodoret, *Haer.* 1.5 [MG 83.352]). See also A.H. 1.25.6. Marcellina, a woman disciple, went to Rome under Pope Anicetus (ca. A.D. 154-ca. A.D. 166). He was married to a certain Alexandria of the island of Cephallania. Epiphanes was their son. See n. 11 to chap. 11. According to Tertullian, *Anim.* 35 (CCL 2.836), Carpocrates himself practiced the magic arts and was immoral. He borrowed his hatred for the God of the Jews and their Law from Saturninus and his principles of total immorality from Basilides. Of all the Gnostics he seems to have been most imbued with Platonic ideas. H. Kraft, "Gab es einen Gnostiker Karpokrates?" *Theologische Zeitschrift* 8 (1952) 434–43, thinks that there was no such heresiarch, only a sect that was given this name when it adopted the Egyptian god Horus-Harpocrates. So reported by G. W. MacRae, "Carpocrates," NCE 3 (1967) 145. See also Rudolph, *Gnosis* 299, who also reports this but believes Carpocrates is real.

2. We base our translation here on remarks made by Rousseau in SC 263.287 (SC 264.333 n. 1).

3. On various interpretations of *panton* here see SC 263.288 (SC 264.333 n. 3).

4. This last phrase is obscure in its conciseness: *et eas, quae similia ei amplecterentur, similiter.* The Greek text, as edited by Rousseau and Doutreleau, is ⟨*kai tas*⟩ *ta homoia autēi aspazomenas* ⟨*homoiōs*⟩. Hippolytus, *Haer.* 7.32.2 (GCS 26.218), has "and [the soul] embraces the beings similar to it [Jesus' soul]." But Epiphanius, *Haer.* 27.2.6 (GCS 25.302), is more complete and suggests the words to be filled in the Latin: "And the souls that are like it [Jesus' soul] which embrace things similar to it, having been freed in the same manner, flew above to the unknown Father." Rousseau's and Doutreleau's work (SC 264.333) would suggest a different translation: "Souls which embrace dispositions similar to his own."

5. Rousseau (SC 263.288–89 [SC 264.335 n. 1]) notes that Epiphanius's reading in Greek corresponds nearly word for word with Lat.

Iren. and wonders if the variations in the Latin represent a translator's misinterpretation or a mishap in transmitting the text.

6. "Wherefore . . . sphere" is extant also in Armenian and is listed by Rousseau and Doutreleau as their sixth Armenian fragment from the Galata 54 MS. For more information on this see SC 263.101-5.

7. Rousseau (SC 263.291 [SC 264.337 n. 1]) feels the expression *tōn entautha* ought to be compared to the words "the soul of Jesus . . . despised" of the previous paragraph for the proper context of the Greek expression. In that case, he argues, the "things here below" would refer to the laws and regulations set up most particularly by the God of the Jews.

8. Utter contempt of Yahweh's Law and violation of it was a duty. See Clement of Alexandria, *Str.* 3.2 (GCS 52[15].197). So Carpocrates taught a repulsive type of redemption. Jesus' contempt for the Law was the salvation of the world. For others to be saved they have to imitate him as their exemplar in this absolute antinomianism. Nothing is said about a redemption through suffering and death.

9. Rousseau (SC 263.291 [SC 264.337 n. 2]) feels the Greek *pros ta ethnē* is correct as the Latin translator has misread *hōs* or *hōs kai* for *pros*. This is important for a correct interpretation of Irenaeus's meaning. Satan is not represented in the A.H. as sending forth pagans. But he sends forth heretics into the midst of pagans. As the pagans cannot distinguish authentic Christians from the heretics, the pagans hold in contempt anything associated with Christianity.

10. Cf. 1 Pet. 2.16. This and the preceding sentence are wrongly run together in Lat. Iren.: *Sed uitam quidem luxuriosam, sententiam autem impiam ad uelamen malitiae ipsorum nomine abuntur.* Epiphanius, *Haer.* 27.4.1 (GCS 25.304), has: "For in no way are they like us; rather they only boast of being called by the Name in order, under the veil of the Name, to work out their own iniquity." That suggested the insertion and punctuation we have given. That the Name is Jesus is clear from A.H. 1.27.4.

11. Cf. Rom. 3.8.

12. Cf. Eph. 5.12.

13. Epiphanius, *Haer.* 27.5.1-9 (GCS 25.306-8), and Tertullian, *Anim.* 35 (CCL 2.836-38), note these same immoral tenets and practices. Carpocrates followed the Pythagoreans in the doctrine about

transmigration of souls, with this big difference: They held that this was a punishment for crime in the previous world; he held it was a punishment for not enough crime in this world. And through this teaching he pushed his principle of immoral actions to the limit. With such a doctrine the existence of hell becomes useless. Nor is there any resurrection, because the body will be left on earth (cf. also Ps.-Tertullian, *Haer.* 3.1 [CCL 2.1405]). Another consequence of his teaching on immorality was that wives ought to be had in common (Clement of Alexandria, *Str.* 3.2 [GCS 52{15}.197]). Their nocturnal assemblies of promiscuity and debauchery were blasphemously called love feasts (agapes) (Clement of Alexandria, *Str.* 3.2 [GCS 52{15}.200]). Here Irenaeus's observation that the writings of the Gnostics contain these things indicates that he read them firsthand.

14. The quotation is a combination of Luke 12.58–59 and Matt. 5.25–26. Perhaps it indicates that the heretics had their own harmony of the Gospels.

15. The Greek of the rest of this paragraph is found in Hippolytus, *Haer.* 7.32 (GCS 26.220), though it differs in places from the Latin. Rousseau and Doutreleau edit this as their sixteenth Greek fragment. See SC 263.98 on this fragment.

16. This last sentence has caused some difficulty. In Latin it runs: *siue ipsae praeoccupantes in uno aduentu in omnibus misceantur operationibus, siue de corpore in corpus transmigrantes uel immissae, in unaquaque specie uitae adimplentes et reddentes debita, liberari, uti iam non fiant in corpore.* Hippolytus, *Haer.* 7.32 (GCS 26.220), omits the clause *uel immissae . . .* and joins the other clauses differently, seemingly getting some words from the similar passage in the beginning of this paragraph. His words are: "Some in the one coming preoccupy themselves by being mixed up in every kind of sin, and so no longer transmigrate from one body to another, but having paid all the debts at once, they will be freed so they no longer have to be in a body." In Lat. Iren. *uel* can be explanatory, and can be translated "or what is the same thing." That helps to simplify the construction, and there is then no need to omit it to translate it by "and" as some have done. "Fulfill the requirements and pay the debts" is literally *adimplentes et reddentes debita.* The Clermont and Voss Codices have *faciant,* which Massuet (MG 7.684 n. 30) and Stieren (1.252 n. 7) accept; but the Arundel Codex

has *fiant*, which Harvey (1.209) as well as Rousseau and Doutreleau (SC 264.340) accept. Lundström (Lundström *Studien* 80) suggests that maybe *faciant* has an intransitive meaning here, namely, *kommen* or *geraten*. But that is not necessary, because *faciant* can mean to live or to operate in a body.

17. This paragraph and a few lines of the next are extant in Theodoret, *Haer.* 1.5 (MG 83.352C). Rousseau and Doutreleau edit this as their seventeenth Greek fragment. For more on this see SC 263.98–99.

18. Lat. Iren., in the light of the Greek in Theodoret, *Haer.* 1.5 (MG 83.352C; see also SC 264.341–42), bears the translation given. Klebba BKV (3.77) has the same. Harvey (1.209 n. 3) followed by ANF (1.351) gets a different meaning out of it: "If iniquity of every kind . . . is practiced by them, under this condition of necessity, I can no longer believe it to be iniquity." That seems to have been suggested by Tertullian, *Anim.* 35.4 (CCL 2.837): "If however the soul is bound to committing all crimes, who will have to be understood as its enemy and adversary?" But, as is evident, Tertullian has the phrase in a different context.

19. This first sentence is preserved in Hippolytus, *Haer.* 7.32 (GCS 26.220). On this text as edited by Rousseau and Doutreleau as their eighteenth Greek fragment see SC 263.98. Cf. *Proof* 3. Clement of Alexandria, *Ecl.* 25 (GCS 17².143), has the same information. In the Orient people were at times marked with a sign known as *stigma* or *sphragis*. For Christians the *sphragis* was the name of Christ that was given at baptism. Cf. W. Bousset, *Kyrios Christos: Geschichte des Christusglaubens von den Anfängen des Christentums bis Irenaeus*, 3d ed. (Göttingen 1926) 227–28; F. J. Dölger, *Sphragis: Eine altchristliche Taufbezeichnung in ihren Beziehungen zur profanen und religiösen Kultur des Altertums* (Paderborn 1911; repr. New York 1967) 39–46.

20. "School." Lat. Iren. has *doctrinae*, but that would normally suppose *didaskalias*. Now, since "school" is much better in the context, it seems the Greek here was *didaskaleion*, as in other cases, which Lat. Iren. inaccurately translated here by *doctrinae*. Cf. n. 3 to chap. 11. Anicetus was pope from ca. 154–166. "Led astray" is *exterminauit*. This word was used also in 1.13.2 to translate *exēpatēse* ("led astray"). It seems to have that meaning here too. Epiphanius, *Haer.* 27.6.1 (GCS

25.308), and Augustine, *Haer.* 7 (ML 42.27), also speak of this Marcellina.

CHAPTER 26

1. This is extant in Hippolytus, *Haer.* 7.33–34 (P₁) (GCS 26.220–21) and *Haer.* 10.21-22 (P₂) (GCS 26.281). For a discussion of differences in the accounts by Irenaeus and Hippolytus, see B. G. Wright, "Cerinthus *apud* Hippolytus: An Inquiry Into the Traditions about Cerinthus's Provenance," SCent 4, no. 2 (Summer 1984) 103–15. Rousseau and Doutreleau designate this as their nineteenth Greek fragment. For more on this see SC 263.99. Others who wrote on Cerinthus are Ps.-Tertullian, *Haer.* 3.2 (CCL 2.1405); Eusebius, *H.e.* 3.28; 4.14.6; 7.25 (GCS 9.1.256, 334; 9.2.690); Epiphanius, *Haer.* 28 (GCS 25.313–21); Theodoret, *Haer.* 2.3 (MG 83.389–92); Filaster, *Haer.* 36 [7] (CCL 9.233). For modern studies see G. Bareille, "Cérinthe," DTC 2.2.2151–55; A. F. J. Klijn, "Cerinto e cerintiani," DPAC 1.648–49; and Rudolph *Gnosis* 165, 299. The exact dates of Cerinthus are unknown. He must have flourished toward the end of the first century. His parents seem to have been Jewish because he was circumcised. Some think that he was born at Antioch; others, in Egypt. At any rate, he lived at Alexandria where he received a rather complete education in pagan and Oriental philosophy and in Philo's attempt to harmonize the philosophers with the Old Testament. He quit Egypt and travelled through Palestine, Caesarea, and Antioch. Later he settled in Asia Minor where he had a school and founded his sect. At the baths of Ephesus John the Apostle met Cerinthus and said with reference to him: "Let us flee lest even the bathhouse collapse because Cerinthus the enemy of the Truth is in there" (A.H. 3.3.4). He was loyal to the law and to circumcision. Still, according to the trend of the times, he was a syncretist. He tried to harmonize the Jewish religion with Platonic Hellenism and the Christian Gospel. According to Irenaeus, A.H. 3.11.1, St. John wrote his Gospel in defense of Christ's divinity against Cerinthus, who for a time was a real danger to Christianity.

According to the report of certain Alogoi and Gaius of Rome, Cerinthus wrote an Apocalypse in which he describes great prodigies. Others, less probably, think these men are ascribing the genuine Apocalypse of John to Cerinthus. Cf. Eusebius, *H.e.* 3.28.1–6; 7.25.1–5 (GCS 9.1.256–60; 9.2.690–92). Cerinthus had at one time converted to Christianity; but the apostles, according to Filaster, *Haer.* 60 [32] (CCL 9.242), condemned him and drove him out of the Church. He was narrow-minded, insisting on the observance of Jewish law by Christians. The followers of Cerinthus, likewise, would have consented to become Christians if they would not have had to give up anything of Judaism. But they regarded Paul as an apostate and so rejected his Letters. This sect gradually died out. Irenaeus does not devote much space to them, perhaps because their system was more or less dead in his time.

2. "And he excelled . . . spiritual" is also extant in Armenian. Rousseau and Doutreleau count it as their seventh Armenian fragment from the Galata 54 MS. For more on this see SC 263.101–5.

3. We base our translation of this sentence on textual emendations discussed in SC 263.292 (SC 264.345 n. 1).

4. Cerinthus also taught millenarianism: Between the end of the world and the Kingdom of God in heaven there would be a period of happiness in an earthly kingdom, where there would be nuptial delights and joyous sacrifices. Irenaeus does not reprove him for this, perhaps because he himself held a mitigated form of millenarianism: cf. A.H. 5.32.1; 5.35.2.

5. Hippolytus, *Haer.* 7.34; 10.22 (GCS 26.221, 281), gives partly what Irenaeus has and partly his own account. See Tertullian, *Praescr.* 33 (CCL 1.213–14); Ps.-Tertullian, *Haer.* 3.3 (CCL 2.1405–6); Origen, *Cels.* 2.1 (GCS 2.126–28); Eusebius, *H.e.* 3.27 (GCS 9.1.254–56); Epiphanius, *Haer.* 30 (GCS 25.333–82); Theodoret, *Haer.* 2.1 (MG 83.388–89); Filaster, *Haer.* 37 [9] (CCL 9.233). See G. Bareille, "Ebionites," DTC 4.2.1987–92; G. Strecker, "Ebioniten," RAC 4.487–500; A. F. J. Klijn, "Ebioniti," DPAC 1.1047–48. Among the first converts from Judaism there were those who though they kept on observing Jewish practices, did not insist on them as essential to salvation, and lived as thorough Christians. Others, however, insisted that along with faith in Christ, circumcision and the other Jewish observances were essential to sal-

vation. The Apostle Paul opposed these so-called Judaizers strenu-
ously and successfully. After the fall of Jerusalem, the first group
realized more fully that the law had run its course; but the others grew
more headstrong in their attitudes and grafted Gnostic errors on their
own system. Already after the death of James, Bishop of Jerusalem, in
A.D. 62 there was trouble. According to Hegesippus, as recorded in
Eusebius, *H.e.* 4.22.5 (GCS 9.1.370), a certain Thebuthis wanted to be
bishop of Jerusalem. When he was thwarted in his hopes, he became
the leader of one of the seven sects that opposed God, His Christ, and
the unity of the Church. Hegesippus seems to refer to what were later
known as Ebionites. They were given this name—which means "the
poor"—because they were Jews. This term was first used to designate
the Jewish converts to Christianity since they followed Christ's
counsel to sell all and have no money (cf. Matt. 10.9). Nearly all the
heresiologists speak of the leader of the Ebionites as a so-called Ebion
or Hebion. But that does not seem to be correct, because Justin, *Dial.*
46, and Hegesippus (cf. Eusebius, *H.e.* 4.22.5) know nothing of such
an individual, though they were acquainted with the sect and mention
other heresiarchs by name. For more on Justin's and Hegesippus's
knowledge on this see Bareille, "Ebionites" 1988–89.

6. See SC 263.293 (SC 264.347 n. 2) for the rationale for the translation "the true God" here.

7. Some of them held that Jesus was born naturally of Joseph and
Mary. In their Bible Isa. 7.14 had "young girl" not "virgin" according
to Irenaeus; cf. also Eusebius, *H.e.* 5.8.10; 3.27.2 (GCS 9.1.448, 256).
Other held that he was born of a virgin (cf. Origen, *Cels.* 5.61 [GCS
2.65]; Eusebius, *H.e.* 3.27.3 [GCS 9.1.256]), though they did not therefore admit that he was God, because they denied that the Christ had
any preexistence. At baptism Jesus became Christ who descended
upon him (Justin, *Dial.* 49 [Goodspeed 147]). Cf. Epiphanius, *Haer.*
30.13.7 (GCS 25.350). The Gospel which they used (see n. 8) adds that
the voice said: "This day have I begotten you" (Ps. 2.7).

8. The Ebionites made much of the Gospel of Matthew, their only
Gospel. See A.H. 3.11.7, where Irenaeus says that they are convinced
by it. Jerome (*Vir. ill.* 2) and many others have identified this Ebionite
Gospel referred to by Irenaeus with the Gospel according to the
Hebrews. M. J. Lagrange too thought this was correct, but he allowed

that Irenaeus might be referring to the canonical Gospel of Matthew, either in the Aramaic or in the Greek. See M. J. Lagrange, "L'Evangile selon les Hébreux," RBibl 31 (1922) 171. Lagrange denied, as Harnack, *Die Chronologie der altchristlichen Literatur bis Irenäus*, pt. 2, vol. 1 of *Geschichte der altchristlichen Literatur bis Eusebius* (Leipzig 1897) 631, had already done, that this Ebionite Gospel was the same as that spoken of by Epiphanius in *Haer.* 30.3.7–9; 30.13.2–7 (GCS 25.337–38, 349–51), because in the one to which Irenaeus refers there was a proof for the one God and Creator, for the infancy and virginal conception (cf. 3.11.7; 3.9.1–3), which are missing in the Gospel as referred to by Epiphanius (Lagrange, "L'Evangile" 171). On this Gospel see also Quasten 1.111–12 and E. Hennecke, *The New Testament Apocrypha*, ed. W. Schneemelcher, trans. R. McL. Wilson et al., 1 (Philadelphia 1963–65) 153–58.

9. The Ebionites naturally had mortal hatred of Paul because of his preaching that the law was no longer valid. They said he was a mere Gentile who had become a Jew with the hope of marrying the high priest's daughter. When he was deceived, he renounced Judaism (cf. Epiphanius, *Haer.* 30.16.9 [GCS 25.355]). He set out to preach Christ without official commission, in fact he was opposed to Peter and James. The Ebionites rejected Paul's Letters not because they denied their authenticity, but because they considered Paul an apostate.

10. Naturally they accepted the Old Testament because for them the old law with all its details was still in full force. Cf. Hippolytus, *Haer.* 7.34 (GCS 26.221). They twisted Matt. 5.17 and 10.24–25 to this meaning. Since few of them could read Hebrew they had to depend on a Greek translation. They would not use the one which the Christians used, the Septuagint, or those of the proselytes Aquila and Theodotion (cf. Eusebius, *H.e.* 5.8.10 [GCS 9.1.446]). So they chose the version made by one of their own, Symmachus (cf. Eusebius, *H.e.* 6.17 [GCS 9.2.554–56]). In reference to the last phrase, Barnabas accuses the Jews of an idolatrous worship of Jerusalem (*Barn.* 16 [ACW 6.60]). It is worth noting too that among the Valentinians both the Ogdoad and Achamoth were known as Jerusalem (cf. Hippolytus, *Haer.* 6.32.9; 6.34.3–4 [GCS 25.161, 163]).

11. For this sect see Hippolytus, *Haer.* 7.36.2–3 (GCS 26.223), whose account is similar to Irenaeus's but not copied verbatim. Ps.-Tertullian, *Haer.* 1.6 (CCL 2.1402–3); Epiphanius, *Haer.* 25 (GCS 25.267–74);

Eusebius, *H.e.* 3.29 (GCS 9.1.260, 262); Theodoret, *Haer.* 1.15 (MG 83.368B); Filaster, *Haer.* 33 [5] (CCL 9.231–32). See also E. Peretto, "Nicolaiti," DPAC 2.2400–2401. Harvey (1.214 n. 1) thinks that Tertullian in *Praescr.* 33.10 (CCL 1.214) classes as one the Nicolaitan and the Cainite sects. Tertullian's words are: *sunt et nunc alii Nicolaitae, Caina haeresis dicitur.* It seems to me that he is merely saying that the present Cainite heresy is similar in character to the ancient Nicolaitan. In regard to the connection between Nicolas the deacon of Acts 6.5 and this sect of Nicolaitans, Irenaeus has usually been interpreted as claiming that they take their origin from him. But N. Brox, "Nikolaos und Nikolaiten," VC 19 (1965) 23–30, thinks that Irenaeus is merely reporting that the Nicolaitans claim him as their founder, namely, a man of apostolic times in order to add prestige to themselves. Yet the matter is not that simple. In the sequel Irenaeus certainly connects these Nicolaitans with those denounced by John in Rev. (Apoc.) 2.6, and he assumes these latter are connected with the deacon Nicolas of Acts. True, he does not brand Nicolas himself as immoral, as many have inferred. Immoral practices he imputes only to his followers, to the Nicolaitans. Hippolytus, then, makes Nicolas responsible for this sect, after he became an apostate (*Haer.* 7.36 [GCS 26.223]). Clement of Alexandria, however, claims the Nicolaitans misused Nicolas's name. He had lived a good life with only one wife (cf. *Str.* 3.4.25–26 [GCS 52 {15}.207–8]). Other heresiologists are silent about any defection of Nicolas and connection with this heretical sect. There are, therefore, those scholars today who question or even deny that Nicolas had any relation with this sect. They claim since John condemned a group called Nicolaitans (Rev. [Apoc.] 2.6, 14–15), and since Nicolas was the name of one of the deacons in Acts 6.5, it was easy for writers much later to connect the two and make the deacon the founder of the heretical sect. Cf. E. Amann, "Nicolaites," DTC 11.1.505. Still we find it hard to admit that Irenaeus, who investigated all his sources carefully and lived not too long after John and Nicolas seemingly would have lived, was merely conjecturing about the relation between the two. So this remains an unsolved problem. According to A.H. 3.11.1, the Nicolaitans were given to Gnostic speculations. Hippolytus agrees with that information in his *Syntagma* according to Epiphanius, *Haer.* 25 (GCS 25.267–74); so do Ps.-Tertullian, *Haer.* 1.6 (CCL 2.1402–3), and Filaster, *Haer.* 33 [5] (CCL 9.231–32). But Clement

of Alexandria and others do not mention this. Irenaeus and Hippolytus speak of the immoral practice and idolatry of these heretics. But
this could have been a conjecture based on Rev. (Apoc.) 2; and "fornication" can figuratively be idolatry, as so often in the Old Testament
and in the Apocalypse. Clement of Alexandria speaks of their community of wives; but he loved secret traditions. Epiphanius seems to have
mixed the two accounts of Irenaeus and Clement, making Nicolas a
fugitive monk of moral perversion and mental aberrations. Cf.
Amann, "Nicolaites" 499–506.

12. On the choice of fornication here instead of adultery see SC
263.293 (SC 264.349 n. 2).

13. Cf. Rev. (Apoc.) 2.14–15.

14. Cf. Rev. (Apoc.) 2.6.

CHAPTER 27

1. Rousseau and Doutreleau edit Eusebius, *H.e.* 4.11.2 (GCS
9.1.322), and Hippolytus, *Haer.* 7.37 (GCS 26.233), as the basis of their
twentieth Irenaean Greek fragment. On this see SC 263.100. Other
ancient authors to consult on Cerdo include Ps.-Tertullian, *Haer.* 6.6
(CCL 2.1409); Tertullian, *Adv. Marc.* 12.3 (CCL 1.443); Epiphanius,
Haer. 41 (GCS 31.90–93); Theodoret, *Haer.* 1.24 (MG 83.372–73, 376);
Filaster, *Haer.* 44 [16] (CCL 9.235–36). For modern studies see G.
Bareille, "Cerdon," DTC 2.2.2138–39; idem, "Gnosticisme," DTC
6.2.1453; C. Giannoto, "Cerdone," DPAC 1.647; Rudolph *Gnosis* 314.
Cerdo was a Syrian, and in Syria he must have learned of Simon's
system, which is reflected in his own. He came to Rome under Hyginus. There he could have met Valentinus. At this time Rome was the
magnet of all innovators. He seems to have flourished in the middle of
the second century. Irenaeus calls Marcion the successor of Cerdo.
There is no record of his having written any work. It is not certain if
he founded a special sect. According to Irenaeus, A.H. 3.4.3, Cerdo
was a restless fellow who became a Christian, but he secretly taught
errors. When he was exposed, he left the Christian community defini-
tively. For Cerdo's doctrine see n. 3. See SC 263.106–7 for information

on Irenaean extracts from this chapter to be found in Armenian translation in *The Seal of the Faith of the Holy Catholic Church*.

2. Lat. Iren. puts Hyginus down as the ninth pope. Eusebius (*H.e.* 5.6 [GCS 9.1.438]) copied this from Irenaeus; so did Epiphanius (*Haer.* 27.6.2 [GCS 25.308–9]). However, he put Peter and Paul as the first in line, and so he really had only eight popes. Irenaeus himself says in A.H. 3.4.3 Hyginus was the eighth, and in A.H. 3.3.3 he enumerates seven predecessors. Perhaps the present passage had eta, that is, eight, which corrupted to theta, that is, nine. This was the solution which Massuet (MG 7.687–88 n. 45) favored. For more on this question see SC 263.293–95 (SC 264.349 n. 3) and E. Caspar, *Die älteste römische Bischofsliste: Kritische Studien zum Formproblem des Eusebianischen Kanons sowie zur Geschichte der ältesten Bischofslisten und ihrer Entstehung aus apostolischen Sukzessionenreihen* (Berlin 1926) passim.

3. Cerdo rejected the entire Old Testament, and sections of the New, namely, Acts, Apocalypse, and the Gospels of Matthew, Mark, and John. He retained, but mutilated, the Gospel of Luke. He also did not accept Jude, James, John, and Peter. He kept Paul's Letters only in part. See Ps.-Tertullian, *Haer.* 6.1 (CCL 2.1408). He taught a dualism —the good God was the Father of Christ; the just God was the God of the law and the prophets. Bareille, "Cerdon" 2138–39, states that in *Haer.* 7.37 (GCS 26.223) Hippolytus says that Cerdo held two first principles—the first one being the good God and the other being the evil God. But in *Haer.* 10.19 (GCS 26.279–80) he speaks of three principles—the good, the just, and matter. This is, however, not a contradiction. The evil and the just God are the same, namely, the Demiurge who with the aid of matter created beings to his own image, though he did a bad job. The good God intervened and sent Christ to save the ensouled. Savior only appeared to be human. He was not born of a virgin. He taught men and women to adhere to him and repudiate the God of the Jews. This was salvation. He did not suffer. Cerdo repudiated marriage because it was a source of corruption. Practically, his system amounted to hatred of the Creator God and cynicism of the worst kind.

4. See Hippolytus, *Haer.* 7.29–31 (GCS 26.210–17), which is, however, not the text of Irenaeus; Hippolytus, *Haer.* 10.19 (GCS 26.279–80), which differs from his own previous account; Tertullian, *Adv. Marc.* 1–5 (CCL 1.441–726); Ps.-Tertullian, *Haer.* 6.2–3 (CCL 2.1408);

Eusebius, *H.e.* 5.13 (GCS 9.1.454); Epiphanius, *Haer.* 42 (GCS 31.93–186); Theodoret, *Haer.* 1.24 (MG 83.372–73, 376); Filaster, *Haer.* 45 [17] (CCL 9.236). Cf. G. Salmon, "Marcion," DCB 3.816–24; G. Krüger, "Marcion," RPT 12.266–77; O. Bardenhewer, *Geschichte der altkirchlichen Literatur*, vol. 1 (Freiburg 1902) 341–46; A. Harnack, *Marcion: Das Evangelium vom fremden Gott. Eine Monographie zur Geschichte der Grundlegung der katholischen Kirche*, TU 45 (Berlin 1921¹ and 1924²; repr. Berlin/Darmstadt 1960) passim; idem, *Neue Studien zu Marcion* (TU 44, pt. 4, 1923) passim; G. Bareille, "Gnosticisme," DTC 6.2.1453–56; E. Amann, "Marcion," DTC 9.2.2009–32; J. Lebreton, *Histoire du dogme de la Trinité: Des origines au concile de Nicée*, vol. 2: *De saint Clément à saint Irénée.* (Paris 1928) 122–31; E. C. Blackman, *Marcion and His Influence* (London 1948) 82–87; Quasten 1.268–72; G. Bardy, "Marcion," DBS 5.862–77; B. Altaner, *Patrologie: Leben, Schriften und Lehre der Kirchenväter*, 8th ed., rev. A. Stuiber (Freiburg 1978) 106–7; Rudolph *Gnosis* 313–16; K. Rudolph, "Gnosis und Gnostizismus, ein Forschungsbericht," ThRdschau 37 (1972) 358–60; B. Aland, "Marcion: Versuch einer neuen Interpretation," ZTK 70 (1973) 420–47; B. Aland, "Marcione-Marcionismo," DPAC 2.2095–98; G. May, "Marcion in Contemporary Views: Results and Open Questions," SCent 6, no. 3 (Fall 1987–88) 129–51; R. J. Hoffmann, "How Then This Troublous Teacher? Further Reflections on Marcion and His Church," SCent 6, no. 3 (Fall 1987–88) 173–91. Marcion was born toward the end of the first century at Sinope of Pontus. His father was the bishop of Sinope. Marcion was educated as a Christian, but his father is said to have excommunicated him for having seduced a virgin (cf. Epiphanius, *Haer.* 42.1 [GCS 31.94]). Some, however, claim that this is to be taken metaphorically: the virgin is the Church whom he corrupted by his heresies. He became an owner of merchant ships and amassed a fortune. He trafficked mostly in Asia Minor. At one time he met Polycarp of Smyrna, who rejected him as the firstborn of Satan (cf. A.H. 3.3.4). Some scholars think this meeting might have occurred in Rome ca. A.D. 154 when Marcion had been excommunicated. Yet Irenaeus related it in a context of Asia Minor. Having spread some of his errors in his travels, Marcion came to Rome toward the end of Hadrian's regime (d. A.D. 138). At first he tried to live friendly with

the Christians. He wanted to be reconciled to them by offering them
200,000 sesterces. See Tertullian, *Praescr.* 30.2 (CCL 1.210). There he
met Cerdo who became his teacher and, in a sense, put system into his
errors. Still it seems that Marcion had his ideas well lined up on
coming to Rome. He attempted to justify Cerdo's ideas about the
incompatibility of the Old and the New Testaments by appealing to
Christ's comparison of the old garments and new patches (cf. Luke
5.36–38). He was refuted by the presbyters and then excommunicated
under Pope Anicetus. After that he founded his own sect, which,
under his direction, became better organized than all the other Gnostic sects. Soon his errors were also propagated in the Orient and he
became a very great threat to the Church. On Marcionism in the
Syriac-speaking area east of Antioch, see H. J. W. Drijvers, "Marcionism in Syria: Principles, Problems, Polemics," SCent 6, no. 3 (Fall
1987–88) 153–72. Toward the end of his life he is reported to have tried
to reenter the Church, but his death, which occurred about A.D. 160,
prevented this. Cf. Tertullian, *Praescr.* 30.3 (CCL 1.210). Though Marcion undoubtedly borrowed some ideas from Cerdo and perhaps Valentinus, still his system was simpler than the complicated imaginative
Valentinianism. He was a Gnostic, but of his own making. In turn, he
depended on some of the philosophers for ideas, but Hippolytus
seems to exaggerate this dependence. Cf. Tertullian, *Praescr.* 7 (CCL
1.192–93). He proposed his heresies in a work called *Antitheses*, which
is lost. See the following notes for more on his doctrine.

5. According to Irenaeus, Marcion held two coordinate eternal
principles: the good God and the just God. According to Hippolytus
(*Haer.* 10.19 [GCS 26.279–80]) there were three eternal principles: the
good God, the just God, and matter. According to Tertullian (*Adv.
Marc.* 1.2 (CCL 1.442–43) there was also an evil God. But there is
really no contradiction here. There were only two Gods: the evil God
used matter as a principle of creation. The just God of Hippolytus is
the same as the evil God of Tertullian.

6. Christ was sent into this world by the good God. He was not
born of a virgin; he merely passed through her as through a channel,
and in that sense only is he of the virgin. In reality he was of heaven
(Hippolytus, *Haer.* 7.31.5–8; 10.19.3–4 [GCS 26.217, 280]) as a kind of

middle character. So one might argue that Marcion was a Docetist. Cf. Blackman, *Marcion* 68, 99–100, 107. The work of the Savior consisted in undoing the work of the Creator, to ruin his institutions, to replace his commandments, to allure men and women for him. The passion was an essential act in redemption; it was the price paid. So Marcion was not an absolute Docetist. Redemption, as Irenaeus reports in A.H. 1.27.3, was completed in Limbo, where the cursed of the Old Testament were saved by faith in Jesus, whereas the just, inasmuch as they had believed the promise of Demiurge, were abandoned by Jesus. On Marcion's notion of redemption see J. Rivière, "Un exposé marcionite de la rédemption," RSRUS 1 (1921) 185–207, 297–323.

7. For the rationale of our translation here see SC 263.295 (SC 264.351 n. 1).

8. Marcion's Gospel, which he claimed was written by God, was in reality the Gospel of Luke mutilated by him, as Irenaeus attests (cf. also A.H. 3.11.7), and as many of the ancient writers relate; see, for instance, Tertullian, *Adv. Marc.* 4.2; 4.5–8 (CCL 1.547–48; 550–58). Cf. E. Amann, "Marcion" 2012–16, and Harnack, *Marcion* 210–15. J. Knox, *Marcion and the New Testament: An Essay in the Early History of the Canon* (Chicago 1942) 31, 161, supports Harnack's position. But Harnack is wrong when he claims that Marcion made the first canon, which was a model for the Church. See a refutation of this by E. Jacquier, *Le Nouveau Testament dans l'église chrétienne*, vol. 1: *Préparation formation et définition du Canon du Nouveau Testament* (Paris 1911) 170–72. Cf. also Tertullian, *Adv. Marc.* 4.43 (CCL 1.661–63) for Marcion's views of the Scriptures.

9. Marcion also compiled an *Apostolicum* which included the ten main Letters of Paul. He rejected the three Pastorals and Hebrews, and he mutilated the ten which he did keep. See Irenaeus, A.H. 3.11.7, 3.11.9, 3.14.4. He also cut out all the arguments from the prophetical writings because, no doubt like his follower Apelles, he considered them "human and false" (cf. Hippolytus, *Haer.* 7.38.2 [GCS 26.224]). He had utter contempt for ecclesiastical tradition. See M. J. Legrange, "Saint Paul ou Marcion," RBibl 41 (1932) 5–30.

10. That was a necessary conclusion if all matter is evil. Those Christians who believed in the cross were saved—but not entirely—

only their souls were saved. They had to observe the New Law out of love, not out of fear as in the Old Testament. All of Jesus' counsels were imposed by Marcion as precepts. Continence was thus obligatory for all, and marriage was condemned as evil because all creatures are evil. Cf. Tertullian, *Adv. Marc.* 1.29; 5.7.6–7 (CCL 1.473–74, 683); Hippolytus, *Haer.* 10.19 (GCS 26.280); Clement of Alexandria, *Str.* 3.3.12.1 (GCS 52 [15].200). Under such pretexts the Marcionites lived licentious lives (Clement, *Str.* 3.4 [GCS 52 {15}.207–14]). Marcion rigorously demanded that the more perfect abstain from meat and wine (Tertullian, *Adv. Marc.* 1.14 [CCL 1.455–56]). Theoretically his asceticism was severe, and Marcion himself gained a high reputation among his followers (Hippolytus, *Haer.* 7.30.3 [GCS 26.216]). But practically it led to lustful abuses and cynicism. See Hippolytus, *Haer.* 7.17 (GCS 26.192).

11. Cf. similar ideas in Theodoret, *Haer.* 1.24 (MG 83.376).

12. Irenaeus made a similar promise later in A.H. 3.12.12, and Eusebius, *H.e.* 5.8.9 (GCS 9.1.446), calls attention to this promise. Some scholars think that Irenaeus never found time to carry this out. Yet, perhaps he did do so by his refutations from the Lord's and the apostles' words in Books 4 and 5. As we noted before, Marcion organized his sect better than the other heresiarchs. See Rudolph *Gnosis* 313 who reports that no Gnostic before Mani had consciously proceeded to establish a church until Marcion. He founded a church and formed communities modelled on those of the Catholics, with bishops, priests, and deacons. That this organization was strong is clear from the fact that it held its own for a long time, even against the persecutions under Valerian and Diocletian, in which some Marcionites shed their blood. Cf. Bareille, "Gnosticisme," DTC 6.2.1454. In the first half of the fifth century there were still some 10,000 Marcionites in the Diocese of Cyrus. The vow of continence was a condition for baptism; apostates from the Catholic Church were not rebaptized. The distinction between the clergy and the laity was not so clear-cut as among Catholics. Women were allowed to perform some liturgical functions, as, for instance, that of baptizing. The teaching of Marcion spread from the capital to other regions of the Roman Empire. That the danger was great for the Church is evidenced by the cry of alarm

among the Catholics and the many apologetic works that the teaching
of Marcion evoked from Justin to Tertullian. Almost in every village
of importance a Marcionite church was erected.

13. Cf. n. 1 to chap. 23.

14. Cf. James 2.7.

15. Cf. Gen. 3.15; Rev. (Apoc.) 12.9.

CHAPTER 28

1. The Greek of this and the following paragraph is preserved by
Eusebius, *H.e.* 4.29.2–3 (GCS 9.1.390). See Hippolytus, *Haer.* 8.16–20
(GCS 26.236–39); Ps.-Tertullian, *Haer.* 7 (CCL 2.1409); Epiphanius,
Haer. 47 (GCS 31.215–19); Clement of Alexandria, *Paed.* 2.2.33 (GCS
12.176); idem, *Str.* 1.15.71 (GCS 52 [15].46); idem, *Str.* 3.5.40 (GCS 52
[15].214); idem, *Str.* 3.6 (GCS 2 [15].216–22); idem, *Str.* 3.9–18 (GCS 52
[15].225–47); idem, *Str.* 7.17.108 (GCS 17².76); Filaster, *Haer.* 48 [20]
(CCL 9.237); Theodoret, *Haer.* 1.20 (MG 83.369, 372). For a com-
pendious account see G. Bareille, "Encratites," DTC 5.1.4–14; H.
Chadwick, "Enkrateia," RAC 4.351–53; F. Bolagni, "Encratismo,"
DPAC 1.1151–53.

2. Cf. Gen. 1.27–28.

3. St. Paul foretold the coming of this heresy in Col. 2.16. It was an
abuse of Christian asceticism. Christ and Paul taught a sane and saving
spirit of asceticism. In the middle of the second century, however,
Cerdo and Marcion taught both that creation was from the just, that is,
the bad God, and that all creatures were bad. As a consequence, they
imposed complete continence and abstinence from meat and wine on
all Christians and insisted that Christ's counsels were of precept and
necessary for salvation. In the last quarter of that century some Christians observed continence and abstinence out of pride. Then they
lined up with the Gnostics and insisted on abstinence from all meat
and wine and the use of sex and also forbade marriage. They were
called Encratites, from the Greek word that means continence. As
poor exegetes they appealed to Scripture to bolster their tenets, but

more to the apocryphal Acts of Paul, and Thomas, and Peter, and John. Chronologically Julius Cassian (an Alexandrian) seems to have been the first leader of the Encratites. But Tatian (see n. 4) was, according to Jerome (*Epist.* 49 [48].2 [CSEL 54.352]), *princeps encratitarum*. After Tatian a certain Severus started another group of Encratites. The Encratites must have been rather widespread and, consequently, rather active, because even in Epiphanius's time some still existed in Asia Minor. Because of their supposed holiness they misled even good Christians, among whom were some bishops. But they were opposed from the beginning by Irenaeus, Tertullian, Hippolytus, and especially Clement of Alexandria.

4. Hippolytus, *Haer.* 8.16; 10.18 (GCS 26.236, 279), varied the wording of Irenaeus but the account is similar. See Ps.-Tertullian, *Haer.* 7 (CCL 2.1409); Eusebius, *H.e.* 4.28–29; 5.13 (GCS 9.1.388, 390, 392; 454, 456, 458); Epiphanius, *Haer.* 46 (GCS 31.202–10); Theodoret, *Haer.* 1.20 (MG 83.369, 372); Filaster, *Haer.* 48 [20], 72 [44], 84 [56] (CCL 9.237, 247, 253–54). See G. Bareille, "Encratites," DTC 5.1.4–13; G. Bardy, "Tatien," DTC 15.1.59–66; F. Bolagni, "Taziano," DPAC 2.3354–57. Tatian was an Assyrian, probably born in Syria of Euphrates about A.D. 120. He received a good Greek education and later read the philosophers, without however really probing their depths. He seems to have traveled for a while from city to city showing off his talents as a peddler of news. He was interested in religious problems and, while in search of the truth, he made inquiry into the mystery religions. At one time he had occasion to read the Jewish and Christian Bible and was struck by the knowledge he found in it. He came to Rome, where he met St. Justin and became a Christian convert. He had great admiration for Justin and spoke very reverently of him even later. According to Irenaeus he apostasized after Justin's martyrdom; Eusebius sets the date at about A.D. 172, which does not contradict Irenaeus, because the latter simply states that it was after Justin's martyrdom, which need not have been shortly after. Tatian wrote a work called *Discourse to the Greeks*. A critical edition of this was done by E. Schwartz, *Tatiani Oratio ad Graecos* (TU 4.1 [Leipzig 1888]). This was supposed to be an apologia for Christianity against the Greek philosophers. Some scholars think it is rather Catholic in tone. Others think that it has a touch of Gnosticism and that it even shows the use of the

apocryphal Gospel of Thomas and the Gospel of Philip. See R. M. Grant, "Tatian (*OR.* 30) and the Gnostics," JThS, n. s., 15 (1964) 65–69; reprinted in his *After the New Testament* (Philadelphia 1967) 208–13. There are three views on when and where it was written. Some think it was written at Rome while Justin was still living (ca. 160), and the presence of some Gnostic tenets would show there was some fluidity of teaching in Rome then. See L. W. Barnard, "The Heresy of Tatian—Once Again," JEH 19 (1968) 1–10. Others claim it was written at Rome but after Justin's death. This would fit in with Eusebius's date for the apostasy of Tatian, as noted above. Still others hold that he wrote it after returning to the Orient about A.D. 172 or as late as A.D. 178. If it was written then, one can easily explain the use of the Gospels of Thomas and Philip, which originated in the Syrian world. Now since Irenaeus brands Tatian as an out-and-out Gnostic, but since such teachings are not found in the *Discourse*, Barnard, "The Heresy" 3–4, thinks Irenaeus was too hard on Tatian. But Irenaeus does not say this *Discourse* was his source—much less does he say it was his only source. He obviously had other information on the openly heretical teachings of Tatian. After returning to the Orient, Tatian probably went to Ephesus, or to Daphne near Antioch. He must have continued there for a rather long period because of his great and long influence. Irenaeus sums up Tatian's errors concisely. Clement of Alexandria (*Str.* 3.12 [GCS 52 {15}.232]) stresses that Tatian held matrimony to be the work of the devil. Bardy, "Tatien" 63–65, feels that Tatian's teaching on the Trinity lacks theological precision. He teaches the Trinity, but speaks of the Word as having a double role: in the Father before creation as the power of all things to be created; in creation, when he was uttered as the first work. He hardly alludes to the Incarnation, but he taught the resurrection of the body. The Holy Spirit gets scant attention. Tatian is remembered today mostly because of his other extant work, the *Diatessaron*. See Introduction, par. 27.

5. Irenaeus is obviously noting this teaching about the "plurality of marriages" (*multas nuptias*) as an error. One may not deduce from this that the Bishop rejects all second or repeated marriages, namely, of widows and widowers. He rejects adulterous marriages, as those of the Samaritan woman of John 4 (to which he refers in A.H. 3.17.2). See

A. Orbe, "S. Ireneo y la iteración de las nupcias," Gregorianum 34 (1953) 653–55.

6. Cf. 2 Tim. 2.18.

CHAPTER 29

1. On this chapter see Epiphanius, *Haer.* 25.2; 26.1 (GCS 25.268–69; 275–86); Theodoret, *Haer.* 1.13 (MG 83.361, 364); cf. G. Bareille, "Barbélites," DTC 2.1.382–84; idem, "Borboriens, Borborites," DTC 2.1.1032–33; L. Cerfaux, "Barbelo-Gnostiker," RAC 1.1176–80; L. Fendt, "Borborianer," RAC 2.510–13; C. Gianotti, "Barbelognostici," DPAC 1.474–75; E. Prinzivalli, "Borboriani," DPAC 1.553. In this chapter Irenaeus is quoting an original Gnostic document known as the *Apocryphon of John*. On this see "The Apocryphon of John" (II,*1*, III,*1*, IV,*1*, and BG 8502,2), introduced and trans. F. Wisse, in *The Nag Hammadi Library*, general ed. J. M. Robinson, 3d ed. (San Francisco 1988) 104. A Coptic version was found in 1896, which goes by the name Codex Berolinensis (or Berlin Gnostic Codex 8502; cf. Quasten *Patr.* 1.276). A printed edition of this was published by W. Till, *Die gnostischen Schriften des koptischen Papyrus Berolinensis 8502*, TU 60 (Leipzig 1955). A second edition revised by H. M. Schenke appeared in 1972. For more on the Berlin Codex 8502 see Rudolph *Gnosis* 28. But three other versions of it were found in the Nag Hammadi discovery. They are called Codex Cairensis II, III, and IV. Codex III is close to the Berlin Codex 8502, and both are independent translations into Coptic of a shorter Greek version of the work, while Codex II and Codex IV are copies of the same Coptic translation of a longer Greek version of the work. R. Kasser published a French translation of all four in "Bibliothèque gnostique II: Le livre secret de Jean (versets 1–124)," *Revue de théologie et philosophie* (hereafter RThPh), 3d ser., 15 (1965) 129–55, and "Bibliothèque gnostique III: Le livre secret de Jean (versets 125–394)," RThPh, 3d ser., 16 (1966) 163–81. An English translation of II,*1* (supplemented where necessary by IV,*1*) is provided by

Wisse in *The Nag Hammadi Library* 105–23. The reason for the difference in length and the other variations have not yet been solved. Cf. H. M. Schenke, "Nag-Hamadi Studien I: Das literarische Problem des Apokryphon Johannis," ZRGG 14 (1962) 57–63. A digest of this by F. Moriarty can be found in *New Testament Abstracts* 6, no. 3 (1962) 362–63, n. 938. For a good analysis of the *Apocryphon of John* see Y. Janssens, "L'Apocryphon de Jean," *Le Muséon* 83 (1970) 157–65 and 84 (1971) 43–64, 403–32. P. Perkins believes, contra F. Wisse, that A.H. 1.29–30 can be properly ascribed to Irenaeus. See P. Perkins, "Irenaeus and the Gnostics: Rhetoric and Composition in *Adversus haereses* Book One," VC 30 (1976) 193–200, and F. Wisse, "The Nag Hammadi Library and the Heresiologists," VC 25 (1971) 205–23.

2. "Barbelo." The spelling of this word is not uniform in the documents; Barbēlō, Barbērō, and Barbēlōth occur. The meaning is also uncertain. Cf. Rudolph *Gnosis* 80. Theodoret, *Haer.* 13 (MG 83.364), says that these sects affected Hebrew names. He wrote Barbēlōth, which has a Semitic ending. Other Hebrew names for the Aeons are recorded later. Bareille, "Barbélites" 383, notes that some scholars, e.g., Hilgenfeld and Lipsius, derive it from the Hebrew "Barba Elō," which means "God is in the Tetrad"; that is, God is in the four Aeons who proceeded from Barbelo. Or, as A. Koch, "Barbelioten," LTK 1.962, explains it: "*In der Vier ist Gott . . . durch 4 weitere Parrungen hindurch das Lichtreich sich entwickeln liessen.*" Harvey (1.221 n. 2) uses the same word but in Syriac, and with the same meaning. F. C. Burkitt, *Church and Gnosis: A Study of Christian Thought and Speculation in the Second Century* (Cambridge 1932) 54–55, 58–60, suggested a Coptic origin, with the word meaning grain, seed, namely, as a seed containing all potentialities. This was accepted by C. A. Baynes, *A Coptic Gnostic Treatise Contained in the Codex Brucianus [Bruce MS. 96. Bod. Lib. Oxford]: A Translation from the Coptic: Transcript and Commentary* (Cambridge 1933) 50. But S. Giversen, *Apocryphon Johannis: The Coptic Text of the Apocryphon Johannis in the Nag Hammadi Codex II with Translation, Introduction and Commentary* (Copenhagen 1963) 165–66, hesitates to accept Burkitt's explanation, and rather supports J. Matter's view, reported by Harvey (1.221 n. 2), which Harvey however rejected as not in tune with the context. This view holds that it comes from the Hebrew *Barath-Ba'alô*, which means "daughter of the Lord," just as Jaldabaloth means "son of chaos." Irenaeus speaks of

Barbelo as "in a virginal spirit," but later in the paragraph he says she was made a "light like Father"; and in 2.30.9 there is mention of a "virginal light," which is certainly Barbelo. In the *Apocryphon of John* 27.19–20 (TU 60.95) she is called "First-Man" and "virginal spirit." But according to Giversen, *Apocryphon Johannis,* 166 the highest, primordial Father is continuously called a virginal spirit in the *Apocryphon*. He could be virginal spirit in the sense that he is "completely unaffected and distant from all that is earthly." And so, Barbelo, who was made like Father, can also be a virginal spirit. At any rate, she has a twofold role: in creation she is the feminine principle; in redemption she clothes Jesus with light and a celestial body. She is the goal of every soul that is saved.

3. For the rationale for this translation see SC 263.302 (SC 264.359 n. 3).

4. The MSS are uncertain whether *magnitudo* and *conceptus* are both in the ablative (which Massuet [MG 7.692 n. 72] favors) or both in the accusative, or *magnitudo* in the accusative and *conceptus* in the ablative, which Harvey (1.222 n. 3) as well as Rousseau and Doutreleau (SC 264.358) accept. This last suggestion seems correct. *Prospicientem in* would seem to call for *magnitudinem.* Cf. 1.29.4: *prospiciebat ad inferiores partes;* 2.17.9: *in quae . . . prospicere* (from 1 Peter 1.12). The Greek of Theodoret (*Haer.* 1.13 [MG 83.361]) makes it plain that *delectationem* should have an active meaning: "while Barbeloth was exulting (*euphrantheisan de tēn Barbelōth*), a conception took place and she gave birth to light."

5. We have added "Will and" following Rousseau's remarks in SC 263.302–3 (SC 264.359 n. 7).

6. At the end of the paragraph Irenaeus lists an Ogdoad of Aeons that came from Father and Barbelo. But was that originally a Decad, with another pair, Truth and Self-begotten, added? Yes, answers Giversen, *Apocryphon Johannis* 175–77. Both Truth and Self-begotten are mentioned in 1.29.2. In Codex II,*1* there is talk of a Pentad and a Decad. Now the androgynous Pentad includes Truth. So the Decad must have had that extra pair. Giversen also thinks that originally the consort of Incorruption was not *khristos,* but *khrēstotēs* (Goodness). This suggestion seems good.

7. Cf. Ps. 8.6–7; 1 Cor. 15.26–28; Eph. 1.22; Heb. 2.8.

8. "Untamable" is *adamas* in Greek. This was the heavenly Man;

Adam was the earthly Man. Cf. Hippolytus, *Haer.* 5.8.2 (GCS 26.89). These notions are also found in the Jewish traditions, written down in the Cabbala. But the idea that Adam had a prototype was contained in the Oriental religions. Cf. Lebreton-Zeiller 2.629.

9. "Were at rest." The Clermont MS (C) has *refrigeranti*, indicating that maybe *refrigerant* is not correct. As a matter of fact, the sudden change to the indicative mood is suspect. In 1.2.6 there is a similar idea: *confirmata quoque in hoc (epi toutōi) omnia et requiescentia ad perfectum . . . dicunt hymnizare Propatorem.* This indicates that in our passage we should read *refrigerantia*, which Lat. Iren. uses as a synonym for *requiescentia*. *In hoc* here represents *epi toutōi*, in the temporal sense of "thereupon." Rousseau and Doutreleau (SC 264.362) also read *refrigerantia*.

10. The heretic Justin, an Ophite, explained the tree of life and the tree of knowledge as angelic beings; cf. Hippolytus, *Haer.* 5.26.6; 5.28 (GCS 26.127, 133). In the Jewish Cabbala the tree of life was in the center of paradise and was identified with the tetragrammaton, "Yahweh," the personal name of God. Cf. Harvey 1.224–25 n. 5.

11. The meaning of "Prounikos" is disputed. Origen, *Cels.* 6.35 (GCS 3.104), says that it is the same as Wisdom of the Valentinians, and that her symbol is the woman with hemorrhage of twelve years. Celsus distorted that by speaking of the power that flows from a certain virgin, Prounikos. Epiphanius (*Haer.* 25.4; 37.6 [GCS 25.271; 31.58]) seems to derive the word from *prounikeuō*, which means to deflower a virgin. It would then allude to the mental fornication of Achamoth when she turned to matter. According to LSJ, s.v. *"prouneikos,"* the word means a hired porter, a low fellow, a lewd person. In Lampe, PGL, s.v. *"Prounikos,"* the first meaning of this word is the name of an aeon that represents sexual knowledge. J. P. Arendzen, "Gnosticism," CE 6.594, holds that it means "the lustful one," who was a virgin goddess, but by her fall from purity was the cause of the material and sinful world. Harvey (1.225 n. 1) claims the word means a runner in a race, and he refers to Achamoth's struggles. That seems farfetched. Observe that the Holy Spirit is the female consort here. See also Rousseau's remarks on "Prounikos" and its use throughout A.H. in SC 263.303 (SC 264.363 n. 1).

12. "Struggled and strained." The Greek is missing for this sentence. Lat. Iren. has *adseuerabat et extendebatur et prospiciebat.* Ac-

cording to Grabe (cf. Harvey 1.226 n. 1) *asseverabat* supposes *diiskhurixeto*, which though it can mean "affirm," has as its first meaning "to lean upon." Harvey (1.226 n. 1) suggests that *dieteinato* ("stretched out over") might have been the original and *extendebatur* was a marginal note, explaining *asseverabat*. But it scarcely seems possible that those Greek words, so different in consonants, were confused. Lat. Iren. must have taken *adseuerabat* in its primary meaning of "do with earnestness," and read a Greek word that has that meaning. Klebba BKV (3.83) implies that in his translation: *"dehnte sie sich mit allen Kräften aus,"* and so does ANF (1.354) in "exerted and extended."

13. On the aptness of "Discord" here, see G. Zuntz, "Erinys in Gnosticism?" JThS, n. s., 6 (1955) 243–44, and SC 263.303 (SC 264.363 n. 2).

14. Cf. Exod. 20.5; Isa. 45.5–6; 46.9.

CHAPTER 30

1. The title placed at the head of this chapter in MG 7.694 includes the Sethians as well as the Ophites. That is in keeping with the information of Theodoret, *Haer.* 1.14 (MG 83.364–65, 368). But the identity of these two sects is not proved. At most, the Ophites might be a more generic title for all serpent-worshiping sects, and the Sethians might have been a particular sect of this group. At any rate, Hippolytus, *Haer.* 5.6–7 and 5.19–20 (GCS 26.77–89 and 116–23), treats them separately, and so do Epiphanius, *Haer.* 37, 39 (GCS 31.50–62 and 71–80) and Ps.-Tertullian, *Haer.* 2 (CCL 2.1403–4). On the Ophites see also Origen, *Cels.* 6.28, 30 (GCS 3.98, 99–100); Clement of Alexandria, *Str.* 7.17 (GCS 17².76); and Filaster, *Haer.* 1 (GCS 9.218). For modern studies see A. Hönig, *Die Ophiten: Ein Beitrag zur Geschichte des jüdischen Gnosticismus* (Berlin 1889) passim; R. Reitzenstein, *Poimandres: Studien zur griechisch-ägyptischen und frühchristlichen Literatur* (Leipzig 1904) 81–101; G. Salmon, "Ophites," DCB 4.80–88; E. Amann, "Ophites," DTC 11.1.1063–75; G. Kretschmar, "Ophiten und Naassener," RGG 4.1659; G. Quispel, "Ophiten," LTK² 7.1178–79; C. Giannoti, "Ofiti-Naasseni," DPAC 2.2458–60. The name of the sect comes from the Greek *ophis*, which means serpent. They worshiped

the serpent for giving knowledge to humankind (cf. Gen. 3); Epiphanius, *Haer.* 37.5.5 (GCS 31.57), describes a curious Eucharistic rite in honor of the serpent. The origin of the Ophites lies buried in obscurity, and authors differ in setting a date. Some claim this sect shows a close dependence on Marcion's antibiblical tenets, and so in point of time would follow this heresy. Others say, rightly, that in substance it is pre-Christian. Worship of the serpent is the most ancient animal worship. It picked up various elements from the mystery religions of Egypt, Phrygia, and Greece. It borrowed from the Old Testament and later from the New. It added elements of the Gnostic heresies to its syncretistic debris. But it remained substantially pagan. Origen and Hippolytus consider it pagan; cf. Amann, "Ophites" 1063–75. Still we do not think that Irenaeus and Epiphanius are wrong in looking at it as a heresy, because some Gnostics who were heretics belonged to this sect. What is the relation of this sect to the Naassenes about whom Hippolytus writes in *Haer.* 5.6–11 (GCS 26.77–104)? Many have identified the two, since "Naassene" comes from *Naḥaš*, the Hebrew for serpent, as Hippolytus already explains. However, Hippolytus's description of them, though similar in some respects, differs from that of Irenaeus on the Ophites. Amann, "Ophites" 1074–75 seems to have hit upon the solution. Hippolytus wrote on the Ophites in his *Syntagma*, as witnessed by Ps.-Tertullian and Epiphanius. For that his information came from Irenaeus. It is a general treatment of the various sects that worship the serpent, called the Ophites. Later he obtained more specific information and wrote in his *Refutatio omnium haeresium* about the Naassenes, the Peratae, the Sethians, and the followers of Justin the Gnostic, all specific sects among the Ophites. On the Christology of the Ophites see the two able studies of A. Orbe, "Cristología de los Ofitas," *Estudios eclesiásticos* 48 (1973) 191–230; "La Cristología de Justino gnóstico," *Estudios eclesiásticos* 47 (1972) 437–57. Irenaeus does not mention this Gnostic Justin by name in his works.

  2. Cf. Gen. 3.20.

  3. For Rousseau's interpretation of this phrase see SC 263.303–4 (SC 264.367 n. 2).

  4. According to Hippolytus, *Haer.* 5.9.13 (GCS 26.100), the Naassenes followed Thales in considering water as the origin of the material world, of which the serpent was a symbol. So the serpent occupied an intermediate position between the deity and matter, and was consid-

ered the image of the intellectual world. Cf. Irenaeus, A.H. 1.30.15. The Peratae held that the serpent represented the Word; cf. Hippolytus, *Haer.* 5.16.12 (GCS 26.113).

5. On the difficulty of the Latin *dilatauit et cooperuit* see SC 263.304 (SC 264.367 n. 3).

6. Rousseau (SC 263.304–6 [SC 264.369 n. 1]) points out the difficulty of interpretation that results from Grabe's and Massuet's emendation: *Corpus autem hoc ⟨quod⟩ exuisse dicunt eam, feminam a femina nominant.* So we base our translation on Rousseau's and Doutreleau's emendation: *Corpus autem hoc filium eius dicunt, eam autem feminam a femina nominant.*

7. All these names are of Hebrew origin, given in transliteration, as even Irenaeus (A.H. 2.35.3) noted: *secundam hebraeam linguam.* The etymology of Jaldabaoth is disputed. Harvey (1.230 n. 1) derives the name from *Yah-El-Da'abôth*, meaning "Lord, God of Fathers." More correct seems to be the derivation given by G. Quispel. He thinks it comes from *yalodah bahôt*, which would mean "Son of Chaos." See G. Quispel, "Gnosticism and the New Testament," VC 19 (1965) 75. This interpretation receives confirmation from Codex II of the Nag Hammadi papyri as noted by J. Daniélou, "Bulletin d'histoire des origines chrétiennes," RechSR 59 (1971) 56; see R. A. Bullard, *The Hypostasis of the Archons* (Berlin 1970) 54. "Yao" is an abbreviation of Yahweh (cf. n. 10 to chap. 4). "Sabaoth" is Hebrew for hosts. In the Scriptures it is often used in the phrase "God of hosts." "Adoneus" is from the Hebrew Adonai, meaning sovereign. "Eloeus" is from the Hebrew Elohim. In fact Hippolytus, *Haer.* 5.26.7 (GCS 26.127), wrote "Elōeim." "Horeus" must also be from Hebrew. Origen, *Cels.* 6.31, 32 (GCS 3.101, 102), wrote *Hōraios.* The letter H could stand for the guttural aleph. Gnostic amulets have a female figure on them and the letters A S T A PH E in Greek. Origen named the seven gods and mentioned that Jaldabaoth is Saturn (*Cels.* 6.31 [GCS 3.101]). Perhaps all seven correspond to planets (cf. A.H. 1.30.9). Jao could be Jupiter; Sabaoth, Mars; Astaphaios, Venus; Adonaios, Sun; Aiolaios (Elohim), Mercury; Oraios, Moon. Cf. J. P. Arendzen, "Gnosticism," CE 6.595–96.

8. Cf. Eph. 1.21.

9. Hence their name of Ophites; cf. n. 1.

10. Cf. Isa. 45.5–6, 46.9.

11. Cf. Gen. 1.26. We have translated this following the textual emendation of Rousseau and Doutreleau (SC 264.370) who put square brackets around *nostram*. For their reasons for wishing to exclude this word, see SC 263.306–7 (SC 264.371 n. 1).

12. Cf. Gen. 2.7.

13. As Harvey (1.232–33 n. 3) notes, this idea comes from rabbinical theology. The Talmud, tract Tanith, says that Adam, when created, reached from the earth to the firmament, according to Rabbi Eliezer; while Rabbi Judah claims that Adam extended from one end of the earth to the other. Rabbi Solomon says that when Adam was lying down, his head was in the east and his feet in the west. In the Cabbala, *Idra Rabba* 40, Adam's body was measured by the worlds through which it extended. This Primal Man is central to certain Gnostic sects, based on Gen. 1.26–27. Cf. K. Rudolph, "Ein Grundtyp gnostischer Urmensch-Adam-Spekulation," ZRGG 9 (1957) 1–20, who notes that there are similarities here to what is in the *Apocryphon of John*.

14. Saturninus and Basilides also spoke of wormlike man; cf. A.H. 1.24.1; Hippolytus, *Haer.* 7.28.3 (GCS 26.208).

15. Cf. Gen. 2.7.

16. This Ophite theory of the generation of angels is very similar to that of the Gnostic Justin, whose account is given by Hippolytus, *Haer.* 5.26 (GCS 26.126–32), except that for the Gnostic Justin, First-beginning was the generative principle of the angels. Cf. *Bereshith Rabbam* on Gen. 3.20, where a puerile rabbinic romance is described that reminds one of these vagaries, as Harvey (1.233–34 n. 3) notes.

17. "Tried" is *argumentata est* in Lat. Iren. This verb is used by Lat. Iren. in only two other places (cf. Reynders, *Lexique comparé* [CSCO 142] 34). In 3.16.6 it is used in the sense of "claim" and in 4.1.1 in the sense of "argue." Neither of these meanings fits here. But in A.H. 1.9.4, Lat. Iren. has *argumentatio* for *epikheireseōs*, namely an attempt. That would fit here. Stieren (1.268 n. 4) suggests, rightly we think, that the Greek was *epikheirēse*. Harvey (1.234 n. 1) disagrees and accepts Massuet's (MG 7.699 n. 34) suggestion of *esophisato, callide molita est*.

18. Cf. Gen. 3.7.

19. For the rationale for our translation "he sinned by making an adulterated copy" for *et haec adulterans peccauit* see SC 263.307–8 (SC 264.375 n. 1).

20. Cf. Gen. 3.15–20. According to the Jewish Cabbala paradise was in the fourth heaven, from where Adam fell, as Harvey (1.235 n. 1) observes. See also n. 13 to chap. 5. This Serpent-Mind, who was the son of Jaldabaoth, acted against his father, because Prounikos had dealt with Adam and Eve through him without the father's knowledge and caused their defection from the father.

21. Namely, in paradise, which was not in this world but in the fourth heaven.

22. Cf. Gen. 3.7.

23. Cf. Gen. 3.7–4.16.

24. "Norea," as in Lat. Iren. She is here the wife of Seth and was apparently, but not necessarily, generated after him as his sister. She together with Seth begot the rest of the human race, who were very bad people. Filaster, *Haer*. 33 [5].3 (CCL 9.231), also takes her to be a woman. Besides, in this section they are following the Bible story, and the woman should be in the immediate context. All this excludes the view that this is Noah. Irenaeus treats of him expressly later. Harvey (1.236 n. 2) thinks Norea comes from *Na 'ărah* (girl), about whom we know nothing. Yet, since the Gnostics picked up any name in the Bible to get their couples, it seems we should look at the immediate context for Seth for a name. Now Seth, as Adam's son, is spoken of in Gen. 4.25, but in Gen. 4.22 (LXX) there is mention of the only woman, besides Eve, in this context. Her name is Noema, which in Hebrew is *Na'ᵃmah*. She would, according to the genealogy of Gen. 4.23, be the great-great-great-great grandniece of Seth. *Na'ᵃmah* could have been in the original myth, which was later misread as *Na'ᵃrah*, and then translated into Greek as *Norea*. Epiphanius, *Haer*. 26.1.3 (GCS 25.275), says the Sethites wrote a book called *Noria*, which contained the errors of this sect. He also identified Norea with Noah.

25. Hippolytus, *Haer*. 5.26.5 (GCS 26.127), speaks of twelve paternal and twelve maternal angels, in the system of the Gnostic Justin. Michael was the first of the paternal angels. "Samahel" does not occur in Scripture. Theodoret, *Haer*. 1.14 (MG 83.366C), has Samanna, which might correspond to the Hebrew *šᵉmoneh* (eight), and that would fit here. But the evidence in favor of Samahel is rather strong. In the Cabbala Sammael was the evil spirit who brought about the fall of man through the serpent. He was called angel of death and the prince of the air. See Harvey 1.236 n. 4. The fact that this serpent is spoken of as

having been cast down must come from Rev. (Apoc.) 12, where the dragon is cast down. In the story of Genesis the serpent is never spoken of that way.

26. Cf. Wisd. of Sol. 10.4.

27. "Jews." Lat. Iren. has *Iudaeos*, but in this area all the leaders of the Jews are mentioned: Moses, Joshua, Samuel. The Judges alone are missing. One can wonder whether *Iudaeos* might not originally have been *Iudices*.

28. Since there are constant allusions to the Scriptures throughout this heresy, there seems to be an allusion here to God's choice of his personal name Yahweh in Exod. 3.6; 6.3, and perhaps to the observance of the Sabbath in Exod. 20.9–11. We accept Doutreleau's and Rousseau's reading of *Deos* (SC 264.378). See Rousseau's justification for this at SC 263.308–9 (SC 264.379 n. 1).

29. For a brief explanation of the significance of this sentence see Rousseau's remarks in SC 263.309 (SC 264.381 n. 1).

30. Cf. Matt. 25.1; John 3.29.

31. Cf. 1 Cor. 15.50. Lat. Iren. has *apprehenderunt*. The difference can scarcely be explained, as Harvey (1.239 n. 6) tries, by saying that Irenaeus is translating from the Syriac, because elsewhere (A.H. 5.9.1; 5.9.4; 5.10.1; 5.13.5) he quotes correctly. Here he might be quoting according to the heretics, or the Latin translator indulged in his elegant variation. Jesus is considered in a twofold manner: his risen self with only the ensouled and spiritual body; and his self with an earthly body as recognized by the apostles. But the Latin construction is not so easy. The antecedent of *eum* is doubtful, as also the subject of *resurrexit*; and so the sense is not clear. Yet past translators simply gave a translation without comment, though the translations did not agree. The Latin is: *Videntes autem discipuli resurrexisse eum, non eum cognouerunt, sed ne ipsum quidem Iesum cuius gratia a mortuis resurrexit*. The context is about Christ's departing from Jesus before the crucifixion, so that Jesus alone died and rose. When, therefore, Irenaeus reports the Gnostic view that the disciples did not recognize him, the "him" is certainly Jesus. But then he adds that they did not recognize Jesus himself. Irenaeus seems to repeat himself, unless one sees the clause that follows as an explanation; namely, they did not recognize the manner in which he rose, that is with a spiritualized and not a worldly body. That fits in well with the sentence that follows;

namely, that the disciples' greatest error was that they thought he rose in a worldly body. The fact that this clause would be an indirect question and should not be in the indicative is scarcely a problem in the varied syntax of Lat. Iren. In this explanation the antecedent of *eum* is always Jesus, and the subject of *resurrexit* is Jesus quite naturally. Other interpretations must suppose that "the man" in Jesus is the subject of *resurrexit*. That is possible, but does not flow easily. For instance, they did not recognize even Jesus, for the sake of whom (Klebba BKV 3.90) or by whom (ANF 1.357) he (perhaps the man in Jesus) rose from the dead.

32. Rousseau (SC 263.310 [SC 264.383 n. 2]) suspects there is textual corruption in these last few words.

33. How this strange error arose is a mystery.

34. For the translation of "intelligence" for *sensibilitas* see A. Blaise, *Dictionnaire latin-français des auteurs chrétiens*, s.v. "*sensibilitas*," and Rousseau (SC 263.310–11 [SC 264.383 n. 4]).

35. Cf. Ps. 109(110).1; Mark 16.19. For "Jesus" in place of "Christ," see Rousseau (SC 263.311 [SC 264.385 n. 1]).

36. Hippolytus, *Haer.* 5.11 (GCS 26.104), says that of the Naassenes. In *Pistis Sophia*, too, there is mention of a seven-headed dragon. Cf. G. Horner, *Pistis Sophia* (London 1924) 161.

37. See Rousseau (SC 263.311 [SC 264.385 n. 2]) for an explanation of this sentence.

38. For a rationale of our translation "however . . . was" see Rousseau, SC 263.311–12 (SC 264.385 n. 3).

39. Cf. Gen. 3.1.

40. According to Theodoret, *Haer.* 1.14 (MG 83.364–65, 368), the Sethians and the Ophites spoke of serpent-wisdom as represented by the bowels.

CHAPTER 31

1. Cf. Ps.-Tertullian, *Haer.* 2.5 (CCL 2.1404); Epiphanius, *Haer.* 38 (GCS 31.62–71); Filaster, *Haer.* 2 (CCL 9.218); Theodoret, *Haer.* 1.15 (MG 83.368). Cf. G. Bareille, "Cainites," DTC 2.2.1307–9; G. Bardy, "Cainites," DHGE 11.226–28; E. Prinzivalli, "Cainiti," DPAC 1.564–

65. There must have been at least a small beginning of this bestial heresy at the time of St. Jude, who wrote: *For admission has been secretly gained by some who long ago were designated for condemnation, ungodly persons who pervert the grace of our God into licentiousness and deny our only Master and Lord, Jesus Christ . . . Yet in like manner these men in their dreamings defile the flesh, reject authority, and revile the glorious ones . . . . But these men revile whatever they do not understand, and by those things that they know by instinct as irrational animals do, they are destroyed. Woe to them! For they walk in the way of Cain* (Jude 4, 8, 10, 11). John, too, in the Apocalypse seems to have had in mind this type of aberration when he condemned the Nicolaitans (Rev. [Apoc.] 2.6, 15). Their tenets and practices are a combination of elements from Cerinthus, Cerdo, Marcion, Carpocrates, Valentinus, Basilides, and Isidore. They blasphemously distorted the Scriptures and outrageously deformed Christianity. Besides the apocryphal gospel of Judas, which Irenaeus mentions, they used other apocryphal works, as, for instance, the *Ascension of Paul.*

2. Womb was Demiurge, the maker of the world. Demiurge and the Old Testament, of which he was the God, as well as Judaism, the Cainites hated wildly. They even claimed that those who had been cursed in the Old Testament are really saved.

3. On baptism see Tertullian, *Bapt.* 1, 10–19 (CCL 1.277, 284–94). For salvation they demanded faith alone without works, except, of course, immoral works. Their doctrines about the hatred of the old law and its God were nothing but an excuse for their immorality. See A.H. 1.25 on Carpocrates and his disciples.

4. Cf. Eph. 5.3. Tertullian gave this idea very concisely in reference to the Valentinians: *Etiam solummodo demonstrare destruere est* (*Adv. Val.* 3.5 [CCL 2.755]).

5. Rousseau (SC 263.313–15 [SC 264.389 n. 1]) believes *patribus* refers to those discussed by Irenaeus in A.H. 1.29–31 and *proavis* to those discussed in A.H. 1.23–28. We follow him and Doutreleau who believe *matribus* is perhaps a corruption of *natos*, and thus we omit it in our translation.

6. We follow Feuardent (cf. MG 7.706 n. 74) and Rousseau and Doutreleau (SC 263.315–16 [SC 264.389 n. 2]) in preferring *detectio* over *delectatio.* See also Rousseau's remarks there on the capital importance

to Irenaeus of an exact knowledge and exposé of heresy as a part of effective pastoral care of someone affected by it.

7. We accept Rousseau's and Doutreleau's reading (SC 264.390) of ⟨*non*⟩ *apta ueritati ostendens dogmata* and base our translation on this change. See Rousseau's arguments for this reading in SC 263.316 (SC 264.391 n. 1).

INDEXES

I. OLD AND NEW TESTAMENTS

2. AUTHORS

3. GENERAL INDEX

Abel, 40, 92, 99
abortion, 42
Abraham, 74, 81, 92, 100, 164
Abrasax, 87, 234, 235, 238
Abraxas, 234
abstinence, 93
Abyss, 137
Achamoth, 34, 35, 36, 38, 39, 40,
    42, 43, 58, 80, 132, 139, 152,
    153, 154, 155, 157, 158, 160, 161,
    169, 170, 205, 207, 209, 216,
    223, 225, 246, 260; formation
    of, 30–33
Achilles, 54
Acts of John, 255
Acts of the Apostles, 249
Acts of Paul, 255
Acts of Peter, 255
Acts of Thomas, 255
Adam, 34, 47, 93, 98, 99, 102, 159,
    172, 185, 260, 264, 265
Adamas, 237, 259
Adonai, 263
Adoneus, 97, 263
Adullam, 221
Adversus haereses, title and
    authenticity of, 2–3; time of
    composition, 3–4; purpose
    and plan of, 6–7; style of,
    7–8; Scripture and tradition

as reflected in, 8–11;
    manuscript history, 11–15;
    printed editions of, 15–18
Advocate, 24, 32, 154
Aeneas, 134
Aeon(s), 23, 24, 25, 26, 27, 28, 29,
    31, 32, 33, 42, 43, 44, 45, 46,
    47, 50, 51, 52, 54, 55, 58, 60,
    61, 62, 66, 68, 69, 71, 73, 76,
    87, 93, 95, 96, 100, 101, 102,
    131, 137, 138, 139, 146, 148, 149,
    152, 153, 154, 157, 158, 170, 178,
    179, 195, 198, 206, 208, 215,
    235, 238, 258, 259
Agamemnon, 48
Ageless, 24
Albigenses, 231
Alexandria, 84, 191, 232, 239, 243
All, 27, 29, 145, 148
Almighty, 46, 49
Alogoi, 244
alpha, 60, 61, 63, 65, 69, 76, 153,
    209, 210
alphabet, Greek, 213
Amos, 100
Anaxilaus, 55, 202
ancient faith, heretical
    derivations from, 80–81
Angel(s), 27, 32, 33, 34, 35, 40, 42,
    56, 60, 81, 82, 83, 84, 85, 86,

Letters of Peter, 249
Letter to Philemon, 9
Libya, 49
Life(ves), 23, 24, 27, 44, 45, 46,
47, 51, 54, 55, 62, 65, 66, 71,
78, 136, 178, 208; Eternal, 94;
Life of God, 205
light, 30, 31, 42, 49, 56, 73, 96, 97;
Light, 31, 32, 44, 45, 46, 47,
52, 78, 94, 95, 187; children
of, 63; moisture of, 96, 98,
99, 100, 101; of Christ, 78;
of the Spirit, 102; of the
world, 36
Limbo, 252
Limit(s), 25, 26, 27, 29, 30, 42, 51,
71, 139, 140, 145, 147, 152, 170,
209
Limiter, 26, 27, 140
Liturgies, 154
Logos, 69, 215
Lord, 21, 22, 41, 42, 43, 44, 70, 74,
75, 76, 77, 78, 81, 90, 91, 92,
173, 253, 258
Love, 24
Luke, 81, 209, 215
Lust, 95
Lyons, 204

Maccabees, 1 and 2, 8
magic, 81, 82, 83, 84, 86; arts, 239
magician(s), 55, 56, 57, 58, 61, 81,
92
Majesty, 94
Maker, 34, 46, 50, 63, 67, 70, 77,
88, 91, 95, 99, 102, 103
Man(en), 23, 24, 25, 27, 34, 44, 45,
46, 51, 52, 54, 55, 61, 62, 65,

66, 71, 94, 95, 98, 134, 136,
178, 208, 259, 260
Mani, 253
manna, 188
Marcellina, 6, 89, 239, 243
Marcion, 91-92, 93, 170, 195, 248,
250, 251, 252, 253, 254, 268;
Gospel of, 252
Marcionism, 251
Marcionites, 253
Marcosian(s), 200, 204, 207, 214,
215, 218, 219, 221, 222, 224
Marcosianism, 6
Marcus, 197, 198, 202, 203, 205,
206, 209, 211; magical and
wicked practices of, 55-59;
speculations about letters
and numbers by, 59-71
Mark, 149
marriage, 93; marriages, plurality
of, 256
Mars, 205, 263. See also Ares
Mary, 39, 66, 90, 100, 185, 188,
235, 245
Master, 49
material, 29, 33, 34, 35, 36, 42, 171
Maternal, 24, 135
matter, 39, 43, 96. See also
substance
mature, 44
Matthew, 90
Matthias, 232
Mediator, 165
Menander, 84, 170, 181, 230, 231,
232, 233
Menelaus, 48
Mercury, 263. See also Hermes
Michael, 100